The Judicialization of Politics in Asia

Over the last two decades courts have become major players in the political landscape in Asia. This book assesses what is driving this apparent trend toward judicialization in the region. It looks at the variations within the judicialization trend, and how these variations affect political practice and policy outcomes. The book goes on to examine how this new trend is affecting aspects of the rule of law, democratic governance and state–society relations. It investigates how the experiences in Asia add to the debate on the judicialization of politics globally; in particular how judicial behaviour in Asia differs from that in the West, and the implications of the differences on the theoretical debate.

Björn Dressel is a Senior Lecturer at the Crawford School of Public Policy at the Australian National University (ANU), Australia.

Routledge law in Asia
Series editor: Randall Peerenboom

1 **Asian Discourses of Rule of Law**
Theories and implementation of Rule of Law in twelve Asian countries, France and the U.S.
Edited by Randall Peerenboom

2 **Human Rights in Asia**
A comparative legal study of twelve Asian jurisdictions, France and the USA
Edited by Randall Peerenboom, Carole J. Petersen and Albert H. Y. Chen

3 **Support for Victims of Crime in Asia**
Edited by Wing-Cheong Chan

4 **Administrative Law and Governance in Asia**
Comparative perspectives
Edited by Tom Ginsburg and Albert H. Y. Chen

5 **Regulation in Asia**
Edited by John Gillespie and Randall Peerenboom

6 **New Courts in Asia**
Edited by Andrew Harding and Penelope (Pip) Nicholson

7 **Legal Education in Asia**
Edited by Stacey Steele and Kathryn Taylor

8 **Legal Reforms in China and Vietnam**
A comparison of Asian communist regimes
John Gillespie and Albert H. Y. Chen

9 **Public Interest Litigation in Asia**
Po Jen Yap and Holning Lau

10 Freedom of Information Reform in China
Information flow analysis
Weibing Xiao

11 Law and Development in Asia
Edited by Gerald Paul McAlinn and Caslav Pejovic

12 The Judicialization of Politics in Asia
Edited by Björn Dressel

The Judicialization of Politics in Asia

Edited by Björn Dressel

Routledge
Taylor & Francis Group
LONDON AND NEW YORK

First published 2012
by Routledge
2 Park Square, Milton Park, Abingdon, Oxon OX14 4RN

Simultaneously published in the USA and Canada
by Routledge
711 Third Avenue, New York, NY 10017

Routledge is an imprint of the Taylor & Francis Group, an informa business

British Library Cataloguing in Publication Data
A catalogue record for this book is available from the British Library

Library of Congress Cataloging in Publication Data
The judicialization of politics in Asia/edited by Björn Dressel.
p. cm. – (Routledge law in Asia; 12)
Includes bibliographical references and index.
1. Courts–Political aspects–Asia. 2. Political questions and judicial power–Asia. 3. Law–Political aspects–Asia. 4. Justice, Administration of–Asia. 5. Asia–Politics and government–21st century. I. Dressel, Björn. II. Series: Routledge law in Asia; 12.
KNC455.J83 2012
306.2′5095–dc23 2011050892

ISBN: 978-0-415-67410-2 (hbk)
ISBN: 978-0-203-11559-6 (ebk)

Typeset in Times New Roman
by Wearset Ltd, Boldon, Tyne and Wear

MIX
Paper from responsible sources
FSC® C004839
www.fsc.org

Printed and bound in Great Britain by
TJ International Ltd, Padstow, Cornwall

Contents

Notes on contributors ix
Preface xiii

1 **The judicialization of politics in Asia: towards a framework of analysis** 1
BJÖRN DRESSEL

PART I
Established democracies 15

2 **The judicialization of Japanese politics?** 17
TOM GINSBURG AND TOKUJIN MATSUDAIRA

3 **Causes and conditions for sustainable judicialization of politics in Korea** 37
JONGCHEOL KIM AND JONGHYUN PARK

4 **The judiciary, policy, and politics in India** 56
SHYLASHRI SHANKAR

PART II
Fragile and young democracies 77

5 **Thailand: judicialization of politics or politicization of the judiciary?** 79
BJÖRN DRESSEL

6 **Indonesia's constitutional court: conservative activist or strategic operator?** 98
SIMON BUTT

7 From judicialization to politicization of the judiciary: the Philippine case 117
ALEJANDRO N. CIENCIA, JR.

8 The judicialization of politics in Pakistan 139
CHARLES H. KENNEDY

PART III
Authoritarian and semi-authoritarian settings 161

9 China's Supreme People's Court within the 'political-legal system' 163
SHUMEI HOU AND RONALD KEITH

10 Cambodia's judiciary: heading for political judicialization? 184
KHEANG UN AND SOKBUNTHOEUN SO

11 Malaysia: limited and intermittent judicialization of politics 202
CHANDRA KANAGASABAI

12 Leadership, law, and legitimacy: reflections on the changing nature of judicial politics in Asia 219
HAIG PATAPAN

Index 234

Contributors

Simon Butt is a Senior Lecturer at Sydney Law School where he is an Australian Research Council Australian Postdoctoral Research Fellow. He teaches and researches in Indonesian law across a wide variety of areas, including constitutional law, law reform, corruption, decentralization and avoided deforestation. He has published widely on Indonesian law, including *Corruption and Law* (Routledge, 2012) and *The Indonesian Constitution* (Hart, 2012, co-authored with Timothy Lindsey). In 2006, he completed his Ph.D., focusing on the Indonesian Constitutional Court.

Alejandro N. Cienca Jr. is Assistant Professor of Political Science at the University of the Philippines-Baguio. He received his MA and Ph.D. in Political Science from the University of the Philippines-Diliman. For his MA thesis and Ph.D. dissertation, he wrote 'Notions of Justice in Cordillera' and 'The Philippine Supreme Court and the Mining Act Ruling Reversal', respectively. He is currently the Chair of the Department of Economics and Political Science (DEPS) of the College of Social Sciences, UP Baguio.

Björn Dressel is a Senior Lecturer at the Crawford School of Public Policy at the Australian National University (ANU) and an Associate Investigator for the Fragile States working group at the Centre of Excellence in Policing and Security (CEPS). His research focuses on issues of comparative constitutionalism, governance and public sector reform in Asia and sub-Saharan Africa. He has published in a range of international journals, including the *Journal of Democracy, Politics & Policy, Contemporary Southeast Asia, Pacific Review and Governance.*

Tom Ginsburg is the Leo Spitz Professor of International Law at the University of Chicago and a Research Fellow at the American Bar Foundation. He holds BA, JD and Ph.D. degrees from the University of California at Berkeley. His recent co-authored book, *The Endurance of National Constitutions* (2009), won the best book award from the Comparative Democratization Section of the American Political Science Association. His other books include *Judicial Review in New Democracies* (2003), *Administrative Law and Governance in Asia* (2008), and *Rule By Law: The Politics of Courts in Authoritarian*

Regimes (with Tamir Moustafa, 2008). Before entering law teaching, he served as a legal advisor at the Iran–U.S. Claims Tribunal, The Hague, Netherlands.

Shumei Hou is a certified lawyer in the People's Republic of China who has practice experience at China's Supreme People's Court. She served as Associate Professor and Head of the Department of Administrative Law at the Henan University of Political Science and Law and has published extensively in Chinese and English journals and was also heavily involved in the training of Chinese judges, lawyers, and public security personnel. Dr. Hou completed her doctoral dissertation at the University of Technology, Sydney on 'Reform of China's Judicial Review System under the WTO Regime' and is currently a postdoctoral fellow at the Griffith University. Her recent articles with Ronald Keith include 'China's Defence Lawyers in the Scales of Criminal Justice', *Journal of Contemporary China*, June 2011 and 'A New Prospect for Transparent Court Judgment in China', *China Information*, November 2011.

Chandra Kanagasabai is an Advocate and Solicitor of the High Court of Malaya who was called to the Malaysian Bar in 1979 after graduating from the University of Singapore in 1979. While in active practice she obtained an LLM from the University of Western Australia in 1998. In 2000 she commenced reading for a Ph.D. at the University of Kent in the UK on a British Chevening scholarship. Her area of research is the judiciary.

Ronald Keith is Professor of China Studies at the Department of International Business and Asian Studies, Griffith University. He has been working on China's legal reform since 1979. His publications include the following three books: Ronald C. Keith, *The Struggle for the Rule of Law in China* (London and New York: Macmillan and St. Martin's Press, 1994); R. C. Keith and Zhiqiu Lin, *Law and Justice in China's New Marketplace* (London: Palgrave, 2001); and Keith and Lin, *New Crime in China: Public Order and Human Rights* (London and New York: Routledge, 2006). Keith and Lin published 'Judicial Interpretation of China's Supreme People's Court as "Secondary Law"', *China Information*, Leiden, vol. xxiii, no. 2, 2009, 223–56. Ronald C. Keith, Lin Zhiqiu and Hou Shumei are currently writing a book for Routledge on China's Supreme People's Court.

Charles H. Kennedy. Hank Kennedy has been a member of the Department of Political Science at Wake Forest University since 1985. Previously he taught at Bowdoin College. He received his Ph.D. from Duke University in 1979. He also holds an MPP in public policy from Duke. Professor Kennedy has written about South Asian political and governmental systems since 1975 and has conducted extensive field research in Pakistan, Bangladesh, and India. He served as the Director of the American Institute of Pakistan Studies from 1988–2001, and was the institute's Secretary from 1982–88. He has written, edited, or co-edited 12 books that deal with South Asia. His most recent include: *Government and Politics in South Asia* (Westview Press, 2009); *Pakistan: 2005* (Oxford University Press, 2006); and *Pakistan at the Millennium* (Oxford University Press, 2003). He is also the author of numerous other scholarly publications. Professor Kennedy also has a long-standing teaching and professional interest in the issues of political Islam, and in US foreign policy with respect to the Middle East and South Asia especially pertaining to Pakistan, Bangladesh, Afghanistan, the Palestinian–Israeli conflict, and Iraq. He currently serves as the Director of the Middle East and South Asia Studies Program at Wake Forest.

Jongcheol Kim is a Professor of Law at the Yonsei University School of Law in Korea and a Distinguished Visiting Professor 2010–11 at the Santa Clara University School of Law in the USA. He received an LLB in 1988 and an LLM in 1990 from Seoul National University College of Law in Korea. He also studied at the London School of Economics and Political Science in the UK for his degrees of LLM in 1994 and Ph.D. in 1998. He worked as a Research Official of the Constitutional Court of Korea in 1999 and has published a number of articles and book chapters in Korean and English in the comprehensive areas of constitutional law, administrative law, and socio-legal theories.

Tokujin Matsudaira is Assistant Professor of Law, Teikyo University, Tokyo. He received his LLB from the University of Tokyo and LLM from the University of Washington. He is the author of several articles in Japanese and English on constitutional theory and law.

Jonghyun Park is an Assistant Professor of Law at the Kookmin University College of Law in Korea and licensed as attorney at law in New York in the US. He is a 2001 graduate of Seoul National University College of Law in Korea and received an LLM in 2003 and Ph.D. in 2009 from Seoul National University Graduate School of Law. He also graduated from the LLM course of Harvard Law School in the USA in 2008. His academic interests are law and politics and comparative constitutional law.

Haig Patapan is Professor in the Department of Politics and Public Policy, Griffith University. His research interests are in political and legal philosophy, comparative constitutionalism, and political leadership. His books include *Judging Democracy* (2000), an examination of Australian judicial politics, jurisprudence, and constitutionalism; *Machiavelli in Love* (2007), a theoretical enquiry into the origins of modern political thought; and a series of co-edited books exploring the changing nature of legitimacy, law, and leadership, especially in Asia: *Globalisation and Equality* (2004); *Westminster Legacies* (2005); *Dissident Democrats* (2008); *Dispersed Democratic Leadership* (2009); *Political Legitimacy in Asia* (2011). His forthcoming co-authored book, *The Democratic Leader* (Oxford University Press, 2012) investigates the unique strengths and limitations of leadership in democracies.

Shylashri Shankar is a Senior Fellow at the Centre for Policy Research, New Delhi. She holds BA degrees from Delhi University, MA (Cantab) from the University of Cambridge, M.Sc. from the London School of Economics and a Ph.D. from Columbia University. She is the author of *Scaling Justice: India's Supreme Court, Anti-Terror Laws and Social Rights* (Oxford University Press, 2009) and of a co-authored forthcoming book—*Battling Corruption: Making the State Responsive to the Poor.* She previously taught at the University of Texas at Austin, and was a Bellagio Fellow at the Rockefeller Center, Bellagio in June 2011.

Sokbunthoeun So is a senior research fellow at Cambodia Development Resource Institute (CDRI) in Phnom Penh, Cambodia. He holds an MA and a Ph.D. in political science from Northern Illinois University. His recent researches focus on land and natural resource governance, decentralized governance, and public sector governance in general. His recent publications appeared in edited book volumes and in various peer reviewed journals including 'Land Rights in Cambodia: How Neopatrimonial Politics Restricts Land Policy Reform', *Pacific Affairs* 84.2 (2011); 'Land Rights In Cambodia: An Unfinished Reform', *Asia Pacific Issues* 97 (2010); and 'The Politics of Natural Resource Use in Cambodia', *Asian Affairs: An American Review* 36 (2009).

Kheang Un is an Assistant Professor of Political Science at Northern Illinois University, USA. He holds a Ph.D. degree in political science and Southeast Asian Studies from Northern Illinois University. Dr. Un served as visiting fellow at the Royal Netherlands Institute for Southeast Asian and Caribbean Studies, the University of Louisville's Center for Asian Democracy, and the Center for Khmer Studies, Cambodia. Dr. Un was a recipient of the 2011–2012 Fulbright fellowship to lecture at the Royal University of Phnom Penh and to conduct research on the issue of democratization in Cambodia. He has published a number of book chapters and scholarly journal articles on contemporary Cambodian politics and political economy. His latest co-edited book is *Cambodia's Economic Transformation* (Nordic Institute for Asian Studies Press/University of Hawaii Press, 2011).

Preface

Over the last two decades, courts and the judiciary have become major players in the political landscape in Asia. Such a trend toward the judicialization of politics is well documented for Europe, Latin America, and the United States, yet the causes, variations, and consequences of its emergence in Asia have been largely unexplored. To the best of my knowledge, there has been no systematic exploration of shifts in power to the judiciary throughout Asia, and certainly no studies linking these developments to the general theoretical debate on the judicialization of politics.

The lack of theoretical and empirical attention to Asia should perhaps not come as a surprise. With legacies of authoritarian executive dominance, an exceptional degree of regime diversity, and institutional arrangements, values, and leadership practices that differ, at times substantially, from those of the West, Asia is a particularly challenging environment for the study of judicial politics. Yet as one of the most dynamic and complex regions in the world, it also offers a fascinating opportunity to explore new judicial dynamics within a rapidly changing environment and across a vast spectrum of contexts; test how effectively theories that evolved elsewhere travel; and thus draw new comparative insights for the academic debate.

It is in this spirit that, rather than prescribing a particular approach, this volume seeks to capture the remarkable complexity of what is happening by presenting a diversity of cases from a variety of regime types in East, Southeast, and South Asia. Although we have assigned the cases to categories of 'established democracies', 'fragile and young democracies', and 'authoritarian and semi-authoritarian regimes', the categories are at best permeable. Indeed given how fast politics in Asia changes, the authors were encouraged to freely expand upon the theme as they trace the changing nature of judicial engagement within a country and explore the causes and the consequences.

The focus of this collection throughout is on what scholars call 'mega-politics'—the growing involvement of judges in core controversies and deep moral dilemmas, from executive branch prerogatives and regime change to restorative justice and elections, and ultimately to questions of nationhood itself. This concentration on mega-politics is particularly interesting because it brings into tight focus the growing political role of the judiciary in policymaking and thus raises critical questions about the nature of governance and political legitimacy. Furthermore, by drawing attention to variations within the judicialization trend, it also helps refine analysis of the causes and effects of the phenomenon as it unfolds. It is thus our hope that this collection will make a timely and seminal contribution to the study of law and politics in Asia.

The papers in this collection were originally presented at the conference on the Judicialization of Politics in Asia at Griffith University in Brisbane, Australia, on 24–25 March 2011. As editor, I am grateful to Professor Pat Weller, Director of the Centre for Governance and Public Policy, and Professor Andrew O'Neil, Director of the Griffith Asia Institute, for financial support. Special thanks also to Kathy Bailey of the Griffith Asia Institute for excellent administrative support. I also offer sincere gratitude to my outstanding colleagues at Griffith University who were willing to comment on individual contributions during the conference: Dr. Edwin Bikundo, Dr. Hun Joon Kim, Dr. Saskia Hufnagel, Dr. Ashutosh Misra, Dr. Michael Clarke, Dr. Roshan de Silva Wijeyeratne, Dr. Stephen McCarthy, Associate Professor Sue Trevaskes, as well as conference facilitators Professor James Allan, Professor Simon Bronitt, Associate Professor Michael Hazel, and Professor Haig Patapan and a number of anonymous peer reviewers.

At my new home at the Australian National University, I am particularly thankful to Professor Tom Kompas, director of ANU's Crawford School of Economics and Government, for granting me the time to complete this project before the start of my teaching duties. Once again, too, I offer sincere thanks to Anne Grant for her superb editorial assistance.

But my greatest thanks must go to the contributors to this volume, not only for their remarkably helpful scholarly insights but also for their patience through the editing process.

1 The judicialization of politics in Asia

Towards a framework of analysis

Björn Dressel

Introduction

Courts and the judiciary have become highly visible in the Asian political landscape. The regular interventions of the Philippine and Indian Supreme Courts in the animated politics of their countries were long considered an exception in the region, but not now. In Korea, Taiwan, and Indonesia new constitutional courts have been crucial in diffusing political crisis and consolidating democratic practice, while in Pakistan the judiciary was critical to clearing the way back to democratic practice. The Malaysian High Court has been embroiled in several politically charged cases, and in Thailand decisions of the Constitutional Court since 2006 have drastically altered the political landscape. Even in more conservative Japan and semi-authoritarian Cambodia and China, there are occasional hints of judicial assertiveness, though so far, for different reasons, those courts have worked to avoid high-profile political cases.

This trend towards the 'judicialization of politics', which Hirschl (2006: 721) describes as 'the ever-accelerating reliance on courts and judicial means for addressing core moral predicaments, public policy questions, and political controversies', has been well documented for the United States, Europe, and Latin America (see Sieder *et al.* 2005; Tate and Vallinder 1995; Epp 1998; Stone Sweet 2000; Feeley and Rubin 1998; Shapiro and Stone Sweet 2002), but its emergence in Asia has largely been unexplored (though see Harding and Nicholson 2010a; Ginsburg and Chen 2009). This should not be surprising: The region is still battling with legacies of executive dominance, weak rule of law, and a degree of regime diversity so unusual that a leading scholar claimed not even 20 years ago that 'a majority of [Southeast] Asian countries are unlikely candidates for the judicialization of politics' (Tate 1994: 188) because so many regimes were neither democratic nor constitutional.

But a lot has changed in the region in the past two decades. As political and economic liberalization advances—though hardly in a linear fashion and with many throwbacks—many regimes have become more concerned about the rule of law, accountability, and rights issues. Indeed, promoting the rule of law has gained traction in the region, sometimes as part of state and constitutional reforms initiated by new democracies emerging from authoritarian rule to enhance the quality of their democracy (Harding and Nicholson 2010b), sometimes as part of the efforts of illiberal regimes to tighten social control, enhance legitimacy, and ensure credible policy outcomes (see Ginsburg and Moustafa 2008). In both cases global and regional discourse about what constitutes 'good governance' has reinforced the trend. As a result, courts have become surprisingly central to the political life of many countries, and the perception is emerging that the region is indeed becoming judicialized (Dowdle 2009).

Yet there is still considerable academic debate and practical concern about the drivers and effects of the trend. For instance, while the literature on drivers of judicialization has generally fallen into two camps—some emphasizing judicialization from below via social demand for rights protection and limited government, others seeing strategic decisions by elites to secure their interests through counter-majoritarian means creating judicialization from above—it is also true, as these case studies illustrate, that many of the models can be applied only with difficulty to Asia. Perhaps even more important, current models provide little insight into how actual judicial performance and behavior can be explained; nor is there agreement on the effects of variances in judicial behavior.

The latter is of particular concern in Asia, where the effects of judicial empowerment have been at best ambiguous. Some courts have actively intervened in politics to enhance governance, for instance providing checks and balances on executive abuse, upholding the supremacy of law, and protecting the rights of citizens. Some, however, have actively subverted the rule of law and undermined mechanisms of accountability in favor of narrow interests or have lent support to the rule *by* law. Still others have been deliberately muted or highly restrained when engaging with core issues of political governance, raising questions about their own autonomy and independence.

The dramatic variations in judicial performance and behavior in Southeast Asia raise serious questions, both empirical and theoretical, that the authors whose studies follow have been willing to confront:

- What patterns of judicialization can be identified and why is it taking different tracks?
- What effects is the judicialization trend actually having on governance? To what extent and under what conditions does it improve prospects for the rule of law and more accountability to society? And when does it lead to more political interference with the courts?
- Finally, how can the Asian experience inform the scholarly debate on the judicialization of politics generally? How does judicial behavior in Asia differ from that in the West? What implications do the differences have for the theoretical debate?

The purpose of this volume is to identify answers to such questions. Bringing together rich country narratives from diverse settings—established democracies (Japan, Korea, India); fragile and young democracies (Indonesia, the Philippines,

Pakistan); authoritarian and semi-authoritarian regimes (Cambodia, Malaysia, China)—the case studies together reveal a comprehensive picture of how courts are operating in a variety of regime types. Written by leading country experts, each chapter explores in detail the evolving pattern of judicial politics in a given country, analyzing its drivers and its effects. Enriched with analysis of critical court decisions and throughout emphasizing 'mega-politics'—the involvement of constitutional or supreme courts in matters of utmost political significance (see Hirschl 2008a: 94)—this volume makes a seminal contribution to the study of law and politics: It is the first systematic exploration of shifts in power to the judiciary in Asia, and it explicitly links developments to the general theoretical debate on the judicialization of politics.

This chapter starts off the discussion by extracting from the literature a basic typology of judicial politics. The purpose is twofold: It is meant to provide a framework of judicial behavior that may help classify the case studies. In drawing attention to the different paths the phenomenon has taken over time in different countries, however, it also hopes to inspire closer attention to variations in the structural and political contexts in which courts operate. This makes it possible to highlight specific drivers—institutional, ideational, and structural—that emerge from the country chapters. Combined with an initial evaluation of the effects of judicial empowerment on governance in Asia, the chapter concludes with some thoughts on how what is happening in Asia can inform the general scholarly debate about the judicialization of politics.

Views from the literature: towards a typology of judicial politics

Although the idea of the judicialization of politics has received considerable academic attention, there is little agreement on how this engagement is best conceptualized, what is driving it, and what its effects are. This may in part be because the concept has often suffered from being stretched to cover different, though sometimes interrelated, processes (see for a good overview Hirschl 2008b). Deserving of thoughtful separation, for instance, are

- the abstract capture of social relations and popular culture by law due to the growing complexities of modern societies—a process perhaps better described as 'juridification' (see for a good overview Teubner 1987; Blichner and Molander 2008);
- the more concrete and much analyzed expansion of the courts into public policy as part of 'ordinary' constitutional rights jurisprudence (positive rights, procedural justice) and the redrawing of boundaries between state organs (separation of powers, federalism); and
- the narrower though salient reliance on courts and judges to deal with core political controversies and deep moral dilemmas related to areas of pure politics ('mega-politics'), such as executive branch prerogatives, electoral politics, and regime change (Hirschl 2008a: 99–100).

In essence, then, we can identify two notions about the judicialization of politics. Narrowly, the term refers to the way judges in exercising judicial review contribute to or at least influence public policy—the process by which courts and judges, especially constitutional or supreme courts, come to dominate the making of public policy, which had previously been the prerogative of legislatures and executives (Sieder *et al.* 2005: 3; Tate and Vallinder 1995). More broadly, though, judicialization is not limited to an expansion of 'judge-made law'; it also encompasses the increased presence of judicial processes and court rulings in political and social life, for instance when social actors use courts and the law to advance their own interests, political actors become more attuned to court actions, and state legitimacy is constructed increasingly in terms of delivering the rule of law (Domingo 2004: 108–10). If we take these two notions together, judicialization generally is marked by more deference to the courts, which allows them to make major political decisions. When courts become active political players, they have more influence on aspects of governance than their traditional role would allow.

At first scholarship on the trend towards constitutional transformation and judicialization anchored it in macro-level processes of democratization and modernization (Shapiro 1999; Sunstein 2001); in a tendency, from the functionalist and neo-institutional point of view, to greater system efficiency; or in the search for solutions to systemic collective action problems (Feeley and Rubin 1998; North and Weingast 1989; Shapiro and Stone Sweet 2002; Weingast 1993). Next, theories about drivers of the trend were expanded to the global spread of rights consciousness and to legal structures to support mobilization by civil society (Tate and Vallinder 1995; Epp 1998; Slaughter 2000). But despite differences in approach and detail, what all these scholars share is a single view: The proliferation and growing assertiveness of judicial and quasi-judicial agencies are expressions of a universal modernization that embraces the rule of law and separation of powers as constructs of viable democratic government, and that these constructs are consistent with a 'demand side' view of judicialization not just from below but even from abroad.

More recently, however, scholars have been drawing attention to the structural dynamics and the actors in the process as part of a supply-side-driven process of judicialization from above. Anchoring the process at the structural level, these micro-level, agent-based approaches argue that self-interested strategic actors might have political reasons for empowering judges. The reasons may be dysfunctional institutions (Guarnieri and Pederzoli 2002; Ferejohn 2002); the wish to delegate authority to courts in order to shift responsibility (Voigt and Salzberger 2002) and build legitimacy for contested policies (Morton 1995; Goldstein 2001); or the personal motivations of judges (Baum 2006; Waldron 1999; Tushnet 1999; Bork 2003). The effort to embed human agency more comprehensively within a structural context can also be seen in the two rational-strategic approaches that are currently dominant: the 'insurance model' that views judicial empowerment as a means of strategic insurance in times of growing electoral competition (Ginsburg 2003; Ramseyer 1994); and the 'hegemonic preservation model' that sees growing judicial empowerment as a means for elites to preserve power as they become more vulnerable to majoritarian politics (Hirschl 2006, 2008b). Thus at the core of these supply-side theories are assumptions of uncertainty and rational calculations by politicians about the benefits of a strengthened judicial role.

Not surprisingly, differences about what is driving the judicialization trend have generated a variety of views about how the trend affects governance. For instance, scholars in the macro-level tradition have often enthusiastically embraced the rise of constitutionalism globally and praised the expansion of judicial review as offering greater protection of citizens and deepening democracy (Ackerman 1997; Dworkin 1990). However, authors of the structural school have been far more cautious. For instance, Ginsburg sees the growing role of the judiciary as conducive to the deepening of democratic governance by transforming political conflict into constitutional dialogue, providing a nonpartisan forum for grievances, and expressing fundamental democratic values. Bork, however, has decried the 'rise of unelected, unrepresentative, unaccountable committees of lawyers' (2003: 22); Morton and Knopff have criticized reliance on 'court room politics [that are] authoritarian in both process and spirit' (2000: 149); and Hirschl suggests the trend may reflect a move towards 'juristocracy' (2008).

While the debate may often have been empirically weak, if not outright normatively charged (see Hilbink 2008), it does highlight theoretical as well as empirical ambiguities about the process of judicialization. For instance, while it would be relatively easy to view judicial actors and processes acting in support of the rule of law in a given country as part of a general process of legalization, the relationship to political accountability and representation is often far more complex, as we can see from long-standing debates within constitutional theory about the balance between judicial guardianship of constitutional principles and majoritarian rule—the counter-majoritarian dilemma—and about who guards the guardians (Friedman 2001; Graber 2008; Bickel 1962 (1986)). Meanwhile, a growing empirical literature on countries in transition is revealing the pitfalls that emerge when the judiciary is repositioned. It reminds us that judicial self-assertion is hardly a linear process, and judicial actors are often deeply embedded in an illiberal past (Domingo 2004: 121). It also exposes the danger that as judicial systems become more politically salient, policymakers may seek to influence the judiciary. This 'politicization' of the judiciary was recognized long ago by such constitutional and legal scholars as Schmitt (1958).

So far the growing body of scholarship has principally been concerned with exploring the origins of judicial empowerment; it has given far less attention to actual judicial performance in terms of either variations in judicial behavior or their effects on governance. Recent scholarly debates have sought to expand and complement some of the current dominant approaches by urging greater contextualization, especially more attention to historical and ideational factors (see Hilbink and Woods 2009; Hilbink 2009); they seem to reflect a discontent with the limits of the current debate while urging a more multidimensional and temporally dynamic approach that works concurrently at different levels (McCann 2009). The debates thus offer interesting avenues for both exploration of judicial empowerment and explanation of actual judicial behavior once judicial review is established.

Recognizing this, let us step back from the scholarly fray in order to think carefully about a new way of looking at the process of judicialization. The literature seems to me to support a move towards a basic typology of judicial politics, two dimensions of which are already visible in the literature:

1 The judicialization of politics is a complex process driven by factors at several analytical levels. It depends to at least some degree on court (de jure) structural independence (institutional); the willingness and ability of judges to intervene (behavioral); and support from political elites to facilitate this process (structural). For simplicity's sake, these interrelated aspects could be collapsed into de facto independence.
2 The involvement of judges in areas of politics can be understood as a continuum ranging from minimal to extensive involvement in such areas as mega-politics.

Working from the two dimensions of de facto judicial independence and engagement in mega-politics, we can build a matrix that illustrates a typology of ideal judicial pattern types, ranging from judicial restraint and judicial muteness to judicial activism and politicization of the judiciary (Figure 1.1).

These patterns of judicial behavior may be slightly overdrawn for illustrative purposes: For instance, the difference between 'judicial restraint' and 'judicial muteness' largely relates to whether the judiciary has the autonomy to withdraw of its own choosing from areas of mega-politics; likewise, where independence is low, depending on the issues the judicial pattern might easily flip between

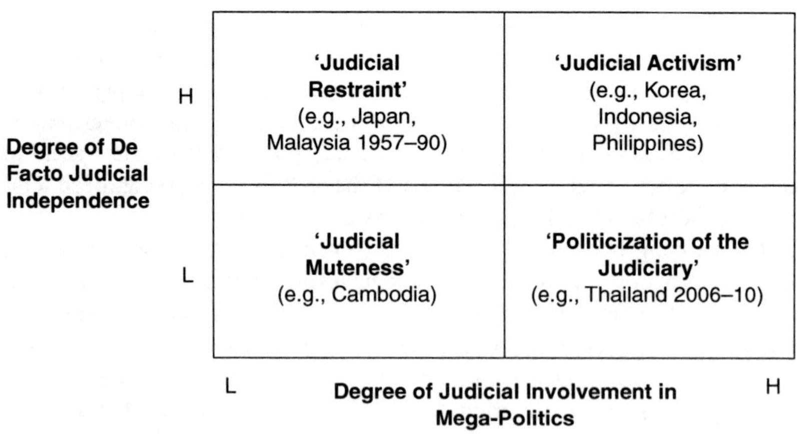

Figure 1.1 Typology of judicial politics in areas of mega-politics.

'politicization' and 'judicial muteness' (or even de-judicialization). Moreover, as the case studies in this collection vividly illustrate, the relationship between judicial systems, law, and politics is highly fluid, and the degree of judicial involvement often swings widely not only from country to country but within a country over time. Judicial engagement in mega-politics may at times be temporary, whether because exceptional events causing political deadlock propel judges into the political fray or because political actors respond to judicial activism with institutional changes that curb the powers of judges. However, it is also clear that as institutional practices become more engrained, the more stable patterns of judicial governance that emerge allow us to characterize the behavior of a country's courts more consistently.

The typology thus helps to bring greater analytical rigor to the study of judicialization and its effects on governance. Above all it provides a more nuanced and temporally dynamic view of the phenomenon. It also helps for analytical purposes to capture a distinct country pattern at a given point *in* time and also makes it possible to identify trajectories of judicial politics *over* time. As a result, the typology thus urges greater analytical attention to the conditions in which certain judicial patterns emerge and the drivers behind change over time. Finally, it might also trigger debate about how these patterns in turn shape modes of governance—for instance in respect to the rule of law, accountability, and the protection of rights. A closer look at some of the findings from the individual case studies illustrates this point.

Drivers and effects of judicial patterns in Asia

To start with, applying the typology to the country cases helps us identify clusters of Asian judicial behavior in areas of mega-politics; for instance:

- **Activist Courts** – Korea, Philippines, Pakistan, Indonesia;
- **Restrained Courts** – Japan, (India?);
- **Muted Courts** – Malaysia, China;
- **Politicized Courts** – Thailand, Cambodia.

Clearly, this is a simplified picture. As the authors reiterate, it is analytically important to differentiate between levels and types of actors in the judicial system; the periods being reviewed; and the areas of judicial engagement.

For instance, supreme and specialized courts such as constitutional courts that have powers of review are more likely to become involved in highly charged political cases than ordinary courts. Similarly, as illustrated in India, history matters: it is only because the Indian Supreme Court had a long-standing history of activism that its current behavior is seen as more restrained. And court behavior can quickly change quite dramatically, as is obvious from the once restrained Thai Constitutional Court, which during the 2006 political crisis was transformed into a highly politicized court, and, at the other extreme, from the Malaysian judiciary, which became increasingly muted when its tendencies towards judicial activism were forcefully stopped by the executive. Finally, even where the judicial pattern has been relatively stable over time, occasional decisions or areas of judicial interventions, like those of the Japanese Supreme Court, might justify a different classification.

Yet whatever the situation, any changes in judicial pattern tend to bring into tight focus the question of what is driving the change. Here the case studies offer valuable insights.

Liberalization, democratization, and regime type

A quick survey of judicialization in Asia would suggest that judicial behavior is primarily an expression of the type of regime in place: more established and vibrant democracies seem to host more activist courts; in semi- and authoritarian settings judges are far less assertive.

This should not be surprising. Indeed as many of the country cases make clear, political liberalization and democratization have brought a repositioning of the judiciary, above all by rewriting the constitution to incorporate judicial review, more explicit rights and liberties, and new safeguards for judicial independence. In the Philippines, for instance, empowerment of the judiciary has been critical to the post-Marcos 1987 constitution and its efforts to leave the authoritarian past behind and prevent executive abuse in the future. Meanwhile in Korea, Indonesia, and Thailand, the new liberal architecture brought in centralized judicial review and new constitutional courts that were envisioned as guardians of the new constitutional order and final arbiters in political conflict.

Yet, as the cases make clear, the relationship between regime type and judicialization is not necessarily causal. While it is perhaps true that judicial empowerment has often sprung from liberalizing reforms, such reforms are hardly sufficient to explain how the courts actually behave. Often courts have been cautious about wading into political controversies and have done so only after some time—often as other political institutions gradually matured. In other instances courts, even specialized ones, have never fully accepted such a role; for instance, the activities of the Cambodian Constitutional Council were stifled not only by the political environment but also by the lack of judicial capacity and will. Perhaps most instructive, the Japanese Supreme Court reminds us that despite considerable democratic maturity and judicial autonomy, courts may choose not to exert their review powers often or engage in core political controversies.

Institutions, ideas, and structures

For understanding how a judicialization pattern emerges and changes over time it may be helpful to look at the interplay between institutional, ideational, and structural factors. Patapan details the complexity of that interplay in the concluding chapter; here I just mention a few key issues.

Institutional variables have considerable influence on patterns of judicialization. For instance, courts need at least some structural independence if they are to emerge as influential actors. That implies the importance of micro-institutional rules that are related, for example, to appointment procedures, composition of the bench, and the autonomy of court budgets. Other relevant rules are those related to judicial review, which not only set the bounds of judicial activity but often also open up new areas of engagement for traditionally conservative institutions. Combined, such institutional arrangements thus provide powerful incentives and constraints on the behavior of both individual judges and courts as institutions. For instance, the differences in how judges are appointed to the Constitutional Courts in Indonesia, Thailand, and Korea have had divergent effects in terms of political interference in the appointment process and the extent to which each court has taken an activist stance. Similarly, decisions by constitutional drafters have often led for the first time to direct engagement of the judiciary in such contentious political areas as electoral disputes and executive prerogatives—not to mention questions of nationhood. Obviously, constitutional decisions are also a major factor not only in whether politics becomes judicialized but in whether courts become politicized.

The effect of institutional rules need not be greater judicial assertiveness in political areas. In Japan, the unusual restraint of an otherwise highly independent judiciary is attributed in part to the tight control of the General Secretariat of the Supreme Court over the selection, appointment, and career trajectories of judges. Similarly, institutional changes to the appointment and tenure system in Malaysia after the first constitutional crisis not only muted the top court but also eroded judicial independence and professionalism all the way down. And such constraints are perhaps most visible in China, where institutional factors have greatly restricted the activities of the Chinese Supreme People's Court.

Where institutional power is more diffused, courts are also generally more likely to be drawn into the political fray. As illustration, in the presidential systems in the region (Korea, Indonesia, the Philippines) courts have often been called upon to arbitrate political stalemate between branches of government and even surrounding the presidency itself. There has been less recourse to the courts in the parliamentary systems in the region (Thailand, India, Malaysia, Japan) due to traditions of parliamentary sovereignty and single party dominance (Congress in India; the Liberal Democratic Party (LDP) in Japan; the United Malays National Organisation (UMNO) in Malaysia; the Chinese Communist Party (CCP) in China), though this has begun to change as the underlying systems do.

Ideas and values have twofold importance in the extent to which courts are engaged in politics. For one thing, the ideational context is critical to understanding the origins of judicial empowerment. This is vividly illustrated throughout the collection. Consider the liberal ideas that culminated in the drafting of the 1997 Thai constitution; the effects of the constitutional crisis provoked by the Wahid impeachment trial in Indonesia; and previous experiences of authoritarian rule in Korea and the Philippines. Ideas, whether home-grown or borrowed from abroad, shape the preferences of actors (see also Peerenboom 2004).

Equally important, ideas and values are also critical in shaping the self-understanding of the judiciary as an institution and thus in shaping patterns of judicial behavior. Ginsburg illustrates that the unusual quiescence of the Japanese Supreme Court in political matters is best explained by the integration of nineteenth-century German organ theory into Japanese constitutional law. The Japanese constitution guarantees the autonomy and independence of such state institutions as the judiciary, but it also limits their activity vis-à-vis each other, resulting in judicial politics that are quite different from what is known in the West (even in Germany). Similarly, for the Chinese Supreme People's Court Hou and Keith argue that the 'three supreme doctrine', among other ideational foundations, may allow the court some internal autonomy but also ties it closely to the stability paradigm of the CCP, thereby assigning it to an apolitical role of guidance and interpretation.

The roles of ideas and institutions may be analyzed separately but they are hard to separate in actuality. For instance, in the Philippines U.S. legacies not only inform the training of judges but also are a powerful factor in the self-identification of the Supreme Court as an activist court. Likewise, in Malaysia courts have been greatly influenced by judicial developments in the Commonwealth, especially since many Malaysian judges have received training overseas. Conversely, where there have been sharp ideational breaks from the past (e.g. Cambodia), or new courts were formed, judicial behavior may take time to form a pattern; the elapse of time can offer considerable leeway for court leaders themselves to shape the trajectory of judicial behavior.

Finally there are broader ***structural dynamics*** that should be considered. Indeed, bold judicial interventions in politics (or the lack thereof) often are rooted within the broader context of state–society relations, and more particularly intra-elite dynamics. As several case studies demonstrate, when political settlements unravel or new elite and social cleavages emerge, courts are often pulled into the political fray, sometimes as independent arbiters, sometimes, where independence is compromised, as an arm of the ruling elites. Hence, judicialization is often facilitated, if not driven outright, by power struggles within the prevailing social dynamics. For instance, think about what was then the Malaysian Federal Court and how it functioned in the leadership contest within the UMNO ruling coalition. Or think about the impeachment proceedings against former President Estrada in the Philippines. Both situations reflected widening intra-elite divisions. There have also been blatant attempts to use the judiciary for political purposes against opposition candidates, most notably in Malaysia, Thailand, and Cambodia.

But judicial actors are not simply pawns in a high-level power play either. Closely tied ideologically and by socialization to ruling political elites, they may fully support regime interests. Or they may pursue interests of their own, particularly with reinforcement from alliances with outside actors. Elite consensus in favor of judicial independence provides space for a range of judicial activities, though a court must choose its direction carefully if it is not to jeopardize the very legitimacy of the judiciary.

As the region undergoes rapid modernization, new sites of political contestation and intra-elite conflict have emerged, often prompting renewed struggles over both the content and the control of law. It is useful to keep in mind the informal dynamics that coexist with the formal realm in Asia. For the judiciary they may take the form of penetration through patrimonial structures or influence exerted by traditional power centers, such as military or royal networks. Because growing international exposure and rising domestic demand for rule-based governance have prompted judicial actors to test boundaries and champion new causes, recognizing the dynamics of both formal and informal structures is crucial to understanding how the judicialization trend is evolving in the region. Equally important is recognizing the complex interplay of these structures with institutional, ideational, and other factors, as Patapan elaborates in the concluding chapter.

Evaluating the effects of judicialization

Evaluating the effects of the judicialization trend in Asia is not easy. Among other things, it raises the issue of what benchmarks to use to assess developments, especially given the diversity of the political settings there. Many scholars look at whether, and what, the higher courts have contributed to such aspects of national governance as accountability, transparency, and respect for rules. They may concern themselves with distinct aspects of the judicialization trend, particularly politicization of the judiciary in favor of narrow interests, or their outright cooptation, which has the effect of muting judicial actors. In such cases, judicial behavior has often exacerbated political conflict by failing to provide impartial justice and ensure that the political system is inclusive.

Instances of growing judicial activism or self-imposed restraint have proved more difficult to evaluate. For instance, while several have stressed that growing judicial assertiveness has been critical to a deepening of the democratic process, heightened accountability for public officials, and greater state responsiveness to issues of socioeconomic rights and service provision, others have been more wary of growing judicial involvement in policy areas or the bold expansion of judicial powers by judges themselves (for example, the 'basic structure' doctrine in India, or the recourse to a 'customary constitution' in Korea). This is partly because judicial actors lack expertise and capacity in public policy making and partly because there is a danger that expanded judicial powers might come at the expense of other institutional actors, particularly those legitimated by popular mandate. But this is also not to say that judicial restraint is always the answer; it, too, bears the risk that contested issues of mega-politics remain unresolved or are badly addressed, which reinforces uncertainty and ultimately erodes legitimacy.

What seems in fact to emerge from the case studies is the pragmatic insight that the effects of judicialization on governance depend on both the strategic behavior of the courts and the constitutional dialogue of other branches of government. Rather than viewing judicial empowerment as a zero-sum game, what matters most is how meaningful dialogue on critical issues is fostered and engages all institutions, to the ultimate transformation of political conflict into constitutional politics. This is particularly so for issues of mega-politics, which by nature are likely to be deeply divisive. Courts must carefully choose their battles and the scope of their interventions; certainly the political capital of the judiciary, the weakest branch of government, is largely derived from its own legitimacy. As regimes in the region mature, early popular court decisions are likely to be replaced with decisions in more complex cases that may prove divisive, but that also increasingly invite political actors to have recourse to the courts rather than risk unpopularity themselves.

Conclusion

From the rich diversity of this volume's case studies there spring new theoretical and empirical insights to enrich the scholarly debate. As the typology of judicial politics presented here suggests, this volume draws attention to nuances and variations *within* the judicialization trend as it unfolds in the region. Moreover, in starkly dissecting patterns of judicialization one by one, it moves the debate from where judicial empowerment originates to how judicial power is actually asserted and the ends to which it has been applied. These studies not only give deeper context to the judicialization trend; they also broaden the arena for much-needed comparative research into how judicialization patterns emerge and change over time.

As these case studies make clear, current theoretical models of judicialization are transferred only with difficulty to the Asian context. We hope the chapters that follow will stimulate further research into the judicialization of politics in Asia—something not only long overdue but, as recent developments illuminate, something that is ever more necessary.

References

Ackerman, B. (1997) The Rise of World Constitutionalism. *Virginia Law Review* 83: 771–97.

Baum, L. (2006) *Judges and their Audiences: A Perspective on Judicial Behavior*, Princeton: Princeton University Press.

Bickel, A. (1962 (1986)) *The Least Dangerous Branch: The Supreme Court at the Bar of Politics*, New Haven: Yale University Press.

Blichner, L. C. and Molander, A. (2008) Mapping Juridification. *European Law Journal* 14: 36–54.

Bork, R. (2003) *Coercing Virtue: The Worldwide Rule of Judges*, Washington, DC: American Enterprise Institute.

Domingo, P. (2004) Judicialization of Politics or Politicization of the Judiciary? Recent Trends in Latin America. *Democratization* 11: 104–26.

Dowdle, M. W. (2009) On the Regulatory Dynamics of Judicialization: the Promise and Perils of Exploring "Judicialization" in East and Southeast Asia. In: Ginsburg, T. and Chen, A. H. Y. (eds) *Administrative Law and Governance in Asia*, London and New York: Routledge, 23–37.

Dworkin, R. (1990) *A Bill of Rights for Britain*, London: Chatto and Windus.

Epp, C. R. (1998) *The Rights Revolution: Lawyers, Activists and Supreme Courts in Comparative Perspective*, Chicago: University of Chicago Press.

Feeley, M. and Rubin, E. (1998) *Judicial Policy Making and the Modern State: How the Courts Reformed America's Prisons*, Cambridge: Cambridge University Press.

Ferejohn, J. (2002) Judicializing Politics, Politicizing Law. *Law Contemporary Problems* 61: 41–68.

Friedman, B. (2001) The Counter-Majoritarian and the Pathology of Constitutional Scholarship. *Northwestern University Law Review* 95: 933–54.

Ginsburg, T. (2003) *Judicial Review in New Democracies. Constitutional Courts in Asian Cases*, Cambridge: Cambridge University Press.

Ginsburg, T. and Chen, A. H. Y. (2009) *Administrative Law and Governance in Asia. Comparative Perspectives,* New York: Routledge.

Ginsburg, T. and Moustafa, T. (2008) *Rule by Law: The Politics of Courts in Authoritarian Regimes*, Cambridge; New York: Cambridge University Press.

Goldstein, L. (2001) *Constituting Federal Sovereignty: The European Union in Comparative Context*, Baltimore: Johns Hopkins University Press.

Graber, M. A. (2008) The Countermajoritarian Difficulty: From Courts to Congress to Constitutional Order. *Annual Review of Law and Social Science* 4: 361–84.

Guarnieri, C. and Pederzoli, P. (2002) *The Power of Judges*, New York: Oxford University Press.

Harding, A. and Nicholson, P. (2010a) *New Courts in Asia*, Oxon and New York: Routledge.

Harding, A. and Nicholson, P. (2010b) New Courts in the Asia-Pacific Region: Law, Development and Judicialization. In: Harding, A. and Nicholson, P. (2010) *New Courts in Asia*, Oxon and New York: Routledge, pp. 1–28.

Hilbink, L. (2008) Assessing the New Constitutionalism. *Comparative Politics* 40: 227–45.

Hilbink, L. (2009) The constituted nature of constituents' interests: Historical and ideational factors in judicial empowerment. *Political Science Research Quarterly* 62: 781–97.

Hilbink, L. and Woods, P. J. (2009). Comparative Sources of Judicial Empowerment: Ideas and Interests. *Political Research Quarterly* 62(4): 745–52.

Hirschl, R. (2004) *Towards Juristocracy: The Origins and Consequences of the New Constitutionalism*, Cambridge, MA: Harvard University Press.

Hirschl, R. (2006) The New Constitutionalism and the Judicialization of Pure Politics Worldwide. *Fordham Law Review* 75: 721–54.

Hirschl, R. (2008a) The Judicialization of Mega-Politics and the Rise of Political Courts. *Annual Review of Political Science* 11: 93–118.

Hirschl, R. (2008b) The Judicialization of Politics. In: Whittington, K. E., Kelemen, D. R. and Caldeira, G. A. (eds) *The Oxford Handbook of Law and Politics*, Oxford and New York: Oxford University Press, 119–41.

McCann, M. W. (2009). Interests, Ideas, and Institutions in Comparative Analysis of Judicial Power. *Political Research Quarterly* 62(4): 834–9.

Morton, F. L. (1995) The Effect of the Charter of Rights on Canadian Federalism. *Publius* 25: 173–88.

Morton, F. L. and Knopff, R. (2000) *The Charter Revolution and the Court Party*, Peterborough, ON: Broadview Press.

North, D. C. and Weingast, B. R. (1989) Constitutions and Commitment: The Evolution of Institutions Governing Public Choice in Seventeenth-century England. *Journal of Economic History* 44: 803–32.

Peerenboom, R. (2004) *Asian Discourses of Rule of Law*, London and New York: Routledge.

Ramseyer, M. J. (1994) The Puzzling (In)Dependence of Courts: A Comparative Approach. *Journal of Legal Studies* 23: 721–47.

Schmitt, C. (1958). Das Reichsgericht als Hueter der Verfassung. *Verfassungsrechtliche Aufsätze aus den Jahren 1924–1954. Materialien zu einer Verfassungslehre*, Berlin: Duncker & Humblot.

Shapiro, M. (1999) The Success of Judicial Review. In: Kenney, S. (ed.) *Constitutional Dialogues in Comparative Perspective*, New York: Palgrave Macmillan.

Shapiro, M. and Stone Sweet, A. (2002) *On Law, Politics, and Judicialization*, New York: Oxford University Press.

Sieder, R., Schjolden, L., and Angell, A. (2005) *The Judicialization of Politics in Latin America*, New York and Houndmills: Palgrave Macmillan.

Slaughter, A. M. (2000) Judicial Globalization. *Virginia Journal of International Law* 40: 1103–24.

Stone Sweet, A. (2000) *Governing with Judges: Constitutional Politics in Europe*, Oxford: Oxford University Press.

Sunstein, C. R. (2001) *Designing Democracy. What Constitutions Do.* Oxford: Oxford University Press.

Tate, N. C. (1994). The Judicialization of Politics in the Philippines and Southeast Asia. *International Political Science Review* 15(2): 187–97.

Tate, N. C. and Vallinder, T. (1995) *The Global Expansion of Judicial Power*, New York: New York University Press.

Teubner, G. (1987) Juridification – Concepts, Aspects, Limits, Solutions. In: Teubner, G. (ed.) *Juridification of Social Spheres: A Comparative Analysis in the Areas of Labor, Corporate, Antitrust and Social Welfare Law*, Berlin; New York: de Gruyter, 3–49.

Tushnet, M. (1999) *Taking the Constitution Away from the Courts*, Princeton: Princeton Univ. Press.

Voigt, S. and Salzberger, E. (2002) Choosing not to Choose: When Politicians Choose to Delegate Powers. *Kyklos* 55: 289–310.

Waldron, J. (1999) *Law and Disagreement*, Oxford: Clarendon Press.

Weingast, B. (1993) Constitutions as Governance Structures: The Political Foundations of Secure Markets. *Journal of Institutional & Theoretical Economics* 286.

Part I

Established democracies

2 The judicialization of Japanese politics?

Tom Ginsburg and Tokujin Matsudaira

Are Japan's politics becoming judicialized? Certainly Japan has been somewhat of an outlier among advanced industrial democracies, in which scholars have documented a decisive trend toward greater scope and authority for judicial decision-making (Tate and Vallinder, 1995; Hirschl 2008). National and supranational courts in North America and Europe regularly decide the largest political and social questions of the day—abortion, gay marriage, the status of religion, even who can take power—questions that Japan's Supreme Court has studiously avoided. Closer to home, the Korean and Taiwanese constitutional courts routinely decide major issues of social policy. Japan's courts seem much more quiescent.

Yet Japan has just experienced a decade of major reforms of legal institutions. The declared goal, as articulated in the 1998 launch of the Justice System Reform Council, was nothing less than the transformation of Japanese society into one that was more law-governed, where ex post judicial remedies replaced ex ante planning in allocating rights and duties. Japan has also experienced major political change with the emergence, however tentative, of what appears to be a two-party system. These factors would lead one to expect a degree of judicialization, since scholars have long predicted that an alternation in political power is a basic factor underpinning judicial power and independence (Ramseyer 1994; Ginsburg 2003).

In this paper we show that in Japan, while some areas have experienced an increased role for judicialized governance, others have not. Relative to other advanced industrial societies, the level of judicialization is low. In examining the reasons for this we find that conventional explanations rooted in politics and institutional structure do not fully account for the phenomenon. Rather, we find, full understanding requires an inquiry into the institutional self-understanding of Japanese courts, which is rooted in the nineteenth century Meiji adaptation of Prussian legal thought. Thus political theory, rather than political structure, seems to provide the explanation we seek.

Our account is consistent with recent work that emphasizes the role of ideational factors in judicial behavior. In her account of Chilean judicial quiescence during the Pinochet regime, for example, Lisa Hilbink focuses on an institutional self-conceptualization of judicial apoliticism (Hilbink 2007) that is rooted in the conservative positivism of a nineteenth century modernizing state. She finds that apoliticism is in fact far from apolitical: by refraining from getting involved in 'political' issues, Chilean judges are reinforcing the status quo. Similarly, the relatively limited judicialization in Japan means that the political process is allowed to play the dominant role in allocation of rights and responsibilities. This is precisely the idea behind the 19th century theory that we elaborate.

In its emphasis on ideational and institutional factors, our story is also consistent with recent work by David Law (2009), who has provided a thick description of the behavior of the Japanese Supreme Court, though the approach is somewhat at odds with prevailing views among other Western scholars of Japanese law. They have tended to emphasize institutional rather than ideational factors in understanding Japanese judicial behavior. John Haley, for example, has emphasized the institutional weakness of the Japanese judiciary to explain its particular role in Japanese society (1991, 1998). J. Mark Ramseyer (1994) has instead emphasized the importance of political pressures from the long-ruling Liberal Democratic Party (LDP), which in his view indirectly controls judicial promotions. These and other scholars have provided a useful corrective to simplistic cultural accounts of Japanese law. But because institutional analysis, in particular its sociological variant, also takes into account the internal understandings of actors who populate institutions, we see the present argument as complementing the dominant narrative rather than replacing it.

To clarify: by judicialization we mean the expansion of judicial involvement in the formation and regulation of public policy. Our emphasis is on decision-making that is within the direct control of judges rather than decisions by other political actors made in the shadow of judicial processes. However, even our simpler concept of judicialization is clearly multidimensional and complex: even within a single country judicialization may affect different policy areas, institutions, and regions differently. It may also ebb and flow, and so we should speak of degrees of judicialization relative to some baseline.

Our chapter is organized as follows. The first section introduces the Japanese judiciary and examines judicialization in Japan in terms of historical as well as contemporary cases. The next reviews theories that purport to explain the low levels of judicialization, finding that those associated with the rational choice school do a much better job of explaining what happened during the long period under LDP rule than what is happening in the contemporary period. We then turn to our primary interest, the ideational factors; and ultimately we draw conclusions.

The status of judicialization in Japan

The Japanese judiciary consists of some 3,000 individual judges—a Supreme Court of 15 justices, eight High Courts located around the country, 50 judicial districts, and some 400 summary courts. Most judges are appointed as assistant judges after completing training at the Legal Training and Research Institute, which is run by the Supreme Court. The institute is also the gateway to careers as prosecutor and practicing attorney. Judges spend their careers in a series of courts, rotating around the country, and are occasionally seconded to other organizations, such as the Ministry of Justice. After 10 years as an assistant, a judge is appointed as a full judge. Formally, judges are subject to reappointment every 10 years, though this is generally a matter of routine. The Cabinet selects members of the Supreme Court, who may have been prosecutors and academics as well as career judges.

A core institution is the General Secretariat of the Supreme Court, staffed by judges themselves. Among other tasks this body makes decisions about judicial rotation and promotion. It is thus central to management and discipline within the judiciary.

In recent years there has been a push to appoint judges from the ranks of practicing attorneys. The Justice System Reform Council, a government commission that recommended a series of major reforms in 2001, called for diversification in the background of judges and greater transparency in appointment and promotion. The main result was establishment of a lower court nomination commission, a majority of whose members are non-lawyers, which is responsible for approving nominees to join the courts. Though this body has rejected a few candidates in recent years, however, the basic bureaucratic structure of the Japanese judiciary has remained intact.

It is a commonplace among English-language scholars of Japanese law that Japanese judges are relatively weak. In his recent analysis of the Supreme Court, David Law (2009; see also Satoh 2008) describes it as the most conservative in the world. It is seen as passive to a fault and incapable of enforcing its decisions. This opinion is no doubt based on the reluctance of the Court to overturn statutes and on some prominent cases in which the political branches seemed to ignore the court. The major exception is John Haley (1998; 2007), who sees the judiciary, though not powerful, as highly autonomous; but even Haley acknowledges the conventional wisdom that it is 'by far the least influential, much less dangerous, branch'.

There is much disagreement about the sources of this institutional conservatism. Shigenori Matsui (2011) argues that Supreme Court judges are reluctant to enforce the constitution because they tend to view it as more an articulation of political principles than a source of law. J. Mark Ramseyer, alone and with various co-authors, has marshaled an array of evidence suggesting that the judiciary conforms to the preferences of the long-dominant LDP, which he argued was able to influence the Supreme Court Secretariat (see, e.g., Ramseyer and Rasmusen 2003). Haley (2007) has challenged this view (see also Upham 2005), arguing instead that Japanese judges 'are among the most honest, politically independent, and professionally competent in the world today'.

Rather than wade into this debate directly, we prefer to simply examine the evidence. As Haley's comments suggest, statements about the Japanese judiciary tend to involve, at least implicitly, a comparison. Typically this is to the courts of the United States, especially those of the activist Warren Court era—perhaps an unfair vantage point for any constitutional court. Even if one broadens the comparison to other top courts in industrialized democracies, however, it is apparent that Japanese courts are relatively insulated from major issues of social and political controversy. As we shall show, this is largely a reflection of prevailing conceptions of the judicial role that have survived massive social and political changes. The next section traces a number of major cases in Japanese history to support the claim of relative quiescence.

Courts in the Meiji and Taisho eras

The Japanese judiciary has its origins in the nineteenth century Meiji modernization of Japan. Because the lack of independent adjudication was one of the main criticisms by foreign powers that imposed unequal treaties on Japan, modernizers made the legal system a focus of reform. Within two decades they created a judicial system that was formally independent of the Ministry of Justice. In a famous incident at Ōtsu in 1891, the Supreme Court resisted political pressure to sentence a rogue policeman to death for his attempt on the life of the Russian crown prince, a crime punishable only by life in prison. This ruling established the principle of judicial independence in Japan and remains a touchstone for institutional autonomy.[1]

Autonomy, however, is hardly equivalent to the exercise of power. Indeed, the history of the Japanese courts up to World War II shows relatively limited involvement with major social and political issues. This was not for lack of problems to solve: industrialization and social change threw up a host of novel issues, not to mention intra-elite struggles. But Japanese courts did not adjudicate disputes between ruling oligarchs (the *genrō*) and the *hosei-kanryo*, who were the lawmaking bureaucrats in the Privy Council, and the Cabinet (see Yamamuro 1984; Colegrove 1931), even though courts in other authoritarian countries have played similar roles (see, e.g., Barros 2002). Nor did the courts play much of a role in resolving major social struggles, even if they were sometimes willing to uphold individual rights.

Take the rural landlord–tenant disputes caused by rapid urbanization, one of the major issues in the early 20th century in Japan. Landlords and tenants had historically negotiated their relationships in the context of semi-autonomous villages, which served both to reinforce social hierarchies and to limit exploitation by landlords. With urbanization landlords were less frequently in continuing relationships with tenants; as the social pressures that restrained their exercise of formal rights were breaking down, there was a concomitant increase in exploitive behavior and formal assertion of rights (Vanoverbeke 2004).

The courts' role in these cases, as in others involving continuing relationships, was to encourage private bargaining, sometimes by invoking the 'consensus of the community' rather than the formal requirements of the Civil Code (Haley 1991: 87–91).[2] But the courts were not sufficient. The political leadership thus set up an alternative conciliation system to honor and encourage the traditional values of harmony, which became the major channel for adjudication of disputes (Haley 1991; Vanoverbeke 2004). Gradually, this conciliation system evolved from being an option for judges to a mandatory system in which parties had little power. The implication was clear: the courts were not a proper forum for adjudicating major social and political disputes. This pattern of channeling disputes away from the courts was to continue in the postwar era (Upham 1987).

Courts in the postwar era

Postwar Japanese courts continued to avoid involvement in major social and political disputes despite major issues of constitutional interpretation. One pattern was for lower courts to be relatively aggressive but then be overruled by a more conservative Supreme Court. This was certainly true in two of the more contentious legal issues in postwar Japanese politics, the interpretation of Article 9 of the Constitution of Japan, and the electoral malapportionment cases.

Article 9

Perhaps the best-known clause of the Japanese Constitution is the article prohibiting the use of war materiel. The article, drafted by the American bureaucrats of the Supreme Commander of the Allied Powers (SCAP) and modified by their Japanese interlocutors, had only been in place briefly when the Korean War forced a revisiting of its premises. Although the provision on the armed forces is clear, the government has continuously sought to expand the role and responsibility of Japan's Self-Defense Forces (SDF), while constitutional literalists have sought to prevent Japan's rearmament.

The Supreme Court was called to adjudicate between these positions as early as the 1959 *Sunakawa* case,[3] which concerned demonstrators challenging a law regulating U.S. base facilities under the 1952 Security Treaty. A lower court had decided that under Article 9 the treaty and the presence of U.S. forces in Japan were unconstitutional. In deciding on appeal that the Supreme Court could overturn only 'obvious' constitutional violations, the majority stated that 'there is a certain element of incompatibility in the process of judicial determination of its constitutionality by a court of law which has as its mission the exercise of the purely judicial function'.[4]

This abdication of court involvement in political questions set the tone for subsequent Article 9 cases. Sometimes the courts relied on standing concerns to avoid reaching the constitutional questions. This was the approach of the Supreme Court in the *Naganuma Nike Missile Site* case (1982), which reversed a lower court finding that the SDF was unconstitutional.[5]

The language of *Sunakawa* is also telling for another reason. The court's insistence on preserving its ability to exercise purely judicial functions suggests that it had in its internal understanding a concept of 'pure' judging. We will return to this concept below.

Electoral malapportionment

Another prominent series of cases concerned the apportionment of electoral districts in Japan. (In fact, two of the eight Supreme Court decisions holding legislative acts unconstitutional concern elections.) The base for the ruling LDP having long been voters in the country, it sought to overweight rural votes. An early challenge to this malapportionment on equality grounds was rejected in the 1964 Supreme Court ruling in the *Koshiyama* case.[6] In rejecting the appeal, the *Koshiyama* court explicitly deferred to the Diet as the political body best able to balance competing considerations.

In 1976 the constitutionality of malapportionment was again an issue in *Kurokawa v. Chiba*.[7] In an election for the House of Representatives, the Supreme Court decided that the disparity in the malapportionment, which amounted to nearly 5 to 1 in the Chiba district, was an unreasonable proportion and strongly implied that the Diet should correct the malapportionment. By most accounts it failed to do so. The LDP, still relying on its core constituency of small farmers, had little incentive to equalize rural and urban votes.

The issue arose again in 1986 in *Kanao* v. *Hiroshima*.[8] The Diet had made no changes to the ratio since the *Kurokawa* decision, and *Kanao* raised the question of a 4 to 1 ratio. This time the court looked at two questions: first, had the Diet had reasonable time to adjust the ratio? And second, was the ratio reasonably within the Diet's discretionary power? Because it had been several years since *Kurokawa*, the court concluded that the Diet had had sufficient time to revise the system—yet it still declined to establish a specific level as reasonable. Furthermore, as in *Kurokawa*, it did not invalidate the election. Since then several cases have discussed the constitutionally appropriate or allowable ratio of malapportionment, but the courts have provided no definitive answer. It appears that the court is hesitant to order the Diet to act. Rather, it has preferred to set loose standards for the Diet to follow and wait for cases to be brought.

A major electoral reform by the Diet in 1994 reduced the number of districts and suggested that the redistricting plan should achieve a ratio of no more than 2 : 1 between the largest and smallest districts. But the Supreme Court later held that, although the law sought to establish a 2 : 1 ratio of malapportionment, in the election before it a greater ratio was allowable in part because of concern that residents of sparsely populated prefectures should continue to have their views reflected in national politics.[9] It thus used a theory of representation to justify malapportionment.

Corporate donations

In the 1970 *Yahata Steel Company* case, the Supreme Court rejected a derivative suit brought by a shareholder against two directors of Yahata Steel who had contributed money to the LDP.[10] The argument was that the donation to political parties deviated from the business purpose prescribed in the company charter and violated the duties of loyalty and care. The court held that there was no distinction between these duties and that corporate contributions to political campaigns were legal. Like natural persons, companies had a right to participate in politics. This decision, which anticipated the U.S. Supreme Court case of *Citizens United* 40 years later, was grounded in private rights of participation and framed as a conflict between those rights.[11] This is an example of a case that appears to uphold liberty but does so in a way that reinforces the existing political structure in Japan so as not to challenge political authorities.[12]

In short, for much of the postwar era Japan's courts have tended to reinforce the status quo in politically charged cases. It is not that law had no role in economic growth and ordering private affairs; however, the particular vision of law that Japan adopted facilitated the developmental state model by insulating the administration from private lawsuits, and courts rarely exercised their power to review legislation. In resolving the civil disputes of private parties, the courts were by all accounts fair and unbiased. Contracts were enforced and property rights protected—key factors for contemporary understandings of the legal bases of economic development (North 1991). Indeed, there was substantial judicial creativity in these private realms in dealing with issues such as landlord–tenant relations or family law that were not explicitly political.

Courts in the Heisei era

The Heisei era (1989–present) has been one of major changes in Japanese legal institutions. Beginning in the early 1990s and accelerating in the second half of the decade, there has been a major movement in Japanese society to expand the role in society of law and, by extension, the courts. Much of this responded to a sense that the earlier developmental model had run its course as Japan entered a long period of recession. As the Justice System Reform Council put it, Japan needed to move from an 'ex ante planning society to an ex post remedies society'.[13] By this it meant that society needed a more liberal basis from which firms and individuals could pursue their vision of the good, subject only to limits imposed by the freedoms of others. When interests clashed, it would be up to the courts, and the legal system with its expanded capacities, to resolve disputes. This vision was the basis of such major reforms of Japanese legal institutions as establishment of a system of lay participation in criminal cases (*saiban-in seido*); creation of a new system of legal education; expansion of prosecutorial review commissions; and many reforms to substantive law. For our purposes, changes to the system of appointing judges that encouraged more practicing lawyers to join the bench were central because they seemed designed to ensure closer links between the judiciary and society and to partially undermine the conservatism induced by the judicial hierarchy.

In the decade since the Justice System Reform Council blessed the reform process many changes have been achieved. Have they been accompanied by judicialization? In the section below, we review major cases of this era, arguing that Japanese courts systematically distinguish between issues of statutory and constitutional rights, which are the proper province of judicial decision-making, and cases involving public policy issues. We show that while the courts are independent and even activist as far as rights issues are concerned, they are still systematically averse to anything that might involve them in 'political' issues.[14] This pattern is what distinguishes the approach of Japanese courts from that of other national judiciaries that have willingly taken a more active role in public policy.

The Shrine Visit cases: Tokyo's Yasukuni Shrine, where the war dead are enshrined, has long provoked controversy among Japan's Asian neighbors. With the rise of a revisionist faction in the LDP, politicians have sought to visit the shrine in their 'private capacity' to honor the war dead. These controversies came to the fore after Junichiro Koizumi was elected Prime Minister in 2001: his visits in 2001 and 2002 provoked serious differences with Korea, China, and other countries.

The shrine visits led to several cases. Most notably, a group of citizens, joined by Shin Buddhists, Protestants, and the war bereaved, sought to enjoin the visits as a violation of the separation of church and state guaranteed by Article 20 of the constitution. The Supreme Court held, on the merits, that the Prime Minister's visit alone did not constitute a tort because the plaintiff could not show that his claim was within the zone of legally protected interests. The court thus decided the issue on a nonconstitutional basis, even though it raised interesting questions about how free a politician was to act in his private capacity.

Recent SDF Cases: The first Gulf War marked the beginning of renewed pressure, both within Japan and from abroad, for the SDF to participate in collective self-defense efforts. Recent deployments in Iraq and Afghanistan stretched the limits further. The decisions of the Cabinet Legislation Bureau, which has a formal role in issuing constitutional interpretations for the government, have generated constitutional challenges.

Even when the lower courts have been asked to determine the constitutionality of military operations, they have shied away from major constraints on government. For example, when the Nagoya High Court heard a 2008 challenge to SDF deployment in Iraq, it denied relief based on lack of ripeness, even though in dicta it found a violation of Article 9.[15] In short, though the courts have made some suggestive statements, they have shied away from shaping policy in this central area, where the constitutional language is fairly clear.

Adjudicating History: Japan's war legacy continues to be a major issue in Asian politics, and some victims have attempted to pursue legal claims, among them foreign 'comfort women', Chinese forced laborers, and Taiwanese soldiers. In the cases brought by Chinese citizens who had been forced to labor in wartime Japan, lower courts refused compensation on the grounds that the claims were barred by the Joint Communiqué between Japan and the People's Republic of China, though they acknowledged the victims' suffering at the hands of the Japanese authorities.[16] The Supreme Court ultimately rejected the appeals. In the 'comfort women' cases, several lower courts found that the Japanese government ought to bear responsibility but concluded that postwar peace treaties barred the victims, who are now Korean or Chinese citizens, from suing the

Japanese government in Japan. They applied the rationale of the court's 2007 decision on Chinese forced laborers.[17] On the other hand, Taiwanese soldiers who had served in the Japanese military were successful in obtaining compensation after the court ruled that the Diet should indeed pay their pensions.

Hansen's Disease: Japan's policies toward those with Hansen's disease (leprosy) were severe late into the 20th century. Mandatory quarantine laws were repealed only in 1996, long after similar policies had disappeared in Europe.[18] Victims were isolated from society and many were forced to undergo sterilization, even though reliable treatments were available by the end of the 1950s. Seeking greater inclusion in society, in the late 1990s the victims turned to the courts in the quest for compensation for denial of constitutional rights (Kingston 2004: 188). In 2001, a large group won a district court case against the government in Kumamoto. The court ruled that the 1953 Leprosy Prevention Law had encouraged discrimination, and that the government should have encouraged integration of Hansen's patients after drug therapy became available in the 1950s.

To the surprise of many, the government of Prime Minister Koizumi decided not to appeal, even though line bureaucrats had hoped it would. Koizumi also apologized, helping to establish his reputation as a reformer (Kingston 2004: 192). This represented a very different tack from that taken with the prominent AIDS-related cases brought by hemophiliacs, which had led to settlements without a government admission of wrongdoing (Bayer and Feldman 1999; Kingston 2004: 168). The Diet subsequently passed a compensation bill and concluded settlements for victims not directly covered.

Equality Cases. Two recent Supreme Court cases regarding equality are worth mentioning (Martin 2010): in 2005 Japanese citizens living abroad won the right to vote in national elections.[19] Then in 2008 the Supreme Court invalidated a provision in the Nationality Law that effectively disqualified children born of Japanese fathers and non-Japanese mothers from acquiring Japanese nationality.[20] Such children are now recognized as Japanese. This decision has been described as 'epoch-making'.[21] In reviewing the decision, it is clear that the Japanese justices take the rights of individuals seriously. The interpretive statement of the *chōsakan* (the staff judge who serves as a clerk in the case) cited other countries' jurisprudence, and Justice Tokuji Izumi's concurring opinion sought to articulate a kind of intermediate scrutiny standard, which if adopted might have widespread implications for equality jurisprudence. The case was significant in that issues of nationality go to the core of Japan's self-conception as a nation. After the decision the Diet was somewhat reluctant to amend the law, though it eventually did excise the unconstitutional provisions.

Other Constitutional Rights: Courts in Japan have been willing to find violations of individual rights when the violations are clear. A major issue involving free expression concerned schoolteachers who refuse to honor the Japanese flag or sing the national anthem, the *kimigayo*, because of its association with wartime militarism. With the election of nationalist demagogue Shintaro Ishihara in 1999, the Tokyo Government became vigorous in pressuring teachers to participate in such activities. In September 2006 the Tokyo District Court found that the city had violated the constitutional guarantee of freedom of thought; however, the Tokyo High Court reversed the decision early in 2011.[22]

In February 2008 the same district court found that the city had exceeded its discretion in punishing certain activist teachers.[23] Relying on their past refusal to honor the flag and anthem at graduation ceremonies, the city had cut their pay and refused to hire them part-time after they had retired. The court held that, although its directive making patriotic displays mandatory was constitutional, the city had exceeded its discretion in punishing the plaintiffs and awarded roughly $258,000 in damages. But this case too was reversed by the Supreme Court, in January 2010.[24] Similar lawsuits elsewhere have failed or been overturned on appeal.

Are there any signs of judicialization? The fact that there has not been a major shift toward judicialization in the Heisei era is somewhat puzzling given the major social and political effort to expand the role of courts. We should perhaps expect this self-conscious effort at institutional design to bear some fruit in the form of a higher profile for the judiciary, but to date there have been relatively few appointments from outside the bench. Because material incentives keep the best private attorneys from seeking to join the courts, the traditional structures remain intact.

There are some tentative hints that increasing public involvement in the judicial system may affect the decisions of legal actors. One example comes from Prosecutorial Review Commissions (PRCs), in which 11 citizens review decisions not to prosecute and have the power to recommend prosecution. Japanese prosecutors have always been willing to go after corrupt politicians: indeed, major figures in postwar politics, such as Kakuei Tanaka and Shin Kanemaru, have felt the sting of criminal prosecution. This speaks to the integrity of the judicial process and the rule of law and suggests that the view that Japanese judicial actors 'avoid politics' is too simple a formulation.

One recent case of significant interest here concerns Ichiro Ozawa, the opposition kingpin who stepped down from his position with the Democratic Party of Japan (DPJ) in summer 2010 after a financial scandal. Prosecutors initially decided that there was not enough evidence to indict him, but a PRC of anonymous citizens recommended another look.[25] Ozawa was indicted for conspiracy in a case involving his staff filing an allegedly false financial report; charges were eventually dismissed. The case was brought by private attorneys recommended by the Tokyo Bar Association and appointed by the Tokyo District Court to represent the PRC (Hongo and Ito 2011). The story suggests that public pressure on occasion can stimulate action by the legal system. Increasing the transparency of the legal system might lead to more such pressure—but that is far from a sure thing, notwithstanding the major reforms.

Another sign of potential for change are statements by certain ex-justices that the court should take on a more active role. It is also worth noting that in March 2011 the Supreme Court ruled that the 1994 electoral system was 'in a state of unconstitutionality' because of vote disparities and called on the legislature to fix it.[26] This was the first time the court had issued such a ruling on the 1994 reform, having previously upheld the system three times. Because the unconstitutional vote disparity of 2.3 was in the range that had previously been ruled constitutional, there is a quantitative indication of creeping expansion of the court's doctrine in this area, though it is too early to say if it constitutes a trend.

Explanations for limited judicialization

The picture emerging from this analysis is that politicization of the Japanese courts is relatively limited. What might explain this? One possible reason might be that there is no Japanese Constitutional Court that can authoritatively restrain political actors in the name of higher law. Yet this explanation is clearly insufficient. Other countries with a unified judicial system have been part of the trend toward judicialization. And the Japanese Supreme Court does have the formal power of constitutional review.[27] To be sure, it has used the power sparingly, striking government action on constitutional grounds in just eight cases since 1946. But judicialization involves more than constitutional review, so the claim that timidity in constitutional adjudication limits the courts in other areas is not convincing.

Furthermore, the claim that constitutional timidity drives the courts ignores significant gaps that have been evidenced between lower courts and the Supreme Court. Lower courts have at times been willing to make controversial anti-government rulings, though these are with some frequency overturned by the courts of appeals.

Other conventional explanations do not fully account for the pattern either. In recent years political explanations rooted in rational choice theory have had a good deal of influence in comparative understandings of judicialization. Ramseyer, who pioneered these theories for Japan, emphasized electoral alternation as a key factor (1994). Hirschl (2004) offers a theory of judicial empowerment that he calls 'hegemonic preservation' centered on departing elites who want to preserve their policies into the future. One of us (Ginsburg) has a version of this argument that he calls political insurance.

All of these influential theories have a common flaw in relation to Japan: they all predict that the decline of the LDP should lead to significant judicial empowerment. Yet although there has been some increase in resources for the judiciary, the judges have not fundamentally changed their passive approach to public policy issues. Hirschl's theory would predict a major effort by the LDP to empower the courts to preserve its policies into the future; Ginsburg and Ramseyer would predict that both major parties would have an interest in such a policy. It may indeed be the case that such an effort has been made. But without a court willing to receive the football, it is hardly worth trying to make the pass. Thus neither the insurance nor the hegemonic preservation theories seem useful for understanding contemporary Japan. It appears that judicial attitudes may be a major constraint. The next section focuses on the relevance here of one particular legal theory.

The role of ideas

The organ theory: Prussian origins

Like other recent accounts of Japanese judicial conservatism, we emphasize the importance of ideas and institutional self-understanding (see Law 2009; Matsui 2011). We differ from other accounts in our emphasis on a particular set of ideas, German in origin, that have been given the most institutional expression in Japanese constitutionalism. These are the ideas underlying the 'organ theory' of Japanese constitutional interpretation. Western scholars of Japan may be familiar with the theory because of the debates over the constitutional status of the emperor that arose when the 1946 Constitution was being drafted (Moore and Robinson 2004), but the theory extends beyond the question of whether or not the emperor was the embodiment of sovereignty or an organ of the constitution itself.

The organ theory draws on nineteenth-century German ideas that saw the state as inherently a central part of the constitutional order. Constitutionalism was not so much a political movement to guarantee democratic self-governance as a set of auto-limitations that the state established in the name of the *Rechtsstaat.* Within the constitutional state, the polity is analogized to a body composed of different organs, each of which must exercise its proper role if the entire system is to function properly. In this conception power is spread throughout the system and not dependent on a higher authority. Just as the brain cannot order the heart not to beat, so it is impossible for co-equal organs to be superior to each other. Instead, each organ receives its power from the source of constitutional authority, whether the emperor as in the Meiji Constitution or the people as in the 1946 document.

This approach is quite distinct from French and American theories of the separation of powers. In the American tradition, separation of powers jurisprudence emphasizes drawing the line between executive and legislative activities, and many of the cases concern legislative over-reaching.[28] In the French tradition, the separation of powers was targeted differently (Billias 1990: 13, 18); since the revolution, it has historically been directed at the judiciary and the historically rooted fear of *gouvernement des juges.* In the Fifth Republic, there has been the additional twist of a quest to ensure, through creation of the *Conseil Constitutionnel*, that the lawmaking power of the legislature does not interfere with that of the executive. In each case, the conception of power is essentially Montesquiean: power comes in just three flavors, and there is little room for the modern administrative state. In each case, a neutral third party—courts in the U.S., the Conseil in France—is set up as a guardian of the separation of powers.

The German tradition is quite different. Because of its late developing, Germany (like Japan) had to organize a state before it really had a modern economy, so there was a sense of necessity propelling the state-building enterprise. Naturally, this led to interest in providing constitutional legitimacy to the administrative apparatus. Instead of viewing society as the ultimate legitimator of the state, the state has an independent organic vitality and is a proper bearer of rights and duties within the polity. The ultimate right of the state is to govern. There is room in the theory for rights and liberties of citizens to exist, but rights are not the starting point or ultimate criterion of constitutional legitimacy, and indeed democracy is in some tension with the statist theory. Private rights and duties are granted by the state, rather than the other way around.

In this tradition courts are not central. Whereas the Anglo-American rule of law tradition emphasizes the common law heritage of external judicial controls on administrative action, the *rechtsstaat* tradition instead emphasizes structural constraints and internalization of norms by government officials. The state itself is defined and empowered through law, and law is the tool to structure its internal relationships, strictly limiting the role of any one actor.

This organic theory of constitutionalism that originated in 19th century German thought fit the needs of the developmental Meiji authoritarian state. For Japan the most influential thinkers were Otto von Gierke and Georg Jellinek (others included Paul Laband and Gerhard Anschutz; see Miller 1965: 9). Von Gierke's great book, *Das Genossenschaftsrecht*, was an exploration of the law of communal associations (Mogi 1932; Emerson 1928: 129–42). According to von Gierke, human society flourished in the possibility of forming collective organizations, and the state emerged only out of a very long process in which such organizations evolved.

The theory was attractive to Japanese thinkers, who found themselves in a similar developmental imperative. The bottom-up character of von Gierke's theory and its communitarian focus aligned well with the Japanese tradition of the self-regulating village (*mura*). The romantic overtones of ethnic solidarity were also a better fit than, say, the French ideas of equality of citizenship and natural rights. The Chinese tradition, in which the state was itself seen as a natural phenomenon, in theory unlimited by higher authority, was also powerful in the Japanese consciousness in the early years of Meiji, which had adopted the *Ritsuryo* structure as a stopgap before Western structures could effectively be imported. The German model became even more attractive after the defeat of France in 1871, imbuing the theoretical compatibilities with an aura of objective superiority.

The organic theory entered the Japanese academic context through Kitokuro Ichiki, a bureaucrat who was also professor of law at the University of Tokyo. He in turn was the mentor of the great constitutional theorist Tatsukichi Minobe (Miller 1965). Minobe tried to rationalize the popular concept of the *kokutai*, or national polity. This theory held that the emperor himself was only an 'organ of the State' rather than an embodiment of sovereignty beyond the state. Minobe drew on the analogy of the head of the human body to describe the role of the emperor: the emperor was the supreme organ, but nonetheless still an organ.

Minobe's view was opposed by imperial absolutists like Shinkichi Uesugi. Rooted in the German historical school, Uesugi promoted ideas of imperial supremacy and absolute monarchy that proved attractive to the militarists who seized power in the 1930s. As Minobe summarized the differences between the two views:

> Among scholars who explain our state law there are those who frequently assert that the monarch is the subject of governmental power. This is an inadmissible error … the state alone is the subject of governmental power, and the monarch is an organ of the state.
>
> (Miller 1965: 27)

Minobe was subjected to withering criticism, even investigation on charges of *lèse-majesté* and political attacks in the Diet in 1935 (Miller 1965: 196–253). But in the aftermath of the military defeat, his organ theory proved useful to understand how a formerly divine emperor could become a constitutional monarch. Minobe's theory was thus redeemed during debates over the 1946 Constitution (Moore and Robinson 2004).

What did the organ theory mean for the judiciary? Recall that the modern judiciary in Japan is a creation of the Meiji era; it was a defensive move to free Japan from the yoke of unequal treaties rather than a longstanding institution with deep cultural roots. Yet, like any constitutional organ, it had a defined role. In the Japanese conception, this was mainly in the realm of private law. Courts were to adjudicate private disputes about legal rights; but they were not thought of as enforcing a social contract or protecting the people from an overbearing state.

Postwar retention of the organ theory

Precisely because they were so reluctant to constrain public authority, Japanese judges were relatively quiet during the militaristic period, and the military regime did not rely heavily on them to carry out its policies. Rather, the military seemed content to allow the courts to operate in their own autonomous realm of private law.

After the war, because the courts had stayed out of public affairs, judges were not targeted for purges as were the military and political organs. Like the rest of the Japanese bureaucracy, there was a good deal of continuity between prewar and postwar personnel—hence no sharp ideological break—so that nineteenth century German positivism survived intact, and with it the organ theory.

This continuity has profound implications for the relationship of government, people, and courts. The central government, representing the Japanese nation-state, still has a monopoly on political legitimacy. It exercises its powers with a presumption of constitutionality.[29] The state strips individuals and groups of *powers*, in return reassigning to them *rights* (Schmitt, 2006: 62–3; see also Hasebe 2004). Property rights are interpreted not as state delegations of sovereign power to individuals but as guarantees of freedom to citizens through juristic institutions in compensation for their depoliticization. Meanwhile, the self-binding state is free to meddle on the periphery of private autonomy so long as it does not disproportionately infringe on citizens' rights. The depoliticized citizenry enjoys private rights but cannot rely on judicial enforcement of rights to displace political decisions.

Japan is now a democracy. Citizens can assume public office and participate in the selection of representatives. But the Diet is also just one organ of the state among many; in principle it is not superior to the bureaucracy, the emperor, or any other organ within its own zone of constitutionally granted authority. The political and administrative branches possess authority that is presumptively constitutional. The judicial branch will overturn their actions only when they immoderately violate the rights of a citizen. U.S.-style judicial review is not well aligned with such a conception, though there is a vein of American constitutional scholarship that promotes the somewhat analogous view that legislative activity is presumptively constitutional.[30]

Postwar Japanese democracy creates no incentive for the high court to judicialize politics. Instead, the court falls back on its traditional conception of a distinction between public political authority and a pluralistic private realm by ensuring that citizens enjoy economic freedom and equality of suffrage. When the subjective rights of citizens are under serious and direct threat, as in the equality cases and many private law matters, the courts will respond. When, on the other hand, citizens are claiming to represent an objective interest common to anyone in the society, such as in the Article 9 cases, the court tends to find the case not justiciable (see also Upham 1987). Not only does this conception tend to limit the scope of legal protection of rights, it also provides few conceptual resources for grappling with, for example, the public policy role of corporations or the public–private partnerships that are pervasive in modern political economy.

The persistence of the organ theory is nowhere better illustrated than in the Final Report of the Justice System Reform Council:

> When likened to the human body, if the political branches constitute the heart and arteries, the judicial branch shall be said to be the veins. The series of reforms…, such as political reform and administrative reform, are, so to speak, an effort to restore and strengthen the functions to make blood flow swiftly by removing extraneous crudescence in the heart and arteries. According to this metaphor, justice reform shall be considered to be aiming at harmonizing the body and improving its health by expanding and strengthening the scale and function of the justice system as part of what the 'shape of our country' should be in the 21st century, with fundamental reflection on whether or not the existing veins were excessively small.[31]

We see these ideas, essentially principles of legal theory, as being at the root of the judicial self-conception in Japan. Judged by formal criteria Japan's judges surely *are* independent, and their record in this regard is admirable. There are no credible reports of judicial corruption; and there has been no overt attempt to influence courts by members of the political class (notwithstanding Ramseyer's convincing evidence about implicit influence through the process of appointment and promotion; Ramseyer and Rasmusen 2003). At the same time the reverse is also true: just as politicians do not interfere with judges, judges do not interfere with politicians. The organ theory goes a long way toward explaining both phenomena; previous work has tended to focus only on one or the other.

Though the organ theory has been challenged at different points in modern Japanese history, it is remarkably persistent. In the prewar era it was challenged by Uesugi and Hozumi from the right as being too liberal and by the liberal left for being too conservative. In the postwar era, liberal academics have also challenged it. In the political sphere, a recent challenger was Ozawa, the now-disgraced DPJ politician. Ozawa sought to revolutionize Japanese politics after the DPJ took over. His basic theme was to make political practice match the actual text of the Japanese constitution. For example, he argued that the cabinet was superior to the bureaucracy—surely a radical position from the point of view of a theory that sees each constitutional organ as having a unique role. He also argued for the supremacy of the Diet in forming the cabinet, in accordance with classical parliamentarism.

Ozawa and the DPJ also argued that the emperor (or rather the Imperial Household Agency) did not have independent authority to refuse a visit of Chinese Vice President Xi Jinping in December 2009 so long as the cabinet asked the emperor to accept. Xi had requested the visit on very short notice, less than the traditional 30 days demanded by the agency. The agency viewed the constitutional provision that the emperor 'shall not have powers related to government' (Article 4) as insulating the emperor from government requests. In contrast, Ozawa argued that this provision meant that the emperor had no authority to refuse a government request, because a refusal would be the exercise of a governmental power. This was, of course, consistent with the organ theory as reinterpreted for the postwar constitutional monarchy. After some political wrangling, the emperor did accede to the request, which provoked significant protest in Japan.

With the exclusion of Ozawa, it seems that the organ theory remains dominant. Until a suitable rival theory is found, Japan will remain an outlier among industrial nations: its judiciary is simply not interested in judicialization. And there is no prospect of one that is.

Conclusion

Compared to other advanced industrialized nations, including close neighbors Taiwan and Korea, Japan has experienced relatively little judicialization. For instance, the Japanese Supreme Court does not adjudicate issues related to who can serve as the head of government, as its counterparts in Taiwan and Korea do. It does not consider major issues of social policy, as do constitutional courts in Germany and Latin America. It is not setting aside major programs of the legislature, as the *Conseil Constitutionnel* in France has done.

Why this situation obtains has stimulated much controversy. Some point to cultural factors, such as the preference for harmony often invoked in discussions of Japan.[32] Others emphasize the lack of a constitutional court and the system of appointments and promotion, through which those who rise in the judiciary tend to reinforce its caution. A related category of explanation emphasizes political controls: because the LDP ruled for so long and could communicate with the Supreme Court Secretariat at the apex of the judicial branch, lower court judges tended to uphold policies consistent with the preferences of the Diet. But the current situation, in which Japan is governed by the DPJ, directly challenges such theories. If the political theories were correct, we should be witnessing at least tentative steps toward judicialization.

We are not yet seeing anything of the sort. Despite a major program of judicial reform, continuity rather than change is the theme.

We join recent analysts in emphasizing ideational factors as explaining the absence of judicialization, but we focus on different ideas. While Matsui's account relies on general ideas of positivism and a belief among judges that the constitution is more a political than a legal document, in our view, regardless of the political structure or positivism per se, Japanese judges have inherited particular conceptions of law and the state that limit their role. This view survived the constitutional transformation of the Allied Occupation. As actors in a discrete organ exercising the state's judicial power, Japanese judges are independent, but they are cabined within a small zone of activity, mainly adjudication of private rights. In conformity with the organ theory, the judges police other branches only when their violations of individual rights are truly egregious *and* when the violation does not conflict with a strong interest of the state. The zone of violations is small indeed.

This is not to say that the nineteenth century German ideas are uncontested. There are bureaucrats and politicians in Japan who do want to move to a more liberal model, which presumably would facilitate a larger role for judicial protection. But even after a self-conscious effort to change the system, the ideas remain deeply rooted.

Japan is exceptional among advanced industrial democracies because it is at most lightly judicialized. It illustrates that the general association between divided politics and judicial empowerment is a matter of tendency, not iron law. Even when they have room to exercise power over important policy matters, judges may not always choose to do so if they do not see policymaking as a judicial role. Self-conception of an activist role seems to be a necessary, if not sufficient, condition for judicialization.

Notes

1 See discussion in Ginsburg, 2010: 19–20. The incident also illustrates the control of senior over lower-ranked judges.

2 *Shakai-tsunen* is a juridical concept interpreted by professional judges. It is not merely deference to social customs; rather, it is a mode by which the Japanese courts reshape society by construing what is to be the society's customary law.

3 Saikō Saibanshō [Sup. Ct.] Dec. 16, 1959, 13 Keishū 3225 (Available online at www.courts.go.jp/english/judgments/text/1959.12.16-1959-A-No.710.html (trans) (Sec 2, paragraph 4 of the majority decision).

4 Ibid.

5 *Naganuma Case*. Saikō Saibanshō [Sup. Ct.] Sept. 9, 1982, 36 Minshū 1679. See also David S. Law, *The Myth of Imposed Constitutionalism*, manuscript.
6 *Koshiyama* v. *Tokyo Election Management Commission*, Saikō Saibanshō [Sup. Ct.] Feb. 5, 1964, 18 Minshū 279.
7 *Kurokawa* v. *Chiba Prefecture Election Commission*, Saikō Saibanshō [Sup. Ct.] July 17, 1985, 39 Minshū 1110.
8 *Kanao* v. *Hiroshima Election Management Commission*, Saikō Saibanshō [Sup. Ct.] July 17, 1985, 39 Minshū 1110.
9 *Yamaguchi et al.* v. *Tokyo Election Administration Commission*, Supreme Court Grand Bench Decision of November 10, 1999, (1) 53 Minshu 8–1577, 1696 Hanji 48, Hanta 114, (2) 53 Minshu 8–1704, 1696 Hanji 46, 1018 Hanta 114 (dismissing approximately 31 appeals of citizen groups from lower court decisions seeking nullification of the House of Representatives election of October 20, 1996).
10 *Judgment of the 'Yahata-seitetsu' Case*, Saikō Saibanshō [Sup. Ct.] June 24, 1970, 24 Minshū 625.
11 *Citizens United* v. *FEC*, 130 S.Ct. 876 (2010).
12 Yoichi Higuchi, *Kenpō toiu sakui* [Constitution as Artificiality] 157, 160 (Iwanami 2009) (arguing that the Court is active in upholding government policies).
13 Shiho Seido Kaikaku Shingikai, Final Report, 2001.
14 We recognize that the distinction between political and non-political issues, like that between public policy and the private sphere, is hardly self-evident. We also recognize that rather than being a real distinction, it is an artifact of the positivist legal theory that has influenced Japan and other states. Our contention is that supreme and constitutional courts in other jurisdictions *have* been willing to decide against the government in the kinds of cases we consider.
15 Nagoya kōtō saibanshō [Nagoya High Ct.] April 17, 2008 (unpublished decision), www.haheisashidome.jp/hanketsu_kouso discussed in Craig Martin, 'Binding the Dogs of War: Japan and the Constitutionalizing of Jus Ad Bellum', *University of Pennsylvania Journal of Constitutional Law*, 30: 267–357.
16 Only a few lower court rulings favored plaintiffs and they have been deemed to be overturned by the 2007 Supreme Court decision. See, e.g., Hiroshima kōtō saibanshō [Hiroshima High Court] July 9, 2004; Saikō Saibanshō [Sup. Ct.] April 27, 2007, 61 Minshū 1188 (available online at http://www.courts.go.jp/english/judgments/text/2007.04.27-2004.-Ju-.No..1658.html); see also Chinese Forced Labor Case Rejected, *The Japan Times*, available online at http://search.japantimes.co.jp/cgi-bin/nn20090310a6.html.
17 See Sup. Ct. April 27, 2007, 61 Minshū 1188; Sup. Ct. April 27, 2007, 224 Saibanshū Minji 325.
18 The 1996 repeal was pushed by later Prime Minister Naoto Kan during his time as Minister of Health and Welfare.
19 In 1998, the Diet amended the Public Offices Election Act to make it possible for Japanese nationals living overseas to vote in Diet elections. However, a supplementary provision allowed overseas voters to vote only in the proportional representation component of the lower house electoral system, not in the single-member elections for the House of Representatives or for councillors elected from prefectures. See Case to seek declaration of illegality of deprivation of the right to vote of Japanese citizens residing abroad, 2001 Saikō Saibanshō [Sup. Ct.] Sept. 14, 2005, 59 Minshū 2087 (available online at http://www.courts.go.jp/english/judgments/text/2005.09.14-2001.-Gyo-Tsu-.No..82%2C.2001.-Gyo-Hi-.No..76%2C.2001.-Gyo-Tsu-.No..83%2C.2001.-Gyo-Hi-.No..77.html).
20 Saikō Saibanshō [Sup. Ct.] June 4, 2008, 2002 Hanji 3 (available online at www.courts.go.jp/english/judgments/text/2008.06.04-2006.-Gyo-Tsu-.No..135-111255.html) (last visited Feb. 15, 2012). See also *The Japan Times*, http://search.japantimes.co.jp:80/cgi-bin/nn20080605a1.html.
21 Martin (2010: 223, n. 149), citing Hasebe Yasuo, Kokusekiho ikkenhanketsu no

shisoyoshiki [The Pattern of Thought in the Judgment Holding the Nationality Act Unconstitutional], 1366 Jurist 77 (2008).

22 In a series of decisions first released on June 2011, the Court found to be constitutional school principals' orders requiring teachers to honor the *hinomaru* and *kimigayo*, reasoning that these orders did not direct violate teachers' freedom of conscience guaranteed by Article 19 of the Japanese Constitution. The Court also cautioned, however, that excessive disciplinary action against teachers who refused to follow the order, for example pay cuts or dismissals, would be considered an abuse of discretion and thus illegal. See Saikō Saibanshō [Sup. Ct.] June 6, 2011, 65 Minshū 1855 (available online at http://www.courts.go.jp/english/judgments/text/2011.06.06-2010.-O-.No..951.html); Sup. Ct. June 14, 2011, 65 Minshū 2148 (available online at http://www.courts.go.jp/english/judgments/text/2011.06.14-2010.-Gyo-Tsu-.No..314.html); Sup. Ct. Jan. 16, 2012.

23 Ibid.

24 http://search.japantimes.co.jp/cgi-bin/ed20110208a1.html.

25 *NHK World*, April 27, 2010.

26 http://findarticles.com/p/articles/mi_m0XPQ/is_2011_March_28/ai_n57158164

27 Kenpō, Art. 81.

28 See e.g. *Bowsher* v. *Synar*, 478 U.S. 714 (1986); *Buckley* v. *Valeo*, 424 U.S. 1 (1976), *INS* v. *Chadha* (Opinion of Powell), 462 U.S. 919 (1983).

29 Kenpo, art. 41(making the Diet 'the highest organ of state power').

30 See Thayer, 1893: 129ff.: courts 'can only disregard the Act when those who have the right to make laws have not merely made a mistake, but have made a very clear one, —so clear that it is not open to rational question.... This rule recognizes that, having regard to the great, complex, ever-unfolding exigencies of government, much which will seem unconstitutional to one man, or body of men, may reasonably not seem so to another; that the constitution often admits of different interpretations; that there is often a range of choice and judgment; that in such cases the constitution does not impose upon the legislature any one specific opinion, but leaves open this range of choice; and that whatever choice is rational is constitutional'.

31 Justice System Reform Council, Final Report, Ch. I, Part 2.1.

32 See Matsui 2011: 23 discussing the views of former justice Masami Itoh.

References

Barros, R. (2002) *Constitutionalism and Dictatorship*, New York: Cambridge University Press (discussing Chile).

Bayer, R. and Feldman, E., eds (1999) *Blood Feuds: AIDS, Blood, and the Politics of Medical Disaster*, New York: Oxford University Press.

Billias, G. A. (1990) 'American constitutionalism and Europe, 1776–1848', in Billias, G. A., ed., *American Constitutionalism Abroad*, Westport, CT: Greenwood Press.

Colegrove, K. (1931) 'The Japanese Privy Council', *American Political Science Review* 25: 589–614; 881–905.

Emerson, E. (1928) *State and Sovereignty in Modern Germany*, New Haven: Yale University Press.

Ginsburg, T. (2003) *Judicial Review in New Democracies*, New York, Cambridge University Press.

Ginsburg, T. (2010) 'Studying Japanese law because it's there', *American Journal of Comparative Law* 58: 15–25.

Haley, J. (1991) *Authority Without Power*, New York: Oxford University Press.

Haley, J. (1998) *The Spirit of Japanese Law*, Athens, GA: University of Georgia Press.

Haley, J. (2007) 'The Japanese judiciary: Maintaining integrity, autonomy, and the public trust', in Daniel Foote, ed., *Law in Japan: A Turning Point*, Seattle: University of Washington Press.

Hasebe, Y. (2004) Book Review, *Journal of Japanese Studies* 30: 189, 192.

Higuchi, Y. (2009) *Kenpo toiu sakui* [Constitution as Artificiality], Tokyo: Iwanami.

Hilbink, L. (2007) *Judges Beyond Politics in Democracy and Dictatorship*, New York: Cambridge University Press.

Hirschl, R. (2004) *Towards Juristocracy*, Cambridge, MA: Harvard University Press.

Hirschl, R. (2008) 'The judicialization of mega-politics and the rise of political courts', *Annual Review of Political Science* 11: 1–44.

Hongo, H. and Ito, M. (2011) 'Ozawa charged over funds misreporting', *Japan Times*, February 1, p. 1.

Kingston, J. (2004) *Japan's Quiet Transformation*, London: Routledge Curzon.

Law, D. S. (2009) 'The anatomy of a conservative court: Judicial review in Japan', *University of Texas Law Review* 87: 1545–93.

Martin, C. (2010) 'Glimmers of hope: The evolution of equality rights doctrine in Japanese courts from a comparative perspective', *Duke Journal of International and Comparative Law* 20: 167–246.

Matsui, S. (2011) 'Why is the Japanese Supreme Court so conservative?', *Washington University Law Review* 88: 1375–423.

Miller, F. O. (1965) *Minobe Tatsukichi: Interpreter of Constitutionalism in Japan*, Berkeley: University of California Press.

Mogi, S. (1932) *Otto von Gierke: His Political Teachings and Life*, London: P. S. King and Son.

Moore, R. and Robinson, D. (2004) *Partners for Democracy*, New York: Oxford University Press.

North, D. (1991) *Institutions, Institutional Change, and Economic Performance*, New York: Cambridge University Press.

Ramseyer, J. M. (1994) 'The puzzling (in)dependence of courts', *Journal of Legal Studies* 23: 721–47.

Ramseyer, J. M. and Rasmusen, E. B. (2003) *Measuring Judicial Independence*, Chicago: University of Chicago Press.

Satoh, J. (2008) 'Judicial review in Japan: An overview of the case law and an examination of trends in the Japanese Supreme Court's constitutional oversight', *Loyola of Los Angeles Law Review* 41: 603–27J.

Schmitt, C. (2006*) The Concept of the Political*, tr. by George Schwab, Chicago: University of Chicago Press.

Tate, C. N. and Vallinder, T. (1995) *The Global Expansion of Judicial Power*, New York: NYU Press.

Thayer, J. B. (1893) 'The origin and scope of the American doctrine of constitutional law', *Harvard Law Review* 7: 129–56.

Upham, F. K. (1987) *Law and Social Change in Postwar Japan*, Cambridge, MA: Harvard University Press.

Upham, F. K. (2005) 'Political lackeys or faithful public servants? Two views of the Japanese judiciary', *Law and Social Inquiry* 30: 421–54.

Vanoverbeke, D. (2004) *Community and State in the Japanese Farm Village: Farm Tenancy Conciliation (1924–1938)*, Leuven: Katholieke Universiteit.

Yamamuro, S. (1984) Hosei-kanryo no jidai [Time of Legislative Bureaucracy], Tokyo: Bokutaku-sha.

3 Causes and conditions for sustainable judicialization of politics in Korea

Jongcheol Kim and Jonghyun Park

Introduction

The judicialization of politics, 'the reliance on courts and judicial means for addressing core moral predicaments, public policy questions, and political controversies', is one of the most significant phenomena of late twentieth and early twenty-first century government (Hirschl 2010: Ch. 8, 119). Through newly acquired judicial review powers or constitutional adjudication, national high courts worldwide have resolved policy issues, even 'mega-politics' issues such as a nation's core policy (executive branch prerogatives); regime change (electoral politics); restorative justice; and questions of nationhood (Hirschl 2006: 723). In Korea, this phenomenon has been led by the Constitutional Court of Korea (KCC) through constitutional adjudication (J. Kim 2008).

After South Korea's authoritarian regime fell in 1987, the people rushed to build a foundation for transforming their political system into a liberal constitutional democracy (Ahn 1997: 74). One task accomplished in this transition was the 1988 revision of the constitution of 1980, a revision that established the KCC and gave it jurisdiction in five fundamental areas, one of which was the power to nullify unconstitutional legislation or other governmental activities (J. Kim 2010a; Park 2008: 63–4).

Since 1988 the KCC has successfully contributed to the evolution of constitutional democracy in Korea by resolving intense and high-profile political controversies as well as ordinary basic rights matters. Above all, since the KCC has ruled on cases determining the constitutional destinies of political branches and core policies, particularly the presidential impeachment and relocation of capital cases in 2004, there can be no serious doubt that the court is a central player in the political process (Park 2009: 4). Although the court has helped to consolidate democracy by judicializing politics, however, critics have warned that the judiciary itself might in turn become politicized.

In this chapter, we analyze the trend towards judicialization of politics in contemporary Korea with special reference to KCC involvement in constitutional matters and policy issues. In so doing, we try to show how Korea illustrates commonalities and national peculiarities within the global trend using empirical studies, particularly historical and case analysis. Beginning with a brief history of constitutional adjudication in Korea, we present developments in the judicialization of politics since 1988 by analyzing KCC decisions and their political implications. After delving into the constitutional and political implications of landmark cases, we move on to identify causes and features of the judicialization of politics in Korea. We conclude by suggesting some conditions necessary to sustain the positive aspects of this global trend in Korea rather than simply summarizing findings and arguments in previous sections.

Early adoption of constitutional adjudication in modern Korea

Since 1948 when the first Constitution of the Republic of Korea was passed, the constitutional adjudication system has been one of the main issues in the history of constitutional revision. Even when the first constitution was being drafted in 1948, there was a special committee for constitutional adjudication separate from the judiciary. Since then, constitutional adjudication (or judicial review) has never been left out of a constitution, although the record in practice was not always good.

For example, although the Constitution Court that the 1960 constitution stipulated to be a final constitutional arbiter, it was never actually established due to the military coup d'état led by General Park Chung Hee (Constitutional Court of Korea 2008: 75–6). The military government did incorporate a judicial review system into the 1962 constitution, and successive authoritarian governments established a Constitutional Committee for adjudication in the 1972 and 1980 constitutions. However, these authoritarian political powers considered constitutional adjudication to be a deviation from efficient execution of state policies (J. Kim 2010a: 117). Given the unfavorable political environment, the Constitutional Committee did not overturn a single case in the 15 years from 1972 to 1987, when the Korean people ended President Chun Doo-whan's iron-fisted rule and it was decided to establish a new court especially for constitutional adjudication.

The 1987 Constitution and the Constitutional Court

One of the most remarkable achievements in the 1987 constitution, the result of the 1987 People's Uprising, was the establishment of the KCC (West and Yoon 1992: 73–119). Its implications are immense. First, it is important that the new institution of constitutional adjudication was created in the undeniable hope of the people that constitutional democracy would be restored. The constitution itself resulted from a longstanding political movement with the people themselves as sovereign. The 1987 uprising was specifically targeted at reinstalling the direct ballot for presidential elections and enhancing protection of basic rights (Park 2008: 89). The expected active role of the KCC as protector of constitutional democracy was a natural reflection of the spirit of the times—then and now.[1]

The growing concern for an active role for the KCC is illustrated in part by its broad and centralized powers, though these were slightly marred in the legislative process. The KCC's scope of review is relatively broad in comparison with counterparts in other democracies. It is entrusted not only with essential powers for review of legislation and adjudication of complaints of unconstitutionality but also with less orthodox powers related to dissolution of political parties, inter-agency competence disputes, and impeachment trials. With these broad and fundamental powers, if supported by the public the KCC might rearrange constitutional arrangements.

So far the KCC has successfully carried out the mission that the constitution imposed as the will of the people (Yoon 2010: 143–4). As of 2010, 22 years after the court was actually established in September 1988, it had accepted 20,055 cases and disposed of 19,395; 10,355 of these were dismissed in the pre-screening process, but the court fully reviewed 8,394 cases. In the cases dealing with the constitutionality of legislation, the KCC declared unconstitutional 456 legal articles in 632 cases. The court has also upheld challenges against governmental powers in 352 cases. Thus about 11.7 percent of the cases it reviewed resulted in the invalidation or partial repudiation of legislation.[2] These cases have stimulated the rapid development of constitutional law, so it is easier to see the growing role of the KCC in the context of a global trend towards judicialization of politics (Goldstein 2004: 612–14; Kennedy 2006: 67–71). Beyond the 'countermajoritarian difficulty' (Bickel 1986: 16–23), the KCC has led Korean constitutional history to the advent of 'juristocracy' (Hirschl 2004: 169).

The judicialization of politics between 1988 and 2010

Whatever its intentions, the KCC has in fact intervened in the policy-making process. The result has been an improvement in the quality of related policies when constitutional doctrines are incorporated into policy decisions. Since traditionally the policy-making process had been carried out by the legislative and executive branches as representatives of the people, this change can be read as the advent of a new policy era; judicial impacts on ordinary policy-makings in the economic, social, and criminal law fields therefore deserve close examination from the perspective of the judicialization of politics.

However, it is difficult to treat this type of judicialization as outstanding evidence of the trend towards juristocracy because the cases are not 'pure' political cases decided on political considerations beyond the traditional normative reasoning of ordinary courts (Hirschl 2006). In the course of democratization, the KCC has often faced hard political questions, and has played a pivotal role in solving them. They include core national policy (executive branch prerogatives); regime change (electoral politics); restorative justice; and questions of nationhood itself. With that in mind, what Hirschl (2006) called the judicialization of 'mega-politics' might be considered a notable aspect of the trend of judicialization of politics in Korea. In this section, therefore, we sketch briefly some achievements of the KCC in terms of the ordinary policy-making process and then examine its role in mega-politics.

Constitutional adjudication and ordinary policy-making

It is notable that in protecting economic rights, especially land use regulation and tax issues, the KCC seemed determined not to violate constitutional principles usually used to protect civil liberties, such as the prohibition against excessive legislative restrictions (the proportionality principle); the principle of expectation interests (confidence in law); the prohibition against blanket delegation; and the rule requiring clarity in statutory expression.

One recent important case here is the 2008 Comprehensive Real Estate Tax Case,[3] in which the KCC ruled that levying a tax on a consolidated family basis is unconstitutional and that imposing the tax on long-term owners of a single home is also incompatible with the constitution. In fact, this tax policy introduced by the former Roh Moo-hyun administration to eradicate speculation in real estate, had been attacked by the conservative opposition as a socialist economic policy.[4] After the presidential election in 2007, the new Lee Myung-bak government and the ruling Grand National Party pledged to abolish the law but needed objective rationales to do that because public support for this law as progressive was still strong. The KCC unconstitutionality decision gave the government the moral and political justification it needed. Although political and constitutional debates on the ruling continue, it is one of the leading decisions showing the KCC's important role in making national economic policies (Park 2009: 205–12).[5]

The KCC has set up significant constitutional guidelines on social policy issues. By effective use of rights discourse it has had a particularly crucial role in protecting the rights of minorities like women and people with disabilities. One leading case is the decision on the House Head System in which a household as a basic unit of the legal family should be formed around the house head, a position that was passed down only through direct male descendants.[6] In this case the KCC held that the Civil Code provisions that constituted the backbone of the House Head System were incompatible with the individual dignity and sexual equality required by Article 36(1) of the constitution on the ground that they discriminated, based on stereotypes concerning sexual roles, against both men and women in determining the order of succession to house head, forming marital relations, and forming relations with children. After the KCC decision, the Civil Code of Korea was amended on 31 March 2005. There is no doubt that this case contributed significantly to improvement of women's social status and rights in all policy-making areas.[7]

Judicial engagement in mega-politics

The KCC and Core National Policy. The best example of the judicialization of core policy-making in Korea is the Relocation of the Capital City Case.[8] During the 2002 presidential election campaign, New Millennium Democratic Party candidate Roh Moo-hyun pledged to move the capital from Seoul to another area to promote equal and balanced development across the country. After Roh was elected, on 29 December 2003 the National Assembly passed a government-sponsored bill to establish a new administrative capital. Political opponents brought a constitutional complaint before the KCC, alleging that it infringed upon their right to a national referendum. On 21 October 2004 the KCC, in an 8–1 opinion, held that the challenged act was unconstitutional. The reasoning was as follows:

1 Since Seoul has been the capital of Korea for over 600 years, a fact the people have recognized, a kind of 'customary constitution' compels that Seoul be the capital.
2 The KCC should protect the national consensus and the custom that Seoul is the capital as a constitutional principle even though it is not written in the constitution.
3 There is no difference in the constitutional effects of the customary constitution and the written constitution.
4 If the nation wants to revise the customary constitution, it should follow the revision procedure in Article 130 of the constitution, which requires a national referendum.
5 Since the challenged act is an attempt to revise the customary constitution without a national referendum, it violates the constitution.

The KCC decision striking down the act stimulated wide-ranging debates between political forces (Park 2008: 78–81). Above all, the adoption of the unfamiliar concept of 'customary constitution' as a standard against which to assess the constitutionality of legislation on core national policy ignited fierce debates among lawyers and legal scholars. Some emphasized the significance of the customary constitution by stressing that the KCC has discretion to find the existence of a customary constitution and apply it. Others argued, among other points, that in a nation like Korea with a civil law system, it is absurd to treat a customary constitution, if there is such a thing, as having the same effect as a written constitution because it was not confirmed by the people as the written constitution was.

In the wake of this ruling, the Roh Government and the ruling Uri Party submitted an alternative bill for an 'administration-centered city' to which all executive departments would move except branches and offices pertaining to such core departments of the state as the presidential office of Cheong Wa Dae, the Supreme Court, the National Assembly, and some ministries dealing with foreign affairs and national security. On 2 March 2005, the bill passed but was soon challenged in another constitutional complaint on 27 April 2005. In this case, the KCC ruled that the new act did not constitute a relocation of the capital.[9]

At this point Korean society started to pay attention to the KCC as a significant policy-making political branch, and the court did not hesitate to broaden its power to intervene in the process of making core policy. Nevertheless, it has avoided ruling on such traditional executive prerogatives as diplomacy and national defense policies. In the Case Concerning the Presidential Decision to Dispatch Korean National Armed Forces to Iraq,[10] for example, the KCC held that highly political matters such as whether or not a decision to dispatch the armed forces violates the constitution and whether the war in Iraq is an aggressive war against international norms should be rendered by the president and the National Assembly, which are directly elected.[11]

KCC and Electoral Politics. The landmark decision illuminating KCC intervention in political change is the Impeachment of President Roh Moo-hyun Case.[12] On 12 March 2004, Roh became the first president in Korean history to be impeached by the National Assembly. Once he was impeached, his presidential powers were suspended.

The starting point of the case was speeches Roh made at political assemblies and statements in press conferences showing he favored the new Uri Party in the scheduled general election. The opposition Grand National Party (GNP) and the New Millennium Democratic Party (MDP), which held a majority in the National Assembly, accused Roh of violating the Public Officials Election Act which prohibits sitting public officials from trying to influence elections or electoral processes. The president refused to accept their demand for apologies or a promise not to repeat such political speeches. On 9 March the opposition in the National Assembly started an impeachment process and on 12 March the assembly, with 193 votes out of 271, passed the resolution of impeachment based on numerous allegedly illegal and improper acts of President Roh before and after his inauguration.

On 14 May 2004 the KCC held that although President Roh was guilty on three counts,[13] the violations did not mount to the level of gravity required to dismiss him from the presidency. The court reasoned that since Article 111 of the Constitution entrusted the power of impeachment to the KCC and Article 53(1) of the Constitutional Court Act (CCA) states that 'when there is a valid ground for the petition for impeachment adjudication, the Constitutional Court shall issue a decision removing the respondent from office', the KCC has the power to determine how grave an illegality must be to justify dismissing public officials from office; the concern is to strike a balance between the relevant interests and constitutional values based on the principle of proportionality (Park 2008: 70–1; J. Kim 2004).

This compromise decision shows the deep concern of the KCC, which was either forced to accept or was itself claiming a role as a constitutional coordinator in the flux of mega-politics. On the one hand, it seemed an attempt to satisfy the opposition parties and their supporters with its findings that President Roh had committed illegal and unconstitutional conducts, so that the motion of impeachment could be regarded as an appropriate response to the conduct, and also with its constitutional order that the president should desist from such illegal activities in future. On the other hand, it seemed to try to please the president's supporters by allowing him to stay in office despite the violations.[14] However, the biggest winner would be the KCC: with this case, it succeeded in creating an image of itself as a key player in the area of mega-politics by declaring that it has final authority to determine whether impeached public officials should be dismissed even if they are guilty of illegal activities.

The KCC and Restorative Justice. After the downfall of the authoritarian Chun Doo-hwan in 1987, victims of former authoritarian governments brought cases to restore justice. In particular civilians affected by the bloody 18 May 1980 Kwangju Democratization Movement and the military coup led by General Chun pressed new governments to punish figures that had been central in the military government.

The ensuing governments had been very reluctant to do so[15] but finally accepted the growing popular demand for restorative justice. On 16 November 1995 President Kim Yong-sam pushed the National Assembly to pass the Special Act on the May 18 Democratization Movement, the thrust of which was to extend the period during which those involved with the 12 December 1979 military coup and the Kwangju Democratization Movement could be prosecuted. The accused challenged the Special Act, arguing that it violated the constitutional prohibition against ex post facto application of the law. Although the five-justice majority supported the applicant's argument, the act was finally declared constitutional because they failed to meet the quorum of six justices required to invalidate laws. In this case, the four-justice minority opinion depended on the restorative justice doctrine (Yoon 2010: 185). Once the KCC endorsed the constitutionality of the controversial law, the prosecutors began investigating the cases and arrested former President Chun and 16 colleagues on charges of insurrection (Yoon 2010: 186–87). On 17 April 1997, the Supreme Court dismissed their appeals of the Appellate Court decision that sentenced Chun to life imprisonment.

The KCC and Questions of Nationhood. Besides issues of 'pure' or 'mega-politics', the KCC was also involved in a most controversial political dealing with 'the very definition, or raison d'être, of the polity' (Hirschl 2006: 735–36).

Korean constitutionalism has a built-in dilemma: it must accept the reality of a divided polity in that two competing regimes each claims that it is the only legitimate polity, defying the other as an unconstitutional anti-state association or organization. The Korean Constitution sets out the sacred mission of reunification of the two Koreas especially in Article 4, after Article 3 declares clearly that the territory of the Republic of Korea (the ROK), internationally known as South Korea, covers the whole Korean peninsula. However, the KCC, along with the Supreme Court of Korea, recognizes the Democratic People's Republic of Korea (the DPRK), internationally known as North Korea, as a unique political organization having a twofold legal entity, the counterpart of the ROK in the political negotiation on reunification, and the other as a subversive organization the political activities of which, as well as the activities of individuals and organizations supporting it, can be prohibited according to procedures prescribed by law.

Korea's National Security Act (NSA) was passed to protect the ROK regime. The KCC has had to determine the constitutionality of provisions of this act on a number of occasions and thus became involved in questions of nationhood. In the Praising and Encouraging Under the National Security Act Case,[16] the court ruled that NSA Articles 7(1) and 7(5), which criminalize the act of praising or encouraging anti-state groups and producing treasonous material, are constitutional so long as they are interpreted to apply only to limited circumstances that threaten national security and free and democratic order. Not surprisingly, the option of criminal punishment and the use of broad and vague terms like 'praising' and 'encouraging' have been abused to oppress political opponents and apply sweeping curbs on freedom of expression not only in authoritarian regimes but even after democratization. In this decision, the court recognized the reality of the continuing South–North military confrontation and resolved to prevent the immense nationwide outcry that was likely to follow a total invalidation of the law even if it had a sound legal basis for finding it unconstitutional.

After this decision, on 31 May 1991, the National Assembly revised the problematic phrasing. As suggested by the KCC it added 'knowingly endangering the national integrity and security, or the basic order of free democracy' at the beginning of Article 7(1), and 'benefits anti-state organizations through other means' was replaced by the more specific 'promotes and advocates for national subversion'.

Causes of the judicialization of politics in Korea

Macro factors

To find causes or backgrounds of judicialization of politics in Korea, first of all, we need to look into the social and political circumstances, which have considerable influence on the judicialization. Many such studies have been carried out in other jurisdictions. Scholars have ascribed judicialization to processes of democratization and modernization (Hirschl 2004), the competitiveness of political parties (Ginsburg 2003, Ramseyer 1994), or struggles to preserve hegemony (Hirschl 2004, 2006). Other scholars have drawn attention to politicians who want to shift responsibility to the judicial branch (Voigt and Salzberger 2002); to construction of constitutional legitimacy for making policy (Morton 1995); and to the strategic behavior of the judicial branch in the political sphere (Guarnieri and Pederzoli 2002, Ferejohn 2002). Most of these hypotheses can be applied to the Korean context.

Above all, we can agree that the emergence of this global trend in Korea is one impact of the process of democratization since 1987. The way democratization operated before and after the 1987 People's Uprising significantly transformed Korean society from a Procrustean, authoritarian, tightly controlled society to a pluralized one governed by constitutional democracy. To cope with this social change, the paradigm of politics also had to change, from a monopoly dominated by autocratic rulers to competition governed by the constitution. The most feasible way to accomplish this task is to intensively constitutionalize politics, in the sense that democratic procedures designed to make political competition free and fair should be institutionalized in a constitution (J. Kim 2010b: 67–94). In turn, this constitutionalization of democratic procedures needs a control system where a new political coordinator is instrumental in accommodating the burgeoning contingency and complexity related to democratization (J. Kim 2010b: 67–94).

In Korea after the 1987 People's Uprising the immediate response to the requirement of constitutionalizing politics was the creation of a specialized constitutional adjudication institution, the KCC. This does not mean that the institution itself can explain its active role. Hirschl is quite right in asserting that there is a close correlation between the culture of political deadlock and an active role for the judiciary in politics (Hirschl 2006: 744ff.). If Korean political culture were more 'consensus politics' than 'conviction politics', there would be less possibility of judicial intervention in 'pure politics'. As a matter of fact, the lack of political stability and efficiency inevitable in a transition period exacerbated a confrontational tendency in Korean politics. In the period of authoritarian rule, issues like presidential impeachment, relocation of the capital, ideological conflicts about restorative justice, political confrontations about reunification or the North Korean problem, and so on were solved according to the convictions of the ruling camp. After democratization, lacking that type of authoritarian control those in the political minority must use all possible means to validate the rightness of their convictions, and the KCC with its wide political jurisdiction is a natural choice as validator.

Furthermore, regime changes in the course of democratization have increased not only the diversity of political ideologies in Korea but also the importance of constitutional competition between competing concepts of both nationhood and political hegemony. This invites the judicialization of politics in a complicated way. First, in politics authoritarianism in Korea has been united with an anti-communist obsession. Before the 1990s it was absolutely impossible to express certain political ideologies because the existence of North Korea and the experience of the Korean War blocked any deep ideological discussions (Cho 1997: 126–7). However, in the course of democratization the dominance of conservative political ideology in Korean politics is fading (C. Kim 2000).

Changes in the political ideological spectrum have been reinforced by regime changes. Consecutive victories in the 1997 and 2002 presidential elections enlarged the political space for liberal reformists and progressives who previously had been stigmatized as pro-North Korean anti-statists. Over the 10 years when the Kim Dae-jung and Roh Moo-hyun governments replaced almost half a century of conservative regimes, the pluralization of politics accelerated to the point that the Democratic Labor Party (DLP), whose manifestos used to specify their pursuit of socialism, succeeded in gaining seats in the National Assembly.[17] Ultimately, conflicts between pre-existing conservative power and emerging progressive power needed judicial clarification of political agendas, which accelerated the judicialization of politics (J. Kim 2005; Park 2008: 97–8).

The growth of civil society has also contributed to the judicialization of politics in Korea. Democratization has empowered civil society, encouraging citizens to be actively involved in the political process, especially through non-governmental organizations (NGOs). NGOs have been active in ensuring a democratic political system by acting as watchdogs as well as working to encourage more participatory democracy (Kim and Moon 2003). In this century the number of NGOs in Korea has exploded from about 9,000 in 1997 to 18,266 in 2003 and 23,017 in 2006.[18] Among current NGOs, the number of civic groups with specific political ideologies is 5,556 and the number of those without a political preference is 17,461. NGOs are active in such policy fields as the economy, education, labor, culture, welfare, press, religion, women, and disability rights. Despite their growing status in the policy-making process, however, NGOs and other civil associations are not decision-makers per se, instead, they function as facilitators in the policy-making process. The KCC can be a useful public forum for civic activists eager to draw public attention to their causes. The constitutional adjudication process offers them an opportunity to diffuse their ideas and even check government decision-makers by making them accountable to the challenges raised in the adjudication process.

Recent rapid growth in the Korean bar has indirectly helped judicial activism to blossom (Ahn 1997: 81). In the last 15 years, the number of licensed lawyers in Korea has almost quadrupled, from over 3,000 in 1996 to over 11,000 in 2010. Every year about a thousand new lawyers join the bar. The increase results from government efforts to reform the judiciary and introduce American-style law schools. The surge in the number of lawyers has necessarily changed how they practice (Ahn 1997: 82): Increasingly, lawyers have been exploring new areas of law, such as consumer, labor, and civil rights law. Many lawyers have joined civic groups working to protect citizens' rights and monitor governmental policies by using the judicial process, including constitutional adjudication.

Micro factors

Analysis of judicial behavior in micro frames as recently featured in research on the causes of the judicialization of politics has been expressed in terms of (a) institutional analysis of the composition and competence of courts; (b) cultural analysis of social circumstances which may impact the behavior of judges; and (c) structural analysis of the operation of courts within the political field. We consider the judicialization of politics in Korea to be partly indebted to favorable institutional arrangements and the concomitant cultural outcomes.

First, the composition of the KCC may lead to judicialization. The court consists of nine justices appointed by the president, of whom three are to be selected by the National Assembly and three nominated by the chief justice of the Supreme Court. Their term in office, which is renewable, is six years (CCA Art. 7(1)). The fact that two-thirds are selected by other political branches may generate a plausible assumption that they can be politically influenced. Indeed, it would be naive to assume that political parties in the National Assembly and the administration select justices without deep political consideration (Park 2008: 94). Also, the relatively short term and the reappointment option may jeopardize the independence of the court by making justices sensitive to the opinions of those with appointive power (J. Kim 2010a: 124).[19]

Second, the jurisdiction of the KCC may be one of the causes of judicialization. Article 111(1) of the current constitution entrusts five areas of jurisdiction to the court: (1) constitutional review of a law; (2) constitutional complaints; (3) impeachment; (4) dissolution of political parties; and (5) disputes about areas and scope of competence between state agencies, a state agency and a local government, or local governments.[20] These functions would alone be enough to suggest the political nature of the court because all of them have a vital influence on constitutional arrangements (Park 2008: 92–3). The KCC has what might be called 'negative legislative power' in that it can review whether a law is unconstitutional. Also, it can be seen as a political decision-maker by intervening in the impeachment process, resolving inter-agency disputes, and dissolving a political party (Yoon 2010: 161–3). Equipped with such broad political powers, the KCC becomes a major constitutional coordinator; in an increasing number of cases, as seen, it has been asked to decide even on matters that used to be the prerogative of the political process.

Third, another factor in ascribing judicialization is the type of standard against which a court's powers are exercised. The KCC is not an exception to the general history of constitutional adjudication, in which adjudicating bodies use substantive subprinciples or rules derived from basic constitutional and statutory principles as standards for adjudication. The principle of proportionality known as the 'principle against excessive restriction' (Constitutional Court of Korea 2001: 125) is one of such principles used most often in constitutional adjudication in Korea (Park 2008: 95). Drawing its constitutional source from the 'necessity clause' of Article 37(2) of the constitution,[21] the KCC has made it clear that this principle gives the court wide discretion to strike a balance between the public interest and the basic rights of the parties in the course of review.[22] No constitutional provision or principle offers objective valuations of the public interest and basic rights; the court itself must make the calculations. This means that the KCC enjoys full discretion to check the constitutionality of every policy without any normative limit. Surely this invites comprehensive judicialization of politics in Korea.

Fourth, public preferences for the judiciary lead to judicialization. In the course of democratization, the Korean public has demonstrated little confidence in any state branches compared to its opinions of actors in the private sector. Among the three branches, however, the judiciary from the beginning has enjoyed a relatively higher evaluation. The public prefers the seemingly neutral decisions of the courts over the decisions of politicians and bureaucrats, who in leading the developmental state are thought to be inevitably corrupted in carrying out their powers to allot social resources and interests to private actors (J. Kim 2008: 103, 116). Elaborating on this preference is the tendency of Koreans to prefer a clear-cut result by exhausting every possible way, political or legal, to achieve their goals, rather than take a middle way by compromising on differences (J. Kim 2008: 103, 116).

Finally, in identifying the roots of judicialization, the perception that KCC justices have of their role should be considered. In the wake of democratization, the role perception of judges also changes. In particular, KCC justices need to concern themselves with what the public expect of them in the course of democratization and with public evaluation of their judgments. For one thing, if they failed to meet the increased public consciousness of rights and democracy, they might not only lose their personal reputations as the highest judges but also face the loss of public confidence in KCC's institutional raison d'être. In fact, in the early years of the KCC, there were public worries that the new constitutional adjudication body might not meet people's demand for it to become a bastion of basic rights and democracy due to some institutional hurdles[23] built in the procedures of adjudication in the hope of inactivating the KCC. However, the eagerness of KCC justices based upon the perception that only active performance might eradicate such worries helped the KCC take a relatively aggressive stance in enlarging its jurisdiction and softening statutory requirements intended to restrict complaints and review to be filed or referred to the KCC (J. Kim 2010a: 128–30), and thus ultimately accelerate judicialization of politics.

Evaluating the judicialization of politics in Korea

As sketched above, one of the most remarkable developments in Korean constitutional history has been the activity of the KCC since 1988. In judging many important laws to be unconstitutional, it has helped to change public and bureaucratic attitudes towards both the constitution and the powers of government (Yoon 1995: 409). Moreover, the KCC has had no hesitation in performing its self-imposed mission as final arbiter of the constitution, to the point that it now has the authority to solve political questions in terms of the constitution. Its activity seems ample evidence that there has been an expansion of constitutionalism (Yoon 2010: 166). One measure of constitutionalism is the degree of protection a society affords to civil rights (Yoon 2010: 167). Through the democratization process and the judicialization of politics, the powers a state may apply to its citizens are now perceived to be limited. Bureaucratic attitudes towards citizens are also changing, with increased importance given to the rule of law and protection of human rights through judicialization of politics.

At the same time there may be concerns about the judicialization of politics in that the trend may gradually undermine the normal functions of politics. The advent of a variety of political ideologies results in frequent conflicts between opposing political powers. In this situation, an ideal solution for a politically mature society might be discourse between powers in the ordinary political arena. However, when there is extreme antagonism and political powers are almost equal, discourse in the political sphere can be so unproductive that participants abandon their political duties and flee to the shelter of constitutional adjudication. Consequently, the judicialization of politics ultimately might severely diminish the political field.

However, if this worry originates from the confrontation of democracy with the rule of law, it is too simple. As mentioned above, the judicialization of politics through a KCC-type of institution presupposes the constitutionalization of politics in that procedures of political decision-making are required to meet constitutional principles. The principles themselves are generally neutral; they propose procedures and values for political judgment and adjustment in dynamic political relations (J. Kim 2005: 240). The function of evaluating the constitutionality of a policy using neutral principles can be considered as a process of selecting a political position within the boundaries of the constitution (Stone Sweet 2000: 204). This can both activate and ameliorate the political arena by improving the quality of political decisions rather than causing a political collapse.[24]

The task of evaluating Korean cases in terms of the judicialization of politics thus needs to look at the distortion of 'judicialization' more than any collapse of 'politics'. The KCC can be blamed, for instance, for its polemical stance in carrying out its duty, because some KCC decisions are based not on detailed constitutional principles but on special interests and partisan motivations. In other words, the politicization of judicial matters weakens KCC authority. While the normative ideal and the institution of the rule of law make the KCC a supreme coordinator of all government powers, the dictates of reality can make this ideal merely a daydream if judges constrain themselves or give in to coercive political pressure (J. Kim 2008: 116).

A good example is the recent case of the Comprehensive Real Estate Tax Act. Just before the KCC issued its decision, it was publicized that Finance Minister Kang Man-soo might have influenced the court's deliberations on the case, since he himself said that according to information from KCC insiders he expected some parts of that tax system to be ruled unconstitutional. Opposition parties instantly berated him for trying to undermine judicial independence and credibility. Naturally, the KCC was also fiercely criticized by the public as well as opposition parties, who feared the court had attempted to misuse its power, contrary to the general expectation that it would lead the judicialization of politics according to constitutional law and principles.[25]

In probing the dark side of the judicialization of politics, the worst case would be that the KCC attempts to manipulate normative contents of constitutional law and politics to justify polemical decisions (Park 2008: 102). Such a camouflage strategy could convert a decision with deep political content into an ordinary judicial decision that seems to be normatively justified. The best example is the Relocation of the Capital case in which the KCC majority based its reasoning on the unfamiliar concept of a 'customary constitution'.

Assumption of a customary constitution as a source of law needs further justification if it is to reach the same status as the written constitution. The majority's complicated explanation has already been summarized, but basically it justifies recognition of a customary constitution on the ground of the principle of popular sovereignty. The majority then argued that even the unwritten customary constitution can only be revised using the procedure for revision of a written constitution.

The logical consequence of this preposition is that even though the people may have the right to choose in which form they constitute the constitution, written or unwritten, they do not have the right to choose the procedure for revising any type of constitution. A problem with the majority logic is that the constitutional revision clauses require both the concurrent votes of two-thirds or more of all members of the National Assembly and a majority decision in a referendum. Therefore, the natural consequence of the majority opinion is that just over one-third of all the members of the National Assembly could block relocation of the capital. Thus we can realize how feebly the KCC majority justifies the customary constitution on the basis of the people's sovereignty. Why can the people themselves not change the customary constitution? Should they be subject to the will of a minority rather than the majority of representatives, when a customary constitution can be formed only by the will of the people?

If, in playing a policy-making role through constitutional adjudication, the KCC takes a strategic approach to reflect political realities in its decisions, or even to manipulate constitutional doctrines or concepts in a sophisticated way to justify some intended conclusion, it would have crossed the line into a 'forbidden castle' where the 'judicial emperor' would appear to be revered by political supporters but sooner or later it could be degenerated into their puppet. Even worse is the nature of the underlying motives. If the intent is to protect the interests of 'discrete and insular minorities',[26] it can be excused in the name of liberal values pertaining to constitutionalism. If, unfortunately, it is motivated by an urge to protect vested socioeconomic interests, such polemical decisions cannot be justified on any grounds.

Conclusion: conditions for the sustainable judicialization of politics

Although the positive influence of the KCC on Korean politics and society should be recognized, it is also true that its remarkable performance has benefited from a favorable environment. The social spirit of the times that is promoting democratization and liberalization has provided a 'blood transfusion' allowing the court to hold itself out as a bastion of constitutional democracy in Korean society. The explicit institutionalization of various areas of jurisdiction has given it a solid backbone so that, unlike its counterpart in the U.S., it can avoid unnecessary debates on how to justify constitutional adjudication. The unpleasant legacy of the old authoritarian regimes—a number of unjust laws and practices—has given it reason to perform in that it does not have to concern itself too much about the impact of activism on the polity when it is getting rid of almost self-evident evils.

However, the KCC has now been in existence for over two decades. Democratization is entrenched in the society as a whole; sociopolitical competition has become intense, with clashes between different ideas of democracy and human rights or more polemical political ideologies. Despite explicit constitutional justifications, the sociopolitical dimensions of KCC decisions routinely generate deeply divided public responses. The court is confronted with more hard cases not only because state authorities have become cautious about yielding their powers in violation of the constitution but also, more significantly, because the docket is seeing more highly confrontational political issues derived from a diversified society.

In dealing with hard cases the KCC cannot avoid its genuine political mission. If it takes this mission seriously in a positive way, its new role as a political coordinator may be realized. If not, it might return to the dormancy of its pre-1987 predecessors. Whichever path it takes, we can assume that the political implications depend on the functional efficiency of its decisions (like other political branches) rather than upon the normative rationales for the decisions (like the traditional judiciary). In other words, justifications of its role in the political process, whether that is active or passive, will be evaluated mainly according to how effectively it can solve or avoid an issue rather than the normative justifications for its choices.

What makes the real differences between the active path and the passive path, however, lies in the long-term effects. Where the KCC is actively involved in mega-politics, it should recognize and accept the danger of politicization. In the opposite case, it can avoid or lessen the danger but has to give up its role in nicely coordinating constitutional arrangements and thereby managing political counterparts.

Is there no middle way? Considering the evolution of constitutional democracy in Korea since at least 1987, it would not be naive to assume that if we can agree with the conditions in which authority for constitutional adjudication is exercised in a self-contained manner, the bright side of the judicialization of politics may prevail over its dark side by diminishing the danger of extreme politicization. The necessary conditions include a democratic constitution on which to base the judicial powers, reservation of the critical public sphere for the judicial powers, and prudential exercise of judicial powers based upon persuasive reasoning (J. Kim 2005). The first two conditions are prerequisites for strengthening its political legitimacy if the KCC is to take an active role as political coordinator. The last, but most important condition is necessary to avoid or lessen the danger of politicization. Even though it claims a political function, the KCC should perform that role in a manner different from that of other political branches. In other words, wisdom, prudence, and persuasiveness are vital virtues for a political adjudicatory body like the KCC. Unfortunately, if we were asked whether, in the recent hard cases dealing with the presidential impeachment and the relocation of the capital, the KCC has met the conditions required for it to perform its role as a political coordinator in a self-contained manner, the answer would have to be in the negative. Nevertheless, we look forward with interest to finding out when the KCC can find the best way to solve political hard cases. Would it be in the near future?

Notes

1 Because of the oppressive political environment, previous constitutional adjudication bodies were derided as merely rubber-stamp institutions for the military dictatorship or as existing in name only; see J. Kim (2010a: 117).

2 See the official statistics on the Constitutional Court website, http://english.ccourt.go.kr/.

3 2006 Hun-Ba 112, 2007 Hun-Ba 71·88·94, 2008 Hun-Ba 3·62, 2008 Hun-Ka12 (Consolidated), 13 November 2008.

4 In Korea, rapid industrialization and urbanization in the course of economic development kept pushing up urban land and housing prices, distorting wealth distribution and leading to social instability. Therefore, economic policies related to real estate become one of the hot potatoes in Korean politics.

5 Another representative constitutional case on economic policy is the Residential Property Ownership Ceiling Case, 94 Hun-Ba 37, etc. (consolidated), 18 April 1999. Here the court invalidated the entire Ceilings on the Ownership of Housing Sites Act for limiting individual ownership of housing sites and prohibiting corporate ownership entirely; see Park 2009: 220–221.

6 2001 Hun-Ga 9.10.11.12.13.14.15 and 2004 Hun-Ga 5 (consolidated), 3 February 2005.

7 Another notable social policy case is the Visually Handicapped Masseurs Case, 2006 Hun-Ma 1098•1116•1117 (Consolidated), 30 October 2008, in which the KCC decided that provisions like Article 61(1) of the former Medical Service Act that exclude the nonvisually handicapped from massage service by allowing accreditation only to the visually handicapped do not contradict the constitution. Although this monopoly policy may clash with other basic rights of nonvisually handicapped people such as freedom of occupational choice, the court held that because the role of masseur is almost the only occupation available for the visually handicapped, a minority that had been discriminated against over the years in terms of education, employment, and many other areas, the constitution justifies this professional monopoly policy as a way for them to realize their substantial equality. For a fuller analysis, see Park 2009: 221–9.

8 2004 Hun-Ma 554, 566 (consolidated), 21 October 2004.

9 2005 Hun-Ma 579, 763, 24 November 2005.

10 2003 Hun-Ma 814, 29 April 2004.

11 The President of the Republic of Korea decided, on 18 October 2003, to dispatch the Korean National Armed Forces to Iraq after consulting the National Security Council, which is responsible for setting policies concerning national security. The complainant filed the constitutional complaint as a Korean national seeking a ruling that the decision was unconstitutional on the ground, *inter alia,* that the President's decision to dispatch forces to Iraq violated Article 5 of the Korean constitution renouncing all aggressive wars.

12 2004 Hun-Na 1, 14 May, 2004.

13 The violations that the KCC acknowledged were threefold. First, he violated the duty of electoral neutrality required by Art. 9 of the Public Official Election Act of Korea by expressing his hope that the people would support the Uri Party. Second, his defiant comments on the warning of the National Election Commission asking him to desist from political speeches related to the general election violated his presidential duty to uphold and protect the Constitution. Third, his proposal of a national referendum on the confidence of the people in his presidency was not compatible with Article 72(1), which allowed only referendums on specific policies and thus encroached upon his duty to uphold and protect the constitution.

14 In fact, it is very difficult to conceive how the KCC could have defied the people's political verdict in that the 15 April 2004 general election had returned a remarkable

victory for pro-Roh political forces; in particular, the Uri Party won 152 seats out of 299.

15 'Ex-Korean presidents implicated', *New York Times*, 30 October 1994.

16 89 Hun-Ka 113, 2 April 1990.

17 In the 2004 general election, the DLP with 10 seats became the third largest party in the National Assembly. It was the first time in modern Korea that any labor party had independent power in the normal political process. Although in the 2008 general election the DLP won just five seats, the existence of this left-wing party in constitutional institutions shows the diversity of politics in Korea.

18 For general information and statistics on NGOs in Korea, see the Committee of Directory of Korean NGOs (2006).

19 For a general explanation, see Yang *et al.* 1999: 17–19.

20 For a brief sketch of jurisdictions, see J. Kim (2010a: 119–24).

21 It provides that 'the freedoms and rights of citizens may be restricted by statutes *only when necessary for* national security, the maintenance of law and order, or for public welfare. Even when such restriction is imposed, no essential aspect of the freedom or right shall be violated' (emphasis added).

22 The proportionality test has four elements: (1) governmental activities must have a legitimate purpose; (2) the means chosen must be appropriate to achieving that purpose; (3) the means used must be the least restrictive of all equally effective options; and (4) the public interest and the degree of infringement are balanced through a relationship of proportionality (J. Kim 2010a: 130). Especially the third and fourth standard gives the KCC wide discretion.

23 For instance, the exclusion of judicial judgments from the jurisdiction of constitutional complaint by Article 68(1) of CCA combined with the statutory exhaustion rule requiring claimants to exhaust all relief processes provided by other laws might prevent most administrative malpractices from being covered by constitutional complaints. For further explanation, see J. Kim 2001; J. Kim 2010a: 129ff.

24 Although the judicialization of politics can be justified under the name of democracy, there is as yet no answer to the question of the extent to which the judiciary can intervene in a political procedure (J. Kim 2005: 244). It would be naive to think that judicial activism can solve all the problems originating in failures of the political branches, although there are a number of positive examples, such as its holdings in the Head of Household case. Even in such cases, however, it should be borne in mind that it was able to do so because the cases brought before it met procedural requirements. Furthermore, the fact that a body has a certain power is one thing; whether this power can be exercised to its fullest is a different matter.

25 Song Sang-ho, "Court to rule on disputed property tax", *The Korea Herald*, 12 Nov. 2008.

26 *United States* v. *Carolene Products Company*, 304 U.S. 144 (1938), Fn. 4.

References

Ahn, K. W. (1997) 'The influence of American constitutionalism on South Korea', *Southern Illinois University Law Journal*, 22: 71–115.

Bickel, A. M. (1986) *The Least Dangerous Branch: The Supreme Court at the Bar of Politics*, New Haven, CT: Yale University Press.

Cho, K. (1997) 'Tension between The National Security Law and Constitutionalism in South Korea: Security for what?' *Boston University International Law Journal*, 15: 125–74.

Constitutional Court of Korea (2001) *The First Ten Years of the Korean Constitutional Court*, Seoul, Korea.

Constitutional Court of Korea (2008) *Twenty Years of the Constitutional Court of Korea*, Seoul, Korea.

Committee of Directory of Korean NGOs (2006) *2006 Directory of Korean NGOs*, Seoul, Korea: Civil Movement Information Center.

Ferejohn, J. (2002) 'Judicializing politics, politicizing law', *Law and Contemporary Problems*, 61: 41–68.

Ginsburg, T. (2003) *Judicial Review in New Democracies: Constitutional Courts in Asian Cases*, Cambridge, UK: Cambridge University Press.

Goldstein, L. F. (2004) 'From democracy to juristocracy', *Law and Society Review*, 38: 611–29.

Guarnieri, C. and Pederzoli, P. (2002) *The Power of Judges: A Comparative Study of Courts and Democracy*, New York, NY: Oxford University Press.

Hirschl, R. (2004) *Towards Juristocracy: The Origins And Consequences of the New Constitutionalism*, Boston, MA: Harvard University Press.

Hirschl, R. (2006) 'The new constitutionalism and the judicialization of pure politics worldwide', *Fordham Law Review*, 75: 721–54.

Hirschl, R. (2010) 'The judicialization of politics', *The Oxford Handbook of Law and Politics*, New York, NY: Oxford University Press.

Kennedy, D. (2006) 'The globalization of law and legal thought: 1850–2000', in Trubek, D. M. and Santos, A., *The New Law and Economic Development: A Critical Appraisal*, London, UK: Cambridge University Press.

Kim, C. J. (2000) 'Korean attitudes towards law', *Pacific Rim Law and Policy*, 10: 1–46.

Kim, J. (2001) 'Some Problems with the Korean Constitutional Adjudication System', *Journal of Korean Law*, 1(2): 17–36.

Kim, J. (2004) 'What does the Korean Constitutional Court miss or misunderstand in the impeachment trial against President Roh Moo-hyun?', *Segye Hunbub Yeon Gu* (*World Constitutional Law Review*), 9: 1–22 (available only in Korean).

Kim, J. (2005) 'Constitutional implications and limits of the judicialization of politics—with reference to judicial activism in the early years of the Roh Moo-hyun Government', *Gong Bub Yeon Gu (Public Law Review)*, 33: 229–51(available only in Korean).

Kim, J. (2008) 'Government reform, judicialization, the development of public law in the Republic of Korea', in Ginsburg, T. and Chen, A. (eds), *Administrative Law and Governance in Asia: Comparative Perspectives*, London, UK: Routledge.

Kim, J. (2010a) 'The structure and basic principles of constitutional adjudication in the Republic of Korea', in Kuk Cho (ed.), *Litigation in Korea*, London, UK: Edward Elgar Publishing.

Kim, J. (2010b) 'The project of "constitutionalized democratic autonomy": Towards a new version of constitutionalism', *Yonsei Law Journal*, 1: 67–94.

Kim, P. S. and Moon, M. J. (2003) 'NGOs as incubator of participative democracy in South Korea: Political, voluntary, and policy participation', *International Journal of Public Administration*, 26: 549–67.

Morton, F. L. (1995) 'The effect of the Charter of Rights on Canadian federalism', *Publius*, 25: 173–88.

Park, J. (2008) 'The judicialization of politics In Korea', *Asian-Pacific Law & Policy Journal*, 10: 62–113.

Park, J. (2009) 'Constitutional adjudication and policy-making—a positive analysis of constitutional policy-making for dissolving the countermajoritarian difficulty', Ph.D. dissertation, Seoul National University of Korea (available only in Korean).

Ramseyer, J. M. (1994) 'Thc puzzling (in)dependence of courts: A comparative approach', *Journal of Legal Studies*, 23: 721–48.

Stone Sweet, A. (2000) *Governing with Judges: Constitutional Politics in Europe*, New York, NY: Oxford University Press.

Voigt, S. and Salzberger, E. (2002) 'Choosing not to choose: When politicians choose to delegate powers', *Kyklos*, 55: 289–310.

West, J. and Yoon, D. (1992) 'The Constitutional Court of the Republic of Korea: Transforming the jurisprudence of the vortex?, *American Journal of Comparative Law*, 40: 73–119.

Yang, K., Kim, M. and Nam, B. (1999) *Report on Reform of the Korean Constitutional Court Act (Hun Bup Jae Pan So Bup Eui Gae Jung Bang Ahn Eh Kwan Han Yun Goo Yong Yuk Bo Go Suh)*, Studies on Constitutional Adjudication 10, Seoul, Korea: The Constitutional Court.

Yoon, D. (1995) 'New developments In Korean constitutionalism: Changes and prospects', *Pacific Rim Law and Policy Journal*, 4: 395–417.

Yoon, D. (2010) *Law and Democracy in South Korea – Democratic Development Since 1987*, Seoul, Korea: Institute for Far Eastern Studies.

4 The judiciary, policy, and politics in India[1]

Shylashri Shankar

Introduction

In 2009 a member of an opposition party who is a leading constitutional and criminal lawyer, a former head of police, a scholar, and three others petitioned the Indian Supreme Court to direct the central government to bring back about Rs.70 trillion black (unaccounted for) money stashed away by Indian nationals in tax havens. Subsequently, one of the Wikileaks revelations listed individuals, many of them Indians, who had black money in Swiss banks. In January 2011 the court chided the Indian government for treating black money as simply a treaty issue related to double taxation: 'We are talking about mind-boggling crime. We are not on the niceties of treaties'.[2]

This and orders calling for investigative agencies to report to the court in specific cases have prompted accusations that the court has become activist, has usurped executive and legislative powers, and has taken over aspects of day-to-day government. 'The judiciary has stepped in, not only to direct the designated authorities to perform their duty, but has also taken over the implementation of the programme through non-statutory committees formed by it,' said former Indian chief justice J. S. Verma in a public lecture in March 2007. The next month Prime Minister Manmohan Singh responded that 'Compelling action by authorities of the states through the power of mandamus is an inherent power vested in the judiciary', but he did warn that 'substituting mandamus with a takeover of the functions of another organ may, at times, become a case of over-reach ... these are all delicate issues which need to be addressed cautiously'.[3]

Contrast the charges of activism and over-activism with an editorial in a prominent academic journal, *The Economic and Political Weekly* (2008):

> Supreme Court judgments in recent years do not indicate any uniform pattern that would either justify the fears of the other two wings of the troika, or strengthen the hopes of the citizens who may be banking on the judiciary as their saviour. The judiciary, the executive, and the legislature have generally managed to work out compromise formulae on disputes that pose a threat to the status quo, with the apex court intervening to save the situation.

Others have pointed out that the Supreme Court has used the power of judicial review sparingly to challenge government policies (Sathe 2002). At best, the court's judgments have had an indirect effect on public policy; the government has adopted the court's suggestions, though only when it was ready to do so. For instance, the 'right to education' that the court articulated in a 1992 judgment became a constitutional amendment only after it appeared as an election promise of a political party. It became law 10 years later.[4]

In the field of socioeconomic rights, where charges of activism have been levelled against the court, a survey of health and education cases reveals that most of the higher court rulings have clarified the content of the right and the statutory obligations of the state rather than creating new duties for the government (Shankar 2009). For instance, court decisions have clarified that a right to education means the right to free and compulsory elementary school education, but not higher education. Even in the environmental cases which are usually cited as examples of judicial activism, the court's involvement merely activated statutory machinery established by environmental laws (Desai and Muralidhar 2000), and it has been pointed out that environmental rights jurisprudence in India is 'yet to come of age', is 'poorly defined', and 'obfuscates hard questions' (Rajamani 2007).

Adherents of either viewpoint might agree with legal scholar George Gadbois (1974) that India's Supreme Court is the most powerful in the world, having virtually become an *imperium in imperio*, an order within an order. They would diverge, however, on whether and how the courts have used their powers. The divergence would stem from their definitions of 'judicial activism'. Choudhary and Hunter (2003) are right to criticize scholars for using judicial activism in a notoriously slippery fashion to mean variously— depending on who is employing it and in what context—departure from well-established precedent, adjudication based on judicial preferences, or judicial reallocation of institutional roles between courts and other branches of government.[5] Choudhary and Hunter quantify their definition of activism as undue incursions by the judiciary into the policy domain of the elected branches by calculating the percentage of cases the government loses less the percentage the government would be likely to lose. But they acknowledge the difficulty of identifying objective criteria that can tell the difference between proper and undue incursions.

Here I focus on what Hirschl (2004) calls the increasing judicialization of mega-politics: the growing involvement of judges in assessing executive branch prerogatives and performance, and the reliance on courts and judicial means for addressing core moral predicaments, public policy questions, and political controversies. The definition of activism I adopt is this: the intervention of the court in areas that are clearly demarcated by the constitution as falling within the jurisdiction of the executive or the legislature. In my view, if the court prescribes a solution in areas where the law is silent or absent and says that it is an interim measure until the legislature creates the law, that does not constitute judicial activism. In *Vishaka* v. *State of Rajasthan*, for instance, the court directed that the guidelines it issued with regard to sexual harassment in the workplace 'would be binding and enforceable in law until suitable legislation is enacted to occupy the field'.[6] Another example: in issuing directives related to blood banks the court asked the central government to 'consider the advisability of enacting separate legislation for regulating the collection, processing, storage, distribution and transportation of blood and the operation of the blood banks in the country'.[7] In *Vineet Narain* v. *Union of India*, the court observed that its directions would fill the vacuum until the legislature or the executive stepped in to cover the gap.[8] Though these cases have often been claimed as examples of judicial activism (legislation by the courts), I would argue that they are not; they are simply stopgaps until another branch accepts its responsibility. The role of the judiciary in these cases is qualitatively different from the one in which judges monitor day-to-day administration of the government.

My definition does have a grey zone related to how to decide whether the court is providing an interim solution or overstepping its jurisdiction. This is highlighted by a petition to a Supreme Court constitutional panel in March 2011, asking 'whether after getting the recommendations of some expert body by a court order, the Court itself can implement the said recommendations by passing a judicial order or whether the Court can only send it to the Legislature or its delegate to consider making a law for implementation of these recommendations'.[9] If the decision is that the legislature ought first to enact a law, clearly that is not judicial activism. But if the court decides to move forward with the recommendations of an expert committee, is it encroaching on the executive's jurisdiction, or providing a stopgap measure? The cases I deal with here sidestep this issue. They are primarily cases where allegedly the court has encroached on the executive's jurisdiction.

My thesis is that despite increasing judicialization, the involvement in politics of India's higher judiciary, particularly the Supreme Court, is marked by a balancing act between supporting government actions and holding the executive accountable for its performance.[10] India's Supreme Court judges seek legitimacy for their decisions by negotiating four elements—laws; institutional norms/experience/rules; political preferences; and public concerns—that may constrain or expand the menu of choices (Shankar 2009). Within the space given by such structural conditions as the rise of weak governing coalitions, the higher judiciary has attempted to balance the constraints imposed by institutional realities (the need to secure cooperation of the executive to enforce its judgments) with the demands for judicial action from such societal actors as the media, political parties, and civil society activists. Higher court judges in India can thus be characterized as negotiators who craft judgments that avoid conflict with the political wings while preserving for the court a pro-citizen reputation.

The rest of the paper elaborates this argument: the next section analyses a recent case dealing with executive accountability and another pertaining to the parliament's jurisdiction. The third section assesses drivers of judicial involvement and restraint, especially the historical context of the rise of judicial review and the growing power of the court over who is appointed to it. Finally, the fourth section assesses the implications of judicialization for state–society relations and democratic governance. Throughout I situate the Indian experience within the scholarly debates and hypotheses about judicial behaviour.

The judiciary and governance

The Constitution of India (1950) established a federal republic with a parliamentary system, a strong central government, and a unified judiciary under a supreme court. The Supreme Court of India, which tops a three-tiered system, has vast powers. It not only functions as both a constitutional court and the court of final appeal, it also has original jurisdiction over disputes between the centre and the states and between states; original jurisdiction (Article 32) to issue orders, directions, and writs to enforce fundamental rights; and appellate jurisdiction over criminal and civil court decisions involving substantial questions of law. In addition, it is to advise on matters referred by the president; and, unusually, it has jurisdiction (Article 136) to grant special leave to appeal from any judgment, decree, determination, sentence or order in any case or matter passed or made by any court or tribunal in the territory of India except a court or tribunal constituted by or under any law relating to the armed forces. Just below the Supreme Court, at the intermediate level an appellate High Court stands at the head of each state's judicial administration.[11] Together, these two tiers form the higher judiciary.

While a precise definition of governance is difficult, it is possible to formulate a general one: 'how the institutions, rules and systems of the state—the executive, legislature, judiciary and military—operate at the central and local levels and how the states relate to individual citizens, civil society and the private sector' (Grindle 2007: 66). Among the basic principles used in assessing democratic governance are the accountability, transparency, and responsiveness of the state to citizens. The three sets of cases discussed below illuminate attempts by the higher judiciary to enhance these principles by balancing support for the government with ensuring that it is accountable to citizens.

Executive prerogatives

In 2007–08 the Indian government sold spectrum licences for 2G (second generation) wireless telephone technology for mobile phone services. The telecom minister, A. Raja, a member of a coalition partner of the ruling United Progressive Alliance (UPA), instituted a first-come-first-served method of selecting companies and also fixed a price (the same as one set in 2001). On 24 September 2007, the Department of Telecom (DoT) issued a press release giving a deadline of a week, after which it would stop accepting applications. Then it advanced the cut-off date to 25 September, saying that there had been a deluge of applications. In January 2008, of the 575 applicants, 121 received licences.

Subsequent investigation revealed that 85 of the licensees did not meet basic eligibility conditions, and some had provided fictitious documents. Together Indian companies had paid only about $2.8 billion for all the licences, and several sold on their licences at high prices to foreign firms (Venkat Raman and Kuncheria 2010). In 2010, an audit by the Comptroller and Auditor General (CAG) said that the government had lost $39 billion in revenues because the processes benefited a few bidders, many of whom were incapable of running mobile networks.[12] The 2G scandal had all the ingredients for high political drama: there were allegations of collusion between businessmen, politicians, and bureaucrats; political fixers who used journalists to install ministers; and justifications offered by the Prime Minister about the need to compromise with corrupt coalition partners to ensure stable government. The opposition parties demanded and got a joint parliamentary committee to investigate.

Meanwhile, another 2G drama was playing out in the courts. The timeline of petitions and judgments demonstrates the judicial balancing act: in 2010, Dr. Subramaniam Swamy, leader of an opposition party, filed a petition for a writ directing the Prime Minister to sanction the prosecution of former minister Raja.[13] The Delhi High Court held that because the case was still under investigation prosecution was 'premature'.[14] Swamy then filed another petition in the Delhi High Court, this one seeking cancellation of the 2G spectrum licences. The court dismissed the petition because Swamy had stated that he would be challenging the constitutional validity of the policy. Speaking for the court, Justice Manmohan emphatically stated that the constitutional question 'should not and cannot enter into the debate'; such adjudication should be limited to exceptional cases, and the 2G case was not one of them.[15]

Meanwhile, in the Supreme Court, the Centre for Public Interest Law (PIL), an NGO, filed a civil appeal against the Delhi High Court dismissal of public interest litigation.[16] Swamy then filed a Special Leave Petition (27535/2010) against the High Court dismissal of his petition for a writ requesting that the Prime Minister prosecute the Telecom Minister. Both cases were heard by the same panel of the Supreme Court.[17] The petitioners thus sought cancellation of tainted licences and a probe into the inaction of the Prime Minister's office in processing sanctions for prosecution of Raja, who had resigned in November 2010.

The Supreme Court's response demonstrates how it tackles countervailing pressures from civil society groups and the government. The court first harshly criticized the government for the way these decisions were made. It directed the Prime Minister's office to file an affidavit explaining the delay in prosecuting Raja and said the government's failure to do so was 'extremely serious'. But it then exhibited some restraint, toning down its criticism of the entire government. Agreeing with the government's view that the minister in charge was solely to blame, it directed its ire at the minister and ensured that he was arrested along with his private secretary and the Telecom secretary (the top civil servant in the ministry). Saying that the companies had a right to be heard, however, the court refused the plea for an interim order suspending the 2G licences of 69 telecom operators that had failed to roll out services. The court's directives to the government were to investigate the procedural lapses in issuing licences and the delay in the executive's office in initiating prosecution.

The court's orders demonstrate the balancing act: in an order dated 24 November 2010, while reserving the matter for judgment the court called for a list of all cases in which sanction had not been accorded for the prosecution of public officials. This was a sweeping example of a situation where the court takes the specific issue before it as indicating a larger problem that needs to be tackled. Simultaneously, responding to the petitioners' pleas to monitor the investigation, it ordered the Central Bureau of Investigation (CBI) to report monthly on the progress of the probe. The court said that the criminal trial would be held on a day-to-day basis, no adjournment on any basis would be allowed, and a special court would be set up.[18] It thus appears that the court was not only monitoring the investigation in detail, where in previous cases it had merely monitored the pace and direction an investigation was taking, but was also monitoring the trial court proceedings. The court emphasized what it perceived to be the lax attitude of the Income Tax Department in dealing with the 2G controversy: 'We are sure [the tax department] would have slept over it [if the court had not intervened]'.[19]

On 11 November 2010 the court issued orders that a special public prosecutor be appointed, even though the government argued that such appointments were the prerogative of the executive.[20] The court justified its order by saying that an exception had to be made due to the 'larger issues of public interest [in] transparent governance' and proper prosecution. A senior government official characterized the order as a 'clear case of judicial overreach'.[21]

Though the Supreme Court has recognized that investigation into criminal matters is essentially and traditionally an executive function,[22] over the years the court has created a pattern of new remedies in criminal matters by taking over investigation in part or even entirely in cases involving public officials; it has issued directions for the constitution of special investigation teams[23] and has in some cases monitored cases itself.[24] In some cases it has even directed external agencies like the CBI to take over or initiate investigations,[25] justifying the intervention on grounds that it was filling the vacuum until the legislature or the executive discharged its role.

In the 2G case, too, the language the court used for the monitoring arrangements made it seem that the directions it was issuing arose from submissions of the government itself and that it simply cohered with the mandate of the government. For instance, while disposing of CA 10660 and SLP 27535, the court said there was no need for a special team because the Solicitor General had already agreed to a court-monitored investigation.[26] The court also mentioned that in view of the submissions of counsel for the government and its agencies, it was necessary to bring the investigation under court monitoring. It rejected the need for a special investigation team on grounds that the CBI and Enforcement Directorate were 'on the right course' and had 'done good work', cautioning that at such a stage 'interference' might 'jeopardize the investigation'.[27]

The Supreme Court's orders in the 2G case demonstrate how the higher judiciary negotiates with the government and civil society in its rulings. In *Swamy* v. *Singh*,[28] the Supreme Court reiterated that the 3-month time limit imposed on the grant of governmental sanction under section 19 of the Prevention of Corruption Act 1988 for prosecution of public servants for corruption must be strictly adhered to. The Court, in its ratio, said that the Prime Minister could not be held responsible for the delay in sanctioning A. Raja's prosecution. It absolved him of this responsibility stating that, 'by the very nature of the office held by him', he was 'not expected to personally look into the minute details of each and every case placed before him and has to depend on his advisers and other officers'. Then, it supported the demand of civil society activists in its judgment on the petition seeking cancellation of 2G licenses.[29] The 122 licenses were cancelled and fines were imposed on several companies. The Supreme Court also held that the trial Court would decide on Swamy's application seeking Chidambaram's (the Finance Minister during the 2G approvals period) prosecution in the 2G case. On 5 February, the trial court held that there was no evidence on record that Chidambaram was acting in pursuance of a criminal conspiracy, 'while being party to the two decisions regarding non-revision of the spectrum pricing and dilution of equity by the two companies'.

While some orders can be classified as judicial activism, others are clearly an attempt to cause minimal embarrassment to the government. The next section explains the reasons for that stance.

Parliamentary matters

The balancing act is apparent in *PUCL* v. *Union of India*, in which a civil society group highlighted Parliament's failure to provide for disclosure of information on assets and liabilities in its amendment of the Representation of People's Act.[30] The act had been amended because of the Supreme Court's ruling in *Union of India* v. *Association for Democratic Reforms*, in which it had directed the Election Commission to collect information from each candidate on past convictions/acquittal/discharge of any criminal offence; pending cases punishable with two or more years of imprisonment; the assets of the candidate, spouse and dependents; and the candidate's educational qualifications.[31]

The Supreme Court took issue with the wording of the amendment and said that previous judgments had established that the legislature had no power to ask instrumentalities of the state to disobey or disregard court decisions. The rationale was that a democratic republic was part of the basic structure of the constitution, for which free and fair elections based on adult franchise were a necessity, and for this reason citizen-voters had to be well informed. 'The voters' right to know the antecedents of the candidates is based on interpretation of Article 19(1)(a) which provides that all citizens of this country would have the fundamental right to "freedom of speech and expression" and this phrase is construed to include the fundamental right to know the relevant antecedents of the candidate contesting the elections.' By exposing the candidate's assets to public scrutiny, voters could get 'clean and less polluted persons to govern the country'.[32]

Here again, while favouring the position of civil society groups seeking more transparency, the court was careful to weave alliances with other activities of the government to justify its ruling. In constructing the arguments in both the 2002 and 2003 judgments, the court referred to similar views expressed by the ad hoc National Commission to Review the Working of the Constitution (2002).

In another case, the Supreme Court upheld the expulsion of members of Parliament who were caught on camera taking bribes, rejecting the contention that it could not review Parliament's power to expel MPs. The response of the then Speaker of the Lower House, an eminent lawyer, shows recognition of the court's tendency to favour restraint while accumulating vast powers. 'It has been held [by the court] that legislatures in India cannot claim immunity from judicial scrutiny even in respect of their internal proceedings ... I do not agree with this ... I do not want to make an issue out of this because I am of the firm opinion that the situation that the court has defined as suitable for judicial scrutiny would never arise.'[33]

Drivers of judicialization

Some scholars have theorized that the strategic behaviour of the executive and the legislature in empowering judges is part of a 'top-down' process (Hirschl 2004) where elected officials might allow judges to make policies so as to avoid responsibility for controversial decisions (Graber 1993), or to protect rights from new or emerging electoral majorities (Hirschl 2004; Gillman 2002). Other scholars have emphasized the motivation of judges themselves (Baum 2007). Still others have emphasized macro drivers (democratization) or 'bottom-up' processes, such as the spread of rights discourses and legal networks (Epp 1998).

The behaviour of Indian judges does not fit neatly into any of these categories. Supreme Court judges have negotiated with different actors, thus highlighting not the rise of a 'juristocracy' but a continuous dialogue with other actors and organs of the state. Indian judges want their judgment to be perceived as legitimate, but legitimacy has to be negotiated; it is not inherent in an institution. One source of the court's legitimacy, Sathe (2002) points out, rests on the people's perceptions that judgments are principled, objective, and just. This involves seeing whether a decision conforms to the spirit of a right. Judgments on public health issues, for instance, articulate major values, such as a 'right to potable water' or to clean streets, but the actual decision focuses on what is feasible. Legal scholar Upendra Baxi (1982) calls such rulings 'juristic activism' because they set the stage for the future direction of the law.

The judiciary and the parliament[34]

To understand why the Indian judiciary accumulates power but is restrained in using it against the executive, we have to comprehend how the constitution conceptualizes judicial powers and how the courts have interpreted it. In 11 sessions from December 1946–November 1949 the 299-member Constituent Assembly (CA) of India met to deliberate on a constitution to come into force after independence from the British in August 1947. Battles raged over the extent of judicial scrutiny of legislation, the definition of federal court powers, the appointment and removal process, and whether judges could take jobs post-retirement. Many CA members were provincial lawyers and legal professionals who because of their political experiences with martial law under colonial rule had become advocates for judicial independence (Beller 1983).

While the Indian constitution has given courts the power of judicial review, the executive has the ability to suspend or repeal that power. This ambiguity in whether the constitution privileges parliamentary sovereignty or judicial review has been manipulated in different periods by both the executive and the judiciary.[35] India's parliamentary system institutes separation of powers, but the effective division is between Parliament and judiciary because the leader of the party that has won the largest number of seats in Parliament is also the executive, the Prime Minister. The President may have veto powers and appoint judges but like the British monarch is merely a titular head.

The CA favoured a system that instituted balance between the three branches rather than checks by one over the other but agreed with the chairman of the drafting committee that the constitution had to walk the fine line between creating a Leviathan and giving the judiciary adequate power to act without fear or favour. The Supreme Court's powers would be determined by law—made by Parliament rather than the constitution—but that document was ambiguous about the extent of judicial scrutiny of legislation, the powers of the federal court, the process for appointing and removing judges, and whether judges could take post-retirement jobs.

These ambiguities provoked conflict between court and Parliament. For instance, the Supreme Court appropriated the power to appoint itself even though the constitution instituted a check on its powers by giving primacy to the executive in appointing judges. The Chief Justice of India (CJI) was to be appointed by the President (on the advice of the Prime Minister and Cabinet) after consultations with other Supreme and lower court judges; other judges were appointed after consulting with the Chief Justice of the court on which they were to sit.[36] In two judgments in 1993 (*Supreme Court Advocates on Record*) and 1998 (*Special Reference No. 1*), the Supreme Court held that the CJI must be supreme if independence and separation of powers were to operate; primacy meant the primacy of the process (not the executive) in which the CJI and four most senior colleagues would be consulted; and the majority was inclined to define 'consultation' as 'concurrence'.[37] Later the court also appropriated the power to transfer judges, saying there was 'no master-and-servant relationship between a Judge and the Government' (*Sankalchand*).[38] Provisions for the accountability of the higher judiciary are confined to impeachment (Articles 124(4) and 217(1) (b)) in extreme cases because 'it was expected that settled norms and peer pressure were sufficient checks' (Verma 2006).

Expansion of judicial powers

Scholars argue that federalism (with its built-in opportunities for jurisdictional conflict); a written constitution (which gives judges the basis for rights-based decisions); judicial independence; and a competitive party system (which could produce weak governing coalitions) all invite challenges from the judiciary (Tate and Vallinder 1995: 30). India's Supreme Court has incrementally appropriated the power to review legislation irrespective of political or structural conditions. Its clout evolved gradually as a result of clashes over the extent of judicial review of some of the 104 constitutional amendments. Scholars have analysed the conflict between the judiciary and the executive/legislature in terms of phases: 1960–64, when the court cautiously and gradually expanded its own authority; 1965–75, a militant ideological phase (Beller 1983); 1975–77, the tale of two courts (Sathe 2002); 1977–80, a resurgence of the court; 1980–84, when the court avoided major confrontation with the Indira Gandhi government (Das 2000); and finally 1985–2011, which saw the dawn and intensification of social action litigation and the court's growing power as Parliament became more fractured.

The initial impetus for expansion of judicial powers came from structural factors, primarily the fraught relationship between judiciary and executive/legislature over abridgment of fundamental rights by legislative amendments and executive actions. Under Jawaharlal Nehru's premiership (1947–64), the Supreme Court and Parliament fought principally over the scope of the right to property and over principles for directives. The basis of the conflict was the way the constitution distinguished between fundamental rights, which were enforceable protections against the state, and non-justiciable directive principles, which defined the future social order. In *Madras* v. *Dorairajan* (1951) the Supreme Court gave primacy to fundamental rights in any clash with directive principles and struck down land reform laws on grounds that they violated the fundamental right to property. In response, Parliament attached to the constitution the Ninth Schedule, which listed acts and statutes that were immune to judicial review even if these conflicted with fundamental rights.

After Nehru's death in 1964, the court entered a militant 'ideological' phase and put itself forward as 'a guarantor of constitutional order in a time of constitutional decay' (Beller 1983: 525). Nehru's daughter, Indira Gandhi, was Prime Minister from 1966–77 and again from 1980 until her assassination in 1984. In the late 1960s and early 1970s, her government embarked on translating her ideological vision into practical policies by nationalizing banks and abolishing privy purses (grants given since 1947 to rulers of princely states of India as part of the terms of their accession to independent India). These policies were challenged in the Supreme Court as infringements on the fundamental right to property (Article 31 and 19(1)). Earlier, in *Golak Nath*, a 6–5 majority held that Parliament was not competent to amend the chapter on fundamental rights and that the validity of constitutional amendments was not beyond the purview of the court. In these cases, too, the majority held that the right to property was a fundamental right.[39]

Gandhi's victory in the1971 parliamentary elections allowed the executive and Parliament to design a full response to the judiciary that included measures to curb the court. New constitutional amendments limited the power of judicial review and specified that the amendment procedures conferred sovereign powers on Parliament. Parliament developed a habit of inserting controversial laws in the Ninth Schedule, which, as Austin (1999) points out, would evolve into a predilection for undermining judicial powers generally and even facilitating attacks on the judiciary as an institution.[40]

During this period the court built up an institutional memory about the dire consequences of challenging a powerful executive. On 25 June 1975, the President, on the advice of Prime Minister Gandhi, suspended Article 21 and imprisoned hundreds of people (mainly political opponents and civil society groups) after an Executive Order proclaimed a state of emergency. Nine High Courts said that detainees could challenge their detention, but they were overruled by the Supreme Court, which then suffered a dent in its authority for allowing civil liberties to be violated. The Prime Minister continued to pack the court with pliable judges and transferring those perceived to be hostile to her policies.[41] Ferejohn (1999) proposed that the greatest danger to judicial independence occurs when the legislature and executive are ideologically unified and the judiciary is composed of judges with a different ideology. That certainly holds for India under Indira Gandhi.

Paradoxically, in this conflict-prone decade, the Supreme Court enhanced its power of judicial review and articulated the integrity of a constitutional rights structure through a 'basic structure doctrine'. Mulling over two amendments designed to reduce the extent of judicial review, in a 1,700-page ruling (7–6 majority) the court overruled a previous judgment on the 'transcendental' nature of fundamental rights and said that Parliament could not 'alter the basic structure and framework of the Constitution.'[42]

The steady expansion of the Supreme Court's powers continued into the 21st century. In the *Coelho* judgment the court expanded the ambit of its influence by stating that the doctrine of basic structure applied to amendments added to the Ninth Schedule after 24 April 1973.[43] It was up to the court to determine whether an amendment was consistent with the basic structure of the constitution. By this unanimous judgment the Supreme Court expanded its review powers to all laws enacted by Parliament.

Although it appropriated the power to determine what constituted 'basic structure', the court has done little with it. Though some accuse the judiciary of using the doctrine 'mostly to protect judicial power by giving the final say to an unelected body of judges' (Ramachandran 2000), an empirical survey of judgments shows that the use of the basic structure doctrine has been 'haphazard' (Mehta 2002) and 'not doctrinal or a general principle' (Jacobsohn 2003). The failure to evolve a consistent jurisprudence on the basic structure of the constitution and on a whole range of issues has become a recurrent theme in discussions of how the court exercises its accumulated powers.

The relationship between the court and democratic politics in India is more complex than the simple counter-majoritarian model would suggest. The tradition of passing on 'the burden of ... decision-making to the Court' goes back to the 1950s and 1960s in affirmative action cases where, as Sathe (2002: 60) says, the political elites wanted an umpire who could adjudicate their contentious issues according to set principles. Successive governments expanded the Supreme Court's jurisdiction over administrative tribunals (industrial labour, income tax, and civil services), bringing it into policy areas previously reserved for the executive branch. This practice expanded to include difficult political questions when the government acceded to court rulings on which groups should benefit from affirmative action (Galanter 1978). This does not mean, however, that the court simply acts on cues from the governing elite; as our case studies show, civil society actors have regularly sought the court's intervention against the government.

Judiciary and civil society

Thus we reach the question of why the court feels impelled to respond to civil society. Immediately after the Emergency, the judiciary (particularly the Supreme Court) had two concerns:

1 It had to regain legitimacy (Baxi 1985; Dhavan 1980; Sathe 2002). It began by legalizing an expanded notion of standing that allowed NGOs and others to bring PIL cases to the court.[44] Constitutional scholar Baxi said in an interview that the court deliberately used the decision to legalize the PIL mode of litigation because it wanted to draw closer to the bar associations, which had initially opposed the expanded nature of standing that the judges had devised. The ruling reflects the emphasis post-Emergency judges placed on collaborating with other legal bodies and the executive. It also demonstrates that the judges knew exactly how far they could go.
2 Having experienced executive authoritarianism and court-curbing moves the court 'resisted confrontation with the government' and opted for a 'wide measure of mutual accommodation' that had 'a whisper of politics as well as a whisper of pragmatism' (Baxi 1980: 202; 1985). This is reflected most vividly in my analysis of social rights litigation in India (Shankar 2009), which reveals that the judges were reluctant to punish government providers (compared to private providers) for failing to fulfil their obligations, preferring instead to use softer remedies, such as instituting committees to correct deficiencies in the state's provision of public utilities.

Behaviour of judges

Indian Supreme Court judges are negotiators who recognize their inability to compel the government to comply with their orders. Even when the court instituted time limits, enforcement depended more on monitoring by the litigant. And even when NGOs supervised progress, the results did not match the promise of the judgment—the gap between legal entitlement and on-the-ground reality is vast.[45]

Litigation patterns also demonstrate a major limitation of courts: judges can only rule on the cases that are brought to them. Most cases brought by NGOs have dealt with urban pollution and sanitation; relatively few have dealt with India's most urgent health problems, such as the need to enhance the quality and provision of medical services in rural areas, overhauling government hospitals and health centres, and providing more doctors in rural and poorer areas.

The Supreme Court's restraint is a result of institutional norms and memories about the perils of challenging executive power.[46] The allocation of cases by the chief justice, lack of enforcement capacity, the emphasis on collaboration rather than dissent within the two- or three-judge panels that typically hear a case, and short stints on the Supreme Court bench (since judges retire at the age of 65) produce overworked judges who barely have time to finish their work.[47] High Court and subordinate judges too are overworked and understaffed.[48] So while Supreme Court judges are aware of their power, they are careful about wielding it in opposition to the other wings of the state because institutionally they are unable to accomplish change on the ground. Judges realize that their decisions may not be enforced, and they will not be there long enough to ensure enforcement.

Even in larger constitutional cases the court has exercised 'maximum restraint' in using the basic structure doctrine against constitutional amendments and has been 'reticent' in striking down an amendment (Sathe 2002: 88). Higher courts 'have unwittingly become conscience keepers of the status-quo except in exceptional cases', said one former justice (Iyer 1987: 144). Thus, while India's Supreme Court has indeed become more powerful, it has been very careful about how it uses that power.

What judicialization implies for governance and democracy

Positive impact

Increasing judicialization has had three positive effects:

1 Judges have woven alliances with other actors—political parties, citizen groups, activists, the media—to keep a watchful eye on how the administration is performing. This has strengthened state–society relations and the scrutiny of misrule.
2 The court has used the force of law to impose deadlines,[49] define elements of governmental accountability,[50] and ask for explanations for noncompliance.[51] This seems to have stimulated government efforts to tighten administrative rules and weed out corrupt officials. Not only has he added control of corruption as a performance management criterion for ministries, the Cabinet Secretary recently decided to hold weekly meetings to dispose of cases pending against top ministry bureaucrats.
3 Judicial actions have prompted the other two branches to scrutinize judicial accountability. Clearly current mechanisms of ensuring accountability are inadequate, considering that despite allegations of corruption in several high-profile cases, no judge has ever been impeached.[52] Investigating allegations of corruption against a judge is difficult. In *Veeraswami*, to protect

> judges from harassment by the executive the Supreme Court ruled that no criminal case alleging that a judge is corrupt could be brought without 'consulting' the CJI.[53] The President of India is supposed to consult the CJI before giving permission to prosecute a judge of a superior court under the Prevention of Corruption Act (1949), but in corruption cases the CJI's opinion is binding.
>
> A Judicial Standards and Accountability Bill is to be introduced in Parliament shortly. It establishes an oversight committee to receive complaints and send them to the relevant committees in the High Courts, which will investigate and within three months recommend further action or closure of the case. If further action is recommended, the oversight committee will appoint a panel of three members. The bill includes a complaints process, a code of conduct, required disclosure of assets, and a time limit for each step of the process.
>
> More negative is that the judiciary still has enough power to in effect be regulating itself. The oversight committee consists of the CJI and two senior judges plus two members appointed by the executive (the attorney general and an eminent member nominated by the President). While the bill does not say whether the committee's decisions have to be unanimous, the norm seems to be that decisions are by majority, which would give judges the deciding vote on whether to take action or investigate their colleagues. A complaint can be dismissed if the High Court committees decide that it has no basis, or if impeachment does not occur in both houses within the same session of Parliament.

These moves—judicial scrutiny of corruption in government and the judicial accountability bill—have enhanced attempts to check corruption within courts. In September 2010 the Supreme Court collegium (the CJI-led panel of senior judges) wrote letters to 20 High Court judges stating that they would be transferred because of 'public interest', and asked them for their preferences. However, at present the penalties imposed on corrupt judges are minimal. The High Court may transfer such judges or keep them idle, but once the furore subsides it brings them back.

A major negative implication of judicialization is the danger of collusion between the judiciary and the other organs of the state. Decisional autonomy does not automatically produce a judge with the capacity for independent thought and judgment; nor does it produce more rights-conscious behaviour. The appropriation of autonomy to appoint judges by the CJI and a collegium and the shift to coalition rule in the last decade have lowered the likelihood of concerted political action or penalties against the court.

Paradoxically, decisional freedom seems to have induced more conservatism in Indian judges on health and education issues. Judges appointed after 1993 were more likely to give state agencies flexibility on health and education and to prescribe collaborative remedies. They were also significantly less likely to uphold PILs and penalize government providers (Shankar 2009). The expansion of media and the enhanced scrutiny on the actions of the state, including the judiciary, have exposed several instances of collusion. The political links of a former CJI's family, the links between another former CJI and private lobbyists, and the system of post-retirement appointments of judges imply quid pro quo connections in the top echelons of the state. Some of the provisions of the judicial accountability bill on conflict of interest would circumvent such collusion.

A more worrying concern is the monitoring by the higher judiciary of day-to-day or month-to-month implementation of its orders. This increases the load on an already overburdened judiciary and will lengthen backlogs in delivering justice. And if despite such supervision the executive fails to comply with court directives, the institutional legitimacy of the judiciary will be besmirched.

Conclusion

Judicial intervention has had both positive and negative effects on governance and state–society relations and on questions of the state's accountability to citizens. In February 2007 Somnath Chatterjee, Speaker of the Lower House, was asked in an interview whether court judgments and the sometimes different perspectives of the legislature and the judiciary were a sign of a robust democracy. A lawyer himself, he replied that some judgments had strengthened the democratic process to the extent that it had cleared doubts about the legislature's powers to deal with its own issues. But other judgments (like *Coelho*) were unnecessary forays into areas that should be defined by the legislature. To a question about whether the tension between the judiciary and the legislature was irreconcilable and whether it would have a negative impact on the democratic system, the speaker replied that 'we tend to read too much into a situation. Our system is basically directed and dictated by the people'.

The speaker is right in taking a less alarmist view of what the judiciary might do with its expanded jurisdiction. For instance, in October 2010 the Supreme Court dismissed a petition seeking review of an earlier decision to allow a state (Tamil Nadu) to provide 69 percent reservation for backward classes[54] (rather than the 50 percent imposed by earlier court decisions). This ruling allayed fears expressed by commentators after the *Coelho* judgment that the court would use its expanded powers of judicial review to uphold fundamental rights (to equality) at the expense of directive principles.

More recently, in a memorial lecture current Chief Justice S. H. Kapadia said that it was the task of the electorate, not of judges, to make the government accountable. He warned the judges that the court was not competent to make policy choices and run the administration and asked them to resist 'the pressure to please the majority':[55]

> In many PILs, the courts freely decree rules of conduct for government and public authorities which are akin to legislation. Such exercises have little judicial function in them. [Their] justification is that the other branches of government have failed or are indifferent to the solution of the problem. In

such matters, I am of the opinion that the courts should be circumspect in understanding the thin line between law and governance.

The increasing emphasis in recent years on the accountability of the executive comes at a price—the erosion of public trust in judicial capacity to ensure implementation of ruling and thus social change. In January 2011 a television opinion poll asked which profession was most corrupt. The results: 66 percent said politicians; only 3 percent said judges.[56] While the public still seems to repose confidence in the judiciary's intentions, and judicial intrusion into governance may be well motivated, by overwhelming judges with an enormous workload and the incapacity of the judiciary as an institution to make policies, the stopgap nature of court solutions, and the destabilizing campaigns initiated by the political branches could well make courts in India a hollow hope.

Notes

1 I am grateful to Subhadra Banda for assistance with the research.

2 Mahapatra, Dhananjay (2011) 'SC pulls up govt on black money issue', *The Times of India*, 19 January.

3 Reported in *The Indian Express*, 6 April 2007.

4 *Unnikrishnan* v. *State of AP* (1993), 1 SCC 645, reviewed the state's right to interfere in the admissions policy and fee structure of private professional institutions. It held that because education is a fundamental right, it could not be an object of profiteering and the fee structure should be compatible with principles of merit and social justice. This allowed the state to intervene in the administration of private higher education. However, the court revised that judgment in *TMA Pai Foundation* v. *State of Karnataka* (2002), where it found the *Unnikrishnan* licence to interfere in private professional institutions unreasonable. A constitutional bench was set up to clarify the *Pai* judgment (*Islamic Academy of Education and Anr* v. *State of Karnataka and Anr* 2003) which allowed private institutions leeway to have a reasonable surplus in the fee structure for future expansion. While the court outlined the limits of regulation for minority institutions that did not receive government funding, it did not clarify the extent of regulation permissible for non-minority institutions that were not funded by the state.

5 As Kmiec (2004) points out, the mere fact that the court strikes down a law does not mean it has engaged in activism. The line between judicial review and judicial activism depends on the speaker's understanding of what the constitution does and does not clearly prohibit. It is also unclear how many invalidations it would take to call the court activist.

6 AIR (1997) 6 SCC 241.

7 *Common Cause Reg, Soc* v. *UOI*, 1996 1 SCC 753.

8 (1996) 2 SCC 199.

9 *University of Kerala* v. *Council, Principals'*, Colleges, Kerala and Ors. (2009)15 SCC 301.

10 Prudence increases from the lower courts to the high court to the supreme court. My argument resonates with the observation of Vanberg (2009) that constitutional court judges are likely to be prudent judges.

11 Apart from writ jurisdiction, the 21 high courts have jurisdiction by assigned territory over the 13,000 lower courts (district, magistrate, and magistrate II and equivalent).

12 In 2003 the NDA coalition had decided to sell bandwidth at 2001 prices, and in 2008, the 2G spectrum was sold at 2003 prices (which were in fact 2001 prices).

13 The first Public Interest Litigation (PIL) case was filed in the Delhi High Court (but we could not find the petitioner's name), challenging the First-Come-First-Served spectrum allocation policy. On 30 May 2009, the Delhi HC, Justices Valmiki Mehta and Mudgal speaking for the Court, severely disapproved of the government's policy, likening it to the sale of cinema tickets. It made observations on the gravity of the case, stating that 'prima facie we find that spectrum has been allocated in a worst manner and public exchequer has been caused severe loss', and characterized the loss as astounding. This judgment was cited by an opposition leader in Tamil Nadu who asked for the telecom minister's resignation. It was not clear what the government did after this judgment. The second writ petition (Civil Appeal No. 2533/2010) was filed by Swan Telecom (the CEO of which is one of the main accused in the criminal case) seeking the dismissal of an order advancing the cut-off date for applications for spectrum allocation. The single judge struck down the order, and the dismissal was upheld by a Division bench.

14 Available online at http://delhihighcourt.nic.in/dhc_case_status_oj_list.asp?pno=543533.

15 Or dt. 18 August 2010 in WP http://delhihighcourt.nic.in/dhc_case_status_oj_list.asp?pno=543533.

16 Special Leave to Appeal (Civil) No(s).24873/2010.

17 Judges of the Supreme Court and High Courts sit in panels (called benches) to hear a case. In the Supreme Court, a small panel of two to three justices is called a Division Bench and a large panel of five or more is called a Constitutional Bench. The Constitution provided for seven Supreme Court judges but the number has increased over the years to 31.

18 '2G scam: Supreme Court to appoint special public prosecutor on Monday', 10 April 2011.

19 '2G scam: SC slams I-T department for slow probe', *India Today,* available online at http://indiatoday.intoday.in/site/story/2g-scam-sc-pulls-up-i-t-department-for-slow-probe/1/137166.html.

20 (2011) 1 SCC 560.

21 'SC names Uday Lalit 2G scam prosecutor, govt bristles', 11 April 2011 – Dhananjay Mahapatra, *The Times of India*, available online at http://articles.timesofindia.indiatimes.com/2011–04–11/india/29405640_1_spectrum-scam-telecom-minister-ak-ganguly.

22 *M.C. Mehta* v. *Union of India (UOI)* (2007) 1 SCC 110: 'Investigation of an offence is … reserved for the executive through the police department, the superintendence over which vests in the State Government.'

23 *National Human Rights Commission* v. *State of Gujarat, (2004) 8 SCC 610.* However, the Supreme Court overturned a High Court directive to constitute a special investigation team in *Divine Retreat Centre* v. *State of Kerala* (2008) 3 SCC 542. The court said 'History teaches us that the independence of the judiciary is jeopardized when courts become embroiled in the passions of the day and assume primary responsibility to resolve the issues which are otherwise not entrusted to it by adopting procedures which are otherwise not known.' The fact that this is in direct contrast to the Supreme Court's judgment in the interim order dated 4 July 2011 in the case of *Ram Jethmalani* v. *Union of India* in WP 176/2009, although delivered by the same judge (Justice B. Sudershan Reddy) is particularly interesting. More recently, in September 2011, the government petitioned the apex court and challenged Justice Reddy's order constituting a special investigation team (SIT) in the black money case on grounds that four precedents cited by the judge (who had since retired) had in fact rejected the idea of courts setting up SITs.

24 In *Union of India* v. *Sushil Kumar Modi and Ors.*, the High Court entrusted investigation in the fodder scam case to the CBI to ensure 'proper and honest performance of duty by CBI'.

25 In *Vineet Narain* v. *Union of India* (1996) 2 SCC 199, the court (p. 200) directed the CBI to conduct a thorough investigation into criminal charges against several high-level government officials and cited 'utmost public importance and national significance'; delay in investigation; and the nexus between high officials and crime, which posed a 'serious threat to the integrity, security and economy of the nation' to help explain why its interference was warranted. It was necessary, it said, to retain public confidence in the impartial working of government agencies.
26 In response to the petition seeking appointment of a group of independent individuals to assist the Court in monitoring the investigation being carried out by the Central Bureau of Investigation (*Center for PIL* v. *Union of India* Civil Appeal No.10660 Of 2010) , the apex court held that the CBI had satisfactorily conducted the investigation. Therefore, it held that 'there is no justification to appoint a group of persons to directly or indirectly scrutinise or supervise the further investigation being conducted by the CBI and other agencies'. However, the Court held that the 'Central Vigilance Commissioner and the Senior Vigilance Commissioner appointed under Section 3(2) of the 2003 Act' was required to render assistance to the Court in order to facilitate the effective monitoring of further investigation, given 'the nature of the case and involvement of a large number of influential persons'.
27 Order issued on 11 July 2011.
28 Civil Appeal No. 1193 OF 2012.
29 *Centre for Public Interest Litigation and others* v. *Union of India* writ petition (civil) no. 423 of 2010. *Dr. Subramanian Swamy* v. *Union of India* writ petition (civil) no. 10 of 2011.
30 *PUCL* v. *Union of India* (2003) AIR (2003) SC 2363, para 16.
31 The plaintiffs contended that 700 legislators and about 30 members of Parliament had criminal records. *Union of India v. Association for Democratic Reforms* (2002) 3 SCR 696.
32 *People's Union for Civil Liberties (PUCL)* v. *Union of India (UOI) and Anr.* (2003) 4 SCC 399, Paragraph 18.
33 Ramakrishnan, Venkitesh (2007) The Supreme Court cannot make laws, *Frontline*, vol. 24, issue 2, 27 January–9 February, also available online at www.frontlineonnet.com/fl2402/stories/20070209003401800.htm, accessed on 5 February 2012.
34 This section relies on Shankar (2009).
35 Article 13, for instance, states that laws must be compatible with the constitution, and interpretation of compatibility would be the task of the judiciary. However, during the Emergency regime (1975–77), the executive suspended the power of judicial review.
36 In *S.P. Gupta and Ors. etc. etc.* v. *Union of India and Ors. etc. etc.* (1982) 2 SCR 365, the court confirmed this.
37 *Supreme Court Advocates on Record Association* v. *Union of India* (1993) Supp 2 SCR 659; Special Reference No. 1 of 1998 (In re) (1998) 7 SCC 739.
38 *Union of India* v. *Sankalchand Himmatlal Seth* (1978) 1 SCR 423.
39 See Seervai (1983) for an analysis of these judgments.
40 The Ninth Schedule comprises 284 Acts and Regulations, 218 of them added after 24 April 1973.
41 Sixteen high court judges who had upheld the challenge to the constitutionality of the Emergency were transferred, and the threat hung over 40 other judges.
42 *Keshavananda Bharati* v. *State of Kerala* AIR 1973 SC 1461. Several scholars (Seervai 1983; Jacobsohn 2003) have analysed the implications of the case for enhanced Supreme Court review.
43 *I.R. Coelho* v. *Union of India* (2007) 2 SCC 1.
44 Justice Bhagwati in *S. P. Gupta* v. *Union of India,* 1981 (Supp) SCC 87.
45 Some of the problems of litigation included the access, the time taken, funding constraints, and the poor efficacy of court judgments (Galanter and Krishnan 2004).
46 It is therefore important to distinguish between different levels of the judiciary. Lower

courts like the high court have been cautioned for their 'adventurism' by the Supreme Court. Many of the environmental judgments and the cases referred to in the opening paragraph were issued by the high courts.

47 Similar arguments have been made by Baxi (1980), Gupta (1995) and Sathe (2002), among others.

48 Figures released by the court in June 2010 indicate that the number of vacancies has gone up in the subordinate courts (3,070) and high courts (287 of the authorized 895). Pending cases too have increased to 41,83,731 in the high courts and 2.78 crore (27 million) in the subordinate courts.

49 See, e.g. *PUCL* v. *Union of India* (right to food), *Or dt. 28.11.2001* (setting a deadline for identifying below poverty line families), and *20.5.2001* (setting a deadline for initiating certain welfare schemes); *People's Union for Civil Liberties* v. *Union of India (UOI) and Ors.*: 2007 (9) SCALE 25 – setting up Anganwadi (health) centres.

50 *Centre for PIL* v. *Union of India* 355/2010 (Or. Dt. 3.3.2011) CVC Matter (holding: the institution is more important than the individual); *Sri Radhy Shyam (Dead) through L.Rs. and Ors.*v. *State of U.P. and Ors.* JT 2011 (4) SC 524 (for land acquired from the poor, greater judicial scrutiny is warranted).

51 Dr. Subrahmanyam Swamy (SLP 27535/2010) 2G case (asking why the Prime Minister had delayed the grant of sanction for the Raja prosecution); *Ram Jethmalani* v. *Union of India WP* 176/1009 (asking why Hassan Ali had not undergone custodial interrogation); *Nandini Sundar* v. *Union of India 250/2009* (seeking an explanation of action taken by the government with respect to arson and violence in three villages in Chattisgarh in March 2011 and the attack on Swami Agnivesh).

52 Media reports have directed the spotlight to these cases. For instance, it was reported that Rs. 1.5 million for payments in a land purchase deal was mistakenly delivered to the wrong judge in the Punjab and Haryana High Court. A three-judge panel was set up but an absence of proof meant that the CBI could not proceed and the judge went back on the bench. The CBI now claims to have enough evidence to link the judge to the money and the land deal, and the CJI has given permission to probe further. In another case of allegations of corruption against a Calcutta high court judge, the upper house of parliament voted to impeach him in August 2011 and before the motion could come up in the Lower House, the judge resigned. During the impeachment debate, the government and the opposition supported a strong judicial accountability bill.

53 The decision is unclear on whether this procedure has to be followed for all criminal cases against judges or only for cases dealing with corruption charges. Before launching into a discussion about consultation, the court said that 'the judges are liable to be dealt with just the same way as any other person in respect of criminal offence. It is only in taking of bribes or with regard to the offence of corruption that sanction for criminal prosecution is required.'

54 The government classifies some of its citizens into Scheduled Caste, Scheduled Tribe and Other Backward Classes based on their social and economic condition.

55 S. H. Kapadia, Fifth M. C. Setalvad Memorial Lecture on Judicial Ethics, 16 April 2011, reported in the *Indian Express*, The Op-Ed page, 18 April 2011, p. 11.

56 Source: http://ibnlive.in.com/videos/141428/poll-media-judiciary-prone-to-corruption.html 11 January 2011.

References

Austin, G. (1999) *Working a Democratic Institution: The Indian Experience*, New Delhi: Oxford University Press.

Baum, L. (2007) *Judges and Their Audiences: A Perspective on Judicial Behavior*, Princeton, NJ: Princeton University Press.

Baxi, U. (1980) *The Indian Supreme Court and Politics*, Allahabad: Eastern Book Company.

Baxi, U. (1982) 'Who bothers about the Supreme Court? The problem of impact of judicial decisions', *Journal of Indian Law Institute*, 24: 848–62.

Baxi, U. (1985) *Courage, Craft, and Contention: The Indian Supreme Court in the Eighties*, Bombay: N. M. Tripathi.

Baxi, U. (1985) 'Taking suffering seriously: Social action litigation in the Supreme Court of India', in Sudarshan, R. *et al.* (eds), *Judges and the Judicial Power*, Bombay: Tripathi.

Beller, G. E. (1983) 'Benevolent illusions in a developing society: The assertion of Supreme Court authority in democratic India', *Western Political Quarterly*, 36: 513–32.

Choudhary, S. and Hunter, C. E. (2003) 'Measuring judicial activism on the Supreme Court of Canada: A comment on *Newfoundland (Treasury Board)* v. *Nape*', 48 *McGill Law Journal*, 525—62.

Das, G. (2000) 'The Supreme Court: An Overview', in Desai, A. H. *et al.* (eds) *Supreme But Not Infallible: Essays in Honour of the Supreme Court of India*, New Delhi: Oxford University Press.

Desai, A. H. and Muralidhar, S. (2000) 'Public interest litigation: Potential and problems', in Kirpal, B. N. *et al.* (eds), *Supreme but not Infallible*, Delhi: Oxford University Press.

Dhavan, R. (1980) *Justice on Trial: The Supreme Court Today*, Allahabad: A. H. Wheeler & Co.

Economic and Political Weekly (2008) 'Confrontation, complicity or selectivity? Isolated acts of judicial activism do not threaten the stability of the troika that runs the Indian state', Editorial, 23 February.

Epp, C. (1998) *The Rights Revolution*, Chicago: University of Chicago Press.

Ferejohn, J. (1999) 'Independent Judges, Dependent Judiciary: Explaining Judicial Independence', *Southern California Law Review*, 72(2–3): 353–84.

Gadbois, G. (1974) 'Supreme Court decisionmaking', *Banaras Law Journal*, 10: 1ff.

Galanter, M. (1978) 'Who are the backward classes?', *Economic and Political Weekly*, 13: 1978, pp. 1812–28.

Galanter, M. and Krishnan, J. K. (2004) 'Bread for the poor: Access to justice and the rights of the needy in India', *Hastings Law Journal*, 55: 789–834.

Gillman, H. (2002) 'How Political Parties Can Use the Courts to Advance Their Agendas: Federal Courts in the United States, 1895–91', *American Political Science Review*, 96(3): 511–24.

Gupta, V. K. (1995) *Decisionmaking in the Supreme Court of India*, Delhi: Kaveri.

Graber, M. A. (1993) 'The Non-Majoritarian Difficulty: Legislative Deference to the Judiciary', *Studies in American Political Development*, vol. 7, Spring: 35–73.

Grindle, M. (2007: 66) 'Good enough governance revisited', *Development Policy Review*, 25: 553–74.

Hirschl, R. (2004) *Towards Juristocracy: The Origins and Consequences of the New Constitutionalism*, Cambridge, MA: Harvard University Press, 2004.

Iyer, K. (1987) *Our Courts on Trial*, New Delhi: B. R. Publishing Corporation.

Jacobsohn, G. J. (2003) *The Wheel of Law: India's Secularism in Comparative Constitutional Context*, Princeton: Princeton University Press.

Kmiec, K. D. (2004) 'The origin and current meanings of "judicial activism"', 92 *California Law Review*, 1441–1476.

Mehta, P. B. (2002) 'The inner conflict of constitutionalism: Judicial review and the basic structure', in Hasan, Z., Sridharan, E., and Sudarshan, R. (eds), *India's Living Constitution: Ideas, Practices, and Controversies*, Delhi: Permanent Black.

Rajamani, L. (2007) 'Public Interest Environmental Litigation in India: Exploring Issues of Access, Participation, Equity, Effectiveness and Sustainability', *Journal of Environmental Law*, vol. 19, issue 3: 293–321.

Ramachandran, R. (2000) 'The Supreme Court and the basic structure doctrine', in Kirpal, B. N. *et al.* (eds), *Supreme But Not Infallible*, Delhi: Oxford University Press, 107–33.

Sathe, S. P. (2002) *Judicial Activism in India*, Delhi: Oxford University Press.

Seervai, H. M. (1983) *Constitutional Law of India*, 3rd ed., New Delhi: N.M. Tripathy.

Shankar, S. (2009) *Scaling Justice: India's Supreme Court, Anti-Terror Law and Social Rights*, New Delhi: Oxford University Press.

Tate, C. N. and Vallinder, T. (1995). 'The global expansion of judicial power: The judicialization of politics', in Tate, C. N. and Vallinder, T. (eds), *The Global Expansion of Judicial Power*, New York, NY: New York University Press, 1–24.

Vanberg, Georg (2009) *The Politics of Constitutional Review in Germany*, Cambridge: Cambridge University Press.

Venkat Raman and Kuncheria, C. J. (2010) 'Supreme Court to oversee telecom scams probe', *Reuters*, 16 December.

Venkatesan, V. (2007) 'Judicial challenge', *Frontline*, vol. 24, issue 2, 27 January–9 February, also available online at www.frontlineonnet.com/fl2402/stories/2007020900 3500400.htm, accessed 5 February 2012.

Verma, J. S. (2006) 'Mechanisms of judicial accountability', CJAR website: http://judicialreforms.org/judicial_account.htm.

Verma, J. S. (2007) Pandit Kunji Lal Dubey Memorial Lecture, Rani Durgavati Vishwavidyalaya, Jabalpur on 24 March, posted online in *The Indian Express*, 7 April 2007, http://airwebworld.com/articles/index.php?article=1222.

Part II

Fragile and young democracies

5 Thailand

Judicialization of politics or politicization of the judiciary?

Björn Dressel

Introduction

Although a variety of patterns of judicialization can be identified in Southeast Asia, arguably it is in Thailand that the judiciary has been most formidably transformed. Pulled into the political fray most recently during the crisis that has gripped the country since Prime Minister Thaksin Shinawatra was ousted in 2006, Thailand's judges have intervened in politics in ways unprecedented not only in Thailand but throughout Southeast Asia and beyond. With close coordination among Thailand's top courts, led by decisions of the Constitutional Court, judges have dissolved major political parties, banned their senior executives from politics, toppled two prime ministers, and directly challenged major government policies. Their decisions have drastically altered the Thai political landscape, with far-reaching consequences for democratic governance.

These cases might be seen as part of a general trend towards the judicialization of politics, which Hirschl (2006: 721) described as 'the ever-accelerating reliance on courts and judicial means for addressing core moral predicaments, public policy questions, and political controversies'. This trend has been well documented for the United States, Europe, and Latin America (Sieder *et al.* 2005; Stone Sweet 2000; Tate and Vallinder 1995), but its causes and consequences in Southeast Asia have rarely been explored. In fact, just 15 over years ago a leading scholar proclaimed that 'a majority of Southeast Asian countries are unlikely candidates for the judicialization of politics' (Tate 1994: 188) because so many regimes in the region were neither democratic nor constitutional. But after a wave of democratization hit the region in the 1990s, a majority of states there altered their constitutions to give more attention to rule of law, accountability, and rights issues. The effect was to empower the courts.

Thailand is a good illustration of this trend. After gradual democratic opening in the early 1990s, frustrations about how Thai democracy was functioning grew (see Pasuk Phongpaichit and Sungsidh Piriyarangsan 1996: 57–107; Pasuk and Baker 2002: 418–30). Thailand's urban liberal elites then pushed for far-reaching institutional reforms—a process culminating in the 1997 'People's Constitution'.[1] While in essence that document was yet another elite project, many observers saw it as a watershed event in Thailand's long history of short-lived constitutions because of the breadth and depth of its reforms (see Connors 2002; Harding 2001; Pinai Nanakorn 2002). Reflecting the belief of the urban middle class that it was possible to 'engineer' democracy, good governance, and the rule of law, the new constitution not only made it possible for the rural poor to have electoral impact, it also introduced for the first time a Constitutional Court, equipped it with judicial review powers, and supplemented it with a system of administrative courts.

Both tiers of courts were meant to fill a major gap in terms of legal redress against public officials while also reinforcing the system of checks and balances the new constitution set up. Its role at first, though important, was somewhat muted, but over time, and with a few salient changes, the Constitutional Court in particular has become a critical political player—indeed, the most politically visible of all the courts. It was instrumental in guiding the political process not only during the events leading up to the military coup against PM Thaksin Shinawatra but ever since.

These developments raise serious questions, such as: What led to the considerable change in judicial behavior? And what have been its effects on Thai politics, and on the rule of law? The question has gained relevance recently because the 2007 Thai constitution[2] explicitly encouraged the courts to take on a political role far beyond anything that was even conceivable previously.

Interestingly current scholarship on Thailand has yet to draw much attention to this phenomenon. For instance, recent studies of the Thai Constitutional and Administrative Courts (Leyland 2009; Harding 2010) have largely been accounts of institutional arrangements and analysis of their jurisprudence from a narrow legal perspective. There have been no attempts to situate the behavior of the courts within the larger sociopolitical context, or to analyze the growing judicial involvement in political matters (for a notable exception, see Ginsburg 2009). Thai specialists, while quick to point out a decline in parliamentary sovereignty caused by deference to the nonaccountable oversight agencies set up by the 1997 constitution (McCargo 2003; Connors 1999), have given scant attention to how this process has actually affected the role of judges and the courts themselves, though some scholars have spoken of an 'activist' Constitutional Court (Ockey 2009: 327) or even suggested the possibility of a broader trend towards judicialization (McCargo 2008: 335–6).

The limited outside scholarly attention to what is happening with the courts is particularly fascinating considering the public and academic attention the subject has received within Thailand, following earlier popularization of the term judicialization (*thulakarnwipat*) by leading academic and public intellectual Thirayuth Boonmee, who suggested in May 2006 that the judiciary could help resolve some of the problems of political reform (Matichon, 1 June 2006). Since then the term has appeared regularly in the media and the topic is also debated in both political circles (see, for instance, Chaturon Chaisang 2009: 79–86) and academic (see Suchit Bunbonkarn 2009; Piyabutr Saengkanokkul 2008; Worachet Pakeerut 2009). Certainly, the issue was not lost on the drafters of the 2007 constitution, which was drawn up under military aegis after the 2006 coup (Borwornsak Uwanno 2009: 42–3; Dressel 2009: 311, 315).

Clearly, not just the fact but the process of judicialization deserves more attention. This chapter therefore tracks the activities of the Thai judiciary with particular attention to the various permutations of the Thai Constitutional Court during the political crisis in 2006–08. While often acting in close concert with Thailand's two other top courts (the Supreme Court and the Supreme Administrative Court), the Constitutional Court offers particularly interesting insights into the judicialization trend not only because it has taken the leading role lately but even more so because of the political repercussions of its decisions.

Analyzing critical court verdicts from a political point of view, this chapter suggests that growing judicial activism and assertiveness in contested areas of political relevance in Thailand, while partly driven by institutional arrangements and the interests of judges themselves, is best understood as a direct outcome of more general intra-elite struggles and the use of the judiciary by Thailand's traditional monarchical networks in their battle over political control. In this analysis we cannot avoid looking not only at the judicialization trend but also at where it seems to be leading: to the growing politicization of the institutions that should be guardians of the rule of law, protecting it from the encroachments of politics. The Thai case shines a spotlight into the shadows behind the judicialization trend, making it clear that judicialization is just one point on a spectrum that may ultimately lead to a serious distortion of the rule of law as it has traditionally been understood.

To advance this argument, we first briefly review the permutations of the Thai judiciary over time, with particular attention to the effects of the 1997 and 2007 constitutions in respect to judicial review. Second, we evaluate the political context of critical verdicts between 2006 and 2008, highlighting the role of the Constitutional Court. We then explore in detail what has driven the changes in the role of the judiciary. Finally, we offer some reflections on what these findings mean, not just for politics in Thailand but also more generally for the theoretical debates on the judicialization of politics.

The roots of judicial review in Thailand

The emergence of Thailand's modern judiciary is closely intertwined with modernizing state-building reforms initiated in the nineteenth century by the Chakri monarchy, whose line continues today. King Mongkut (Rama IV, 1851–68) initiated cautious reforms directed to centralizing and rationalizing the Thai state by reforming the traditional system of justice exercised by elders and patrons in the community. However, these efforts were not formalized consistently until the ascendancy of King Chulalongkorn (Rama V, 1868–1910), and in particular his son Prince Ratchaburi Direkrit (1874–1920), the first royal to study abroad—he studied law. In 1891 King Chulalongkorn established an official Ministry of Justice (MOJ), and under the direction of the prince over the next two decades the courts were gradually brought under the firm control of the ministry (and thus the monarchy), with its administration winning praise from foreign observers as one of 'the cleanest and straightest Siam has ever seen' with judges that 'would compare favorably with the members of the judiciary of many European countries' (Graham 1924: 372–3).

Meanwhile, fears of foreign encroachment on Thai sovereignty–several European governments established courts to handle cases involving their own citizens—accelerated the momentum and gave direction to judicial reforms through, for example, adoption in 1908 of Western-style court procedures and the decision in the early 1920s to promulgate a civil law code system rather than the British-style common law system that Prince Ratchaburi had preferred. But the separation of the judiciary more clearly from the royal bureaucracy was not a clean break. In 1912 the Court of Justice was given some responsibility over judicial affairs but control over the judiciary (including training) was highly centralized within the MOJ, and judicial independence was a matter of theory only.

The situation was changed little when the 1932 coup staged by Western-educated civilian and military reformers against King Prajadhipok (Rama VII, 1925–35) transformed Thailand into a constitutional monarchy. While coup leaders with legal training like Pridi Banomyong (1900–83) did adopt a modern code of law, expand legal education, and promote the constitution as an alternative source of legitimacy, the powers and structures of the judiciary were virtually unchanged—a trend that would continue for most of the twentieth century.

Not until the 1997 constitution was drafted was there profound change. The urban elites who wanted to address Thailand's persistent problems of instability, corruption, and executive abuse, saw judicial reform as an integral part of their political reform project. The constitution for the first time formally separated the courts from the MOJ to make them more independent. It also established a new Constitutional and Administrative Court (complementing the Court of Justice), which not only introduced judicial review for the first time but was envisioned by the drafters as the future guardian of the new liberal constitutional architecture and the hub of a network of new oversight agencies to strengthen rule-based governance (Leyland 2008; Harding 2010).

Remarkably, there had been no precedent for an independent body entrusted with constitutional and judicial review in any of the 18 constitutions that had governed politics in Thailand after it became a constitutional monarchy in 1932 (Chai Anan 2002: 106); the ad hoc Constitutional Tribunal that appeared in some of Thailand's constitutions after 1945 (i.e., in 1949, 1952, 1968, 1974, 1978, 1991) was quite different because it shared judicial review powers with parliament until 1991 and its term was linked to that of parliament (see: Banjerd Singkaneti 1998: 22–8). Moreover, it was a direct challenge to Thailand's long-standing 'bureaucratic polity' in which elites reserved to themselves the right to interpret the law and alter constitutional rules. It is thus not surprising that the idea of the Constitutional Court was subject to intense debates when the 1997 constitution was being drafted. Only after concessions were made with respect to access, powers, and composition of the bench—senior Supreme Court judges were particularly vocal in opposing the idea of centralized judicial review—was the court eventually enshrined in the constitution (Klein 2003: 37).

Despite some inevitable compromises, the 1997 constitution nevertheless gave the court relatively broad jurisdiction and solid safeguards for its independence. The court was composed of 15 judges appointed by the king on the advice of the Senate for a single, nonrenewable, term of nine years, with retirement mandatory at age 70 (Chapter VIII, Articles 255, 260). Seven of the judges were drawn from the career judiciary (five from the Supreme Court and two from the Administrative Court) through internal elections; of the other eight, five were experts in law and three in political science who were nominated by a special Selection Committee and confirmed by the Senate. The court's budget autonomy was guaranteed, with an independent administrative unit functioning as its secretariat. Access to the court was provided for parliament, the executive, lower courts, and other watchdog bodies, but not for individual citizens.

Its jurisdiction was broad by international standards: With final authority over all matters of constitutional interpretation, its jurisdiction covered the constitutionality of laws and regulations; rulings on references from lower courts; and disputes about the competence of organs of the state (Chapter VIII, Articles 255–70; also Rules of the Constitutional Court Procedures, B.E. 2546 [2003]). However, reflecting the earlier compromises, executive actions and decisions other than emergency decrees (the prerogative of the Administrative Court) were exempt; nor could the Constitutional Court consider criminal cases of official corruption or overrule final judgments of the Supreme Court. Compensating for these limitations, however, were far-reaching ancillary powers related to impeachment of officeholders and assessment of qualifications to hold office, and to specific disputes about the legality of elections and election results and dissolution or merger of political parties, which were governed by the Political Party Act B.E. 2541 (1998) (especially sections 17, 27, 72–3).

The Constitutional Court quickly gained a reputation for relative independence and efficiency. Accepting 417 cases out of 560 petitions between April 1998 and December 2004, the justices issued rulings in 398 cases. A majority dealt with the constitutionality of laws (54 percent), followed by cases related to party dissolution (16 percent), disputes between state organs (11 percent), and asset and liability declarations of officeholders (7 percent) (Office of the Constitutional Court 2005: 72–3). Most of these decisions, except for a very few involving prominent politicians (e.g., Deputy Prime Minister Sanan Kachornprasat, Decision No. 31/2543: 10 August 2000) were not challenged—although not unnoticed.

Some observers quickly identified a pattern of judicial restraint, particularly with regard to human rights, where the absence of a right of individual petition severely constrained the role of the court, and in review of legislation, where the court seemed to align itself regularly with the government (Klein 2003: 13). Others pointed to differences within the bench, particularly between the narrow legal formalism of the career judges and the often broader interpretations of the political scientists. If some of the latter seemed to vote regularly with the government, that may be because their appointments, compared to those of the career judges, may have been more political. It may also be that the entire bench had a tendency to value the primacy of the state over the rights of citizens (see

Klein 2003: 66; Pasuk and Baker 2004: 175). There was general agreement, however, that the court had done much to help consolidate the political transition, particularly since many of its early decisions in support of the Election Commission of Thailand (ECT) proved crucial for stabilizing the electoral process, especially in the run-up to the 2001 parliamentary elections (Klein 2003: 46–53).

However, public perceptions of the court were soon to alter dramatically. In 2001 the National Counter Corruption Commission (NCCC) charged then-Prime Minister Thaksin Shinawatra with concealment of assets during his brief spell as Deputy Prime Minister in 1997–98 (it was claimed that assets were registered in the names of the housekeeper, maid, driver, security guard, and business colleagues). A ruling against him could carry a five-year ban from politics just after his resounding victory (by Thai standards) as prime minister. When he appealed against his indictment, claiming 'honest negligence', the court in a tight 8:7 decision ruled for Thaksin (Decision No. 20/2544: 3 August 2001).

The much-anticipated verdict, pronounced during an unprecedented public mobilization campaign by the defendant and his supporters, was widely interpreted to be the result of political pressures on the justices. It was the first time in 18 NCCC cases that the court had failed to endorse the commission's findings. Reported comments of the justices about political considerations (Constitution Court judge Chumphol na Songkhla was widely quoted as having said, 'Who are we to judge that Thaksin is guilty? He was elected by 16 million Thais'), and attempts at political interference and intimidation reinforced the perception that the court had not been impartial, though a close reading of the 1,200-page ruling suggests that the verdict was driven less by the conclusion that Thaksin was innocent—a question the court did not answer—than by unusual internal voting rules that effectively transformed minority opinions into a majority ruling (for a thorough discussion of the procedural complexities of the Thaksin case, see Klein 2003: 73–6).

Procedural details aside, there is little doubt that the decision severely compromised the reputation of the court. In fact, given Thaksin's increasingly assertive leadership style and heavy-handed interference in the areas of human rights, press freedom, and constitutional practice, it was not unreasonable for members of the public to infer that the court, and the other independent oversight agencies, could not provide effective checks and balances against executive abuse, especially since the government increasingly influenced appointments to these agencies through its gradual control over the Senate, which despite being designed as a nonpolitical body quickly became captured by government (Pasuk and Baker 2004: 175–6). Indeed in 2003 four appointments to replace retiring judges raised concerns about the quality and independence—three were known to have had close ties with the Prime Minister; the other lacked any qualifications in constitutional law—though this did not mean that all decisions went in favour of the government.

Meanwhile, the public standing of the Supreme Administrative Court was rising. It was widely perceived as being more professional and more insulated from executive interference than the Constitutional Court, particularly after it ruled against the government in the contested privatization of the Electricity Generating Authority of Thailand (EGAT) in 2005.[3]

This background helps explain many of the modifications the 2007 constitution made to the court's institutional arrangements. This constitution was drafted in only six months under the auspices of the military junta's Council for National Security (CNS); the tightly controlled drafting exercise lacked the inclusiveness of its predecessor, and it was approved in a referendum that was highly controversial. The new constitution (Article 206) reduced the number of justices from 15 to just nine, five of whom are now appointed from sitting judges (three from the Supreme Court, two from the Supreme Administrative Court). Of the other four, two must be qualified in law and two in political science, public administration, or another social science, and all must be experienced in state affairs. The process for Senate selection of these judges was depoliticized and the qualifications raised; lawyers must now have at least 30 years of continuous experience (Article 205 (3)). Petitions by individuals to the court were allowed for the first time, which filled a major gap in previous arrangements (Article 212).[4]

Combined, these changes may have reflected an intention of the drafters—many of them lawyers—to tighten the membership of the court, strengthen its powers, and make it less amenable to political interference. Unfortunately, however, the 2007 constitution also explicitly enhanced the *political* role of the court, and the judiciary in general. For instance, the presidents of the highest courts are now involved in selecting senators and candidates for the independent agencies (see Articles 113, 243, 246, 252, 256). The courts may also propose bills and laws directly to the House of Representatives (Articles 139 (3) and 142 (3)). Most controversial, the Constitutional Court was given the power to dissolve a political party if one of its executive members is found guilty of election fraud (Article 237). Together all these changes considerably altered the balance of power between the judiciary and other branches of government and laid the foundation for the growing judicialization of politics in Thailand.

Judicial policy making, 2006–08[5]

A series of bold judicial interventions between 2006 and 2008 illustrates how the Constitutional Court has emerged as an increasingly important element in Thailand's political landscape and has led the way for other Thai courts to intervene in core political matters. These interventions have not only expanded the previous scope of judicial engagement but also seriously politicized jurisprudence. Thus they raise concerns about the role of the courts, legitimate or not, in the Thai political system.

Annulment of the 2006 General Election

The first manifestation of the new judicial assertiveness was the Constitutional Court's decision in May 2006 to annul the April general elections. The Thaksin government had decided, controversially, to counter growing allegations of disloyalty to the monarchy, corruption, and conflicts of interest (particularly after the tax-free sale of Thaksin's Shin Corp business to a foreign investor) with a call for a snap election in April 2006—even though it had won an overwhelming election victory only a year earlier, and parliament still had three more years to serve. Major opposition parties, after failing to convince the government to postpone the elections until a binding platform of political reform was agreed, decided to boycott the elections, claiming that first the prime minister should step down in light of possible parliamentary and judicial scrutiny of his actions. However, their recognition of a likely failure to win the upcoming elections and political calculations about the benefits of the boycott might have been its real cause (Nelson 2006: 9).

Whatever the reasons, as public protests widened and the extra-parliamentary opposition mobilized royal ideology in its support (see Connors 2008), the boycotts clearly threw the country into constitutional crisis, because an election in which only one major party ran, Thaksin's Thai Rak Thai (TRT), clearly raised questions about its legitimacy. (The few minor parties that did participate were all aligned with the TRT.) And when the election came, so many parliamentarians failed to get the 20 percent of the vote required for them to be seated that parliament could not convene (see for a detailed chronology of events, Nelson 2006).

Although some solution to the electoral deadlock was urgently needed, the Constitutional Court's 8:6 decision[6] to void the election was remarkable for a number of reasons. For instance, the legal reasoning was unusually broad: For one thing, the justices argued that the 37-day period between dissolution of the House and election day, though technically not violating the constitution, had led to political problems severe enough for the election to be disqualified. Another rationale was that the positioning of ballot boxes violated the secrecy of the vote. Ultimately the court found that 'The election yielded results which are unfair and undemocratic, and are therefore unconstitutional, being inconsistent with Articles 2, 3, 104 (3) and 114 from the beginning of the election process, i.e., from the scheduling of the elections, the application of candidates, the ballots, and the announcement of the election results'.[7] This view was promptly validated by the Administrative Court.[8]

Both these interpretations directly contradicted opinions of the Election Commission of Thailand. Moreover, there seemed to be an unusual degree of coordination between various courts: the Administrative Court had decided in April to cancel the rerun election in selected constituencies, the Constitutional Court annulled the general election in May, and the Criminal Court brought action against the Election Commissioners (see below), in July.

Many observers were convinced that these decisions had their basis in speeches by the revered King Bhumipol Adulyadej (Rama IX) to judges of the Administrative and the Supreme Court (Montesano 2007: 315). In the first, to members of the Administrative Court, the king said:

> Now I will talk about the election. The court itself has the right to discuss the election, especially the candidates who received less than 20 per cent of the vote.

> Is this an issue relevant to you? In fact, it should be. The issue of the sole-candidacy elections is important because they will never fulfil the quorum. If the House is not filled by elected candidates, democracy cannot function. If this is the case, the oaths you have just sworn would be invalid. You have sworn to work for democracy. If you cannot do it, then you may have to resign. You must find ways to solve the problem. [...]
>
> Should the election be nullified? You have the right to say what's appropriate or not. If it's not appropriate, it is not to say the government is not good. But as far as I am concerned, a one-party election is not normal. The one-party situation is undemocratic.[9]

Similarly, the speech to the Supreme Court stressed the need for the judges to intervene. Rejecting demands for direct royal intervention (as had happened in the past), the king argued that the public 'pins their hope on the courts' and demanded that the courts 'have to consider how to work this out'.

That the royal message got through was shown just days later when the Chief Justice of the Supreme Court called a meeting of the heads of the Administrative, Supreme, and Constitutional Courts. The meeting was not only followed by the Constitutional Court's decision to annul the 2 April elections but also by the heads of the three courts calling for the Election Commissioners to resign, possibly exerting undue pressure.[10] When they failed to do so, in an unprecedented coordination of action among the courts in July 2006, they were first disqualified and then hurried off to jail for four years for malfeasance (for a detailed account of the rather extraordinary series of events, see Nelson 2006).

Dissolution of Thai Rak Thai

In May 2007 the Constitutional Tribunal ruled that Thaksin's TRT party must be dissolved, and barred 111 of its executives from holding public office for five years.[11] This was the first case heard by the nine-member tribunal that had been set up by the leaders of the September 2006 coup after they dissolved the Constitutional Court. Many of the tribunal's members were known to be critical of the Thaksin government; for instance, Thanit Kesawapitak had suggested that the tribunal consider dissolving the party, and Nurak Marpraneet had been part of the military-appointed Constitutional Drafting Assembly. Charges had been filed against TRT, the Democrat Party (DP), and several minor parties for alleged irregularities during the abortive April 2006 general election, and the case was seen as a major test of the judges' impartiality—especially since the interim constitution gave them discretion to dissolve a political party if a single one of its executives was found guilty of election fraud (see: CDR Announcement No. 27, Article 3).

The 6 : 3 decision was once again extraordinary: The tribunal found TRT and its allies Pattana Chart and Chart Thai guilty of conspiring to gain administrative power by illegal means. It concluded that TRT executives had provided funds to smaller parties during the election and executives of the smaller parties had tinkered with party membership records.

The verdict came only days after another royal speech to members of the Administrative Court in which the king urged the judiciary to continue working toward a solution to the political crisis (he said, for instance, 'I have the answer in my heart, but have no right to say it'). Politically, it effectively decapitated Thailand's largest and most popular political party, which had won resounding victories by Thai standards in 2001 and 2005. In fact, not only was the highly popular Thaksin Shinawatra now ineligible to run for office, so was virtually anyone else who had held a leadership position in his party or cabinet.

The unanimous dismissal in the same ruling of all charges against the military-favoured DP (despite at least some evidence of DP members engaging in similar illicit activities, not to mention suggestions that they had engaged in deliberate efforts to frame the TRT party), followed by a decision of the military-appointed Assets Examination Committee to seize almost US$1.7 billion worth of Thaksin family assets, certainly reinforced the concern that as the December 2007 elections approached the judges were supporting the junta's political agenda.

The terms of the actual decision do little to dispel this impression. The unusually laborious verdict took more than 11 hours to read out. The justices seem to have been at great pains to justify their ruling and downplay defence arguments that the case was moot because the election had already been annulled. Thaksin's team had raised serious procedural concerns, given that the legal basis for dissolving the party effectively made an act punishable that was not an offense when committed. The tribunal responded that

> The principle prohibiting retroactive enforcement of law that will cause adverse effect on individuals emanates from the 'no punishment without law' principle; however, such principle applies only to criminal acts [...;] the revocation of electoral rights is not a criminal sanction but it is a legal measure which resulted from the laws empowering such parties' dissolution.[12]

For many in the legal profession this was hardly convincing reasoning—especially since the verdict accused the former Prime Minister of posing a danger to democracy through corruption and cronyism. That certainly suggested that the tribunal had bent the legal rules to achieve a politically desired outcome.

The Samak case and the dissolution of the PPP

Finally, two cases decided in late 2008 by a reconstituted Constitutional Court suggest that the previous judicial interventions into electoral politics were not aberrations but part of a continuous pattern of judicialization. The first found Prime Minister Samak Sundaravej guilty of a conflict of interest for hosting a popular cooking show on TV; the second dissolved the People's Power Party (PPP), the political successor of the TRT. Both again had profound political consequences.

The junta had organized general elections in December 2007. Once again, to the profound shock of the junta and others, the TRT, reconstituted as the PPP, won by a landslide (the PPP won 233 seats out of 480, leaving the DP at 164 seats a distant second). This prompted Thailand's dismayed urban elite to public protests under the umbrella of the People's Alliance for Democracy (PAD). As PAD supporters and the PPP-led government were locked in a fierce stand-off, the Constitutional Court, with a new bench and new powers granted to it by the 2007 constitution, again jumped into the fray.

There was not much hope for, or likelihood of, judicial restraint. In what was widely perceived as a warning shot at the government, in May 2008 the Constitutional Court had already declared unconstitutional the government's signing of a joint communiqué in support of Cambodia's application of the Prehar Vihear temple complex, of which Thailand had previously claimed ownership, for recognition as a World Heritage site.[13] That opened the door to possible impeachment of Foreign Minister Noppadon Pattama and other members of the already beleaguered Samak government. In the case we are discussing, however, the Senate and the ECT had come to the Constitutional Court charging that the Prime Minister had violated constitutional conflict of interest provisions by hosting his semipolitical cooking show. The unanimous 9:0 verdict[14] against Samak was remarkable not just for its bold political implications—forcing the Prime Minister to resign for what many considered a minor abuse of power—but once again for the legal reasoning (see Kittisak Prokati 2011). The court held that Samak's activity on the show was the work of an 'employee', a finding the constitution required for a verdict of guilty, as Art. 267 prevents any public officeholder from holding 'any position in [...] an organization carrying out business [...] nor be an employee of any person'. It was only able to do this by deviating from the actual definitions set out in Thailand's civil code and labor laws, instead relying by its own admission on a simple dictionary. With what one judge later described as 'judicial creativity', the court thus forced the resignation of the first Prime Minister elected under the 2007 constitution.

With the Samak case having already set a new benchmark for judicial interventionism, there was little public surprise when the Constitutional Court ruled 9:0 in December 2008[15] to dissolve the PPP and two of its political allies after the Supreme Court convicted PPP leader Yongyut Tiyapairat of buying votes in the December 2007 general elections. Issued at the height of a tense stand-off between the government of Prime Minister Somchai Wongsawat and PAD supporters, who were occupying the international airport, the verdict effectively ended the PPP-led government's efforts to alter the constitution in a way that would have robbed the Constitutional Court of some of its new powers. It also dealt the final blow to a weakened government, forcing Samak's successor, Prime Minister Somchai, to resign and clearing the path for a DP-led coalition government.

The way the court handled the case once again did little to counter the impression that the verdict was politically motivated. Legal observers were stunned, for instance, when the justices abruptly ended testimony by defence witnesses—and then returned hours later with a verdict less than three pages long that ignored profound questions about how vote-buying fit into the anti-democratic behavior required by the Political Party Act (Articles 91 and 98) or how to balance dissolving a party with the constitutionally guaranteed freedom to form a party.

This series of high-profile Constitutional Court decisions illustrates the emergence of a high-speed trend toward judicialization of Thai politics. The court's bold interference in electoral politics profoundly altered Thailand's governance landscape: it effectively decapitated what had been Thailand's largest and most successful political party for 10 years and barred its leaders from politics for years. Forcing the resignation of two prime ministers—and keeping pressure on the still popular former Thaksin Shinawatra to remain in self-imposed exile—the Constitutional Court, with help from other courts, has in effect reversed elections to tilt the political balance toward the DP-led government. As a result, Thailand's political system has become less competitive and less representative, to the benefit of the country's traditional urban elites.

While it may be true that the period described here was unusual in terms of the severity of the political crisis, without which the judiciary probably would not have been prompted into action, it is probably also true that the court's decisions exacerbated the crisis. For the first time judges—not the king or the military—have been seen to intervene decisively in Thailand's political affairs.

The trend has continued well beyond the cases analyzed, and other courts are now following the lead of the Constitutional Court. For instance, in September 2009 the Supreme Administrative Court stunned the DP-led government of Prime Minister Abhisit when, amid the unfolding global financial crisis, it issued a temporary injunction against 76 major investment projects worth Bt400 billion (US$12 billion) at and around the Map Ta Phut industrial estate.[16] The court effectively jeopardized a fiscal stimulus of about 4.5 percent of GDP and left the government exposed to mounting investor concerns (Phatra Securities 2009). And in early 2010 the Supreme Court's Division for Holders of Political Positions delivered its much-anticipated verdict on the freeze of Bt76 billion (US$2.3 billion) of Thaksin's assets.[17] The thrust of the decision—seizing about half the assets as correlating to his time as prime minister—may seem in some ways less remarkable than the unprecedented assertiveness of this court in more directly political matters, but the effects were equally political (Pavin Chachavalpongpun 2010).

The reputation of the Constitutional Court was further undermined when in late 2010, shortly before its controversial decision on mere procedural grounds to reject the dissolution of the DP for election violations (thus allowing the DP to stand in the 2011 elections),[18] video footage emerged showing the Secretary to the Court President discussing details of the case with a DP parliamentarian; later footage also implicated several judges on the court in leaking exam papers to preferred candidates during efforts to recruit court officials in 2008. As judicialization seems to be spreading ever more widely through the court system, the signs of growing politicization have increasingly compromised the professionalism of institutions like the Constitutional Court.

The question still to be answered is this: How can we account for the actions of the Constitutional Court since 2000 that catalyzed the trend?

Explaining judicial behavior

From the analysis of the behavior of the Constitutional Court in 2006–08 there emerge several factors that can be seen to have supported the judicial activism and assertiveness of Thailand's courts in core political controversies.

For one thing, the institutional powers granted to a court clearly do matter. Before courts can test and perhaps expand their constitutional boundaries, they rely first on the powers they have been given. Traditionally Thai courts exercised judicial restraint in political matters. The new judicial activism in these areas grows out of the new powers—many of them ancillary—granted to judges under first the interim and then the 2007 constitution (see, for a discussion of the growing global trend of equipping constitutional courts with ancillary powers, Ginsburg and Elkins 2009). Similarly, in giving the judiciary a role in such policy-making areas as appointment of senators and ability to introduce legislation, the 2007 constitution in effect reduced the separation of powers and invited them to become politically active—to a point that seems to be making many judges themselves increasingly concerned about political interference.

How Constitutional Court judges are appointed is also a factor. For instance, the mix of career and noncareer judges on the bench has certainly provided room for some of the nonlawyers to take a more activist approach. The fact that Constitutional Court judges are appointed for a single nonrenewable term and are further term-limited by age has had a somewhat paradoxical effect. While in principle the rule is meant to discourage political calculations among the judges related to renewal of their terms, it may instead have undermined institutional continuity and thus allowed greater executive influence over the court. In fact, since the court was founded, not a single judge has completed a full nine-year term. The coup that dissolved the court was of course a factor, but the obligatory retirement age and voluntary resignations had already decimated the original bench, leaving only four of the original bench still serving. Thus the court has lacked both a consistent cohort of justices and strong internal leadership by a long-serving court president.

And what about the personal motivations of the judges themselves? By tradition and training Thai judges are inclined to formal legalism and judicial restraint, which previously made them reluctant to engage with questions of political significance (see for a good overview of the Thai judicial system and curriculum, Institute of Developing Economies 2001). But particularly in the highest courts, it has become obvious that some judges have personal views about such matters as the activist role of the judiciary or the tenure of former Prime Minister Thaksin—a problem amplified by the new process for appointing judges. For instance, as the composition of the bench for the military-appointed Constitutional Tribunal made clear, several judges appointed were selected not only for their professional qualifications but for their known positions in opposition to the former prime minister and his government. Again, with respect to the Constitutional Court appointed in 2008, some of the new justices, like Jarun Pukditanakul, are well-known Thaksin critics and outspoken advocates of a more assertive judiciary. This suggests that the process of judicialization is at least in part driven by judges themselves. In reaction, perhaps, many career judges are reluctant to take a seat on the Constitutional Court because they consider it too political.[19]

Finally, let us look at the broader structural context. There is little doubt that the intervention of the monarchy triggered much of the judicial assertiveness in political cases. This should not be surprising. Not only is it very rare for the king's authority to be challenged but the relationship between the monarchy and the Thai judiciary has, as already demonstrated, traditionally been close. The king himself has taken a close interest in the judiciary, having earlier studied law; his granddaughter, Princess Bajrakitiyabha, has ventured into legal studies; she earned a doctoral degree from Cornell University and joined the Office of the Attorney General as an attorney in 2006. With admiration for the law fairly pervasive in the royal family, it is thus perhaps not surprising that over the last decade several top judges have filled positions on the Privy Council—the nerve centre of an otherwise informal monarchical network structure. This has further entrenched the relationship between court and judiciary (what McCargo [2005] has called the 'network monarchy'). Within Thai political culture, judges can hardly avoid being receptive to the subtle signals sent by Thailand's informal but de facto power center.

But the intervention of the monarchy during the political crisis is just one aspect of today's intra-elite struggles that pitch the traditional military and royal networks, supported by the urban middle class, against Thaksin and his inner circle, whose modern bourgeois interests, backed by decisive popular electoral support, directly challenged the old power arrangements (Pasuk and Baker 2005). In fact today—because of a looming royal succession crisis, the mobilization of Thailand's marginalized, and the failure of the military to garner much public support for their coup—in order to safeguard the old order Thailand's traditional elites have turned to constitutional reform that empowers judicial and quasi-judicial actors (Hewison 2007; Dressel 2009). The activism of the Thai judiciary can thus be seen as a proxy for the larger battle for political hegemony. Judges have become essential to the elite project of consolidating the post-coup political order. Unfortunately, in the process the courts have become directly politicized. In turn this has undermined the rule of law, replacing it with what is in effect a rule by judges. Ultimately, the effect has been to exacerbate a more general crisis of legitimacy, not only for the courts but for the governance of Thailand as a whole (see Dressel 2010a).

Conclusion

This chapter has used a series of cases heard by various permutations of the Constitutional Court to examine the trend towards the judicialization of politics in

Thailand—a trend that deserves more scholarly attention than it has yet received, and certainly has yet to run its course. We provide evidence for the growing involvement of the courts in such core political matters as electoral disputes, executive actions, and broader public policy choices. This chapter shows that the new trend is to a large extent driven by a combination of new powers granted to the court, the interests of some judges themselves, and (underlying both) the growing intra-elite tensions that have prompted Thailand's traditional royal networks, with the support of many liberal urban elites, to use the judiciary as a proxy in the struggle for political power in Thailand.

The situation in Thailand provides insights for the general theoretical debate on the judicialization of politics (see good overview: Hirschl 2008a). Traditionally, many scholars have anchored the trend towards judicialization within macro-processes like democratization, modernization, or the spread of rights consciousness, but recently attention has shifted to agency-based models and political determinants (see for a selection of this burgeoning literature: Ginsburg 2003; Whittington 2007; Clayton and Gillman 1999; Lovell 2003; Graber 1993).

For instance, facets of the Thai case seem to be well captured by Ran Hirschl's work (Hirschl 2004, 2006, 2008b), which has challenged recent scholarly enthusiasm for the expansion of global rights. Focusing on the interests and strategies of key political actors, he argues that constitutional reform and the related empowerment of the judiciary are not so much progressive per se as a reflection of elite efforts to maintain the status quo. His 'hegemonic preservation thesis' seems particularly apt for explaining the efforts of Thailand's political elites to mitigate the uncertainties of the electoral process through constitutional arrangements in 1997, and their even more determined efforts in 2007. The outcome is that they have reduced the influence of representative institutions and constrained the operations of democratic politics (Connors 2002; Ginsburg 2009; Hewison 2007).

Perhaps, though, Thailand deserves a more nuanced view than currently dominant models like Hirschl's might suggest. Often overlooked is the flip side of judicialization that is particularly clear in Thailand: the politicizing of the judiciary. Many significant political verdicts in Thailand have been hard to reconcile with accepted standards of procedural justice. It is in fact tempting to argue that the Constitutional Court has moved beyond judicialization into areas that suggest abuse of justice or 'un-rule' of law.

Empirically, the Thai case underlines the point that judicialization and the rule of law do not necessarily go hand in hand. Other factors, often extra-constitutional (like the role of the monarchy in Thailand), may have far-reaching effects on the process. What is happening in Thailand is a reminder that legal and judicial transplants from elsewhere in the world, such as constitutional and administrative courts, need to be analyzed carefully and perhaps adapted rather than adopted. In a new context, these institutions are likely to function very differently from the way they do in their home settings.

And given contextual factors unique to Thailand, most obviously the influence of the monarchical networks, the case also urges closer theoretical attention to some of the historical, ideational, and relatively informal (e.g., clientelistic) aspects of the political context that may determine judicial behavior, such as elite settlements and structures, informal power centers like the Thai monarchy, and the ideological attitudes of elites towards democratic governance. Areas like this have yet to be fully accounted for in scholarly debates (see, for similar reasoning, Hilbink 2009). This is particularly important if one is interested in moving the debate from the sources of court empowerment to how courts actually perform.

Notes

1 Constitution of the Kingdom of Thailand (B.E. 2540), as published in the Government Gazette, Vol. 114, Part 55a, dated 11 October B.E. 2540 (1997).
2 Constitution of the Kingdom of Thailand (B.E. 2550), published in the Government Gazette, Vol. 124, Part. 27, dated 24 August 2007 (B.E. 2550).
3 Case No. 5/2549, 2006; for discussion of this and the equally politically charged iTV and Shin Corp cases in 2004 and 2006, see McCargo and Pathmanand (2005: 47–53).
4 See 2007 Constitution, Article 212. However, though this is directly molded on German constitutional law, it seems to be an awkward mix of what is known in German constitutional law as *Normenkontrolle* (i.e., testing of individual norms of constitutional conformity) and *indviduelle Verfassungsbeschwerde* (i.e., the claim by a plaintiff of the violation of constitutional rights).
5 Part of this section draws on Dressel (2010b).
6 Decision No. 9/2549 (2006).
7 Decision No. 9/2549 (2006), unofficial translation.
8 Decision No. 607–608/2549 (2006).
9 Unofficial translation of the king's speech to the Administrative Court, quoted from *The Nation*, 27 April 2007.
10 For an unofficial transcript of the conversation between Supreme Court Judge Pairote Navanuch, Supreme Court Secretaray Virat Chinvinijkul and a senior government official on the eve of the 2006 Election Commission dismissal, see Asian Legal Resource Centre (2007).
11 Decision No. 3–5/2550 (2007).
12 Quoted from the English translation in: Borwonsak (2009: 36).
13 Decision No. 3–5, 2550 (2007).
14 Decision No. 12–13/2551 (2008).
15 Decision No. 20/2551(2008).
16 Court Order 592/2552 (2009).
17 Case No. 1/2553 (2010).
18 Decision No. 15/2553 (2009); in: *European–Asian Journal of Law and Governance (EJALG)*, vol. 1, no. 1 (Summer 2011), pp. 133–64.
19 Constitutional Court judge Boonsong Kulbupha's request for a transfer was widely interpreted as motivated by the growing politicization of the court, see 'Constitution Court judge "wants out"', *Bangkok Post*, 24 July 2008.

References

Asian Legal Resource Centre (2007) 'Recording of conversation between Supreme Court Judge Pairote Navanuch, Supreme Court Secretary Virat Chinvinijkul and a senior government official on the eve of the 2006 Election Commission dismissal', Article 2, 6: 64–8.

Banjerd, S. (1998) *Das Thäilandische Verfassungstribunal im Vergleich mit der Deutschen Verfassungsgerichtsbarkeit [The Thai Constitutional Tribunal in Comparison to the German Constitutional Court System]*, Frankfurt am Main, Berlin, Bern, New York, Vienna: Lang Verlag.

Borwornsak, U. (2009) *Economic Crisis and Political Crisis in Thailand: Past and Present*, Bangkok: King Prajadhipok's Institute.

Chai, A. S. (2002) *State-Building, Democracy and Globalization*, Bangkok: IPPS.

Chaturon, C. (2009) *Thai Democracy in Crisis: 27 Truths*, Bangkok: A. R. Information & Publication Co., Ltd.

Clayton, C. W. and Gillman, H. (eds) (1999) *Supreme Court Decision Making: New Institutionalist Approaches*, Chicago: University of Chicago Press.

Connors, M. K. (1999) 'Political reform and the state in Thailand', *Journal of Contemporary Southeast Asia* 29: 202–26.

Connors, M. K. (2002) 'Framing the "People's Constitution"' in McCargo, D. (ed.), *Reforming Thai Politics*, Copenhagen: NIAS.

Connors, M. K. (2008) 'Article of faith: The failure of royal liberalism in Thailand', *Journal of Contemporary Asia* 38: 143–65.

Dressel, B. (2009) 'Thailand's elusive quest for a constitutional equilibrium, 1997–2007', *Contemporary Southeast Asia* 31: 296–325.

Dressel, B. (2010a) 'When notions of legitimacy conflict: The case of Thailand', *Politics and Policy* 38: 445–69.

Dressel, B. (2010b) 'Judicialization of Politics or Politicization of the Judiciary in Asia? Considerations from recent events in Thailand', *The Pacific Review*, vol. 23, no. 5, pp. 671–691.

Ginsburg, T. (2003) *Judicial Review in New Democracies. Constitutional Courts in Asian Cases*, Cambridge: Cambridge University Press.

Ginsburg, T. (2009) 'Constitutional afterlife: The continuing impact of Thailand's post-political constitution', *International Journal of Constitutional Law* 7: 83–105.

Ginsburg, T. and Elkins, E. (2009) 'Ancillary powers of constitutional courts', *Texas Law Review* 87: 1431–61.

Graber, M. A. (1993) 'The nonmajoritarian difficulty: Legislative deference to the judiciary', *Studies in American Political Development* 7: 35–73.

Graham, W. A. (1924) *Siam: A Handbook of Practical, Commercial, and Political Information*, 3rd edition, London: Alexander Moring Limited, The De La More Press, vol. 1, pp. 372–3.

Harding, A. (2001) 'May there be virtue. New Asian constitutionalism in Thailand', *Australian Journal of Asian Law* 3: 236–60.

Harding, A. (2010) 'The Constitutional Court of Thailand 1998–2006. A turbulent innovation', in Harding, A. and Nicholson, P. (eds), *New Courts in Asia*, Oxford and New York: Routledge.

Hewison, K. (2007) 'Constitutions, regimes and power in Thailand', *Democratization* 14: 928–45.

Hilbink, L. (2009) 'The constituted nature of constituents' interests: Historical and ideational factors in judicial empowerment', *Political Science Research Quarterly* 62: 781–97.

Hirschl, R. (2004) *Towards Juristocracy: The Origins and Consequences of the New Constitutionalism*, Cambridge, MA: Harvard University Press.

Hirschl, R. (2006) 'The new constitutionalism and the judicialization of pure politics worldwide', *Fordham Law Review* 75: 721–54.

Hirschl, R. (2008a) 'The judicialization of mega-politics and the rise of political courts', *Annual Review of Political Science* 11: 93–118.

Hirschl, R. (2008b) 'The judicialization of politics', in Whittington, K. E., Kelemen, D. R. and Caldeira, G. A. (eds), *The Oxford Handbook of Law and Politics*, Oxford and New York: Oxford University Press.

Institute of Developing Economies (2001) 'The judicial system in Thailand: An outlook for a new century', available online at: www.ide.go.jp/English/Publish/Download/Als/pdf/06.pdf.

Kittisak, P. (2011) 'Remarks on ruling of the Thai Constitutional Court No. 12–13/2551', *European–Asian Journal of Law and Governance* 1: 123–32.

Klein, J. R. (2003) 'The battle for the rule of law in Thailand: The Constitutional Court of Thailand', in Raksasataya, A. and Klein, J. R. (eds), *The Constitutional Court of Thailand. The Provisions and the Working of the Court*, Bangkok: Constitution for the People Society.

Leyland, P. (2008) 'Thailand's constitutional watchdogs: Dobermans, bloodhounds or lapdogs?', *Journal of Comparative Law* 2: 151–77.

Leyland, P. (2009) 'The emergence of administrative justice in Thailand under the 1997 constitution', in Ginsburg, T. and Chen A. H. Y. (eds), *Administrative Law and Governance in Asia*, New York: Routledge.

Lovell, G. I. (2003) *Legislative Deferrals: Statutory Ambiguity, Judicial Power, and American Democracy*, New York: Cambridge University Press.

Matichon (2006) 'Thirayudh Boonmi chu tulakanphiwat kae wikhrit-pathirup kanmuang' [Thirayudh Boonmi pushes judicialization to solve crisis and reform politics], June 1.

McCargo, D. (2003) 'Balancing the checks: Thailand's paralysed politics post 1997', *Journal of East Asian Studies* 3: 129–52.

McCargo, D. (2005) 'Network monarchy and legitimacy crisis in Thailand', *Pacific Review* 18: 499–518.

McCargo, D. (2008) 'Thailand. State of anxiety'. In Singh, D. and Salazar L. C. (eds), *Southeast Asian Affairs 2008*, Singapore: Institute of South East Asian Studies.

McCargo, D. (ed.) (2002) *Reforming Thai Politics*, Copenhagen: NIAS.

Montesano, M. (2007) 'Thailand: A reckoning with history begins'. In Singh, D. and Salazar, L. C. (eds), *Southeast Asian Affairs 2007*, Singapore: Institute of Southeast Asian Affairs.

Nelson, M. H. (2006) 'Political turmoil in Thailand: Thaksin, protests, elections, and the king', *eastasia.at* 5(1).

Ockey, J. (2009) 'Thailand in 2008: Democracy and street politics'. in Singh, D. (ed.), *Southeast Asian Affairs*, Singapore: ISEAS.

Pasuk, P. and Baker, C. (2002) *Thailand: Economy and Politics. 2nd ed.*, Kuala Lumpur: Oxford University Press.

Pasuk P. and Baker, C. (2004) *Thaksin. The Business of Politics in Thailand*, Bangkok: Silkworm Books.

Pasuk P. and Baker, C. (2005). 'Business populism" in Thailand', *Journal of Democracy* 16: 58–72.

Pasuk, P. and Sungsidh, P. (1996) *Corruption and Democracy in Thailand*, Chiang Mai: Silkworm Books.

Pavin, C. (2010) 'Verdict on Thaksin's billions: An inherently catch 22 situation?', *The Straits Times*, 18 February.

Phatra Securities (2009) 'Research notes, Thailand economics: Prospects for 2010',

3 December, available online at: www2.phatradirect.com/phatra/Research/upload/0000105005/1202ECON-2010%20forecast.pdf (accessed 21 January 2010).

Pinai, N. (2002) 'Comparative constitutionalism: The remaking of the constitutional orders in South-East Asia', *Singapore Journal of International & Comparative Law* 6: 90–116.

Piyabutr, S. (2008) 'The Judiciary and Democracy', *Prachatai*, 20 April, available online at: http://prachatai.com/english/node/601 (accessed 15 January 2010).

Sieder, R., Schjolden, L. and Angell, A. (eds) (2005) *The Judicialization of Politics in Latin America*, New York and Houndmills: Palgrave Macmillan.

Stone Sweet, A. (2000) *Governing with Judges: Constitutional Politics in Europe*, Oxford: Oxford University Press.

Suchit B. (2009) 'Democracy and rule of law in Thailand: Judicialization of politics or politicization of the judiciary', lecture at Georgetown Law School, 5 November, at www.thaiconsulatela.org/pdf/PM-DemocracyandRule.pdf (accessed 6 February 2012).

Tate, N. C. (1994) 'The judicialization of politics in the Philippines and Southeast Asia', *International Political Science Review* 15: 187–97.

Tate, N. C. and Vallinder, T. (eds) (1995) *The Global Expansion of Judicial Power*, New York: New York University Press.

Whittington, K. E. (2007) *Political Foundations of Judicial Supremacy: The Presidency, the Supreme Court, and Constitutional Leadership in U.S. History*, Princeton: Princeton University Press.

Worachet P. (2009) *Choodfai Nai Sailom [Ignite in the Wind]*, Edited by A. Sawaengsook, Bangkok: Openbooks.

6 Indonesia's Constitutional Court

Conservative activist or strategic operator?

Simon Butt

For three decades under Soeharto (1966–98) Indonesia was an authoritarian state. There were no effective checks, institutional or democratic, on the exercise of government power. Formally, the state was bound by the 1945 Constitution, but the judiciary lacked power to enforce it and was not independent (Lev 1978; Pompe 2005). The government, usually with military support, strictly controlled elections, directly appointed members of national assemblies, restricted the activities of opposition parties, curtailed or extinguished political freedoms, controlled the media, and repressed dissent, often violently (Budiman 1994; Lubis 1993).

Since Soeharto resigned in May 1998, however, Indonesia has undergone an enormous number of constitutional, democratic, and decentralising reforms (Hosen 2010). The Constitution now contains a Bill of Rights that draws on the Universal Declaration of Human Rights (Lindsey 2002). The electoral system was overhauled, and many new political parties have emerged to participate in free and fair elections (see www.freedomhouse.org). Many functions of government—including some lawmaking powers—have been devolved to almost 500 governments in provinces, districts, and cities.

Critical to the overhaul of the Indonesian polity has been judicial reform, notably the establishment in 2003 of the Constitutional Court (the MK: *Mahkamah Konstitusi*).[1] The MK has four functions that place it at the forefront of Indonesian politics and legal and democratic progress:

1. Constitutional review: The MK ensures that statutes passed by Indonesia's national parliament comply with the constitution. It is the only court to have had this power since Indonesian independence was declared in 1945.[2]
2. Investigate allegations of electoral impropriety or error and if necessary reallocate parliamentary seats.
3. Resolve disputes about the jurisdictions of state institutions and the dissolution of political parties.
4. 'Provide a decision' if the national parliament suspects that the president or vice-president has committed treason or corruption, another serious crime or form of misconduct, or otherwise no longer fulfils the constitutional requirements for holding office.

This chapter seeks to assess what the MK has contributed to Indonesian constitutionalism and democracy. It also attempts to situate the court within the typology of judicial politics outlined in the introduction. Given its celebrated independence (Butt and Lindsey 2008; Butt 2007b) the court clearly does not fall into the judicial muteness or politicised category. At first blush, it might seem to fit comfortably within the judicial activism category: It has confidently decided 'mega-politics' disputes—particularly democracy-related cases, such as electoral and candidacy disputes. It has upheld the new Bill of Rights, notably rights related to freedom of speech and the right to vote, and has declared invalid laws that it found to conflict with it. In particular, the court has entered the debate about the role of religion in the Indonesian state—perhaps the most vexed political issue in modern Indonesian history. The MK has even identified constitutional rights and state obligations not spelled out in the Constitution and then upheld them or enforced them against the state. It has also resisted parliamentary attempts to restrict its jurisdiction.

On the other hand, in some cases the court has worked to avoid striking down statutes even after deciding they were unconstitutional. For instance, it has limited decisions so that they only become operative into the future, allowing unconstitutional statutes to remain in force for a specified time and declaring statutes 'conditionally constitutional' or 'conditionally unconstitutional'.

Such measures might be considered attributes of a politicised rather than an activist court. At first blush, they seem to indicate that the court has respect for the legislature and wants to cause it as little disruption as possible. But I intend to demonstrate here that most of the MK's avoidance measures reflect a strategic pragmatism that may in the long run allow the court not just to maintain but perhaps even intensify its activism. I argue, in fact, that the MK's declarations of conditional constitutionality or unconstitutionality are disguised activism. In these decisions, even though the court does not strike down provisions of a statute before it, it often does effect de facto legal change by requiring that the statute be interpreted in a specific way. In doing so it often functions as a sort of second parliament, amending legislation to ensure that it complies with the Constitution. But the 2003 Constitutional Court Law was itself amended in 2011 in a way that, I argue, seeks to prevent the court from continuing to issue conditional constitutionality decisions. So perhaps this avenue of activism is now closed off.

I begin by discussing the history behind the court's establishment and factors that seem to drive its approach to its work. I then examine its activism and 'avoidance measures' by discussing key decisions in electoral disputes and judicial review applications. Finally, I assess the effects the court's activism has had on the Indonesian polity.

Background

Mietzner (2010) finds the roots of the MK in political disputes that occurred immediately after Soeharto's departure that underlined the need for new mechanisms to resolve political conflict. He comments that 'Key socio-political forces quarrelled over unclear laws and regulations, triggering conflicts that threatened to derail the democratisation process' (Mietzner 2010: 410).

The much-contested 1999 general election result is an example of such a conflict (Mietzner 2010: 410), but the conflict most often cited as leading to the establishment of the court was the 'constitutional crisis' surrounding former President Abdurrahman Wahid's removal from office in 2001 (Lindsey 2002: 244; Harijanti and Lindsey 2006: 147; Widjojanto 2004: 211; Asshiddiqie 2004: 11). Wahid's party had obtained only 13 percent of the vote in the 1999 general election but for various reasons the People's Consultative Assembly (MPR: *Majelis Permusyawaratan Rakyat*) saw him as an acceptable compromise president. But Wahid found it difficult to cobble together the parliamentary majorities he needed to get laws passed, and by mid 2001 the wheels of government had largely ground to a halt (Lindsey 2002: 257). Wahid was also implicated in corruption scandals. Fearing that the MPR would try to remove him, he sought pre-emptively to dissolve parliament but was unable to convince the military to support him. Instead, the MPR did remove him and installed Megawati. The affair was marked by so much confusion and controversy that it provoked heavy debate about the need for an impartial institution to help settle high matters of state.

Such disputes account only for the court's powers to decide electoral disputes and parliamentary impeachment motions, however. They do not explain why the court was given judicial review powers—one of its most important and most active functions.

Ever since independence Indonesian judges, lawyers, and scholars had been arguing that the Indonesian Supreme Court or a specific-purpose Constitutional Court was needed to ensure that laws enacted by parliament conformed to the Constitution (Lev 1978; Husein 2005: 72–3; Asshiddiqie 2004: 5), but Soeharto had put in place structural and ideological mechanisms that effectively quashed reform (Butt 2007b). The regime leaned heavily on a national mantra that economic development (*pembangungan*) required political stability, which dissent and opposition would undermine.

This was reinforced by the way some New Order government ideologues interpreted the national ideology, *Pancasila*,[3] as being aligned with the concept of 'integralism'. Professor Soepomo, a distinguished legal scholar, had proposed this as a basis for the Indonesian state during constitutional debates in the lead-up to independence in 1945 (Feith and Castles 1970). Integralism enshrined the concept that state and citizens together constituted a single entity (see generally Simanjuntak 1994). According to Soepomo, because the state was at one with the people, it must be sensitive to the community sense of justice, but it must also transcend all groups in every field. This totalitarian or integralistic ideal required a firm executive. There was also no need to protect individual human rights from the state because the individual was an organic part of the state. Neither *pembangunan* nor *Pancasila* left any space for opposition to the government in the form of judicial review, let alone judicial independence.

When Soeharto fell, the *pembangunan* mantra and his interpretation of *Pancasila* fell into deep disfavour, previously centralised power was dispersed, and important structural reforms were made to Indonesia's judicial system. A raft of new statutes was enacted relating to the Supreme Court and the courts below it. A primary purpose of these 'one-roof' (*satu atap*) reforms was to provide a legal basis for the transfer of control over the organisational, administrative, and financial affairs of the lower courts from the executive branch to the Supreme Court.[4] This, it was hoped, would help improve judicial independence by releasing the courts from the formerly tight supervision under Soeharto.

The effective allocation of the power of the state to a number of sources—particularly a democratically elected parliament and the courts—has dismantled the core feature of the integralistic state: political power concentrated in the hands of the president and his elite (Waddell 2005: 52). In these conditions reformist calls for judicial review, no longer repressed, carried great force.

Establishing a new court with jurisdiction to check government power and decide electoral disputes had great popular and parliamentary support—it seemed one way of ensuring that post-Soeharto Indonesia did not slip back into authoritarianism (Eldridge 2001; ICG 2001). Simply granting the Supreme Court jurisdiction to resolve electoral and institutional disputes, hear judicial review applications, and consider impeachment motions was not a viable option. Even though its independence was to be formally enshrined in the Constitution and new laws, the Supreme Court's reputation for impartiality and competence was in tatters after decades of institutional neglect and corruption (Pompe 2005). The only choice, it seemed, was to establish a new court to exercise these powers.

The political conflicts, the reconfiguration of the Indonesian polity, and post-Soeharto *reformasi* fervour combined to support establishment of the MK. In particular, the mechanism for appointments to the MK was designed to ensure the independence of its judges. The three primary arms of government—the national parliament, the president, and the Supreme Court—each choose three judges for the nine-judge bench.[5] This mechanism has produced a diverse bench—judges have been academics, former judges, politicians, even retired army officers; it is also said to make judges feel more secure in handing down decisions that might not please their nominating institution in that they can be selected for a second term by one of the other arms of government (Mietzner 2010: 404).

Many of the court's achievements—particularly the reputation it has acquired for being trustworthy and competent—are attributable to the skill and commitment of its founding chief justice, Jimly Asshiddique, who had been a respected professor of constitutional law at the University of Indonesia. From the moment the court went into operation, Assiddique was able to draw significant political support for it even though its very function was to restrict the exercise of political power. Though the MK's beginnings were humble,[6] it now has a sizeable budget that allows it to pay its judges and staff more than those of other judicial institutions—even the Supreme Court—and that funded construction of one of the most impressive buildings of any state institution since Soeharto's fall (Mietzner 2010: 405).

Asshiddique was also undoubtedly instrumental in ensuring that MK decisions are better reasoned and more accessible than the decisions of other courts, though often the legal reasoning remains questionable (Butt 2007b,

2011). In particular, under his leadership the court set out some of the jurisprudence discussed below, for instance by deciding that Indonesia's version of the rule of law (the *negara hukum*, 'law state') is a constitutional principle from which rights and obligations flow, and by upholding human rights and democratic principles. Under a different leader the MK might well have taken a more conservative path. That would not have been surprising given Indonesia's history of judicial subordination to government.

Asshiddique resolutely and successfully guarded the integrity of the court, and Mahfud, his successor, followed that precedent. Though most other Indonesian judges are generally assumed to be corrupt, the integrity of MK judges has not been seriously questioned, although there have been allegations of impropriety. In October 2010 it was alleged that an MK judge had been bribed with one billion rupiah in an electoral case, but a fact-finding team was unable to find any corroborating evidence (Savitri 2010; Desyana 2010). In another 'scandal', Judge Arsyad Sanusi resigned in February 2011 after it was alleged that his daughter and son-in-law had accepted bribes from an applicant in a 2009 Constitutional Court case. Again, after investigation no proof was found that Justice Sanusi even knew about the bribe, let alone received it. Nevertheless, he decided to resign to sustain the court's reputation (*Hukumonline* 2011a).

Judicialisation?

I now turn to several of the most high-profile and controversial cases the MK has handed down, starting with judicial review cases, in which it has struck down legislation impeding human rights mentioned in the Constitution; imposed unwritten constitutional obligations upon the state; and even assessed government economic policy and budget allocations. (It is not possible here to give detailed consideration to the court's reasoning, however.) I then turn to democracy-related cases—disputes about vote-counting, the constitutionality of electoral laws, and candidacy.

Judicial review

Article 50 cases. From its earliest days the MK has resisted parliamentary attempts to limit exercise of its jurisdiction. Article 50 of the MK Law—the statute that established the court and covers its composition and procedures—limits the court to reviewing statutes enacted after the first amendment to the Constitution in 1999. In a series of cases, a majority of the MK first ignored and later invalidated Article 50.[7] It held that because the Constitution imposed no such limitation upon the exercise of its jurisdiction, parliament could not seek to impose it. The MK has reviewed many statutes enacted well before 1999.

Human rights. By invalidating national legislation the MK has upheld a number of the human rights listed in the Bill of Rights. It has, for example, upheld the rights to free speech,[8] to be free from the operation of retrospective laws,[9] to access information,[10] and to be free from discrimination.[11]

However, the court has also regularly applied Article 28J(2) of the Constitution, which states, 'When exercising their rights and freedoms, each person must submit to limits determined by legislation with the sole purpose of guaranteeing recognition and respect for the rights of others'.

In these cases, the court has avoided striking down the statute in dispute, on the grounds that it is directed towards protecting the human rights of others or has another purpose, such as public order.[12]

Implied rights and state obligations. In several cases, based primarily on two constitutional provisions the MK has imposed obligations on the state that the MK found to be implicit rather than explicit in the Constitution. The first provision is the preamble, which states that the government is 'to protect all Indonesians and their native land and to further public welfare, the intellectual life of the people, and to contribute to the world order of freedom, peace and social justice'. The second is Article 1(3), which states that Indonesia is subject to the rule of law. From these provisions the MK has implied broad state obligations, including obligations to protect citizens from corruption,[13] to protect the domestic broadcasting industry from foreign domination,[14] and to provide a fair trial, access to justice, legal aid and the presumption of innocence.[15] It has done this largely without fanfare and without stirring controversy about whether it is overstepping its jurisdictional boundaries.

Economic rights and issues. Article 33 of the Constitution requires that the economy be structured as a 'common endeavour' and that the state control natural resources and sectors that provide the necessities of life. On several occasions, the MK has been asked to consider whether that article provides scope for privatisation of important industries and natural resources, namely electricity, oil and natural gas, forestry resources, and water. In its first case in this area, for example, the court decided that the 2002 Electricity Law, which sought to loosen state control of the sector and allow for significant private ownership and involvement, fell foul of Article 33.[16] It invalidated the entire statute.

By contrast, in the Water Resources (SDA) Law case, the majority upheld the constitutionality of the statute, finding that it did not in fact relinquish government control over water resources.[17] The law, the judges said, had merely made it possible for the state to grant to the private sector a right to exploit water. The government retained power to make policy and regulations, manage water resources, and grant permits for water exploitation.

These cases raise questions about the extent to which the court should engage, if at all, in public policy debate. On the one hand, the court has strongly emphasised that it lacks jurisdiction to assess state or government policies conveyed through legislation.[18] Yet surely in these cases it has done just that. In the Electricity Law case in particular, the MK stance seems to have been that privatisation cannot guarantee the prosperity of the people, as required by Article 33(2) (Butt and Lindsey 2008).

Education budget. The Indonesian Constitution requires that the national parliament allocate at least 20 percent of the state budget to education. The Indonesian Teachers' Association and others regularly asked the court, in cases filed almost annually since 2004, to invalidate state budgets that fail to meet this target.[19] (Because the budget is a statute, the court can assess it.) These cases are about as straightforward as legal cases can be: the constitutional target seems clear; the budget does not meet the target; therefore, the budget does not comply with the Constitution. Realising, however, that budgets are hotly political and usually delicately balanced, each year the court has declined to invalidate them, citing the likelihood of ensuing financial chaos. Instead, the court has urged the government to increase the budget allocation for education from year to year. The national parliament eventually allocated 20 percent of the state budget to education starting in 2009, though partly by including teacher salaries in the calculation (Desafti 2010).

Freedom of religion and the place of Islam. The Constitution confirms the right to freedom of religion in at least three different places. Article 29(1) says that the 'state guarantees the freedom of every person to embrace their respective religion and to worship in accordance with that religion'; Article 28E(1) says that the 'state is to guarantee the independence of every citizen to embrace their respective religion and to worship in accordance with that religion and belief'; and Article 28I(1) says that this right 'cannot be limited in any way'.

Indonesia has more Muslims than any other nation, and about 90 percent of its estimated 240 million people consider themselves Muslims. Yet Indonesia is not an Islamic state. It is a country of significant diversity—ethnic and linguistic as well as religious. Even within Indonesian Islam there is significant diversity of thought and belief (Feener 2007). The government recognises and enforces Islamic rules against Muslims in limited fields—primarily family matters and Islamic finance—but the rules have been watered down to reflect moderate interpretations of *Syariah*. Still, the place of Islam is a very sensitive issue that the state usually seeks to avoid as far as possible (Butt 2010a).

Some Indonesian Muslims, said to be a minority, still seek a greater place for Islam and more conservative Islamic law in the Indonesian state and government. For many of them, Islam provides a comprehensive set of rules—civil, criminal, and public—for life. Some have brought challenges before the MK to what they see as state interference in their right to religious freedom (Butt 2010a). The court appears to have been concerned to douse such arguments and maintain the status quo.

Polygamy has been one controversial issue. Indonesian law does not ban polygamy. It is permitted, but only with the consent of a religious court. The law makes obtaining such consent difficult. In one case a man sought to challenge these polygamy restrictions.[20] He argued that Islam required him to observe Islamic law and that, in the interpretation he followed, Islamic law permitted polygamy. The restrictions were therefore unconstitutional.

Surprisingly, in its decision the MK focused on Islamic law rather than the right to religious freedom. After discussing various Koranic verses, the court found that Islamic law did not in fact require polygamy. It also decided that the state had authority, under Islamic law, to set requirements for citizens who wanted to enter into a polygamous marriage. In any event the state had not prohibited polygamy.

In another MK case[21] a young graduate of an Islamic school (*Madrasah*) in Serang, Banten, argued that full adherence to Islam required full adherence to the corpus of Islamic law, including matters of public law and criminal law and its punishments. The relief he sought was to expand the jurisdiction of the religious courts so that he could realise his constitutional rights. Not surprisingly, the MK rejected this claim, pointing out that under the Constitution the national legislature had power to limit the jurisdiction of all Indonesian courts. The Court concluded:

> Indonesia is not a religious state which is based only on one religion; but Indonesia is also not a secular state which does not consider religion at all. It does not hand over all religious affairs entirely to individuals and the community. Indonesia is a state which is based on the Almighty God. The state protects [the rights of] all religious adherents to carry out the teachings of their respective religions. In relation to the philosophy of Pancasila, national law must guarantee the integrity of the ideology and the integration of the nation and develop religious tolerance based on justice and civility. National law, therefore, can be an integrating factor which is a glue and unifier of the nation. The state's service to citizens does not depend on whether adherents to a particular religion, ethnic group, or race are in the majority or minority.
>
> (3.18)

Democracy-related cases

A number of MK cases have involved democracy-related issues, such as disputed election returns, candidacy, and disputes about the electoral system generally.[22]

Disputed returns. After the 2004 and 2009 elections for the national legislature almost all the competing political parties filed objections with the MK that eventually numbered in the hundreds (Harijanti and Lindsey 2006: 148; Mahfud 2009: 27–9; Asshiddiqie 2009: 11; Sukma 2009: 322). Most alleged 'irregularities', ranging from the deliberate and illegal, such as fraud, to the inadvertent and unavoidable, such as counting errors and logistical problems (Ramage 2007: 136, 138; Webber 2006: 399; Sukma 2009: 325). In 2004 the court upheld 38 of 252 petitions; in 2009 it upheld 70 of 657 (Mietzner 2010: 407).

The MK has also settled complaints brought by presidential candidates. For instance, Wiranto, former commander-in-chief of the Indonesian Army (TNI: *Tentara Nasional Indonesia*), ran for president in 2004, lost, and challenged the results (Harijanti and Lindsey, 2006: 140). In 2009 he was back before the court for the same reason, though this time as the running mate of Jusuf Kalla, former vice-president to Susilo Bambang Yudhoyono. Also in 2009 former President Megawati Soekarnoputri and her vice-presidential candidate, Prabowo Subianto, challenged the presidential election results. The court rejected all these cases, and the plaintiffs accepted its decisions (Mietzner 2010: 407).

Candidacy cases. The MK has also ruled on whether particular individuals can stand as candidates. In 2004, for example, former President Abdurrahman Wahid unsuccessfully challenged a statute that appeared to prohibit him from standing for president again on the basis that he was physically incapable of performing the role (Harijanti and Lindsey 2006: 140). Of more note was a 2004 case in which the court decided that people who had been members of the Indonesian Communist Party or other prohibited organisations, or had been involved in the 1965 coup could be nominated for candidature in local, regional, and national elections.[23] Strictly speaking, this was a judicial review case, however, because the MK decision invalidated legislation that prohibited these groups from being nominated. According to the court, the law breached the constitutional right of Indonesians to participate in government and to be free from discrimination.

In two separate cases,[24] applicants challenged provisions of Law 10 of 2008 on Elections for the National Parliament, Regional Representative Council, and Local Parliaments that prohibited candidates from running if they have been convicted of a crime that carried a maximum of five years' imprisonment. The court decided the provisions were conditionally constitutional—that is, constitutional as long as they were not applied to political crimes and minor offences.

The *sisa suara* case. Under Indonesia's electoral laws, the number of votes required for each parliamentary seat (the 'seat threshold', *Bilangan Pembagi Pemilihan*), national or regional, is determined by dividing the number of registered voters in an electoral area by the number of seats allocated to that area. Once votes meet the threshold, a party obtains a seat. Of course, not all seats can be filled in this 'first phase': some parties will not receive enough votes to obtain a seat; others obtain seats but their 'left over' votes are insufficient to obtain a further seat. The court was asked to determine how 'surplus votes' (*sisa suara*) would be used to allocate parliamentary seats.[25]

This dispute concerned the way the Indonesian Electoral Commission (KPU: *Komisi Pemilihan Umum*) chose to allocate these surplus seats in this 'second phase'. The KPU had decided, by internal regulation (Reg. 15 of 2009), that the remaining seats would be allocated more or less proportionally by reference to the surplus votes alone. Votes used to obtain a seat in the first phase were in effect exhausted and could not be used again in this second round.

Several members of the Democratic Party (PK: *Partai Demokrat*) who had missed out on a seat because of this allocation method asked the Supreme Court to assess whether the regulation complied with Indonesia's Legislative Election Law (Law 10 of 2008). The Supreme Court decided that it did not, interpreting the law to require that seats left over from the first phase be allocated by reference to the proportion of all the votes a party received, including those that had already gone towards obtaining a seat. This result clearly favoured major parties because their votes would, in effect, be counted twice: once to determine whether they had met the quota for a seat and again when the proportion of votes they had obtained overall would be used to determine how many surplus seats they would obtain. The Supreme Court decision was clearly significant: 66 seats in the national parliament (DPR: *Dewan Perwakilan Raykat*) would need to be reallocated and about 1,300 in regional parliaments. President Susilo Bambang Yudhoyono's PD would have benefited most, gaining an additional 31 seats, and Megawati's PDI-P and Golkar would have gained about 16 to 19 seats each.

Several parties that would have lost seats under this arrangement appealed to the MK. The court upheld their claim, holding that the Legislative Election Law, which the disputed KPU regulation had sought to implement, was so unclear as to fall foul of the constitutional guarantee of 'legal certainty'. Instead of invalidating the provisions, however, the court held them to be 'conditionally constitutional'—that is, valid as long as they are applied in terms of the MK's interpretation of them. Pointing to recent scholarship on the rights of minorities in democracies, the court held that parties with 50 percent or more of the threshold would receive a seat. If seats remained, these would be allocated in a third phase. The MK's interpretation resembles the KPU regulation that the Supreme Court had struck down. To do otherwise, the MK noted, would allow a vote that had already been converted into a seat to be used twice—something that had no place in a proportional electoral system like Indonesia's that is based on democratic principles.

Electoral roll case.[26] The MK was asked to invalidate Articles 28 and 111(1) of Law 42 of 2008 on Presidential and Vice-Presidential Elections which required citizens to register with the KPU in order to vote. The court decided that the constitutional right to vote could not be impeded by administrative requirements. It ordered that citizens who held a valid identity card or passport had to be allowed to vote even if they were not on the electoral roll.

Timidity and conservatism?[27]

Although it has attracted support and respect from the Indonesian public and the legal sector, the MK has regularly faced hostility to its decisions from politicians. This is hardly surprising: until the court was established, government officials and parliamentarians were accustomed to operating largely unscrutinised, and they were certainly not used to having their laws invalidated.

From its earliest days it became clear that the MK needed to find ways to soften the effect of its decisions on the legislature. If the court failed to accommodate the environment in which it operated, it faced irrelevance and disrespect (if it continued to make decisions that the government ignored or circumvented) or even disbandment (if powerful politicians became so irritated by its decisions that they moved to have the court dissolved). Several institutions born during the post-Soeharto *reformasi* fervour had trod less carefully, prompting a political backlash strong enough to threaten their efficacy and in some cases their very existence (Butt 2007a, 2011).

In its very first reported case the MK struck down Law 20 of 2002 on electricity.[28] The law had been enacted for several reasons. One was to increase the power and reach of Indonesia's electricity network. (Indonesia's electrification rate is around 65 percent, one of the lowest in the region.) Another was that

International Monetary Fund (IMF) financial assistance for resuscitating Indonesia's economy after the financial crisis of 1997 was contingent on Indonesia meeting various 'conditionalities', one of which was privatisation of various areas of the electricity sector. The Electricity Law therefore sought to break down the state monopoly of the provision of electricity.

The MK's decision was not well received by members of the legislature and the executive. Politicians strenuously criticized the court, charging that it lacked the expertise to make decisions about matters of economic policy; with only nine judges, it was also argued, the MK lacked democratic legitimacy to invalidate the statutes of a 550-member elected parliament. Moreover, the court had prevented the government from complying with the IMF conditionalities without considering the consequences; and privatisation was in any case critical to ensure that Indonesia would have sufficient electricity to meet demand.

The response was decisive. Within two months of the decision, the government had issued a regulation that in effect reinstated the thrust of the invalidated law. Because it was similar to the Electricity Law, it is probable that the regulation also breaches Article 33 of the Constitution. But the MK has no jurisdiction to examine the legality of government regulations; it can only assess the constitutionality of statutes.

Strategic pragmatism

Since the Electricity Law case, the MK has adopted at least four techniques that appear geared towards making its decisions more politically palatable, particularly to the legislature. Here the Indonesian court is not alone; many continental European states employ similar techniques (Stone Sweet 2000; Nardini 1999; Koopmans 2003). However, on closer inspection, in Indonesia at least most of these techniques are pragmatism in disguise; they might even be considered hidden activism.

One way the MK has softened the impact of its decisions is by declaring that they will operate only into the future. In other words, even if the court finds that a law is inconsistent with the Constitution, its invalidation operates only from the date the court hands down its decision. Anything done under the law before then is not tainted by the illegality and so does not need be to 'undone'. An example of the ramifications of this approach is the Bali Bombing case,[29] where the MK decided that the law under which the Bali bombers were investigated and ultimately convicted was unconstitutional because it was enacted after the bombings took place, breaching the constitutional prohibition on criminal laws with retrospective application. However, it was not necessary to set the Bali bombers free or retry them. Because they had been convicted under the law before the MK invalidated it, their convictions stood.

This tempering technique is highly problematic: there seems little to be gained from asking the court to assess whether a law is consistent with the Constitution if an applicant cannot use a favourable MK decision to force the government to undo an action it has taken. Only people to whom the unconstitutional law would be applied in the future gain from the benevolence of the applicant whose approach to the MK led to the law being struck off the books. Meanwhile, the government can pass a law that egregiously breaches human rights and apply it with impunity until someone asks the MK to strike it down. Even if the party is successful, any action taken under the law before the MK makes that decision will be considered 'legal'.

A second MK technique is to declare that a statute is not consistent with the Constitution but then refuse, because the consequences of invalidating it would be too great, to strike the law down, instead asking the government to make further attempts at compliance.[30] As we have seen, the court took this approach in the Education Budget cases. A third method is to declare that a statute breaches the Constitution but refuse to strike it immediately, choosing instead to set a deadline for the national parliament to pass a new, constitutional, law.

Since these first three techniques are probably themselves unconstitutional or otherwise illegal, they raise significant questions about the court and its role. The Constitution requires the MK to ensure that the national parliament follows the Constitution. When the parliament fails to do so and the court chooses not to intervene (as in the budget cases) or chooses to give a deadline for the parliament to replace an unconstitutional law, it seems to be failing to do its duty. It is allowing laws to continue in force that it has determined are beyond the parliament's lawmaking power. Further, by giving its decisions prospective effect only, the court seems to implicitly sanction actions the government may have already taken under an unconstitutional statute. On one view, then, the MK, though charged with enforcing the Constitution, is itself breaching it. This would appear to leave the rule of law—which requires at a minimum that the government, including the courts, abide by the law, particularly the Constitution—teetering on the brink of irrelevance.

Perhaps, though, such criticisms should be reserved for constitutional courts which, although operating in political systems in which judicial review and accountability mechanisms are well accepted and established, persist in using similar tempering techniques. It may be unfair to judge the MK using the standards of countries that have more compliant and respectful governments, and where political considerations are not so overwhelming. Perhaps because the court has shown enduring signs of promise, expectations of what it can achieve in Indonesia's political environment are simply unreasonably high. In my view, the MK's current approach is quite realistic. The court is building for itself a reputation for handing down impartial and reasoned decisions without drawing excessive pushback from government. As it establishes itself, and as government compliance with its decisions becomes the norm, it can begin issuing more zero-sum decisions. Ironically, then, the MK may be tempering its own activities to ensure its continuing activism. Perhaps if it is to have any chance of making the government follow the letter of the Constitution in the future, the court must itself deviate from the Constitution at least for now.

Expanding jurisdiction?

The final technique to be discussed is perhaps the one the MK uses most. In many cases the court has decided that a law is 'conditionally constitutional'—that is, it is constitutional and can stay on the books so long as it is implemented in a way the court thinks is constitutional.

The surplus votes case is one example of this. In another case,[31] the court declared that, although it had concerns about the Water Resources Law similar to those it had about the Electricity Law, the MK would not invalidate it provided that the government issued regulations which were consistent with the Constitution. In yet another case,[32] the court was asked to assess whether a law which allowed film censorship breached the constitutional right to free speech. The court criticised the law for being behind the times in terms of democracy and freedom of expression but nevertheless declared it to be conditionally constitutional—that is, constitutional provided the censorship board implemented it in ways that reflect democratic principles and human rights norms.

On the one hand the conditional constitutionality technique appears to show deference to parliament. With it the court airs the constitutional problems it has found in a statute but does not require that parliament take any action, thereby avoiding the time and effort associated with parliamentary processes. Action is required only of the party or institution that implements the law.

On the other hand, this method also seems to allow the MK in effect to amend statutes. Though often the court claims that it is not a 'positive legislator'—it can only invalidate unconstitutional laws—when it declares a statute to be conditionally constitutional, it seems to be assuming that very function. By imposing an interpretation of the law that differs from the terms of the law, it is in effect making a de facto change to the law (Butt 2011). Likewise, when the MK makes the constitutionality of a statute conditional upon its implementing regulations themselves being consistent with the court's interpretation of the statute, the MK appears to assume some form of control over regulations. Yet, as we saw with the Electricity Law case, it lacks jurisdiction to review regulations.

Conclusion

Despite being less than a decade old, the MK has proved itself to be critical to post-Soeharto electoral democracy and the move towards constitutionalism. Since Soeharto's fall, Indonesia has become one of the world's most democratic countries—certainly if the sheer number of elections held there is any indicator. Indonesians now vote in more free, fair, and competitive elections than citizens of 'nearly any other democracy' (Ramage 2007: 136).

Electoral democracy has brought new challenges, however. Indonesia's political landscape is highly fragmented. Seats are at a premium, making elections particularly competitive and leading to disputes about the results for which resolution is crucial. Scholars (Ipp and Hoverter 2005: 834; Williams 2007: 938) have argued that relatively peaceful elections in conflict-prone areas and highly pluralist states, such as Indonesia, are attributable at least in part to the availability of professional resolution of electoral disputes. Without enforceable political and democratic rights—and credible electoral contests, institutions, and dispute adjudication—the legitimacy of elections is at risk.

The MK has, it seems, done more than ensure that Indonesian elections are free and fair. It has been vital to keeping the peace between political parties and ensuring election legitimacy (Mietzner 2010). Contesting political parties have largely accepted its decisions (Ramage 2007: 138; Webber 2006: 339), presumably because the decisions were seen as professional and impartial. That is why members of the court refer to the MK as the 'guardian' of Indonesia's democracy (Mahfud 2009; Asshiddiqie 2009; Asshiddiqie 2008; Mahkamah Konsitusi 2009).

The judicial review decisions discussed show that the MK can be considered an activist court. It has struck down numerous statutory provisions for breaching the Constitution or the Bill of Rights. In so doing the MK has been instrumental in dismantling integralism and building a culture of constitutionalism among Indonesia's lawmakers. (By all accounts, MK decisions are forcing some parliamentarians to at least flick through the Constitution before they sign off on laws; and they are said to be making parliamentarians more careful about what they attempt in parliament and say in parliamentary debates, lest the MK ask for a transcript and reveal debates at trial for all to see.) And even though some of its tempering techniques may seem to reflect political compromise, they may indeed reflect the court expanding its jurisdiction but they may instead be necessary for the court to consolidate its position within the Indonesian polity.

Equally important is that the MK provides a very public forum in which high-order legal issues are openly explored and grievances between citizens and the government can be fully aired, if not always satisfactorily resolved. Its decisions are broadcast live on television and streamed over the Internet. Its tempering techniques do not seem to deter citizens, organisations, and other institutions from using it—they flock to the court to bring cases. Perhaps the court as a forum in which the government is held to account to citizens for the laws it makes is so far its greatest achievement.

Yet despite its activism approach to judicial review, it is easy to overstate the MK's contribution to Indonesian constitutionalism. Its powers are limited; it can review the constitutionality only of statutes enacted by the national parliament, although the bulk of Indonesian law is found in executive and departmental regulations, such as government and presidential regulations and ministerial decrees (Thoolen 1987: 58). It also lacks jurisdiction to review the many thousands of bylaws that local governments have enacted since the decentralisation reforms (Butt 2010b). Only the Supreme Court can review these types of 'lower-level' laws, and even then only in relation to statutes. There is, therefore, no judicial mechanism for testing the constitutionality of laws of a lower rank than statutes.[33] Yet the need for effective review of regulations is arguably more acute than for review of statutes, because regulations are often issued without parliamentary scrutiny and debate. Unless the MK's jurisdiction is expanded to cover them, in general constitutionalism in Indonesia will remain weak.

Recently, the national legislature has, in amendments to the Constitutional Court Law in 2011, struck back at the MK's conditional constitutionality decisions. Indeed, former Law and Human Rights Minister Patrialis Akbar introduced the amendments as being a step to prevent the court being a 'positive legislator' (Hukumonline 2011b). Of particular note is Article 57(2a) of the 2011 Amendment, which says

> Constitutional Court decisions are not to contain:
>
> a declarations other than those referred to in Article 57(1) and (2).
> b orders to lawmakers.
> c formulations or norms to replace the norms of legislation that are declared to conflict with the Constitution.

Articles 57(1) and (2) state:

> 1 If the Constitutional Court declares that the contents of a subsection, provision and/or part of a statute conflict with the Constitution, then the contents of that subsection, provision and/or part of the statute no longer have binding force.
> 2 If the Constitutional Court declares that requirements, based on the Constitution, for the enactment of the statute were not fulfilled, then that statute no longer has binding force.

Article 57(2a) appears to squarely confront the MK's declarations of conditional constitutionality and unconstitutionality. When it has made the constitutionality of a provision subject to its interpretation in a specific way—such as by adding or deleting parts of the provision—the court indeed seems to be replacing parliamentary legislation with its own. These provisions seem, therefore, to require that MK choose between invalidating provisions of questionable constitutionality—which in most cases would require a legislative response—or leaving them in force.

Chief Justice Mahfud has announced that the MK has accepted the amendments even though they would likely make it difficult to provide substantive justice (Hukumonline 2011b). However, it seems likely that, given its past efforts to protect its jurisdiction, or at least to delineate the boundaries of that jurisdiction, the MK will search for a way to circumvent this restriction, too.

Notes

1 The third amendment to Indonesia's constitution, approved on 9 November 2001, provided for establishment of the MK; the fourth amendment (10 August 2002) required that it be created by 17 August 2003, with the Supreme Court (*Mahkamah Agung*, MA) exercising its jurisdiction in the meantime (Constitution, Transitional Provisions, Article III). The law creating the MK (No. 24 of 2003) was passed on 13 August 2003. Soon after, its judges were installed by presidential decree and the court began accepting cases.

2 The Federal Constitution, which was in force for only one year (1949–50), permitted judicial review of state, but not federal, statutes (Articles 130(2) and 156(1) of the Interim Indonesian Constitution of 1950).
3 *Pancasila* (literally 'The Five Principles') embodies a commitment to the following principles:

   1 *Ketuhanan Yang Maha Esa* (Belief in Unitary Deity);
   2 *Kemanusiaan Yang Adil dan Beradab* (A Just and Civilised Humanity);
   3 *Persatuan Indonesia* (The Unity of Indonesia);
   4 *Demokrasi*; and
   5 *Keadilan Sosial* (Social Justice).

4 The process began with Law No 35 of 1999, which amended the Judicial Power Law of 1970. There followed Law No 4 of 2004 on judicial power, which replaced the 1970 law; Law No 5 of 2004, which amended Law No 14 of 1985 on the Supreme Court; Law No 8 of 2004, which significantly amended the General Courts Law (Law No 2 of 1986); and Law No 9 of 2004, which amended Law No 5 of 1986 on the administrative courts.
5 Article 24C(3) of the Constitution; Articles 4(1) and 18(1) of the MK Law.
6 The court started out in 2003 with an office in the MA building but without any administrative staff, then shifted to a Jakarta hotel for about a month. From there it moved into an office complex for six months, holding court at the People's Consultative Council (*Majelis Permusyawaratan Rakyat*, MPR)/national parliament building. Not until January 2004 did the MK obtain its own building (Asshiddiqie 2004: 14–15).
7 MK Decision 004/PUU-I/2003; MK Decision 013/PUU-I/2003; MK Decision 066/PUU-II/2004.
8 See, for example, MK Decisions 6/PUU-V/2007 and 012–022/PUU-IV/2006.
9 See, for example, MK Decision 013/PUU-I/2003.
10 See, for example, MK Decisions 9/PUU-VII/2009 and 98/PUU-VII/2009.
11 See, for example, MK Decision 011–017/PUU-I/2003.
12 See, for example, MK Decisions 013–022/PUU-IV/2006 and 14/PUU-VI/2008.
13 MK Decision 006/PUU-I/2003.
14 MK Decision 005/PUU-I/2003.
15 See, for example, MK Decision 006/PUU-II/2004.
16 MK Decision 001–021–022/PUU-I/2003.
17 MK Decisions No 058–059–060–063/PUU-II//2004 and 008/PUU-III/2005.
18 MK Decision 006/PUU-I/2003.
19 See, for example, MK Decision 011/PUU-III/2005; MK Decision 026/PUU-III/2005.
20 MK Decision 12/PUU-V/2007.
21 MK Decision 19/PUU-VI/2008.
22 For discussion of other democracy-related cases, see Mietzner (2010).
23 MK Decision 011–017/PUU-I/2003.
24 MK Decisions 14–17/PUU-V/2007 and 15/PUU-VI/2008.
25 MK Decision 110–111–112–113/PUU-VII/2009. Discussion of this case draws on Butt 2009.
26 MK Decision 102/PUU-VII/2009.
27 Parts of this section draw on Butt (2007b).
28 MK Decision 001–021–022/PUU-I/2003.
29 See, for example, MK Decision 013/PUU-I/2003.
30 See, for example, MK Decision 012–016–019/PUU-IV/2006.
31 MK Decision 058–059–060–063/PUU-II/2004 and 008/PUU-III/2005.
32 MK Decision 29/PUU-V/2007.
33 Indonesia's 'hierarchy of laws' (*tata urutan peraturan perundang-undangan*) sets out state institutions and individuals that can make laws in Indonesia, the types of laws

they can make, and the relative authority of those laws. The most recent version of the hierarchy, in Article 7(1) of the Lawmaking Law (Law No. 4 of 2004, amended in 2011), is as follows:

1 The 1945 Constitution (*Undang-undang Dasar 1945*);
2 MPR Decrees (*Ketetapan MPR*);
3 Statutes (*Undang-undang*)/Emergency Interim Laws (*PERPU*);
4 Government Regulations (*Peraturan Pemerintah*);
5 Presidential Regulations (*Peraturan Presiden*);
6 Provincial Regulations (*Peraturan Propinsi*);
7 City/District Regulations (*Peraturan Kota/Kabupaten*).

References

Asshiddiqie, J. (2004) 'Setahun mahkamah konstitusi: Refleksi gagasan dan penyelenggaraan, serta setangkup harapan', in Harun, R., Husein, A., and Bisariyadi (eds), *Menjaga Denyut Konstitusi: Refleksi satu tahun Mahkamah Konstitusi*, Jakarta: Konstitusi Press.

Asshiddiqie, J. (2008) *Menuju negara hukum yang demokratis*, Jakarta: Sekretariat Jenderal dan Kepaniteraan Mahkamah Konstitusi.

Asshiddiqie, J. (2009) 'Creating a Constitutional Court for a New Democracy', paper presented at Melbourne Law School, March 11.

Budiman, A. (1994) *State and civil society in Indonesia*, Clayton, Victoria, Australia: Centre of Southeast Asian Studies.

Butt, S. (2007a) 'The Constitutional Court's decision in the dispute between the Supreme Court and the Judicial Commission: Banishing judicial accountability?', in McLeod, R. H. and MacIntyre, A. J. (eds), *Indonesia: democracy and the promise of good governance*, Singapore: Institute of Southeast Asian Studies.

Butt, S. (2007b) 'Judicial review in Indonesia: Between civil law and accountability? A study of Constitutional Court decisions 2003–2005', Law Faculty, Melbourne University.

Butt, S. (2010a) 'Islam, the state and the Constitutional Court in Indonesia', *Pacific Rim Law & Policy Journal*, 19(2): 279.

Butt, S. (2010b) 'Regional autonomy and the proliferation of perda in Indonesia: An assessment of bureaucratic and judicial review mechanisms', *Sydney Law Review*, 32: 177.

Butt, S. (2011) *Corruption and Law in Indonesia*, London: Routledge.

Butt, S. and Hansell, D. (2004) 'The Masykur Abdul Kadir Case: Indonesian Constitutional Court decision No 013/PUU-I/2003', *Australian Journal of Asian Law*, 6: 1.

Butt, S. and Lindsey, T. (2008) 'Economic Reform When the Constitution Matters: Indonesia's Constitutional Court and Article 33', *Bulletin of Indonesian Economic Studies*, 44(2): 239–62.

Desafti, A. (2010) 'Court ruling won't affect education budget', *Jakarta Post*, 3 April.

Desyana, C. (2010) 'Dugaan Suap Hakim MK Tak Terbukti, Mahfud Batal Mundur', *Tempo*, 9 December.

Eldridge, P. (2001) 'Human rights in Post-Soeharto Indonesia', *Brown Journal of World Affairs*, 9: 127.

Feener, R. M. (2007) *Muslim Legal Thought in Modern Indonesia*, Cambridge, UK: Cambridge University Press.

Feith, H. and Castles, L. (1970) *Indonesian Political Thinking, 1945–1965*, Ithaca, NY: Cornell University Press.

Harijanti, S. and Lindsey, T. (2006) 'Indonesia: General elections test the amended Constitution and the new Constitutional Court', *International Journal of Constitutional Law*, 4: 138–50.

Hosen, N. (2010) *Human Rights, Politics and Corruption in Indonesia: A Critical Reflection on the Post-Soeharto Era*, Dordrecht, Netherlands: Republic of Letters.

Husein, Z. A. M. (2005) *Berjalan-jalan di Ranah Hukum*, Jakarta: Konstitusi Press.

Hukumonline (2011a) 'Putusan Majelis Kehormatan MK Bakal Digugat', 14 February.

Hukumonline (2011b) 'MK Legowo Sambut UU Baru', 22 June.

ICG (2001) *Indonesia: Impunity Versus Accountability for Gross Human Rights Violations*, Jakarta: International Crisis Group.

ICG (2006) *Islamic Law and Criminal Justice in Aceh*, Southeast Asia/Brussels: International Crisis Group.

Ipp, O. and Hoverter, T. (2005) 'Identifying international principles for resolving election disputes', *Administrative Law Review*, 57: 829.

Koopmans, T. (2003) *Courts and Political Institutions: A Comparative View*, Cambridge; New York: Cambridge University Press.

Lev, D. S. (1978) 'Judicial authority and the struggle for an Indonesian Rechsstaat', *Law and Society Review*, 13: 37.

Lindsey, T. (2002) 'Indonesian constitutional reform: Muddling towards democracy', *Singapore Journal of International and Comparative Law*, 6: 244–301.

Lubis, T. (1993) *In Search of Human Rights: Legal-Political Dilemmas of Indonesia's New Order, 1966–1990*, Jakarta: PT Gramedia Pustaka Utama in cooperation with SPES Foundation.

Mahfud, M. (2009) 'The role of the Constitutional Court in the development of democracy In Indonesia', World Conference on Constitutional Justice, Cape Town, South Africa, 22 January.

Mahkamah Konstitusi (2009) *Enam tahun mengawal Konstitusi dan Demokrasi*, Jakarta: Mahkamah Konstitusi.

Mietzner, M. (2010) 'Political conflict resolution and democratic consolidation in Indonesia: The role of the Constitutional Court', *Journal of East Asian Studies*, 10: 397–424.

Nardini, W. J. (1999) 'Passive activism and the limits of judicial self-restraint: Lessons for America from the Italian Constitutional Court', *Seton Hall Law Review*, 30: 1–63.

Pompe, S. (2005) *The Indonesian Supreme Court: A Study of Institutional Collapse*, Ithaca, NY: Southeast Asia Program, Cornell University.

Ramage, D. (2007) 'Indonesia: Democracy first, good governance later', *Southeast Asian Affairs 2007*: 135–60.

Savitri, I. (2010) 'Akil Mochtar: Tudingan refly bisa bunuh karakter hakim', *Tempo*, 12 December.

Simanjuntak, M. (1994) *Pandangan negara integralistik: sumber, unsur, dan riwayatnya dalam persiapan UUD 1945*, Jakarta: Pustaka Utama Grafiti.

Stone Sweet, A. (2000) *Governing with Judges: Constitutional Politics in Europe*, Oxford; New York: Oxford University Press.

Sukma, R. (2009) 'Indonesian politics in 2009: Defective elections, resilient democracy', *Bulletin of Indonesian Economic Studies*, 45: 317.

Thoolen, H. (1987) *Indonesia and the Rule of Law: Twenty Years of 'New Order' Government: A Study*, London: F. Pinter.

Waddell, S. (2005) 'Shifting visions of the social and legal order in Indonesia: Implications for legislative style and form', *Australian Journal of Asian Law*, 7: 43.

Webber, D. (2006) ‘A consolidated patrimonial democracy? Democratization in post-Suharto Indonesia’, *Democratization*, 13: 396–420.
Widjojanto, B. (2004) ‘Mahkamah Konstitusi, Harapan Baru Pembangunan Negara Hukum?’ in Harun, R., Husein, A, Bisariyadi (eds), *Menjaga Denyut Konstitusi: Refleksi satu tahun Mahkamah Konstitusi*, Jakarta: Konstitusi Press.
Williams, K. (2007) ‘The growing litigiousness of Czech elections’, *Europe-Asia Studies*, 59: 937–59.

7 From judicialization to politicization of the judiciary

The Philippine case

Alejandro N. Ciencia, Jr.

Introduction

The drafters of the 1987 Constitution saw creation of an independent and empowered judiciary as Philippine society's main defense against authoritarianism and corruption. For the delegates to the post-Marcos 1986 Constitutional Commission, if the goals of democracy, rule of law, peace, equality, and justice were to be achieved, the Philippine judiciary had to be insulated from political or partisan influences. The constitution's explicit grant of expanded review powers and its varied policy prescriptions have resulted in what some observers see as growing judicial intrusion into the prerogatives of political bodies—judicialization of politics, a phenomenon currently most apparent in the Philippine Supreme Court.

The judicialization of Philippine politics post-Marcos was a gradual process. In the early years of Corazon Aquino's presidency, the Supreme Court functioned as a passive arbiter of conflicts and appeared to be generally supportive of the president. In time, it began to exercise its new review powers, invalidate decisions by political bodies, and insert itself into policy-making. It would justify this alleged intrusion into policy-making as simply fulfillment of its duty as the guardian of the constitution and the main insurer of law and justice.

Now that the Supreme Court is considered the final arbiter of conflicts, the expansion of judicial power and the judicialization of politics in the Philippines have transformed it from an arena for contestation into the object of political contestation itself. Almost 25 years after being reconstituted with new powers, the Philippine Supreme Court is now politicized, seen by the public as a coopted institution and uninsulated from partisan influences—an outcome the drafters of the constitution clearly did not envision.

This paper seeks to analyze causes and consequences of the judicialization of politics in the Philippines since 1987. The author's preferred definitions of judicialization and politicization are specified at the outset. These are followed by a brief discussion of the history of the post-Marcos Supreme Court. The paper then uses a number of landmark decisions to support the claim that judicialization is indeed taking place in the Philippines. Drivers of the process are then analyzed, the main argument being that the text of the Philippine Constitution is the real force driving judicialization. The paper then examines the broad consequences of judicialization, considers its connection with recent developments that suggest an evolving politicization of the judiciary, and looks at what is driving this process. The paper concludes by exploring lessons scholars of judicial politics can draw from the Philippine case.

Tate (1994: 190) suggests that judicialization occurs when 'the Court [assumes jurisdiction over] a wide variety of policy processes that would otherwise be the responsibility of the executive and legislature, that is, the majoritarian institutions'. Like Tate, Hirschl (2008) sees judicialization as characterized by a growing reliance on judicial bodies and processes. Unlike Tate, however, Hirschl (2008: 2) looks closely at a particularly fascinating type of judicialization—the 'judicialization of mega-politics'—the reliance on courts and judicial processes to address 'core moral predicaments, public policy questions, and political controversies' and 'matters of outright and utmost political significance that often define and divide whole polities'. He cites as examples 'electoral outcomes and corroboration of regime change to foundational collective identity questions, and nation-building processes pertaining to the very nature and definition of the body politic as such' (Hirschl 2008: 2).

As for 'politicization of the court', the author understands it as the growing recognition by the public of the court as a partisan player in politics alongside the erosion of court's public image as an impartial and independent arbiter of disputes (Haynie 1998: 462). The application of this concept to the present study will be discussed further below. But to distinguish judicialization from politicization of the court at this point, the former refers to the growing reliance on courts and their processes to decide on matters that traditionally fall within the jurisdiction of executive and legislative bodies. The latter meanwhile refers to growing perception of the court as a partisan and possibly a coopted decision-making body instead of an impartial and independent arbiter of conflicts.

Judicialization in the Philippines post-Marcos

To understand the process of judicialization in the Philippines and its recent shift toward politicization of the judiciary, a quick review of Supreme Court history since 1987 and a discussion of significant rulings may be helpful. The government structure set up by the 1987 Constitution is characterized by separation of powers, an emasculated presidency, bicameralism, and a multiparty system. Early in the presidency of Corazon Aquino, the first president after Marcos, and particularly under the watch of Chief Justice Claudio Teehankee Sr., the functions of the Supreme Court varied.

At the outset, it served a legitimating function when it unanimously confirmed Aquino as president both de facto and de jure in *Lawyers' League for a Better Philippines* v. *Corazon C. Aquino* (1986).[1] To a greater extent, however, the court served an arbitral function in disputes between the executive and the legislative branches. Particularly contentious was whether presidential appointments needed congressional confirmation. Called upon to resolve deadlocks resulting from such disputes, the court tended to favor the position of the president, to the dismay of legislators. In *Sarmiento* v. *Mison* (1987), for instance, the court upheld President Aquino's power to appoint the customs commissioner without congressional confirmation.

Predictably, the most significant cases presented for judicial review in the early years of the Aquino presidency concerned the ousted Ferdinand Marcos, his family, and alleged cronies; the validity of martial law-era policies and court rulings; and efforts to rectify transgressions associated with the Marcos dictatorship. In most of these the Court espoused an anti-Marcos position. To justify its rulings, it would often assert that it was simply being faithful to the 1987 Constitution, presenting itself as guardian of the constitution.

Still, it bears recalling that the 1987 Constitution was designed to be anti-authoritarian and anti-Marcos. The composition of the Supreme Court as reconstituted in 1987 revealed a similar anti-authoritarian, anti-Marcos predisposition. At least five of the original members of the Supreme Court were reputed to be Marcos critics. Teehankee and Vicente Abad Santos had been dissenters in the Marcos-era Supreme Court. Pedro Yap, as a delegate to the 1971 Constitution Convention, had voted against provisions of the 1973 Constitution which gave Marcos total control of the Philippine government. Marcelo Fernan had been a member of the opposition in the National Legislature and Andres Narvasa had been a member of the Agrava fact-finding body that found the military culpable for the assassination of Benigno Aquino Jr. in 1983. The other members of the court were reputedly independent-minded legal scholars and human rights or libertarian advocates.

Chief Justice Teehankee was highly supportive of President Aquino and worked to ensure that court rulings were unanimous. When Marcelo Fernan became Chief Justice in mid-1988, however, he ushered in a court that was less sympathetic to the president and more inclined to invalidate her appointments and subject government economic policies to judicial review.

In *Civil Liberties Union* v. *Executive Secretary* (1991), the Fernan-led Court rejected presidential orders allowing cabinet members to assume additional governmental positions. In *Brillantes* v. *Yorac* (1990), it invalidated Aquino's appointment of the respondent as acting chair of the Commission of Elections (COMELEC). Voting 9–6 in *Laurel* v. *Garcia* (1990), the court prohibited the president from selling Philippine property in Roponggi, Japan. In *Garcia* v. *Board of Investments* (1989)—a decision widely criticized by businesspeople as judicial meddling in economic policy-making—it rejected a foreign investor's decision to relocate its petrochemical plant. Significantly, in cases that evoked bad memories of martial law and the Marcos dictatorship, the Fernan court issued decisions that libertarians and human rights advocates found alarming. For instance, it upheld the legality of military checkpoints in *Valmonte* v. *De Villa* (1989) and warrantless arrests in subversion cases in *Umil* v. *Ramos* (1991).

But the Fernan court did not always nullify government policy choices. In *Bautista* v. *Salonga* (1989), the court affirmed the president's appointment of the petitioner, thus sustaining the *Sarmiento* v. *Mison* ruling that some types of presidential appointment do not require congressional confirmation. In *Association of Small Landowners* v. *Secretary of Agrarian Reform* (1989), the court unanimously sustained the constitutionality of the Comprehensive Agrarian Reform Program (CARP). In *Marcos* v. *Manglapus* (1989), a divided court upheld President Aquino's refusal to allow the Marcos family to return to the Philippines. The *Manglapus* majority argued that in matters of national security the president enjoyed 'residual powers'. It was at this point late in Aquino's presidency that the court began to test the limits of its expanded judicial review powers and to demonstrate its independence, to the extent that on a number of occasions it incurred the ire of policy-makers, the business community, and the public. The deferential Teehankee court had been replaced by a less supportive Fernan court.

Fidel V. Ramos assumed the presidency in 1992 as a plurality president, having won less than 25 percent of the votes. Clearly, he was not as popular as his predecessor and benefactor, Corazon Aquino. Nonetheless, he had the support of legislators, particularly those in the Lower House of Congress, who at the time were led by his trusted ally and Lakas[2]-National Union of Christian Democrats (NUCD) party-mate, Jose de Venecia, the speaker from 1992 to 1998. Under Ramos the government embarked on a mission to transform the Philippines into a newly industrialized country (NIC) by 2000. To do so Ramos advocated economic reforms which, among other things, required adoption of liberalization, deregulation, and privatization policies.

Andres Narvasa was chief justice when Ramos was president. On his watch the Supreme Court often found itself reviewing government policies. For the reform-oriented Ramos, the court was largely an obstructionist veto-player, but it did not always invalidate his government's policy choices. For instance, it upheld the constitutionality of the Ramos-endorsed value-added tax in *Tolentino* v. *Secretary of Finance* (1995) and sustained the Senate's ratification of membership in the World Trade Organization (WTO) in *Tañada* v. *Angara* (1997). But in *Manila Prince Hotel* v. *Government Service Insurance System* (1997), the court allowed a Filipino corporation, rather belatedly, to match the winning bid of a Malaysian company for 51 percent of the shares in Manila Hotel. The Ramos administration saw the ruling as inconsistent with its privatization and economic liberalization policies. The court justified its decision as upholding the Filipino First policy espoused by the 1987 Constitution.

In *Tatad* v. *Secretary of Energy* (1997), the court also invalidated the first oil deregulation law (Republic Act 8180) on the ground that it violated the economic rights of the Filipino people. The Ramos administration saw the invalidation as impeding its deregulation efforts. Then *Santiago* v. *Comelec* (1997) gave the Ramos administration its most resounding rejection with the ruling that the Initiative Referendum Act (Republic Act 6735) was insufficient as a means of amending the constitution. Thus it thwarted efforts to remove from the constitution economic protectionist or nationalist provisions and sections limiting the terms of elected officials, demonstrating yet again its independence, particularly from the president.

Joseph Ejercito Estrada succeeded Ramos as president in 1998. Early in 2001 his presidency was cut short when allegations of corruption resulted in impeachment proceedings, and he was eventually ousted via 'people power'. Ultimately the impeachment trial provided the backdrop for activist intervention by the Supreme Court, facilitating his ouster. Earlier in November 2000, anti-Estrada congressmen had garnered the necessary number of signatures to send articles of impeachment to the Senate. While Estrada appeared to have the support of enough senators to stave off removal from office, when the Senate acting as an impeachment court refused to open a sealed envelope allegedly containing revealing evidence, the prosecution walked out of the trial and people took to the streets to demand Estrada's resignation. Fearing violence and political instability, the Supreme Court, led by Chief Justice Hilario Davide, stepped in; on 20 January 2001 it administered the oath of office to Gloria Macapagal-Arroyo as the new president. More than a month later, in *Estrada* v. *Arroyo* (2001) the Supreme Court declared that ousted President Estrada had in fact resigned the presidency at the height of what is now generally known as EDSA II,[3] paving the way for Vice-President Arroyo to succeed him as the constitutionally mandated successor. Arguably, the Supreme Court decision to endorse Arroyo was judicialization at its peak.

When Macapagal-Arroyo assumed the presidency in 2001, she intended to continue the economic reforms pursued by her Lakas-NUCD party-mate, former president Fidel Ramos. Interestingly, most of the major cases that preoccupied the Davide-led Supreme Court during the first half of the Macapagal–Arroyo presidency were economically significant. In a number of decisions over a very short period of time, the court invalidated multibillion-dollar contracts the government had signed with private entities and foreign business interests. Among these decisions were *Chavez* v. *Public Estates Authority – Amari* (2002); *La Bugal-B'laan Tribal Association, Inc.* v. *Ramos* (2004 January); *Information Technology Foundation of the Philippines* v. *Comelec* (2004); and *Agan Jr.* v. *Philippine International Air Terminals Co., Inc.* (2004). In addition to *Estrada* v. *Arroyo*, which challenged the legitimacy of the Arroyo presidency, in her early years as president, the court also had to settle other political cases, such as *Francisco Jr.* v. *House of Representatives* (2003) that challenged the constitutionality of the efforts of members of the House of Representatives to impeach Chief Justice Davide.

Though Arroyo was declared winner of the 2004 presidential elections, allegations of electoral impropriety (e.g., the Hello Garci scandal of 2005) and charges of corruption against her and her family members would soon plague her presidency. To secure her political survival, Arroyo moved to repress protests and demonstrations and prevented cabinet members from testifying in legislative inquiries. For most of the latter half of her presidency, the court used its review powers in political and civil liberties cases most of which sprang from Arroyo's efforts to protect her presidency. The most notable of these decisions were *BAYAN v. Ermita* (2006), which voided the Arroyo government's calibrated preemptive response (CPR) policy that prohibited street protests without permits; *Senate* v. *Ermita* (2006), which invalidated the president's Executive

Order 464 requiring executive officials to secure presidential consent before appearing at legislative hearings; and *David* v. *Arroyo* (2006), which sustained the president's power to declare a state of emergency, although it ruled illegal arrests and raids made pursuant to Proclamation 1017.

Other political decisions followed. For instance, *Lambino* v. *Comelec* (2006) dismissed as a 'constitutionally infirm [people's] initiative' the Malacañang-supported signature drive to jumpstart transformation of the bicameral presidential system into a unicameral parliamentary system; and *Province of North Cotabato* v. *Government of the Republic of the Philippines* (2008) invalidated the memorandum of agreement on ancestral domain between the Philippine government and the Moro Islamic Liberation Front (MILF). In all these cases the Supreme Court ruled against President Arroyo, reaffirming its image as an independent body and asserting its key role as guardian of the Constitution. But—in a decision reversing its original ruling in *Senate* v. *Ermita* (2006)—in *Neri* v. *Senate* (2008) the court upheld petitioner Romulo Neri's invocation of executive privilege during a Congressional hearing on the scandal-plagued ZTE-National Broadband Network (NBN) Project. As will be seen below, *Neri* has a significant place in the history of the Court.

Clearly, to this point the post-Marcos court had not been sparing in its exercise of judicial review. However, it must be emphasized that it did not always invalidate government action. Moreover, in many instances where government action *was* invalidated, the court appeared to have convincing constitutional or other legal grounds, according to observers and commentators (e.g., Bernas 1999, Bernas 2000, Cruz and Datu 2000, Bernas 2003, Panganiban 2004, Bernas 2007, etc.). Sometimes, however, the justifications the Court provided were not at all persuasive. For instance, legal scholars have found less than satisfactory the ruling on Estrada's resignation in *Estrada* v. *Arroyo* (see Paguia 2003, Bernas 2001, Cruz 2001). In any event, the preceding section has cited various occasions which suggest that Philippine politics was being judicialized. The following section discusses factors that contributed to that process.

Drivers of judicialization in the Philippines

The 1987 Constitution provided the impetus for judicial intrusion into Philippine politics. It essentially created a Supreme Court designed to serve as 'a check on the executive and legislative powers' (Agabin 1996: 193). In Section 1, Article VIII, it explicitly gave that court and lower courts the power of judicial review:

> The judicial power shall be vested in one Supreme Court and in such lower courts as may be established by law.
>
> Judicial power includes the duty of the courts of justice to settle actual controversies involving rights which are legally demandable and enforceable, and to determine whether or not there has been a grave abuse of discretion amounting to lack or excess of jurisdiction on the part of any branch or instrumentality of the Government.

The constitution broadened the concept of judicial review. It not only authorized the judiciary to look into the actions of any branch or instrumentality of government to determine whether the actions were constitutional, it explicitly mandated that judges 'settle actual controversies involving rights which are legally demandable and enforceable'. In the category of 'legally demandable and enforceable' the drafters envisioned human rights and civil liberties; the clause was inserted because the drafters wished to avoid a recurrence of Marcos-era rights violations where courts easily dismissed human rights cases as involving a 'political question' that a judicial body should not decide (Agabin 1996). Protection of human rights would no longer be considered a political question.

Note, too, that judicial review is defined as a 'duty': The constitution has imposed on the Philippine Supreme Court and lower courts the duty to determine whether any branch or instrumentality of government has committed a grave abuse of discretion. This implies that if the Supreme Court should refuse to look into how the political branches are exercising discretion, it would be violating its constitutional duty. Section 1, Article VIII, thus justifies not only judicial intrusions but also *recurrent* judicial intrusions.

Agabin (1996) adds that provisions in the 1987 Constitution have increased the likelihood of the Supreme Court invalidating decisions and actions of the Philippine president or Congress. Comparing the present constitution with previous ones, he finds, significantly, that the voting requirement for nullifying a treaty, international or executive agreement, or law has changed from two-thirds of the entire court to a mere majority of those who actually take part in deliberations.

Apart from stipulating that the courts have the duty to exercise judicial review, the 1987 Constitution also makes fairly specific statements about economic policy and the delivery of social justice.[4] When these provisions are juxtaposed against the stipulation that the Supreme Court has a duty to exercise judicial review, it is easy to conclude, as Agabin (1997) did, that the constitution invites judicial intrusion *especially* in matters of economic policy. He elaborates:

> Our constitution is replete with provisions for the regulation of the economy and of the state's positive obligation to promote social justice. As its framers like to put it, our present constitution is 'pro-people, pro-poor, and pro-Filipino.' This means that the Philippine Supreme Court, unlike the United States Supreme Court, cannot promote the development of capitalist institutions at the expense of the people. It cannot assume the function of protecting the market from various regulatory incursions if these conflict with the economic policies incorporated in the constitution. While the constitutional tools which may be used to protect free enterprise have been copied in the present constitution, like the due process clause, the equal protection clause, the contracts clause, and the takings clause, these have been neutralized not only by reversals by the Supreme Court but also by countervailing policies in the constitution itself. Unless we reduce the constitution to a mere imitation of

> its American counterpart, the Supreme Court cannot behave like the US Supreme Court during the Gilded Age when it tilted the balance in favor of free markets over the sovereignty of the people.
>
> (Agabin 1997: 183–4)

It bears noting although Agabin considers the Philippine constitution to be 'pro-people, pro-poor, and pro-Filipino', Associate Justice Dante Tinga thinks otherwise. In *La Bugal* v. *Ramos* (December 2004), he describes the 1987 Constitution as containing a mix of 'protectionist' and 'liberal economic' policies.[5] But despite their disagreement about the constitution's policy direction, Agabin and Tinga agree that it contains policy prescriptions. Thus when the court is acknowledged as the chief interpreter of a constitution that happens to be replete with policy prescriptions, in performing its assigned task of interpretation the court unavoidably makes policy pronouncements. Meanwhile, if the constitution is thought of as a confusing mix of policies, when the court moves to fix constitutional confusions, for all intents and purposes it is defining policy. The constitution's explicit support for certain policies invites judicial intrusion into what is generally regarded as part of the political realm. The constitution's recognition of new rights—for example, the rights of indigenous peoples—can also engender litigation, especially when the new rights threaten rights protected by older jurisprudence. Increased reliance on litigation, along with a more expansive notion of rights, fosters judicialization.

The constitution also provides for a more independent Supreme Court. De Leon (2002: 240–1) enumerates provisions that safeguard the Court's independence:

1. Sections 2 and 5 of Art VIII: 'Congress may not deprive the Supreme Court of the constitutional powers granted to it';
2. Section 4[1]: 'Congress cannot prescribe the manner in which the Supreme Court should sit, and determine the number of Justices composing the court';
3. Section 5[6]: 'the Supreme Court is given the authority to appoint all officials and employees of the judiciary';
4. Section 11: 'the members of the Supreme Court and judges of lower courts enjoy security of tenure';
5. Section 10: 'the salaries of members of the judiciary cannot be decreased during their continuance in office';
6. Section 2, Art XI: 'the members of the Supreme Court can only be removed through the difficult process of impeachment'; and
7. Section 3, Art VIII: 'the judiciary enjoys fiscal autonomy'

De Leon (2002: 240–1) adds:

> The constitutional policy of an independent judiciary is further strengthened by the provisions transferring [from the Department of Justice] to the Supreme Court administrative supervision over all courts and personnel

> thereof (Sec. 6, Art VIII) and the authority to assign temporarily judges of lower courts to other stations as the public interest may require (Sec. 5 [3], Art VIII), and the provision giving specific authorization to the Supreme Court to order a change of venue or place of trial to avoid a miscarriage of justice (Sec. 5 [4], Art VIII). The prohibition against members of Congress personally appearing as counsel before any court (Sec. 14, Art VI), while designed to shield them from corruption, works equally to promote the independence of the courts.

The strengthening of judicial power by the present constitution has to be appreciated in relation to the weakening of the political bodies that a number of constitutional provisions stipulate. The most significant appear to be those provisions which impose limits on the terms of elected officials and limits on the executive's exercise of martial law powers. Empowering the judiciary while weakening the political branches clearly encourages judicialization.

The Philippine constitution has also granted the Supreme Court what appear to be law-making powers. According to Section 5, paragraph 6, Article VIII, the Supreme Court has the power to

> Promulgate rules concerning the protection and enforcement of constitutional rights, pleading, practice, and procedure in all courts, the admission to the practice of law, the Integrated Bar, and legal assistance to the underprivileged. Such rules shall provide a simplified and inexpensive procedure for the speedy disposition of cases, shall be uniform for all courts of the same grade, and shall not diminish, increase, [or] modify substantive rights. Rules of procedure of special courts and quasi-judicial bodies shall remain effective unless disapproved by the Supreme Court.

In 2008 the Supreme Court promulgated the *writ of amparo* to contain an alarming rise in extrajudicial executions. This was followed by the *writ of kalikasan* in April 2010 to address urgent environmental concerns. In other jurisdictions, such actions would be seen as symptoms of judicial activism because they preempt executive and legislative action on such matters.

As might be expected, jurisprudential principles or doctrines can also be used to justify judicial activism. Orosa (2004: 601–10) identifies a number of jurisprudential doctrines that the Philippine Supreme Court has invoked to justify its 'activist' rulings, among them (a) the constitution is supreme; (b) the welfare of the people is the supreme law (*salus populi est suprema lex doctrine*); and (c) the doctrine of 'transcendality' or 'transcendental importance', which is often invoked to justify the setting aside of procedural requirements. Of course, precedents and *stare decisis* can be invoked to support activist rulings—a previous activist decision can serve as precedent for future activist decisions. The accumulation of activist rulings epitomizes the process of judicialization.

As mentioned earlier, the separation of powers that characterizes the presidential system of government is highly vulnerable to gridlock. The seemingly intrinsic propensity of the presidential or the separation-of-powers system to find itself in gridlock fosters judicialization because sooner or later the court will be called upon to resolve deadlocks, as it did in 2001 when it intervened to facilitate Estrada's ousting.

Thus, constitutional, institutional, and structural factors favored the rise of judicial activism and the advance of judicialization in the Philippines. Still, it is the text of the constitution, supported by reliance on the concept of constitutional supremacy, which is the major driving force behind the judicialization of politics. As Agabin (1997) suggests, the Philippines 'constitutionalized' judicial activism. The build-up of judicial power and the weakening of the prerogatives of Philippine political branches are attributable to the desire of delegates to the 1986 Constitution Commission to prevent a return to authoritarianism. An empowered and independent judiciary with broad and explicit review powers was envisioned as a safeguard against dictatorship and corruption. (Note, however, that Ferdinand Marcos himself placed a premium on constitutionalism—or at least its appearance.)

The 1935, 1973, and 1987 Philippine Constitutions have all granted the Court the power of judicial review. The present chapter does not deny that. It argues that the 1987 Constitution has expanded the Court's judicial review powers but it is not saying that the constitutional provision on judicial review alone accounts for the process of judicialization. The expansion of the court's judicial review and other powers coincided with the relative weakening of the other branches and this provided the impetus for judicialization. This chapter does not also discount the role of individual agency. The author believes that justices' attitudes towards incumbent authorities and institutions and their predilections towards activism or restraint also bear on the court's behavior.[6] In the hands of attitudinally restraintist justices who look favorably on incumbent authorities, particularly the president, expanded judicial review powers are unlikely to result in judicialization. Still, studies in judicial behavior find that justices have a general tendency to advance their policy goals (Segal and Spaeth 2002, Maltzman *et al.* 2000, Epstein and Knight 1998). This chapter thus argues that when constitutional and institutional arrangements allow the exercise of expanded judicial powers, policy-oriented justices who possess such powers are likely to involve themselves in matters traditionally brought to executives and legislators for action or resolution.

The consequences of judicialization

This section will speak briefly about how judicialization affects democratic governance, the rule of law, economic development, and the like, but would prefer to draw greater attention to the general effect of judicialization on the behavior of societal actors. It appears counterintuitive to assume that judicialization and democratic governance go hand in hand. At the outset, there are questions about how the opinions of a small group of appointed justices can substitute for those of elected representatives, how unelected justices can be held accountable for bad decisions, and the extent to which the court would be willing to make its procedures and deliberations more transparent and participatory for the general public. Undoubtedly, there have been times when the sentiments of the Filipino people were more in tune with those of the justices than with their 'representatives'. But there clearly is danger in vesting too much power in one department of government, whether it be the executive, the legislative, or the judiciary.

Rule of law, though a slippery idea, is generally associated with the impartial application of stable rules (Weingast 1997). It is often equated with the perception that rules are applied consistently and justices rule consistently. The brief historical review of the post-Marcos Supreme Court showed that reversals do occur and the policy direction of court rulings can vary from time to time. Periodic ruling reversals, the shifts in policy direction the court has endorsed in its decisions, intermittent episodes where the court invalidates executive or legislative actions, conflicts between how the court and political bodies read the laws, the frequent rulings by a divided court, the failure of authorities to enforce court decisions, the refusal of citizens to follow court rulings, and the leniency authorities display towards convicted celebrities and influential individuals—all these have impressed on the Filipino public the fact that the rules governing Philippine society are in fact not stable and their application is rarely impartial. Rule of law is lacking. In this context judicialization makes the legal environment even more unpredictable.

With regard to the economy, the widespread sentiment is that judicialization is detrimental to coherent policy-making and the attainment of economic policy goals. Bakker (1997: 98) reports that it was judicial intrusion which prevented President Ramos from implementing a coherent economic policy in the 1990s, making it impossible for him to achieve his developmentalist vision of Philippines 2000.

At any rate, the most immediate consequence is that judicialization can pave the way for judicial pre-eminence. Indeed, the expansion of review power in the Philippines has led scholars to announce the arrival of 'judicial supremacy' (Agabin 1996) or 'kritarchy' (Orosa 2004). As we have seen, by performing its legitimating function the court can actually play the role of king-maker, as in 2001 when it declared Gloria Macapagal-Arroyo president of the Philippines. It can also assume a direct role in policy-making, primarily as a veto-player, as can be seen in the rulings on the validity of huge contracts the government had entered into with other entities. The mere fact that the policies, decisions, and actions of the president or Congress can be subjected to judicial review allows the court to assume a pre-eminent political role if it wants to.

At this point, let us consider two rather intriguing developments: (1) the alarming increase in extrajudicial executions while the Philippines was becoming judicialized; and (2) the apparent cooptation of the court by former President Arroyo. These two processes point up the actual role of courts in Philippine society. Courts are venues where societal actors bring legal cases in the hope of advancing their interests. People who believe that the courts cannot assure protection of their interests are likely to seek other venues or resort to extrajudicial, even violent, means to advance those interests. Where the rule of law is wanting, judicialization catalyzes evolution of the courts from being simply a venue for dispute resolution to being the object of dispute themselves. Judicial capture becomes a goal. Even more, for political actors desperately seeking to ensure their political survival, judicial capture becomes an imperative. Hence, efforts to coopt the courts.

In the final years of her presidency, Macapagal-Arroyo was such an actor. Fearing criminal prosecution once her presidential immunity expired, among other things she used her appointment powers to put allies in key places—justices on the Supreme Court; a former subordinate, Renato Corona, as chief justice; and a family friend as ombudsman—hoping that the deeply-held Filipino values of gratitude and personal loyalty would pay off in both the short and the long run. As will be argued below, in confluence with other developments Arroyo's actions stimulated the shift from the judicialization of politics to the politicization of the court.

The politicization of the Philippine Supreme Court

Political scientists have long acknowledged that courts are political bodies. If one defines politics as 'the authoritative allocation of values for a society' (Easton 1953: 129) or 'the process by which resources are distributed within a society' (Haynie 1998: 459), courts clearly are political. Political scientists also question the portrayal of judicial decision-making as a mechanical activity—the mechanical application of the letter of the law, because they find that oftentimes judges also take into account the policy consequences of their decisions. Judges are policy-oriented actors. Hence, they are political.

Still, scholars acknowledge the importance to the court of maintaining its reputation as an apolitical institution (Haynie 1998: 462). The court's legitimacy and influence often depends on its ability to maintain the image of being apolitical—making decisions exclusively on the basis of the law independent of political pressures and without regard for policy consequences and other political consideration. Politicization of the court connotes the undermining of the court's apolitical image as arbiter of conflicts. This understanding of politicization of the court should suggest that for the author the court has always been a political institution although it was not always seen by the public as such; and politicization of the court can be said to be occurring during periods when the court's public image of independence and impartiality is questioned.

Judicial independence is most apparent when the court rules against the preferences of political bodies, particularly the president and Congress, and the public—as represented by Philippine society's opinion-makers—finds the court's justifications for such invalidations to be faithful to the Constitution. Meanwhile, lack of judicial independence is often alleged when the court fails to offer convincing justifications for its decisions especially when it upholds actions of the political branches which the public finds questionable, oftentimes for being incompatible with its understanding of the constitution or law. Similarly, judicial impartiality is assumed when the court invalidates actions of the political bodies and succeeds in providing persuasive justification for its decisions. Lack of judicial impartiality is often alleged when the court fails to offer persuasive and legally sound rulings, especially when such rulings are seen as favoring or benefiting particular political personalities at the expense of the public and/or fidelity to the constitution.

Politicization is a matter of perception and degree. In as much as courts are unavoidably political, it appears that courts ought to be differentiated in terms of the extent to which they are seen by the public as such. The degree of politicization can also vary across time. One can speak of varieties or gradations of politicization of courts. There are courts that are deferential to the executive and legislative branches of government but are seen by the public as independent and uncoopted, and their agreement with governmental bodies is generally regarded as constitutionally warranted. The Teehankee Court appears to represent this type.

There are courts that occasionally invalidate actions of governmental bodies but the public generally sees such invalidations as constitutionally warranted. Such courts may be characterized as generally credible, independent, and non-deferential. Then there are courts that are regarded by the public as lacking credibility. A sub-type of these includes courts whose members are not beholden to any political body or entity but the public often finds their rulings to be legally unsound. Such courts may be described as independent and unfettered but lacking credibility.

A second sub-type refers to courts that seem to have been coopted by political bodies or personalities, oftentimes the president. Such courts tend to favor the positions of governmental bodies but the public sees such actions as inconsistent with its understanding of the constitution and the law. Such courts lack independence and credibility. The Supreme Court during Martial Law was such a court.[7] Fairly recent events suggest the reappearance in the Philippines of a court coopted by a president. A third possible sub-type would refer to courts that have been coopted by particular interests in society like crime syndicates. They may be unsympathetic to the executive and legislative bodies and the public often finds their rulings to be legally unsound.

As early as 2009 observers began talking about an 'Arroyo Court' (see Rufo and Romero 2009: 18). The pronouncement was prompted by the realization that the Court would soon have a disproportionate number of Arroyo appointees, and thus by inference Arroyo partisans. Although Benigno Aquino III is now the president, of the 15 current members of the Court, Arroyo appointed 14. In her nine years as president Arroyo had the opportunity to appoint 23 justices to the Supreme Court (Vitug 2010: 94).

A quick survey of Supreme Court decisions which can be regarded as politically significant for former President Arroyo from November 2009 (while she was still president) to February 2011 (with Aquino as president) yielded eight en banc cases. In six of them the Court upheld the position that favored her. In *Biraogo* v. *Truth Commission* (December 2010), which questioned Aquino's

Executive Order No. 1 creating a commission to look into allegedly anomalous deal-making by her administration, the court found the order to be unconstitutional. In *de Castro* v. *JBC* (March 2010 and April 2010), which challenged the power of an outgoing president (Arroyo) to appoint the next chief justice despite a ban on appointments during elections, the court upheld that power—thus allowing her to appoint Corona as chief justice while preventing the new president from choosing someone more sympathetic. In *Aquino & Robredo* v. *Comelec* (April 2010), then-Senator Aquino questioned the validity of an Arroyo-approved legislative measure reapportioning the Province of Camarines Sur for electoral purposes. The court found the measure to be valid. Arroyo's son, Dato, now represents that district in Congress. In *Bello* v. *Comelec* (December 2010), which questioned whether Arroyo's other son, Mikey, was eligible to represent a party-list group of security guards in Congress, the court dismissed the petition as premature. In *Rubrico* v. *Arroyo* (February 2010), the court excluded Arroyo from the list of respondents in a *writ of amparo* petition.

Arroyo was, however, rebuffed in *Funa* v. *Ermita* (February 2010), a petition questioning her power to appoint Elena Bautista, another close ally, to two concurrent government positions. In *Gutierrez* v. *House of Representatives* (February 2011), the court lifted its status quo ante order which had stalled the Lower House's efforts to impeach Ombudsman Merceditas Gutierrez, a close Arroyo family friend.

Although the court did not always support Arroyo, it favored her in what seem to be the most politically sensitive cases: *Biraogo* v. *Truth Commission* and *De Castro* v. *JBC*. Losing *Biraogo* would have put her at the mercy of a commission created by a rival apparently bent on prosecuting her. *De Castro* v. *JBC* was a major victory mainly because Filipino legal luminaries consider her position in the case to have been constitutionally untenable (see Bernas 2010, Dedace 2010). *Funa* v. *Ermita*, a case she lost, may be inconsequential. At the time *Gutierrez* v. *House* seemed to be a big defeat for her, but recent events have made it irrelevant: Ombudsman Gutierrez resigned on 29 April 2011, paving the way for President Benigno Aquino to make the appointment. In any event, though, there are clearly grounds for seeing the current court as still an Arroyo Court.

At this point it may be useful to examine other relevant data on rule of law in the Philippines and the performance of the Philippine Supreme Court. Global Integrity Report (2004, 2006, 2007, 2008, 2010) noted a significant drop in the Philippines' score for 'rule of law' from 80 in 2004 and 2006, to 52 and 51 in 2007 and 2008 respectively, and a slight increase to 62 in 2010. Meanwhile, the Philippine survey body, Social Weather Stations (SWS) (2011), reports a considerable change in the public satisfaction scores of the Philippine Supreme Court. For most of the period from November 1990 to May 2005, the Court obtained the highest public satisfaction ratings among governmental bodies which also include the Senate, House of Representatives, and the Cabinet. But from August 2005 to June 2011, the Court's ratings would be surpassed by the Senate's. The Global Integrity Report data may be seen as reflecting in part the court's reputation as guardian of the rule of law while the SWS data suggests an erosion of the court's prestige and credibility.

The judicialization of politics Tate observed in 1994 has evolved into the politicization of the Philippine judiciary. To understand how this came about, here is a quick recapitulation of pertinent decisions and events:

1 Supreme Court participation in the ousting of President Joseph Estrada in 2001 and its decision in *Estrada* v. *Arroyo* led to the Court's alignment with the administration of his successor and rival, Gloria Macapagal-Arroyo. On 1 May 1 2001, pro-Estrada supporters, mostly poor, launched their own version of People Power which ended in violence, destruction of property, and declaration of a state of rebellion. Some people began to question whether People Power was a legitimate means of removing an unpopular president.

2 In response to the attempts, endorsed by Estrada loyalists, to impeach members of the court in the middle of 2003, culminating in impeachment of Chief Justice Hilario Davide that November, the Supreme Court used its constitutional powers to preempt the impeachment process. It then clarified the law on impeachment in *Francisco* v. *House of Representatives* (2003). Allies of President Arroyo would exploit loopholes in this ruling to thwart attempts to impeach her.

3 In the aftermath of the 'Hello Garci' scandal of 2005, which led to the resignation of a number of members of her cabinet and the government's adoption of a repressive stance against her opponents, the court made efforts to distance itself from Arroyo, repudiating her in several landmark political and civil liberties cases in 2006.

4 Another scandal, the ZTE-NBN deal, erupted in 2007. Romulo Neri, former director of the National Economic Development Authority (NEDA), testified in a Senate hearing about being bribed to approve a multimillion-dollar deal with a Chinese telecommunications firm and informing President Arroyo about it. When senators began to grill him about Arroyo's participation, he invoked 'executive privilege'. When Neri refused to attend subsequent Senate hearings, the Senate filed a case against him with the Supreme Court. In what would probably have been Arroyo's last stand, the court (with the help of at least three new appointees) saved her in *Neri* v. *Senate* (2008). With Arroyo still in survival mode and Philippine society unwilling to oust her via another People Power uprising, Filipinos waited out her presidency.

   At least two considerations discouraged massive participation in another People Power uprising: (a) the realization that it was People Power that had brought Macapagal-Arroyo to the presidency, and (b) the perceived lack of a competent, constitutionally acceptable replacement (the vice-president was not considered acceptable).[8]

5 The retirement of a number of justices in the last years of her presidency allowed President Arroyo to use her appointment powers to constitute a

sympathetic Supreme Court with a sympathetic chief justice, Renato Corona.

President Arroyo was exceptionally fortunate that after the Supreme Court rapidly invalidated her actions in a number of high-profile political/civil liberties cases in 2006, it upheld Neri's invocation of executive privilege in *Neri* v. *Senate* in 2008. Voting 9–6 the court overruled its previous executive privilege case, *Senate* v. *Ermita*, which had put a premium on governmental transparency. *Neri* v. *Senate* underscored the opposite by again setting limits on the public's right to information.

The major reason for change in stance was the change in the bench. Three justices (Panganiban, Sandoval-Gutierrez, and Garcia) who had upheld governmental transparency in 2006 had retired before *Neri* v. *Senate* was decided; four Arroyo appointees (Nachura, Reyes, Leonardo-de Castro, and Brion) had joined the court. Some of the continuing justices also changed their votes. Apart from the exertion of external political pressure, which is often alleged when justices change course, it is also possible that the justices who switched were concerned that an anti-Arroyo decision could trigger greater political instability. Unlike the political pressure hypothesis, this view assumes that the justices were motivated by a commitment to keep the polity stable. In any case, the court's ruling in *Neri* v. *Senate*, which became final in September 2008, marked the return of a court sympathetic to President Arroyo.

A number of factors may account for the pro-Arroyo voting tendencies of the current members of the Supreme Court. One explanation is that Arroyo appointed to the court people who shared her policy views. This account posits that justices are principled and independent decision-makers who decide a case as they see it. The alternative view is that a host of external factors—cultural values, institutional arrangements, institutional incentives and constraints, etc.—affect the independence of justices and their decision-making. The Filipino value of 'utang na loob' or debt of gratitude can prevent an appointee from voting against his or her benefactor, the president, while the value of 'pakikisama' or camaraderie tends to discourage disagreement with other appointees and with the appointing authority.

Still, there are accounts which emphasize the crucial role of institutional arrangements. Spaeth (1979: 113) has argued that certain features of the American political system foster the independence of U.S. Supreme Court justices, such as (a) lack of ambition for higher office; (b) lack of electoral accountability; and (c) the Supreme Court being the court of last resort. One can of course add life tenure and perhaps even ample compensation and benefits. Taking that viewpoint into consideration, it would appear that some features of the Philippine Supreme Court do not bode well for judicial independence—the insulation of justices from external and partisan pressures. The absence of life tenure and the comparatively low salaries of Filipino justices may not have a perceptible bearing on judicialization but certainly contribute to the lack of independence and the possible cooptation of the court. When justices do not feel adequately compensated, are insecure about their lives after serving on the Supreme Court, or are contemplating post-court political careers, it is not inconceivable that they might be susceptible to partisan or populist pressures or the desire to gain the favor of the appointing authority—the president.

At worst justices may be tempted to engage in inappropriate behavior. For instance, in February 2009 the court announced that it had found one of its justices guilty of leaking a yet unpromulgated court decision for pecuniary considerations (Pazzibugan 2009). The incident raises disturbing questions about how well insulated justices are from external inducements and about their sense of security.

A major concern for advocates of judicial reform is the process of judicial appointments. The president appoints members of the judiciary. To help the president choose appointees, the constitution created the Judicial and Bar Council (JBC), which prepares a list of possible candidates for the president to choose from. The constitution does not require the consent of the Commission of Appointments for appointees to the Supreme Court.

The JBC consists of (1) the chief justice as *ex officio* chairman; (2) the Secretary of Justice; (3) a representative of the Congress as an *ex officio* member; (4) a representative of the integrated bar; (5) a professor of law; (6) a retired member of the Supreme Court; and (7) a representative of the private sector. The president appoints JBC members with the consent of the Commission of Appointments, though appointees to the bench do not require confirmation.

To insulate judicial appointments from politics, the delegates to the 1986 Constitutional Commission discarded confirmation by politicians in the Commission of Appointments. There are recurring observations, however, that the process has not really been insulated from partisan influences. It has been suggested (see Bakker 1997; Vitug 2010) that the process has fostered the cooptation of justices by making them feel indebted to the appointing president or making them vulnerable to quid pro quo deals. In the absence of a thorough and merit-based process for screening potential justices, personal connections seem to be the primary consideration in recommending and choosing appointees, making the process highly susceptible to presidential cooptation.

There is a 'realist' view that judicial appointments are intended by the appointing officer to be partisan. The court that Corazon Aquino constituted in 1986 was designed to be anti-Marcos, or at least tilted against him. In the Philippines, in choosing appointees to the court, the president apparently selects those who can be regarded as allies against a perceived rival or threat. Hence, Aquino chose critics of Marcos. It is revealing that at least three of Macapagal-Arroyo's Supreme Court appointees— Minita Chico-Nazario, Teresita Leonardo-De Castro, and Disodado Peralta—had been judges on the lower Philippine court which tried Joseph Estrada for plunder. It also bears noting that Leonardo-De Castro and Peralta, as members of the *Sandiganbayan*, had found Estrada guilty. Meanwhile, one Arroyo appointee, Antonio Eduardo Nachura, had been a member of the lower house prosecution panel that prosecuted Estrada for impeachment.

Appointing allies against a common enemy or threat makes political sense; an alliance forged in such a manner promises mutual protection. Judicial appointments serve as political security for presidents who perceive enemies. This section argues that while there are institutional norms and practices which foster judicial activism and judicialization, there are also arrangements and practices which nurture the cooptation of justices.

The apparent cooptation of the court may be attributed to a confluence of events, including cultural and institutional factors. Still, the role of presidential appointment seems to stand out. President Arroyo had the strange luck of appointing a number of neophytes to the court during the latter years of her presidency. Studies have noted the impact of 'freshman effects' on justices' voting behavior (See Epstein *et al.* 2008). Most neophyte justices are alleged to undergo a period of adjustment or 'acclimation' during their early years on the court and justices' judicial philosophies gain stability only after some time. This suggests that the votes of judicial neophytes are mostly malleable and susceptible to go with the majority. If the acclimation hypothesis is correct, the apparent cooptation of the court may be nothing but the result of freshman effects en masse. Acclimation may be part of this confluence of factors which resulted in the apparent cooptation of the court.

As to whether the cooptation of the Philippine Supreme Court is a fleeting or lasting phenomenon, in the Philippines presidents see court appointees as allies and possible sources of protection. The potential for presidential cooptation of the court is inherent in the appointment process. When political disputes become contentious, presidents can be expected to take full advantage of their appointment powers to exert influence on the court. But when political contests cease to be zero-sum games, the court can be expected to operate with more independence.

Will the present court continue to be the Arroyo Court in the immediate future? The sudden resignation of Merceditas Gutierrez as ombudsman suggests that members of the Arroyo 'alliance' may not be determined to protect her at all costs. Justices have been known to vote against their appointing benefactors, and rivalries and alliances in the Philippines tend to be fleeting. There are reasons to suspect that Arroyo's hold on the current members of the court will at some point slacken. But given political pressures and partisan influences and its preeminence in legal and constitutional disputes, the temptation to coopt the court will always be there.

With regard to lessons from the Philippine experience for scholars of judicial politics, while the judicialization of politics may be a global phenomenon, that does not necessarily mean that the force driving it is the same everywhere. The spirit behind it may be a confluence of many different factors. At any rate, whether singular or a host of factors, the explanation for judicialization in a particular geopolitical setting has to be investigated in that particular setting. Though the phenomenon may be global, the explanation must be local, even if not necessarily exclusive to that setting. As Hirschl (2004) suggests, the explanation must also take into account the element of timing.

There is danger in overlooking the context-specific features of a given case of judicialization. To treat the Philippine Supreme Court as a mere copy of its counterpart in the United States would be a mistake. Even apart from cultural factors, the institutional constraints and incentives bearing on the behavior of Filipino justices are not the same as those on their American counterparts.

It would also be a mistake to treat 'constitutionalism' as a concept that raises no problems, or to assume that all constitutions have similar contents. Hirschl (2004) argues that promotion of neoliberalism is the driving force behind the new constitutionalism and the judicialization of politics, particularly in Israel, New Zealand, and South Africa. If that is the case, judicialization in the Philippines is clearly not a manifestation of the 'new constitutionalism': With its protectionist policy prescriptions the Philippine constitution is hardly a neoliberal document. In fact, neoliberals in the Philippines (along with politicians who detest term limits) are the ones who clamor most persistently for amending or replacing the present constitution.

Conclusion

The Philippine constitution itself provides the legal basis for judicial intrusion into what would be regarded in most other jurisdictions as the realm of politics. Philippine politics values constitutionality—or at least its appearance. Even the authoritarian Ferdinand Marcos hid his activities behind a facade of constitutionality and legality. In addition to 'constitutional' factors, the confluence of other institutional and structural features of judicial decision-making has nurtured the process of Philippine judicialization. The separation of powers system of government, with its penchant for finding itself in gridlock, has created a political environment favorable to judicial intrusion.

Judicialization, along with reliance on the concept of 'constitutional supremacy', has made courts the object of political capture and control. The confluence of personal considerations, cultural factors, and institutional arrangements has transformed the judicialization of politics into the politicization of Philippine courts. On its face, judicialization, while premised on the rule of law, seems to produce the opposite: It seems rather to breed legal uncertainty and instability. As a process, judicialization has to be studied in relation to the environment which nurtured it. This will require analysis of the context-specific and time-specific features of judicialization.

Notes

1 The Philippine Supreme Court cases cited are available at http://sc.judiciary.gov.ph/.
2 'Lakas' is the Filipino term for 'strength'.
3 EDSA is the acronym for Epifanio de los Santos Avenue which served as the venue for 'people power' uprisings in the Philippines. EDSA I refers to the 1986 people power uprising that led to Ferdinand Marcos' ousting.
4 The 1935, 1973, and 1987 Constitutions contain specific policy statements pertaining to the economy and social justice. It is not the presence of specific policy statements

alone which produces judicialization. Their presence alongside the stipulation that judicial review is a 'duty' favors judicialization. Examples of policy statements can be found in the following constitutional provisions: (1) Paragraph 2, Section 10, Art XII: 'In the grant of rights, privileges, and concessions covering the national economy and patrimony, the State shall give preference to qualified Filipinos.' Citing this provision, the Court in *Manila Prince Hotel* v. *GSIS* (February 1997) prevented a Malaysian firm from buying the Manila Hotel; and (2) Section 19, Art XII: 'The State shall regulate or prohibit monopolies when the public interest so requires. No combinations in restraint of trade or unfair competition shall be allowed.' On the basis of this provision the Court in *Tatad* v. *Secretary of the Department of Energy* (November 1997) ruled that the First Oil Deregulation Law was unconstitutional because it promoted unfair competition in the oil industry.

5 Tinga, on the one hand, cited constitutional provisions which advance economic protectionism like paragraph 1, Section 2, Art XII: 'The State may directly undertake such activities, or it may enter into co-production, joint venture, or production-sharing agreements with Filipino citizens, or corporations or associations at least sixty per centum of whose capital is owned by such citizens', and, on the other hand, those that encourage foreign participation like paragraph 4, Section 2, Art XII: 'The President may enter into agreements with foreign-owned corporations involving either technical or financial assistance for large-scale exploration, development, and utilization of minerals, petroleum, and other mineral oils according to the general terms and conditions provided by law, based on real contributions to the economic growth and general welfare of the country.'

6 Similarly, individual agency has a bearing on the way justices respond to attempts by other interests to coopt them. Some justices would succumb to cooptation while others would resist.

7 The cooptation of the Supreme Court is not a new phenomenon. The author does not also suggest that attempts to erode the court's image as impartial arbiter were observed only during the latter part of Arroyo's presidency.

8 Noli de Castro, the vice-president at the time was perceived by the Philippine middle class and business community to be incompetent and inexperienced ('Philippine VP de Castro Seen as Risky Replacement for Arroyo' (2005).

References

Agabin, P. (1996) 'The politics of judicial review over executive action: the Supreme Court and social change', in Agabin, P. *Unconstitutional Essays*, pp. 167–98. Manila: University of the Philippines Press.

Agabin, P. (1997) 'Judicial review of economic policy under the 1987 Constitution', *Philippine Law Journal*, 72: 176–94.

Bakker, J. W. (1997) *The Philippine Justice System: The Independence and Impartiality of the Judiciary and Human Rights from 1986 till 1997*. Leiden, Netherlands: Centre for the Independence of Judges and Lawyers.

Bernas, J. G. (1999) *A Living Constitution: The Ramos Presidency*. Pasig City, Philippines: Anvil Publishing, Inc.

Bernas, J. G. (2000) *A Living Constitution: The Cory Aquino Presidency*. Pasig City, Philippines: Anvil Publishing, Inc.

Bernas, J. G. (2001) '13–0: 'What does it mean?', *Today*, 4 March.

Bernas, J. G. (2003) *A Living Constitution: The Abbreviated Estrada Presidency*. Quezon City: ADMU Press.

Bernas, J. G. (2007) *A Living Constitution: The Troubled Arroyo Presidency*. Quezon City: ADMU Press.

Bernas, J. G. (2010) 'Shadow of a doubt', *Philippine Daily Inquirer*, 21 March. Available online at: http://opinion.inquirer.net/inquireropinion/columns/view/20100321-260099/Shadow-of-Doubt. (accessed 8 February 2012).

Cruz, I. A. (2001) 'The Estrada Case', 11 March. Available online at: http://separateopinion.wordpress.com/2010/07/02/the-estrada-case-marc ... (accessed 8 August 2011).

Cruz, I. A. and Datu, C. C. (2000) *A Brief History of the Supreme Court (from Arellano to Narvasa)*. Manila: Rex Printing Company, Inc.

de Leon, H. S. (2002) *Textbook on the Philippine Constitution*, Manila: Rex Book Store.

Dedace, S. (2010) 'Christian Monsod: SC under Arroyo is like a Marcos court', *GMA News Online*, 18 March. Available online at: www.gmanews.tv/story/186447/christian-monsod-sc-under-arroyo- (accessed 8 August 2011).

Easton, D. (1953) *The Political System: An Inquiry Into the State of Political Science*. New York: Knopf.

Epstein, L. and Knight, J. (1998) *The Choices Justices Make*. Washington, DC, USA: Congressional Quarterly Inc.

Epstein, L., Quinn, K., Martin, A. D., and Segal, J. (2008) 'On the perils of drawing inferences about Supreme Court Justices from their first few years of service', *Judicature*, 91: 168.

Global Integrity Report (2004) The Philippines: Integrity Scorecard. Available online at: http://back.globalintegrity.org/reports/2004/2004/scoresd466.html?cc=p ... (accessed 8 August 2011).

Global Integrity Report (2006) Philippines: Integrity Scorecard. Available online at: http://back.globalintegrity.org/reports/2006/PHILIPPINES/scorecard.cfm (accessed 8 August 2011).

Global Integrity Report (2007) Philippines: Integrity Scorecard. Available online at: http://report.globalintegrity.org/Philippines/2007/scorecard (accessed 8 August 2011).

Global Integrity Report (2008) Philippines: Integrity Scorecard. Available online at: http://report.globalintegrity.org/Philippines/2008/scorecard (accessed 8 August 2011).

Global Integrity Report (2010) Scorecard: Philippines 2010. Available online at: www.globalintegrity.org/report/Philippines/2010/scorecard (accessed 8 August 2011).

Haynie, S. (1998) 'Paradise lost: politicisation of the Philippine Supreme Court in the post Marcos era', *Asian Studies Review*, 22: 459–473.

Hirschl, R. (2004) "The political origins of the new constitutionalism", *Indiana Journal of Global Legal Studies*, 11: 71–108.

Hirschl, R. (2008) 'The judicialization of mega-politics and the rise of political courts', *Annual Review of Political Science*, 11: 1–44. Available online at: http://ssrn.com/abstract=1138008.

Maltzman, F., Spriggs, J. F., and Wahlbeck, P. J. (2000) *Crafting Law on the Supreme Court: The Collegial Game*. New York, New York, USA: Cambridge University Press.

Orosa, T. J. C. (2004) 'Constitutional kritarchy under the grave abuse clause', *Ateneo Law Journal*, 49: 565–615.

Paguia, A. F. (2003) *Estrada v. Arroyo: Rule of Law or Rule of Force?* Manila: Icon Press Inc.

Panganiban, A. (2004) 'Gravely abusive contracts: the role of the Supreme Court in promoting judicial statesmanship', *Ateneo Law Journal*, 49: 4–31.

Pazzibugan, D. (2009) 'Ex-SC justice banned for life to practice law', *Philippine Daily Inquirer*, 14 August. Available online at: http://newsinfo.inquirer.net/inquirerheadlines/nation/view/20090814-220222/Ex-SC-justice-banned-for-life-to-practice-law (accessed 8 February 2012).

Philippine Supreme Court Cases, available online at http://sc.judiciary.gov.ph/.

Rufo, A. C. and Romero, P. S. (2008) 'In the High Court, some justices are more loyal than others', *abs-cbnNEWS.com/Newsbreak.* 23 October. Available online at: www.abs-cbnnews.com/special-report/10/23/08/high-court-some-justices-are-more-loyal-others (accessed 15 March 2010).

Social Weather Stations (2011) Fourth Quarter 2010 Social Weather Survey, 27 January. Available online at: www.sws.org.ph/pr20110127.htm (accessed 30 July 2011).

Segal, J. A. and Spaeth, H. J. (2002) *The Supreme Court and the Attitudinalist Model Revisited.* New York, New York, USA: Cambridge University Press.

Spaeth, H. (1979) *Supreme Court Policy Making: Explanation and Prediction.* San Francisco, California, USA: W.H.Freeman and Company.

Tate, C. N. (1994) 'The judicialization of politics in the Philippines and Southeast Asia', *International Political Science Review*, 15: 187–97.

Vitug, M. D. (2010) *Shadow of Doubt: Probing the Supreme Court.* Quezon City: Public Trust Media Group Inc.

'Philippine VP de Castro Seen as Risky Replacement for Arroyo' (2005) VOANews.com, 16 July. Available online at: www.voanews.com/english/news/a-13-2005-07-16-voa7.html (accessed 8 February 2012).

Weingast, B. (1997) 'The political foundations of democracy and rule of law', *American Political Science Review*, 91: 245–63.

8 The judicialization of politics in Pakistan

Charles H. Kennedy

Introduction

In its 63-year independence Pakistan has had a very complicated and fluid constitutional history (see, e.g., Khan 2001 and Newberg 1995). It has had five formal constitutions, one inherited at independence (the Government of India Act of 1935, modified by the India Independence Act of 1947) and four indigenously crafted documents in 1956, 1962, 1972, and 1973. At times it has also operated without a written constitution (1958–62; 1969–71), under a 'suspended' constitution (1977–1985) and a 'modified' though 'restored' constitution (1985–97)—the last of which was significantly altered by the passage of the Thirteenth Amendment (1997–99).

Between October 1999 and August 2008 the state was dominated by other legal devices: two Provisional Constitution Orders (PCOs; 1999, 2007), and a Legal Framework Order, which were substantively incorporated into the constitution through the passage of the Seventeenth Amendment. In March 2007 President Musharraf took the ill-advised step of suspending the Chief Justice of the Supreme Court, Muhammad Iftikhar Chaudhury. After Chaudhury's court-ordered reinstatement, Musharraf promulgated the 2007 PCO, which effectively dismissed many (63) of the judges in Pakistan's superior judiciary by requiring them to take a fresh oath of office. They were replaced by judges willing to take the new oath. After President Musharraf was obliged to leave office in August 2008, the issues of the dismissed judges and of the broad powers that civilian President Zardari inherited from Musharraf were joined. The judges were restored in March 2009; and in April 2010, Parliament passed the Eighteenth Amendment, which 'restored' the constitution to a Prime Ministerial form of government. Indeed, functionally Pakistan has undergone 14 different constitutional structures since 1947.

Currently, Pakistan has a bicameral Parliament with a National Assembly and a Senate. The National Assembly consists of 342 members: 272 are directly elected in a first-past-the-post system from single member constituencies; 60 seats are reserved for women and 10 for non-Muslim minorities, which are allotted to the respective political parties to fill according to proportional representation determined by the overall percentage of votes received in the general election. The National Assembly selects the Prime Minister and serves a maximum term of five years or until the government chooses or is forced by a vote of no-confidence to hold a general election. The 102-member Senate is indirectly elected by the four provincial assemblies (23 from each—Punjab, Khyber Pukthunwha, Sindh, and Balochistan); 8 are selected from the Federally Administered Tribal Areas and 2 from Islamabad. Senators are elected for fixed six-year terms, with elections being held every two years for one-third of the members. The National Assembly is the dominant house—all money bills must originate there—but the Senate must concur with legislation so proposed. Both houses must approve amendments to the constitution. Since April 2010 with the passage of the Eighteenth Amendment, the Prime Minister is the head of government with the indirectly elected President's role reduced primarily to that of a head of state. The most recent election was held in February 2008 and a Pakistan People's Party (PPP)-led coalition elected Syed Yusuf Raza Gilani as prime minister in March. Another PPP politician, Asif Zardari, was selected as President following the resignation of Pervez Musharraf in 2008. The pattern of each of the four provinces mirrors that of the federal government—each has a provincial assembly whose members elect a Chief Minister.

Pakistan has seven federal courts—five High Courts (Punjab, Capital Territory—Islamabad, Khyber Pakhtunwha, Sindh, Balochistan); a Federal Shariat Court; and a Supreme Court. The appointment of judges to each of these benches is determined by Article 175A of the Constitution (as amended by the Nineteenth Amendment on 1 January 2011) in which respective Judicial Commissions (led and dominated by respective Chief Justices) submit recommendations to a federal Parliamentary Committee for approval. The High Courts' jurisdiction extends to its relevant province or territory in which it has standing to challenge or to entertain grievances against federal, provincial, and local government actions; they supervise all courts within their respective jurisdiction and they serve as a court of appeal to District and Sessions Courts. The Federal Shariat Court has broad jurisdiction to examine and determine if any law or provision of law is repugnant to the Holy Injunctions of Islam and to specify remedies for such offending laws to be made in consonance with its findings. (Article 203D). The Supreme Court is the apex court of the state. It has carved out very broad powers of judicial review in recent years; enjoys original jurisdiction to adjudicate disputes between provinces; is the court of last appeal against decisions of the High Courts; and through its Shariat Appellate Bench serves as the court of last appeal against decisions of the Federal Shariat Court (FSC).

Pakistan's superior courts have taken a somewhat tortuous path to their current judicial activism. Their role, and challenge, has often been to launder egregiously extra-constitutional acts of both military and civilian leaders to make them clean and constitutional. The task has been extremely complicated; it has often required considerable judicial creativity, not to mention tactical retreats, feints, veiled or not so veiled threats, promises, and implicit compromises or 'deals' with military dictators, reformed but still authoritarian former military dictators, and recalcitrant (democratically elected yet authoritarian) civilian political leaders.

Despite the distinction and sincerity of Pakistan's superior judiciary and legal community, and despite their voluminous and at times eloquent (if sometimes painfully) verbose case law, Pakistan's superior courts did not show much judicial backbone until the *Mian Nawaz Sharif* decision in 1993. Until then the Supreme Court (SC) had adopted two responses to egregious departures from the constitution:

Response A: Accept extra-constitutional political choices as regrettable, sometimes disturbing, and even at times reprehensible but ultimately necessary to maintain legal continuity and keep state institutions functioning. Some illustrative cases:

- *Tamizuddin Khan:* In 1954 Governor-General Ghulam Muhammad, tacitly supported by the military, dissolved the Constituent Assembly because 'the constitutional machinery has broken down' and declared a state of emergency. Assembly President Tamizuddin Khan argued before the Chief Court of Sindh that Muhammad did not have the power to dismiss the assembly. That court agreed but was overruled by the Federal Court,[1] which took the path of least resistance and tacitly validated Muhammad's action.
- *Dosso:* In 1958, after a military coup the President of Pakistan, Iskandar Mirza, annulled the 1956 constitution and declared Chief of Army Staff (COAS) General Mohammad Ayub Khan Chief Martial Law Administrator. The Supreme Court ruled in *Dosso*[2] that a military coup was a valid way to change government particularly if the new government fundamentally maintained the institutional structure of the state (e.g., Laws [Continuation in Force] Order, 1958). The court thus interpreted the adoption of the 'law of necessity' as unavoidable to avoid legal chaos; therefore, it had no choice but to validate the constitutionality of the coup.
- *Nusrat Bhutto:* When General Zia-ul-Haq declared martial law, deposed and imprisoned Prime Minister Z. A. Bhutto, and suspended the 1973 Constitution, the Prime Minister's wife, Nusrat Bhutto, appealed to the Supreme Court, which (following *Dosso*) found the coup valid,[3] based on documentation that Bhutto and his party, among other derelictions, had rigged the 1977 elections and engaged in massive corruption.
- *Zulfiqar Ali Bhutto:* The Lahore High Court—reconstituted by judges willing to take a new oath under a new government—found Z. A. Bhutto and four others guilty of ordering the murder of a political rival, Ahmed Raza Kasuri. On appeal the SC, now led by a Zia-ul-Haq appointee Anwar-ul-Haq, upheld the death penalty conviction 4–3.[4]

Response B: Declare executive acts 'extra-constitutional' eloquently and boldly, but too late to do anything about them. Illustrative cases:

- *Asma Jilani:* In 1969 at the request of President Ayub Khan, COAS General Yahya Khan staged a coup to protect the administration from a variety of threats; he established martial law, dismissed the cabinet, and dissolved national and provincial assemblies—but left the courts and the law alone. After general elections in 1970 and a disastrous civil war that led to the independence of Bangladesh, Yahya Khan was forced to resign.

After his departure the SC addressed the constitutionality of his 1969 assumption of power in the *Asam Jilani* case[5]; it found, forcefully, that the 'doctrine of necessity' that supported *Dossa* was bad law; Yahya Khan was a 'usurper' who had seized the government without any legal justification; but laws made and actions taken while Yahya was in charge had to be accepted as valid to avoid disastrous political and legal consequences.

- *Saifullah Khan:* General Zia ul-Haq became president in 1982, and the Eighth Amendment passed in 1985 gave the president power to dissolve national and provincial assemblies, which he did in May 1988. A writ to challenge the dissolution was promptly filed before the Lahore High Court, which ruled the dissolution unconstitutional. It was on appeal to the SC when Zia was assassinated in August, leaving Pakistan without a president, prime minister, national and provincial assemblies, and provincial chief ministers. Because the Senate was not subject to dissolution, the constitutional succession brought into the presidency the Senate chairman, Ghulam Ishaq Khan, who promptly called for assembly elections.

  The SC upheld the Lahore ruling,[6] saying dissolution was only acceptable 'when the government has broken down completely', and even then the president must name a caretaker cabinet. However, like the Lahore court the SC found that the 'national interest' would not be served by reinstating the assemblies because a new election campaign was under way.

Starting with the *Saifullah Khan* decision in 1989 the court was consistently seeking a dignified and useful role for itself as 'referee' between president and prime minister: The president had authority to dismiss the prime minister and chief ministers but had to make a good case for doing so, and when his reasoning and the responses to it confronted each other, the SC was final arbiter (see Kennedy 1995). In allowing the court to assume this role, the prime minister and the president had opened the door for what at first was a trickle but later a flood of judicial activism. But before we explore that further, let us consider the very important role of the FSC in establishing the independence of the superior judiciary.

Islamization and judicial activism

The tortured history of 'Islamization' in Pakistan is far too broad to contemplate here. The inability of Pakistan to adopt its first indigenous constitution until nine years after independence can largely be explained by the rift between 'Islamic moderates' (often called 'secularists' by their detractors) and 'Islamists' (often called 'fundamentalists' by their detractors). With the 1956 constitution the moderates won out, but we will start our brief discussion in the early 1980s, when Zia-ul-Haq assumed power.

In 1980 Zia created a Federal Shariat Court (FSC) with appellate and revisional jurisdiction over acquittals from lower courts (High Courts and sessions courts) in cases based on Zia's new Islamic criminal laws (the *Hudood* laws); exclusive jurisdiction to hear 'Shariat petitions' brought against 'any law or provision of law' as repugnant to the Holy Qur'an or Sunnah; and jurisdiction on its own motion (*suo* moto) to identify such repugnancy. Zia expected implementation of his Islamization program to be incremental, prudential, and cautious. For instance, while he granted the FSC extraordinarily wide jurisdiction, he narrowly limited how it might apply the term 'law'. Also, Zia appointed FSC jurists from High Court judges who were recognized as moderates; and also provided that FSC findings could be appealed to a new Shariat Appellate Bench (SAB) of the SC.

Between 1980 and 1986 the FSC scrutinized several thousand laws, ordinances, orders, and regulations; in dozens of cases the authority responsible for an offending law was obliged to make revisions. Ultimately, however, the court found definitively that over 99 percent of Pakistan's laws were in consonance with Islam.

Moreover, few bringing Shariat petitions found relief. Between 1979 and 1987, 330 petitions were filed; nearly half (122) dealt with land cases, most of the rest were concerned with Islamic criminal law and punishments; civil service grievances; family laws; social practice; and *riba* (bank interest; for details, see Kennedy 1992). By invoking Article 203B, which conveniently limited its jurisdiction, the court avoided addressing all such topics save civil servant grievances, though in its attempts to improve conditions of employment for government servants it was quite activist.

Somewhat ironically the FSC became far more expansive of its interpretation of its role after its founder Zia died in 1987. It played a significant part in rescinding tenancy rights to the pre-emption of land, and ultimately in the wholesale gutting of the progressive, yet flawed, Land Reforms introduced during Zulfikar Bhutto's governments in 1972 and 1977 (Kennedy, 1993a). It also was a main actor in the complicated and tortured attempts to ban *riba* from the economy of the state; attempts that were later upheld and then reversed on appeal by the Shariat Appellate Bench of the Supreme Court (Kennedy 1993b; 2004).[7]

Another of Zia's Islamic initiatives was the *Hudood* ordinances introduced in 1979. These were four hastily drafted ordinances that covered *zina* (sexual crimes—rape, fornication, sodomy, adultery, and related issues); *qazf* (the imputation of immodesty to a woman with respect to *zina*); prohibition (alcohol and narcotics); and property (theft). In hearing appeals the FSC over the decades has softened the fervor of district judges and prevented the harshest penalties (stoning; cutting of hands) from ever being carried out.

After nearly three decades of concerted opposition against the *Hudood* laws by feminist and human rights groups, the Parliament passed an act Protection of

Women (Criminal Laws Amendment) in December 2006[8] which among other things put *Hudood* crimes back under the Pakistan Penal Code, redefined certain crimes under *zina*, and established appeal to the High Courts, thus reducing the jurisdiction of the FSC.

Late in 2010, the FSC, perhaps heartened by the expanding reach of the Supreme Court released its monumental response to the Protection of Women Act—*Abdur Razaq Aamir* v. *Federal Government of Pakistan.*[9] Its argument centered on the contention that the FSC's jurisdiction was sanctioned and protected by the constitution and therefore could not be curtailed by subordinate legislation. The judgment also pointed out that the FSC can review its own decisions Article 203-GG; and its power of review is not subject to an act of Parliament. Gratuitously, it added that the Council of Islamic Ideology, established and protected by the constitution, was defined as a wholly advisory body with its reports and findings subject to review by the Parliament and the courts.[10]

The *Abdur Razzaq Aamir* case reminded those who had forgotten that the FSC was also to be reckoned with in terms of judicial activism. It has since its inception had discretionary authority to pretty much do as it pleases. Ultimately its findings and standing to entertain cases can only be reviewed by the SAB, which is appointed by the Chief Justice from among Muslim SC justices. Thus, the FSC and SC may either reinforce their collective interests in increasing their authority against potential competing state institutions; or they can limit each other's judicial activism. The *Addur Razzaq Aamir* decision, currently on appeal to the SAB, may suggest whether the courts will cooperate or compete.

'Enlightened' military authoritarianism

In 1997 Nawaz Sharif returned with a vengeance (see Kennedy 2009; 2006). In the 1997 elections he and his Pakistan Muslim League – Nawaz (PML-N) won far more seats than the two-thirds necessary to amend the constitution. Rapidly and forcefully Sharif orchestrated unanimous passage of the Thirteenth Amendment, which by repealing Articles 58(2)b and 112(2)b effectively ended the power of the president to dismiss the national and provincial assemblies. It was also a frontal assault on the SC, stripping it of its powers as referee between the prime minister and the president. The passage in July of the Fourteenth Amendment, which prohibited 'floor crossing' (thus enforcing party discipline) relieved the Nawaz government of any civilian threat; it now need not fear either a presidential dissolution or a no-confidence vote in the National Assembly.

The judiciary struck back. On 29 October a three-judge SC panel headed by Chief Justice Sajjad Ali Shah accepted a petition challenging the constitutionality of the Fourteenth Amendment, declared the amendment *sub judice*, and suspended its operation until it ruled on the challenge.

Not surprisingly Nawaz took offense.[11] After he denounced both the court's ruling and the integrity of the chief justice, on 2 November the chief justice cited him for contempt of court. But during the first day of the contempt trial a group (mob) of PML-N loyalists (thugs) occupied the Supreme Court building. A few days earlier, two other SC judges had filed a petition challenging the right of Sajjid Ali Shah to serve as chief justice (he had been promoted during Benazir Bhutto's second government) because he had not been the senior SC judge when he was elevated and issued an order that no fresh cases be directed to him. Subsequently, the full SC found Shah's appointment illegal, and Ajmal Mian succeeded him. Now Nawaz Sharif and his government were effectively immune from challenge not only by the National Assembly but also by a now intimidated SC. But Sharif had neglected to immunize himself from the military.

On 12 October 1999, COAS General Pervez Musharraf staged a bloodless military coup, using essentially the same script as his predecessors. Like Zia, he promulgated a Provisional Constitution Order (PCO) that put the constitution in 'abeyance', and though 'maintaining function and exercise of [all courts'] respective power and jurisdiction' prohibited any court from challenging any of his actions or proclamations or those of any other persons exercising authority in his name.[12]

Petitions challenging the PCO were filed with the SC, but before hearings commenced, on 28 January 2000 Musharraf forced members of the superior judiciary to take a fresh oath, this one to uphold the PCO. Six SC justices, including Chief Justice Saeeduzzaman Siddiqui, and nine High Court justices refused and were retired. Irshad Hasan Khan became the new chief justice.

The reconstituted SC then defended its decision to entertain petitions filed against the PCO because 'undertaking a fresh oath of office does not in any way preclude the judges of this court from examining the questions raised ... which have to be decided ... so as to resolve the grave crises and avoid disaster'. Then, although it found that removal of judges through the device of the fresh oath was an unconstitutional departure from the rules found in Article 209, the court declared it could not offer a remedy because it is 'hit by the doctrine of past and closed transactions and cannot be reopened'.[13] It went on to validate the 1999 PCO because the COAS had no choice but to take such unconstitutional means given wholesale corruption; the contempt shown by Nawaz Sharif for the superior judiciary; and so forth. That is, the army and General Musharraf had validly assumed power by means of an extra-constitutional vehicle, but they had done so in the sincere interest of the state and its people (the 'touchstone of State necessity'). However, the SC found that civilian rule should be restored in the shortest possible time, which it set at three years.

Tidying up the mess[14]

General Musharraf may have sincerely wanted to leave office, but the task, particularly after the US asked Pakistan to be its primary partner in the 'Global War Against Terror' proved highly complicated and required extreme creativity. Musharraf faced four immediate obstacles: (1) he had to become the president; (2) he had to significantly revise the constitution to remove the Thirteenth and Fourteenth Amendments; (3) he had to hold elections by 12 October 2002; and (4) he had to convince the new National Assembly to validate his re-engineering.

First, on 1 May 2002, borrowing from the Ayub and Zia playbook, he called a referendum, asking the voters to elect him to a five-year term as president so that he could consolidate his 'reforms and reconstruction of institutions of state for the establishment of genuine and sustainable democracy … and to combat extremism and sectarianism.' Reportedly, 97.5 percent of those who voted said yes.

President Musharraf moved quickly to reconstruct the constitution. In June he ordered the National Reconstruction Bureau (NRB) to craft a package of constitutional reforms and make them available online for public discussion. On 21 August he formally promulgated the NRB's recommendations as Legal Framework Order (LFO), 2002, which among other things established the size of the prospective national and provincial assemblies; validated all laws, actions, orders, and so forth issued since Musharraf and his government assumed office; and declared that all superior judges who had taken the most recent oath were regular members of the judiciary.[15] On 9 October 2002 he promulgated the Legal Framework (Amendment) Order, lifting the retirement age of the superior judiciary from 65 to 68.[16]

Next, Musharraf arranged to hold elections on the LFO schedule. He also significantly tilted the playing field in the direction of the Pakistan Muslim League (Qaid-i-Azam 'Q'), his own party, through the Political Parties Ordinance, which mandated that parties elect their leaders and draft (time-consuming and divisive) formal party platforms. It also restricted the length of electoral campaigns and subjected would-be candidates to time-consuming oversight by the Election Commission (see Botteron 2006). Musharraf's Conduct of General Elections Order, 2002, required that all candidates to national and provincial assemblies hold a bachelor's degree or its equivalent from a recognized *madrassa*. Not surprisingly, given these reforms and considering that opposition leaders Benazir and Nawaz were exiled, the PML (Q) won a plurality of seats in the National Assembly. Mir Zafarullah Khan Jamali was asked to form the government.

Finally, the contentious new National Assembly agreed to validate Musharraf's new constitutional system—at a price. In exchange for support of the LFO, which was presented to the assembly as the Seventeenth Amendment, the opposition parties insisted that Musharraf relinquish this position as COAS by the end of 2004. Thus the Seventeenth Amendment was passed on 30 December 2003, and on 1 January 2004 Parliament gave Musharraf a vote of confidence, which continued his term as president.

The Seventeenth Amendment confirmed the re-establishment of a president-dominant system, but Musharraf was reluctant to resign as COAS and in October managed to cobble together a National Assembly majority to pass the President to Hold Another Office Act, 2004. Although this bought him time, it did not end the controversy, because Article 63 of the constitution plainly states no one can hold at any one time more than one 'properly paid position in the service of Pakistan' (see Kennedy 2005).

With his four urgent goals accomplished, Musharraf in 2004 found himself heading up a new presidential-dominant political system where the National Assembly was weak, ineffective, and hopelessly contentious—a system in which the military, with Musharraf still COAS, played a dominant though indirect role—but with a relatively effective, if less than democratic, government. Musharraf was lauded in the international press as having saved Pakistan's troubled democracy, having the backbone to stand up to terrorists and for making Pakistan a firm ally of the US–NATO coalition in Afghanistan.

Meanwhile, the superior judiciary had willingly accepted, or had been intimidated into going along with, the general's plans. After its less than heroic defense of its judicial autonomy by taking the fresh oath and its validation of the PCO's 'necessity' in the *Zafar Ali Shah* case, the SC followed with several at best equally timid responses to Musharraf. In 2002, the court had gone along with the dubious proposition that an educational requirement for election enhanced democratic representation, and though it found the fact that Musharraf unconstitutionally held two official positions, it reasoned that since the PCO had put the constitution in abeyance, it had no remedy to correct the ill.[17] Even more timidly, in the *Pakistan Lawyers' Forum* case of 13 April 2005, the SC wholly validated the Seventeenth Amendment by claiming sycophantically that Pakistan had 'emerged from a period of constitutional deviation' and that by 'striking down the Seventeenth Amendment [the SC] would destroy the entire system.'[18]

But then Musharraf made a serious mistake.

Suspension of the Chief Justice

In 2007, with a single action Musharraf's carefully crafted system unraveled. Before embarking on a campaign for a new five-year term of office as president, he decided to force out the 'unpredictable' Chief Justice Ifthikar Muhammad Chaudhry. Chaudhry had taken the judge's oath in January 2000 as a member of the Balochistan High Court and on 4 February had promptly been elevated to the SC. On 7 May 2005 he had become chief justice.

Until then Chaudhry's record was unremarkable. He had supported SC decisions for Musharraf in all the significant cases which had challenged Musharraf's rule, and apparently it was this reliability and his unexceptional career that had encouraged Musharraf to make him chief justice. At the time Chaudhry had just turned 57; the retirement age for judges of the Supreme Court is 65.

But after being named chief justice, Iftikhar Chaudhry became quite a different man. Soon after assuming the post he set up a Human Rights Cell (HRC) in the Supreme Court; its job was to receive petitions from those aggrieved or those knowledgeable of human rights offenses (broadly defined). Since 2005 the SC has received tens of thousands of petitions. The court chooses to address those which have the most merit; and in some cases members of the court grant remedies directly or punish those responsible for offenses.

Chaudhry also initiated the practice of having court employees track media reports of crimes against women and children, abuses of justice, corruption, and abuse of power by civil servants and elected public officials and then claiming jurisdiction on its own motion to investigate and where warranted issue judicial orders. The foundation for this judicial activism was an expansive reading of

Article 184(3), which grants the court standing in cases which have public importance or which challenge fundamental rights expressed in the constitution.

Between May 2005 and March 2007, the court considered thousands of petitions and issued dozens of decisions. The most famous, the *Pakistan Steel Mills* case, involved the sale of Pakistan Steel Mills to a dummy firm based in Mauritius which was a front for Arif Habib, an infamous criminally indicted loan defaulter. Members of government had been paid handsomely to look the other way. The decision issued on 23 June 2006 was a profound embarrassment to Musharraf and the PML(Q), which had prided itself on being less corrupt than its predecessors.[19]

Musharraf suspended the Chief Justice on 9 March 2007. Chaudhry contested his suspension as being without cause and filed a petition to the SC challenging it.[20] Supporters defined his refusal to resign as 'heroic' and many were galvanized. Prominent in the resultant street demonstrations were lawyers as well as members of opposition political parties (the PPP and the PML(N)). On 12 May, at the invitation of the Karachi Bar Association Chaudhry visited Karachi, where his motorcade from the airport was attacked. When the dust settled 42 people had died and more than 150 were injured. The Sindh provincial government, along with Musharraf, was blamed for inadequate security. Ten weeks later on 20 July a full bench of the SC (without its chief justice) declared 10–3 that Musharraf had acted beyond his authority and lifted the suspension.

This was a truly historic decision. The court had stood up against a president, who was also still COAS; the event was characterized as restoring judicial autonomy and as a victory for the nascent lawyers' movement.

Ever resourceful, Musharraf found a remedy. On 5 October 2007 he promulgated the National Reconciliation Ordinance (NRO), which among other things terminated all pending legal proceedings related to financial improprieties initiated between 1 January 1986 and 12 October 1999.[21] Benazir Bhutto had been forced into exile in 1998 to avoid prosecution on numerous charges of corruption and other illegalities during her two terms as prime minister. The NRO allowed her to return to Pakistan without risking jail and would free her husband, Asif Zardari, from confinement. A day later, on 6 October, President Musharraf was re-elected by the members of the National Assembly, Senate, and provincial assemblies with 55 percent of the vote. By putting up a candidate to contest the election, unlike other opposition parties, Benazir's PPP thus legitimized the election.

Despite this clever (though transparent) deal, Musharraf's woes were far from over. Emboldened by popular support and led by the firebrand Chaudhry, who was deeply perturbed by his suspension, the SC struck back. Indeed, even before the NRO was promulgated, on 23 August 2007, the court in *Pakistan Muslim League v. Federation of Pakistan*[22] allowed Nawaz Sharif, who after the 1999 coup had accepted exile in Saudi Arabia rather than jail at home, to return to Pakistan. The eloquent and detailed decision by Justice Javed Iqbal found the agreement Nawaz Sharif had been obliged to sign to be invalid, as was his documented promise to stay away for at least 10 years.[23]

Further, on 28 September 2007 the court had invalidated the President to Hold Another Office Act as being in violation of Article 63 of the constitution, which cannot be amended simply by act of Parliament. It also opined that the president was barred from seeking a third term in office unless the constitution was amended.[24] But in a parallel decision, also decided on 28 September, the court ruled that it had no standing to remedy effects of the President to Hold Another Office Act because the act did not challenge any fundamental right.[25] On 12 October, as expected, the SC accepted appeals challenging the validity of the NRO.[26]

In retrospect Musharraf had no choice but to suspend the runaway judiciary. On 3 November he declared a state of emergency and issued a new Provisional Constitution Order (PCO).

Breaking new ground

This was a first in Pakistan's ever-creative constitutional system. The constitution was suspended by the 2007 PCO, which was in effect a military coup made by a standing COAS against a government whose civilian president happened to be the same COAS: Musharraf had replaced his own government with his own government. Although the PCO followed the well-worn tracks of such documents, legitimizing the coup on the basis of a 'breakdown of law and order' that posed 'a grave threat to the life and property of the citizens of Pakistan', the real target was a Supreme Court 'working at cross purposes with the executive and legislature in the fight against terrorism and extremism'.

The mechanism to cleanse the body politic of the recalcitrant judiciary was to require judges to take yet another new oath of office under the terms of the 2007 PCO. This time it would be like rebooting a computer: shut down the machine of state, make judges of the higher benches take a fresh oath of office which would oblige them to accept (again) that they had no power to 'make any order against the President or Prime Minister or any person exercising power or jurisdiction under their authority' and throw in for good measure a rider that no court could challenge the validity of the PCO itself.

Within a few hours of this PCO being promulgated, Chief Justice Chaudhry and six other SC judges refused to take the oath, issued an order declaring the PCO illegal, and enjoined members of the superior judiciary from taking the new oath.[27] Of the 19 SC justices, 15 did not take the new oath, along with 44 High Court judges.[28]

The new Supreme Court, augmented by oath-taking judges elevated from the High Courts, moved quickly. On 6 November new Chief Justice Hamid Dogar, the most senior of the SC judges who had taken the oath, countermanded the Chaudhry court's 3 November order on the grounds that it was made after the 2007 PCO had been issued.[29] By the Dogar court's logic, apparently the only way to declare a coup extra-constitutional would be before it happens. On 19 November the court dismissed several petitions challenging Musharraf's recent election as president on the grounds that (1) the two-office rule does not apply to a president; (2) because of the PCO the term limit issue does not prohibit his re-election; (3) he was a pious Muslim (even if, as counsel for the petitioner argued, he had lied about leaving office after three years); and (4) he met the educational requirements with a BS (honors) in war studies from the University of Balochistan and a 1983 M.Sc. in war studies from Qaid-i-Azam University.[30]

On 23 November the court found that the new oath of office was a valid exercise of power because (1) there was precedent (PCO, 1977 and *Zafar Ali Shah*); (2) the Chaudhry court had ignored 'due process' by extreme judicial activism as demonstrated by the HRC, which had led to an 'arbitrary selection of cases'; and (3) the court's reliance on an expanded interpretation of Article 184(3) does not apply to individual grievances.[31]

The actions of the new SC paved the way for Musharraf to dismiss the National Assembly (it had completed its five-year term) and name a caretaker prime minister. The new court had also given him the space to resolve the 'uniform issue' and resign as COAS, naming General Asfaq Pervez Kayani as his successor. With these matters taken care of, Musharraf withdrew the 2007 PCO on 15 December. Rebooted, the government had been returned to its original state but without 63 troublesome superior court judges. As 2007 was closing, Musharraf seemed invincible. The National Assembly to be elected should be less contentious; at worst the PML(Q) would share power with one of the other two major political parties, but both their leaders (Benazir Bhutto and Nawaz Sharif) were banned from serving another term as prime minister; under its tainted new chief justice the SC was now docile; and Musharraf could remain in control indefinitely as president. But the well-designed plans of even a very clever politician and general are vulnerable to surprises.

On a campaign trip in Rawalpindi on 27 December 2007 Benazir Bhutto was assassinated. The persons responsible were not brought to justice, and Musharraf's government was blamed for ineffective security. The dismissal of the superior justices was sparking increasing protests, led by the lawyers and their associations but now joined by both opposition parties. And it was too late to delay or abort the general election. In the February 2008 election Bhutto's PPP won a plurality of seats, the PML(Q) suffered significant losses, and in March the PPP was able to put together a government headed by long-term PPP leader and loyalist Syed Yusuf Raza Gilani. Even the Dogar Court began to show signs of independence. In February it rejected a petition filed against the dismissal of the superior court judges but found that although the dismissal of the judges (and by implication the PCO itself) was illegal, the court had no remedy but to allow the reprehensible act to stand owing to the 'past and closed transactions' doctrine.[32]

Divided along normal party lines, the new civilian government could agree on little except two things: (1) President Musharraf should leave office; and (2) the superior court justices who had not taken the PCO 2007 oath order should be restored to their courts. The latter dovetailed neatly with the former. The judges issue was palpable proof of Musharraf's authoritarian past, it had drawn attention to the murky means by which he had gained another term as president, it challenged not only the legitimacy of his government but also the notion that

Pakistan was a democracy—but, most important, it had energized the opposition to work together to oust him.

The opposition, formed around the movement that had hastened restoration of the chief justice, had been growing. Supported first by lawyers and by both the PPP and the PML(N), it grew to incorporate women's groups, human rights groups, and students. Defrocked members of the superior judiciary also participated. The movement received very positive support from Pakistan's media, and the story was picked up by international media. For the most part the movement, although raucous, remained non-violent. As spring moved into summer, Musharraf became increasingly isolated and under siege.

In April even the Dogar Court took a swipe at Musharraf by overturning the educational requirements for elective office. The court ruled that it had standing under Article 184(3) because the issue involved both 'public importance' and fundamental rights. It presented evidence that the educational requirements were both restrictive with respect to class—only 4.1 percent of registered Pakistani voters and 1.6 percent of all Pakistanis—possess the requisite degrees; and with respect to region—the percentages are far lower in Balochistan and Azad Kashmir. Of course, this decision was warmly welcomed by the PPP and the PML(N), the original targets and victims of the educational requirements.[33]

Enter Zardari

On 7 August 2008 proceedings were initiated to impeach President Musharraf. On 18 August he resigned. It is generally believed that the military encouraged his resignation. On 6 September Parliament elected Asif Zardari, Benazir Bhutto's widower, president.

Although much of the support for Musharraf's resignation came from those who had demanded that the higher court judges be restored to office, President Zardari was loath to take that step. Perhaps he feared that a restored judiciary might find the NRO (the ordinance which had stopped proceedings against those deemed corrupt) unconstitutional; that would have meant that he had to either flee the country or go to jail. Moreover, a restored court would probably have considerable independent authority, having been associated with the downfall of Musharraf and being generally perceived as anxious for the restoration of democracy. And Zardari certainly was aware of the long-standing conflict between an assertive SC and the Bhuttos (the SC had upheld a murder conviction against his father-in-law and sustained the dismissal of his wife's two governments; more personally, it had accepted the contention that her government was enthusiastically corrupt and that Zardari himself was the ringleader of such corruption.) He also faced significant challenges from Nawaz Sharif and the PML(N). He decided to drop reinstatement of the judges from the PPP agenda and its implicit deal with the PML(N), the 'Charter of Democracy', and see if he could ride it out.

The Dogar Court did its best to help. In two cases decided on 25 February 2009, the court considered the political fate of the Sharif brothers, Shahbaz and Nawaz. Both wanted to lift the ban on their becoming elected officials; Nawaz had been banned as a consequence of his conviction in a case associated with the 1999 coup; and Shahbaz because he was part of the family that had (as admitted in Nawaz's confession) been engaged in monumental corruption when Shahbaz was Chief Minister of Punjab and Nawaz was Prime Minister. The court refused to lift the bans. Complicating the matter was that both petitioners had refused to attend hearings before first the Lahore High Court and later the SC, so the proceedings had been dragging on for over a year.[34] From a political perspective this kept the Sharifs, leaders of the largest opposition party in the National Assembly, from formally representing the PML(N) [the 'N' stands for Nawaz].

As Zardari delayed, the Movement for the Restoration of the Judges ('the Young Lawyers' Movement') continued to grow, and with party workers of the PML(N) and PPP, now factionalized along partisan lines, actively participating both for and against the movement, it became increasingly violent. With the active involvement of the Sharifs and supported by former judges and prominent legal practitioners, the movement planned a Great March from Lahore to Islamabad to push its agenda. With carnage likely, President Zardari relented: On 16 March he restored the judges to their former positions with their seniority intact. He also left in place the judges who had taken the oath, expanding the size of the superior courts through a rider in a finance act which was passed by Parliament.

The restored Chief Justice and the Supreme Court

The first major decision of the restored court was to claim standing to address whether the Sharif brothers were eligible for public office. In an opinion by Justice Tassadeq Hussain Jillani, the SC found that (1) rather than being contempt of the court, the absence of the Sharifs from the High Court and Supreme Court hearings was calculated to show support for justices who had refused to take the fresh oath of office; (2) given their motives, their case was not time-barred; (3) in any case the High Court did not have original jurisdiction under Article 199, but (4) the SC did have jurisdiction under Article 184(3) because the case was of public importance and freedom of association (Article 17) was involved.[35] Some argued, amid brisk discussion of related issues, that the decision fulfilled a debt of gratitude for PML(N) support for the displaced judges; others viewed it as payback for the absence of PPP support.

Another crucial decision of the reinstated court was the *Sindh High Court Bar Association* case, which addressed various aspects of the PCO, 2007. It is unusually long (455 pages) but at times eloquent, and it is dense with factual analysis of the history of the interaction of judiciary and executive. Some of the major findings:

1. The *Tika Khan* cases in which the Dogar Court had validated the PCO were deemed null and void, as were all of the other acts taken under the PCO, 2007.
2. Those who refused to take the new oath had never ceased to be members of the judiciary, so such positions had never fallen vacant. Therefore, Dogar was never in fact Chief Justice; all appointments to the superior judiciary

made in consultation with him (3 November 2007–22 March 2009) were unconstitutional; and the judges concerned were to be returned to their previous benches.

3 Those justices who took the new oath of office under the 2007 PCO would be dismissed and prosecuted for contempt of court under Article 204.
4 The SC was restored to the mandated 16 judges (Article 176), including the Chief Justice, from the 30 judges specified by the PPP-sponsored Finance Act.

The opinion, written by Chief Justice Chaudhry, is unremitting in its condemnation of the acts of Musharraf and the courts. It also shows no sympathy for judges who had taken the fresh oath—not only had they taken it under an extra-constitutional order, but they had defied a direct order of the CJ and his six SC colleagues issued on the day the 2007 PCO was announced. By taking the oath they stood in contempt of court—they were not only backing a usurper, they were destroying the integrity and autonomy of the court.[36]

On appeal the Supreme Court on 13 October 2009 reiterated that two classes of former jurists were in contempt of court: (1) those who had taken the fresh oath of office; and (2) those appointed by Dogar when he served as chief justice. The SC would dismiss the contempt charges if these judges withdrew their appeals and expressed 'unconditional apologies' to the real SC, or, if they had already retired, simply expressed their 'unconditional apologies'. Two days later, responding to a rumor that the PPP-led government was contemplating a new act that would restore the judges who had taken the 2007 oath,[37] Chaudhry returned the 'threat' by stating that such an act would be unconstitutional and that media commentators who had spread the rumor should be prosecuted.[38]

On 16 December 2009 the Court allowed appeals against the NRO, calling it entirely illegal because it was merely a 'deal made between two persons' (Musharraf and Benazir). Among other problems, the NRO gave benefits illegally and irrationally to a 'special class' of people who had been under indictment between 1 January 1986 and 12 October 1999 (politicians, industrialists, bankers and so forth). Altogether, the NRO was extra-constitutional, *ultra vires*, and void *ab initio*. Accordingly, all the cases and files of the NAB and the Ehtesab Bureau should be reopened and indictments pursued, fines collected and the guilty brought to justice.[39]

Educational qualifications redux

The Chaudry court also decided to accept an appeal from a losing candidate in the 2008 election who claimed that his opponent had fraudulently claimed in his application to have the necessary earned BA degree. Although the SC had invalidated the education qualification for candidacy, it found that the respondent had nonetheless committed a 'corrupt practice' by making a false statement about his educational qualifications that was punishable for imprisonment up to three years and the defendant being barred for 10 years from further electoral office.[40] The court also directed the Election Commission to initiate action against all persons accused of such corrupt practices.

Following this decision the Election Commission found that it could verify all but 147 (over a third) of the qualifications of successful candidates and turned the issue back to the National Assembly. Subsequently the Parliamentary Education Committee directed the Higher Education Commission (HEC) to help verify the educational achievements of all successful candidates for office. This has not been easy. The Zardari-led government has been loath to allow Pakistani universities to comply with the HEC request; as of mid-March 2011, the HEC was still awaiting information on 60 politicians.[41]

Throughout the SC has been proactive in prosecuting cases in which fraud has been proven. For instance, on 4 August 2010, the court directed that a criminal case be filed against a member of the National Assembly (MNA) and that the state recover all monies including pay and allowances since he was elected MNA.[42] Previously, on 25 March 2010 the SC accepted the case of a defeated candidate who charged that the winner had claimed a bogus MA in Islamic Studies. With the degree issuing educational institution failing to respond to the court's inquiries, the court conducted an unofficial examination, asking the defendant questions that anyone knowledgeable about Islam would have easily been able to answer but which the defendant could not. The court declared the MNA's credentials to be fraudulent, the MNA resigned his position, and a by-election was conducted.[43]

Displeased with the slow pace of the HEC process, the SC on 5 November 2010 issued an order declaring that *anyone* had standing to bring a case against MNAs to the SC for quick disposal.[44]

The work of the human rights cell

One basis for President Musharraf's suspension of Chief Justice Chaudry on 9 March 2007 was that on his own authority the latter had established the HRC, which was accepting cases brought to it or seeking information on cases publicized in the media. Conversely, Chaudry claimed that the court had standing to consider such cases on its own authority and that such cases fell under an expansive interpretation of Article 184(3), which granted the SC original jurisdiction on matters of public importance or those that challenged fundamental rights.

During Chaudry's tenure as Chief Justice, the HRC has heard over 10,000 cases with incredible range. These are some highlights:

1 Human Rights Case no. 5091 (PLD SC 232) ordered police officials to proactively pursue cases associated with bonded labor.
2 *Govt of Punjab* v. *Abid Hussain et al.* (PLD 2007 SC 315) ordered the federal government to provide mechanisms for convicted indigents to pay court-ordered compensation to their victims (*diyat* and *arsh*), such as soft loans; granting parole to allow indigents to work; allowing convicts facing imprisonment of 10 or more years a three-year release period to allow them to work off their *diyat*; and programs to pay victims or their heirs compensation from such paroles, loans, or work-release programs.

3 Human Rights Case no. 4115 of 2006 (PLD SC 2008 71) upheld an appeal against a High Court ruling that had not counted time served as part of a convict's jail term.

4 Suo Motu case no. 10 of 2007 (PLD 2008 SC 673) ordered various provincial governments and the Islamabad Capital Development Authority (CDA) to investigate and explain the rise in sugar prices and crack down on hoarders (matters of food and well-being, according to the decision, being of public importance).

5 *Zafar Iqbal Shagra* v. *Federation of Pakistan* (PLD 2009 SC 363) appointed an SC judicial commission to examine government policies related to oil and natural gas price fixing during Musharraf's presidency and to give an opinion on whether prices set (a) were reasonable; (b) resulted in a 'profit' to the government; and (c) passed on market-based lower prices to the consumer—the commission costs to be borne by the government regulators.

6 *Human Rights Commission of Pakistan* v. *Government of Pakistan* (PLD SC 507), on appeal from the Sindh High Court, ordered that the Bonded Labor System (Amendment) 1992 applied to all cases in which a tenant was required to remain on lands to pay off debts owed to the landlord, and stated that landlords had no detention rights whatsoever against tenants.

7 Suo Motu case no. 5 of 2010 (PLD 2010 SC 731) found that the Ministry of Petroleum had accepted from a gas company non-transparent bids that were corrupt, and ordered the officials involved in corruption be dealt with by law.

8 Human Rights Cases nos. 4668 of 2006, 1111 of 2007 and 15283-G of 2010 (PLD 2010 SC 759) found that the Islamabad CDA had (a) illegally granted permission for a fast-food outlet to be built in an area zoned for a public park; (b) awarded permission to a food chain without an open bid; and (c) allowed the building of a bowling alley and construction of a private club on public land, and ordered that the government officials concerned be dealt with by legal authorities.

9 *Bank of Punjab* v. *Haris Steel Industries* (PLD 2010 SC 1109), which was related to the Steel Mills case, ordered that (a) the NAB must employ a permanent rather than an interim chairman; and (b) the prosecutor general employed by the NAB must be replaced because the NAB Ordinance did not allow for his term to be extended. When Deedar Shah was appointed permanent chairman, the SC on 10 March 2011 ruled the appointment invalid because Shah was not impartial: he had been the chief justice of the Sindh High Court in the 'hijacking case' against Nawaz Sharif; had been a PPP MNA; and was a close associate of the Bhutto family.

10 Human Rights Case 16360 of 2009, and *Others* v. *Secretary of Health, Government of Pakistan* (PLD 2011 SC 37) ordered that hospitals grant female health workers the minimum wage despite an independent contractual agreement with them.

11 *Ejaz Akbar Kasi* v. *Ministry of Broadcasting and PTV* (PLD 2011 SC 22) ordered that 10 long-time contractual employees be made regular employees for seniority and retirement purposes.

12 Suo Motu case no. 24 of 2010 (unreported) was decided on 27 January 2011. In its continuing investigation of corrupt practices the SC in 2010 discovered that 10 police officers had been employed on contract past the government retirement age of 60, thus violating the Civil Service Act, 1973, and the Establishment Code. The court noted that for 'establishing rule of law and constitutionalism it is necessary that the relevant provisions should be followed strictly in letter and spirit; otherwise it would not be possible to provide an effective machinery in law'. It added that re-employment under contract blocks promotion of younger officers and is a detriment to good governance. Accordingly the SC ordered the Establishment Division and the Chief Secretaries of provincial governments to ensure that all rehiring of employees using contracts conforms to established law.[45]

The Eighteenth and Nineteenth Amendments

Parliament passed the Eighteenth Amendment on 8 April 2010. Among other things, the amendment (1) eliminated the power of the president to dissolve the national and provincial assemblies; (2) eliminated term limits for prime ministers; (3) established that chief ministers, but not governors, can dissolve provincial assemblies and that governors must be appointed by the 'President on the advice of the Prime Minister' rather than the 'President at his discretion'; (4) significantly increased the powers of provincial governments vis-à-vis the federal government; (5) restricted the authority of the FSC to the federal list; (6) restricted the term of a caretaker cabinet (following a vote of no-confidence or dismissal of government) to 60 days and prohibited any extension; (7) required that military heads be appointed by the 'President with the advice of the Prime Minister'; (8) validated all actions, laws, etc. from 12 October 1999–31 October 2003; (9) established that judges who took the oath of office under the 2000 Judges Oath (connected to PCO 1999) remain judges—those who did not cease to have any claim to office; and (10) validated the results and conduct of the 2008 general elections.

The Eighteenth Amendment also provided for appointment of superior court justices through Article 175A, which established judicial commissions at the federal and provincial levels. The federal Judicial Commission was to consist of the chief justice, the two most senior SC justices; one former chief justice (appointed by the president); the Federal Minister of Law and Justice; the Attorney General; and one senior advocate appointed by the SC Bar Council. Thus, the commission would have had three SC representatives; three members of the government; and one member from the Pakistan Bar Council. Appointments to the High Courts and FSC would be similarly constructed.

Appointments by the judicial commissions would be sent to a parliamentary committee consisting of four members of the Senate and four members of the National Assembly. Of the eight members, four would come from the governing party and four from the opposition. The Parliamentary Committee would then have to positively confirm Judicial Commission appointments by a two-thirds majority within 14 days, otherwise the Judicial Commission must send a new nomination.[46]

On 30 September 2010, the SC accepted challenges to the Eighteenth amendment. The Court found that the amendment violated provisions of the Judges case;[47] the CJ in consultation with the president was responsible for judicial appointments; that the Parliamentary Committee could too easily reject recommendations of the Judicial Commission; and the role of the cabinet as appointed by the Prime Minister and President would politicize the process. Accordingly, the court ruled that Article 175A of the Constitution as revised by the Eighteenth Amendment was unconstitutional and ordered that it be revised to maintain judicial autonomy.[48]

In response Parliament passed the Nineteenth Amendment Bill on 20 December 2010. The new amendment incorporated the recommendations of the SC and significantly amended the process of selecting a Federal Judicial Commission, to consist now of the chief justice, the four most senior SC judges; one former chief justice selected by the current chief justice; the Federal Minister of Law and Justice; the Attorney-General; and a senior advocate of the Pakistan Bar Council. That is, the nine-member council consists of six judges; two cabinet members; and one representative of the Bar Council. The composition of the Parliamentary Committee was left unchanged, as was the requirement for a Parliamentary Committee decision within 14 days. However, the new Article 175A provided that Parliamentary Committee only can reject a nomination of a judicial commission with a three-fourths majority (6 of 8).[49]

Conclusion

Therefore from the vantage point of mid-2011, Pakistan's superior judiciary, and particularly the Supreme Court has carved out a level of institutional autonomy and pursued a pace of judicial activism certainly without precedent in Pakistan and arguably beyond the pace and scope of the other case studies discussed in this volume. But, there is considerable disagreement as to what has driven such change. One view would explain the phenomena as largely owing to some combination of the tenacity, skill, leadership, courage, and at times obsession bordering on megalomania, of the current Chief Justice, to counter threats to the judicial autonomy of the Court, threats which he views at times as personal affronts, and to establish what he terms the Rule of Law. This is most tellingly demonstrated by a reading of his major decisions since the restoration of the Court in March 2009, which combine a Messianic zeal for justice with a dollop of revenge.

A second view would explain the phenomena as largely owing not to the actions of the Court or its members but rather to the failures of civilian and military leadership in the state to counter the inroads of the courts on their turf. One version of this view would posit that the Courts have seized the field owing to bad luck—most notably the untimely death of Benazir Bhutto upsetting the carefully crafted military–civilian paradigm of Musharraf. Another version would posit that the judicialization of politics is largely owing to the monumental mistakes of Musharraf, his suspension of the Chief Justice, which was compounded still further by his dismissal of the recalcitrant judges through the requirement of oath taking under the 2007 PCO.

Still another version of this view posits that the civilian institutions of the state have become so irredeemably corrupt and inept under both the PPP and PML(N) civilian regimes, that they simply cannot regulate their own activities and must therefore rely on the courts to do the job. Of course, in this regard judicial activism looks a good deal more attractive to the opposition than to the standing government.

Quite apart from the drivers or the political motivation of the actors involved in the process, one cannot but be supportive and impressed by the ideals of the Chaudhry Court particularly as demonstrated by the cases associated with the Human Rights Cell. The Court has in effect assumed the role of a powerful federal ombudsman identifying and attempting to right the wrongs of individuals caught up in the injustices of the system. But, sadly the Court lacks the resources to effectively implement or enforce its numerous directives to recalcitrant military and civilian leaders.

But, the Court's pronouncements have certainly had the effect of energizing civil society movements in the state. They have also had the effect of significantly improving the public perception of the judiciary which has served to empower the Court in their chronic battle against venal politicians. But, somewhat perversely it seems to this observer that the more effective the Court becomes in building legal walls against the depredations of its Parliamentary rivals that it may encourage the continued dominance of the military.

Indeed, critics of the Chaudhry Court often point out the obvious fact that its expanding authority is linked to an implicit accommodation with the military—a military that sees merit in a weak legislature. Ultimately, the Court's increased autonomy rests on the sufferance of the military as does the persistence of other civilian institutions.

Notes

1 *Sindh High Court Bar Association* v. *Federation of Pakistan PLD* 2009 SC 879. The 1956 Constitution renamed the Federal Court the Supreme Court.

2 *State* v. *Dosso PLD*, 1958 SC 533; see also Khan (2001: 2112–15; Newberg 1995: 73–77).

3 *Begum Nusrat Bhutto* v. *Chief of Army Staff and Federation of Pakistan PLD* 1977 SC 657.

4 *State* v. *Zulfiqar Ali Bhutto and others PLD* 1978 Lahore 523; Zulfiqar Ali Bhutto v. State PLD 1978 SC 40.

5 *Asma Jilani* v. *Government of Punjab PLD* 1972 SC 139.

6 *Khawaja Muhammad Sharif* v. *Federation of Pakistan PLD* 1988 Lahore 725; *Federation of Pakistan* v. *Muhammad Siafullah Khan PLD* 1989 SC 166.

7 The leading cases are *Mahmood-ur-Rehman Faisal* v. *Secretary Ministry of Justice and Parliamentary Affairs PLD* 1992 FSC 1; *Dr. M. Aslam Khaki* v. *Syed Muhammad Hashim PLD* 2000 SC 225; and *United Bank Limited* v. *Farooq Brothers PLD* 2002 SC 800.

8 Protection of Women (Criminal Laws Amendment) Act VI of 2006 PLD 2007 Central Statutes 82.
9 *Abdur Razzaq Aamir* v. *Federal Government PLD* 2011 FSC 1 at 48–50.
10 Abdur Razzaq Aamir at 98–101.
11 See *Dastoor* v. *Federation of Pakistan PLD* 1988 SC 1263.
12 Provisional Constitution Order no. 1 of 1999 PLD 1999 Central Statutes 446. In an amendment (Chief Executive's Order no. 10 of 2000) Musharraf deemed himself 'Chief Executive of the Islamic Republic of Pakistan'.
13 Zafar Ali Shah PLD 2000 869. Paragraph 284.
14 My treatment in this section borrows liberally from Kennedy (2009; 2006).
15 Legal Framework Order (Chief Executive Order # 24 of 2002) (21 August 2002).
16 Legal Framework (Amendment) Order (Chief Executive Order # 29 of 2002) (9 October 2002).
17 *Qazi Hussain Ahmed, Amir Jamaat-i-Islami* v. *General Pervez Musharraf PLD* 2002 SC 853.
18 *Pakistan Lawyers' Forum* v. *Federation of Pakistan PLD* 2005 SC 719.
19 Pakistan Steel Mills case re Constitution petition no. 9 (23 June 2006) www.supreme-court.gov.pk.
20 *Justice Ifthikar Chaudhry* v. *President of Pakistan PLD* 2007 SC 578. On 8 May the SC under interim CJ Rana Bhagwandas, a Hindu, issued an order suo motu to charge and imprison four government security personnel who had 'manhandled' Justice Chaudhry when he was forcibly removed from the court on the day of his suspension. Suo-motu case #1 of 2007 PLD 2007 SC 688. On 13 July the court dismissed a petition that challenged the eligibility of Bhagwandas serving as the CJ because was 'non-Muslim' (PLD 2008 SC 77).
21 National Reconciliation Ordinance (5 October 2007), www.pakistani.org.
22 *Pakistan Muslim League (N)* v. *Federation of Pakistan PLD* 2007 SC 642. Discussion of ambit of Article 184(3) at 657–670; statement signed by Nawaz Sharif at 671–2.
23 Ibid.
24 *Jamaat-i-Islami* v. *Federation of Pakistan PLD* 2009 SC 549. [note that this decision was not published until 2009].
25 *Jamaat-i-Islami* v. *Federation of Pakistan PLD* 2008 SC 30 at 69.
26 *Mubashir Hasan* v. *Federation of Pakistan PLD* 2008 SC 80.
27 For the complete order, see *Wajihuddin Ahmed* v. *Chief Election Commissioner PLD* 2008 SC 25 at 27.
28 The four justices of the SC who took the new oath were: Abdul Hameed Dogar, Muhammad Nawaz Abbasi, Faqir Muhammad Khokhar, and M. Javed Buttar.
29 *Wajihuddin Ahmed* v. *Chief Election Commissioner PLD* 2008 SC 25.
30 *Wajihuddin Ahmed* v. *Chief Election Commissioner PLD* 2008 SC.
31 *Tika Iqbal Muhammad Khan* v. *Pervez Musharraf PLD* 2008 SC 178 at 251–2.
32 *Tika Iqbal Muhammad Khan* v. *Pervez Musharraf PLD* 2008 SC 615.
33 *Muhammad Naseer Mahmood* v. *Federation of Pakistan PLD* 2009 SC 107. The case overturned *Pakistan Muslim League (Q)* v. *Chief Executive of Islamic Republic of Pakistan PLD* 2002 SC 944.
34 *Federation of Pakistan* v. *Muhammad Shahbaz Sharif PLD* 2009 SC 237; *Federation of Pakistan* v. *Mian Nawaz Sharif PLD* 2009 SC 284; *Federation of Pakistan* v. *Mian Nawaz Sharif PLD* 2009 SC 531.
35 *Federation of Pakistan* v. *Mian Nawaz Sharif PLD* 2009 644.
36 *Sindh High Court Bar Association* v. *Federation of Pakistan PLD* 2009 SC 789.
37 *Justice Khurshid Bhinder and others* v. *Federation of Pakistan PLD* 2010 SC 483.
38 *Sindh High Court Bar Association* v. *Federation of Pakistan PLD* 2010 SC 1151.
39 *Mubashir Hassan* v. *Federation of Pakistan PLD* 2010 SC 1; *Mubashir Hassan* v. *Federation of Pakistan PLD* SC 265.
40 *Muhammad Rizwan Gill* v. *Nadia Aziz et al. PLD* 2010 SC 828.

41 Author's interviews with officials (February–March 2011). It is often alleged that President Zardari is particularly hostile to such proceedings because he himself does not possess the necessary educational requirements. Some of those interviewed suggested that the nonresponsive vice-chancellors either owed their appointments to Zardari or were afraid of the consequences if they responded honestly to the HEC.
42 *Haji Naseer Mehmood* v. *Mian Imran Masood et al.* PLD 2010 SC 1089.
43 *Nawadzada Iftikhar Ahmed Khan* v. *Chief Election Commissioner PLD* 2010 SC 817.
44 *Najibullah* v. *Aamir Yar PLD* 2011 SC 1.
45 Suo Motu case no. 24 Human Rights cases 57701-P and seven others (attested copy) decided on 21 January 2011, on page 5 of text.
46 Eighteenth Amendment Article 175A.
47 *Al-Jehad Trust* v. *Federation of Pakistan PLD* 1996 324. This was a case that deemed Benazir Bhutto's attempts to circumvent seniority in the appointment and promotion of judges was unconstitutional.
48 *Nadeem Ahmed* v. *Federation of Pakistan PLD* SC 1165.
49 Constitution Article 175A.

References

Botteron, C. (2006) 'Validating educational qualifications as a prerequisite to hold elective Office: The Supreme Court and the Pakistan Muslim League (Q) decision', in Kennedy, C. H. and Botteron C. (eds), *Pakistan: 1995*, Karachi: Oxford University Press.

Kennedy, C. H. (1992) 'Repugnancy to Islam: Who decides?', *International and Comparative Law Quarterly*, 41: 769–88.

Kennedy, C. H. (1993a) 'Islamization of real estate: Pre-emption and land reforms, 1978–1992', *Journal of Islamic Studies*, 4: 71–83.

Kennedy, C. H. (1993b) 'Judicial activism after Zia: Towards the prohibition of *Riba'*, in Kennedy, C. H., *Pakistan: 1992*, Boulder: Westview Press.

Kennedy, C. H. (1995) 'Presidential–Prime Ministerial Relations: The Role of the Superior Courts', in Kennedy, C. H. and Rais, R. B., *Pakistan: 1995*, Boulder: Westview Press.

Kennedy, C. H. (2004) 'Pakistan's Superior Courts and the Prohibition of Riba', in Hathaway, R. and Lee, W. (eds), *Islamization and the Pakistan Economy*, Washington, DC: Woodrow Wilson International Center for Scholars.

Kennedy, C. H. (2005) 'Pakistan 2005: Running very fast to stay in the same place', *Asian Survey*, 41: 105–111.

Kennedy, C. H. (2006) 'A User's Guide to Guided Democracy: Pervez Musharraf and the Pakistani Military Governance Paradigm' in Kennedy, C. H. and Botteron, C. (eds), Pakistan: 1995 Karachi: Oxford University Press.

Kennedy, C. H. (2009) 'Constitutional structures', in Malik, Y., Kennedy, C. H., Oberst R., *et al., Government and Politics in South Asia*, 6th edition, Boulder: Westview Press.

Khan, H. (2001) *Constitutional and political history of Pakistan*, Oxford: Oxford University Press.

Newberg, P. (1995) *Judging the State: Courts and Constitutional Politics in Pakistan*, Cambridge, UK: Cambridge University Press.

Zafar, S. M. (2000) 'Constitutional development in Pakistan, 1997–1999,' in Kennedy, C. H. and Baxter, C. (eds), *Pakistan 2000*, Lanham: Lexington Books.

Part III

Authoritarian and semi-authoritarian settings

9 China's Supreme People's Court within the 'political-legal system'

Shumei Hou and Ronald Keith

Introduction

Hirschl's 'judicialization of politics' argues that in Asia within the last two decades, court intervention into 'deadlocked politics' is 'less exceptional' and that courts are asserting independent political personality through judicial review. This approach looks for examples of court intervention in 'pure' or 'mega politics' that influence 'core regime legitimacy and collective identity' (Hirschl 2006: 721).

In China, however, heavy politicization of the judiciary is more the rule than the exception. Currently, there is, for example, a revived exercise of leadership by the Party Central Committee's Legal-Political Committee (*zhengfa weiyuan-hui*) over China's Supreme People's Court (SPC). The strength of such political leadership has varied over time. During the Jiang Zemin years of Chinese Communist Party (CCP) leadership there was less political intervention, whereas, under the more conservative Hu Jintao leadership, there has been more political intervention. On the other hand, there have been instances of creeping or light judicialization as the SPC has taken creative initiative to guide the court system through judicial interpretation and has begun issuing 'leading cases' (*anjian zhidao*). That is why this analysis raises the question of where (or perhaps whether) the SPC should be placed on the continuum of judicialization and politicization that recognizes possible contemporaneous expression of what are severely imbalanced tendencies.

There are institutional, ideological, and political reasons for the primary trend towards heavy politicization. In the first place, the CCP created the court system. The SPC has to cope with the institutional reality that 'judiciary and administration are inseparable' (*sifa yu xingzheng bufen*) (Keith 1994: 82–83). The CCP has consistently disavowed American-style separation of powers (*quanli fenli)*, though Article 135 of the State Constitution obliges the SPC, the Supreme People's Procuratorate (SPP), and the public security organs to work within an administrative separation of functions predicated on the mass-line organizational 'principle of separation of responsibilities, mutual restriction and mutual coordination' (*fengong fuze, huxiang peihe, huxiang zhiyuede yuanze*) (National People's Congress of the People's Republic of China 2000: 83).

Moreover, according to Article 3 of the 1980 State Constitution, all state organizations, including the SPP and the SPC, are subject to 'democratic centralism' (*minzhu jizhong*). Formally the SPC has the ability to 'supervise' and 'guide' the people's court system, though no formal power to review national legislation; it also has informal capacity to improvise review through judicial interpretation of the law (see Backer 2009–10; Keith and Lin 2009; Peerenboom 2010). It does not consciously intervene in deadlocked politics but there have been cycles of self-conscious 'judicial activism'.

The imbalance between heavy politicization and light judicialization is discussed here with reference to public positions taken by succeeding court presidents on the SPC's relation to party politics and ideology that are contextualized within China's 'political-legal system' (*zhengfa xitong*). The system, which the party's Seventeenth National Congress reaffirmed as a key example of a system with 'Chinese characteristics',[1] refers to the relative independence of courts, procuratorates, justice bureaus, and public security organs within the dual management and guidance of same-level and higher political-legal committees and of people's governments.

Jean-Pierre Cabestan, director of the French Centre for Research on Contemporary China, has criticized the role played by the CCP's political and legal affairs committees as an 'obstacle to the emergence of independent courts' (Cabestan 2005, 46). He notes that under China's 'authoritarian and repressive legal system', rules outlined in the constitution have been 'rendered meaningless as they are circumvented by more powerful political and Party norms' (Cabestan 2005: 45). Gunter Schubert in his critique of Beijing scholar Pan Wei's 'consultative rule of law' makes a similar point to the effect that legal reform of authoritarianism and upgrading of public administration will not sustain CCP rule in the long run (Schubert 2005: 7)

The former dean of the Peking Law School, Zhu Suli, has discussed what he calls 'party-ization of the judiciary' (*sifa danghua*), but he rebuts what he sees as Western distortion of the relation between law and politics in China. Objecting to 'questionable presuppositions' that (a) there is 'a unique political influence that comes from the CCP'; (b) 'that it is possible to create a standard model of a judiciary from political influence'; and (c) that it is possible and necessary for researchers to examine and measure such influence independently, Professor Zhu stated that while the Party's influence is 'ubiquitous', so far as the judiciary is concerned it is 'general and diffuse' (Hou and Keith 2012). Zhu then took on his critics on the issue of party interference with the judiciary:

> Today, although the CCP has adopted 'relying on the law to rule the country' (*yifa zhiguo*) and judicial independence is inscribed in the Constitution, party organizations and individuals persist in influencing and interfering with the judiciary. However, although these interferers are sometimes leading cadres who 'wave the flag' of the local Party organization, it does not mean that an individual's interference represents the Party's or that

> particular Party organization's interference. To the contrary, some of them are violating CCP principles, policies, and disciplinary rules.
>
> (Zhu 2007)

What follows situates China's paramount court, the SPC, within the changing political-legal system before moving on to consider particular SPC judicial interpretations, leading cases, and statements of supervision that concern the protection of rights and interests and related operational problems of judicial transparency and enforcement. The analysis suggests that the SPC is a heavily politicized extension of China's formal political-legal system predicated on general CCP leadership; however, the SPC has at times exercised its distinctive judicial and supervisory self-initiative in leading the court system to meet the needs of society. Distinctions between tendencies to judicialization and politicization are most evident with respect to recent cycles of SPC leadership, spanning the court presidencies of Xiao Yang, 1998–2008 and Wang Shengjun, 2008–the present.

The SPC approach to law and politics

The explanation for heavy politicization and light judicialization lies in the history of changes in Chinese institutions and politics. China's political-legal system incorporates party and state organizations that coordinate to provide justice in society; over time the system has witnessed qualitative institutional change and perhaps unexpectedly different cycles of SPC 'judicial activism'.

In Mao's time the court system was a weapon that supported mass activism in defeating the class enemies of China's new revolutionary regime. Legal institutions, including the SPC, had to comply strictly with party ideology: The law was subordinate to politics. Justice in the courts was not to stand in the way of the just cause of mass action.

Even when the judicial system was being built up in the early 1950s, SPC President Shen Junru, the only non-party member to serve as court president, warned judges to eschew 'boundless magnamity' (*kuanda wubian*) towards class enemies and counterrevolutionaries. He considered the people's judicial organs to be part of the people's dictatorship, which does not operate on the same basis as the capitalist concept of *sifa duli* (judicial independence). In the context of national political consolidation of the new regime, trials were to proceed on the basis of regulation as reflected in the 'centre's unified centralization' (*zhongyangde jizhongtongyi)* (Shen Junru's speech in Administrative Office of the Supreme People's Court 2010: 21).

The 1954 constitution qualified Mao's early 1950s mass populism with a new emphasis on justice institutionally delivered based on equality before the law (*falu pingdeng*). The SPC was given new standing as the highest court in the land, responsible for supervision of the national system of people's courts; it was specified that the SPC and the SPP would 'exercise their powers independently'.

Thereafter SPC operations closely followed the cycle of domestic politics. Rising class struggle in the mid 1960s worked against 1954-style institutionalization. This trend reached its zenith in 1975 with the drafting of a 'leftist' constitution that was to meet the requirements of the masses with the CCP as the 'leading core of the Chinese people' (*Zhongguo renminde lingdao hexin*). The 1954 Constitution was pared down from 106 to 30 articles to simplify judicial process and make it accessible to the masses (Zhang 2003). Article 25 of the 1975 Constitution dismissed the 1954 administrative checks and balances between organizations and gave Public Security the procuratorate's responsibility for supervision. The SPC became just another court that 'must follow the mass line', especially with respect to the struggle against counterrevolutionaries.[2]

Reacting to the collapse of rights and the legal system in the 1966–76 Cultural Revolution, Deng Xiaoping came up with reasoning that approximated 'government of law, not men', criticizing 'leftist' misappropriation of the mass line for the sake of arbitrary political persecution. In December 1978 Deng supported a new strategy based on 'entwined' legalization and democratization: 'Democracy has to be institutionalized and written into law, so as to make sure that institutions and laws do not change whenever the leadership changes or whenever the leaders change their views' (Keith 1994: 9).

Deng scrapped the more blatantly 'leftist' elements of the 1975 and 1978 constitutions, rejecting improper political interference in the legal system. 'Judicial independence' was addressed in Articles 5 and 126 of the 1982 Constitution. Article 5 proclaimed: 'No organization or individual may enjoy the privilege of being above the Constitution and the law.' Article 126 elaborated that 'The people's courts shall, in accordance with the law, *exercise judicial power independently* (*duli xingshi shenpan quan*) and are not subject to interference by administrative organs, public organizations, or individuals [italics added].' The party may have had to adjust its viewpoint, but it still looked down from the heights on the constitution as a *deus ex machina*. The 1975 and 1978 constitutions had acknowledged the Party as the 'leading core of the people', and that formulation was carried forward implicitly in the 1982 constitutional reference in Article 3 to all state agencies subscribing to 'democratic centralism'.

The relation between law and party leadership was addressed frankly: 'Independence' was not an absolute condition; it had become a conditional need to ensure respect for the authority of the law and the rational division of labor within the judicial system. In hindsight its leaders conceded that the party had been improperly intervening in the work of the courts, and that future counter-revolution ('opposition to socialism') was to be addressed through the court system. In 1980 Professor Dong Likun (Dong 1980: 14) explained the party's new thinking:

> The party's most important task … is to guarantee the independent performance of the judicial organs.… Those who believe that only the party committee can judge cases and that they are party leaders only if the party interferes in judicial work just don't understand this principle [of judicial

> independence].... For a long time we ignored the specific function of the judicial organs and were unable to guarantee thorough implementation of the state laws. This fundamentally weakened party leaders.

The political-legal system underwent a major change with the inception of legal reform in December 1978 at the Third Plenary Session of the CCP Eleventh Central Committee Meeting. Some of the SPC's basic terms of reference, especially its formats for interpretation and supervision, expanded to address the fast-changing needs to deepen economic reform and the related constant adjustment of 'rights and interests' to insure political stability.

A 1979 party circular had specifically forbidden party intervention in court sentencing (Keith and Lin 2006: 13). In June 1986 Deng (*Selected Works*, Vol. III) complained that the issue still had not been resolved. He criticized 'substituting the Party for the law' (*yi dang dai fa*), stating,

> If the Party intervenes in everything, it will not help the people understand the importance of the rule of law. This is a question of the relations between the Party and the government, of the political structure of our country.... Right now the party is concentrating on rectifying the conduct of its own members, but at the same time we are trying to strengthen the rule of law in society at large. Our country has no tradition of observing or enforcing laws.
>
> (Deng 1993: 166)

In Deng's view, party members had to learn what not to do, and the masses needed to understand the implications and benefits of the 'rule of law'. The subsequent 1986 CCP Central Committee Notice to the Entire Party to Stand Up for the Socialist Rule of Law presumed that the party would 'act according to law', because the law was of the party's own making. It was assumed that the CCP must show the people the worth of the law by demonstrating that it would itself act according to law.

Peerenboom glossed the related 'supremacy of law' in China in the following way:

> One of the main theoretical and practical issues in establishing rule of law has been how to reconcile the leading role of the Party with the basic rule of law principle of the supremacy of law. Theoretically, the issue has been resolved by allowing the CCP to set the general direction for society while requiring that the Party's policies must be translated into law that is legally binding.
>
> (2004: 116)

This interpretation was confirmed on 4 June 1987 by SPC President Zheng Tianxiang, who in referring to 'grabbing construction in one hand, and the legal system in the other' (*yishou zhua jianshe, yishou zhua fazhi*), explained the constitution's notion of the supremacy of law:

> The constitution and laws were approved by our country's highest legislative authority under the active leadership of the Party Centre. The constitution and laws are the true expression of formalization in law of the Party's mass line, strategies, and policies (Zheng's speech in Administrative Office of the Supreme People's Court 2010: 224)

As the Cultural Revolution receded in time, so did the old revolutionary generation. The CCP then turned its attention to the dangers of deepening corruption. In 1989 Jiang Zemin reiterated Deng's 1986 instruction, claiming: 'We will never allow the party to take the place of government, never allow the party to take the place of law'. In the 1990s, however, he argued that the law, in and of itself, would not solve the party's number one problem, corruption, especially as it was spreading into the judiciary itself. The law does not apply itself; its application requires moral human agency. Jiang's solution was to synthesize the rule of law (*fazhi*) and the rule of virtue (*dezhi*) (Keith and Lin 2006: 28). Reacting to the 'absurd fallacies' of the Falun Gong and Western country tactics of 'peaceful evolution' (*heping yanbian*), Jiang sought to reinforce the rule of law by linking it with Chinese morality—'Chinese characteristics' (*Zhongguo tese*).

In 1996 Jiang still championed the formulation 'rule the country relying on law and establishing a socialist legal system countrywide' (*yi fa zhi guo, jianshe shehuizhuyi guojia*), which was later highlighted in the constitutional amendment of 1999. Also, at the 15th Party Congress of 1997, after Deng's death, Jiang reiterated his support for 'systematic guarantees for the judicial organs to exercise independently and openly [this is the original Chinese translation of the English] adjudicatory power'. In 1999 Jiang (Keith and Lin 2006: 16) endorsed the 'socialist rule of law' amendment but he reinforced the relation of the rule of law to CCP-determined morality: 'It is equally important to govern the country with high morals and persistently strengthen social moral construction. Ruling the country according to law and governing the country with high morals complement and promote each other (Keith and Lin, 2006: 16).'

Party leaders at the March 2001 session of the NPC agreed that the rule of law and the rule of virtue are coeval, especially given the mounting contradictions associated with the accelerated transition to the socialist market economy. Jiang resurrected traditional 'good person politics' (*xianren zhengzhi*) in a seemingly neotraditional pursuit of 'harmony'. This irony was not lost on Chinese reform jurists concerned about the combined rules of law and virtue (*fazhi yu dezhi*) (Keith and Lin 2006: 17–18). Wen Xiaoli, for example, argued that separation of the law from morality, and in particular separation of the rule of law from the rule of virtue, was a necessary requirement of 'modernity'. He warned that excessive emphasis on morality would foster a resurgence of the 'rule of man' as against the 'rule of law' (Keith and Lin 2006: 17).

Recent SPC court leadership

If there is one constant in the SPC's mandate, it is supporting political stability by meeting the needs of the people; however, how the SPC relates to the people in accomplishing this task has been a matter of political discussion. In China people's rights and interests (*quanyi*) are often equated with human rights (*renquan*); and protection of these rights and interests is justified as necessary to political stability and national economic development. With reform there was a new emphasis that protecting rights and interests made a contribution in responding to people's needs in a time of profound transition.

Xiao Yang's strong interest in legal reform was suggested when during the 1996 revisions to the Criminal Procedural Law and Criminal Law, as Minister of Justice, he welcomed procedural revision that helped protect human rights:

> What needs to be specifically pointed out is that this amendment conforms to international practice and commonly observed judicial principles; and therefore proves beneficial to a strict enforcement of the law, to the protection of human rights, and to our efforts to reinforce our international cooperation and struggle in the fields of jurisprudence and human rights.
>
> (Keith and Lin 2001, 185, fn. 27)

Minister Xiao also vigorously defended the principle of legality when he proclaimed: '...the principle of convicting a crime and meting out punishment according to the law has replaced reasoning by analogy'(Keith and Lin 2001, 211). He believed that this reform was every bit as important as the elimination of the presumption of guilt in the Criminal Procedural Law.

During Xiao's subsequent tenure as SPC court president in 1998–2008 the SPC adopted judicial activism (*sifa nongdong*), supporting professionalization of the judiciary and an expanded role for judicial interpretation and supervision through a new system of 'leading cases'. This reform stressed the importance of judicial judgment that respects 'trial independence'. Xiao's court aspired to meet the people's needs with an arms-length emphasis on professionalism and due process (see Trevaskes 2011; Hou and Keith 2011; Liebman 2007). This was not just a technical matter as it touched on the essential relation of politics to law.

Deng's legal reforms stressed the rule of law, trial independence, and professionalism as against inappropriate Party intervention and misappropriation of checks and balances within the justice system. In 2001 Court President Xiao cited the lessons of history: 'When the law rises, a country is governed; when the law falls, a country is weak' (*Zuigao renmin fayuan liren yuazhang wenxian*; 2010: 286). In the hindsight of 2004 failure to consolidate proposals for a new panel to oversee review of the constitution, Xiao's words may have seemed prophetic.

However, though Xiao emphasized the rule of law, he did not hesitate to affirm its development with 'Chinese characteristics'. In July 2002, he advised China's judges: 'You must proceed from reality, holding on firmly to China's national conditions and exploring with great effort the road to the professionalization of judges based on Chinese characteristics; do not simply copy foreign models' (Xiao Yang's speech in Administrative Office of the Supreme People's Court 2010: 293). In November 2002, he cited the party's subscription to 'liberating the mind' and 'seeking the truth from the facts', but he also noted with approval the close relation between politics and law in China: 'Judges in foreign countries on the whole do not do not participate in politics and their thought is comparatively conservative. China's judges must go into politics and move with the times' (Xiao Yang's speech, Administrative Office of the Supreme People's Court 2010, 308).

In his 2004 visit to Yale University, with the U.S. Chief Justice in attendance, Court President Xiao explained the difference between the Chinese and Western approach to justice in a way that was reminiscent of Jiang Zemin's synthesis of the rule of law and rule of virtue:

> From the perspective of setting the goals of the rule of law, the law's basic essence lies both in judicial organs and in the judges' thoughtful discretion, but the tradition in China is that of a 'customary society' and the law in and of itself cannot therefore serve as a so-called 'miracle cure' because basic elements, such as ethics and feelings, are part of the judicial process.
>
> (Xiao Yang's speech, Administrative Office of the Supreme People's Court 2010, 313)

Since the 17th National Party Congress in October 2007, and especially since the appointment in March 2008 of Wang Shengjun as court president, there has been a palpable increase in the politicization of the SPC and the court system based on party leadership. In the last months of Xiao's tenure, his boss, Luo Gan, chairman of the CCP Political and Legal Affairs Committee, picked up on Hu Jintao's report to the 17th National Party Congress which called for strengthening of Party oversight of legal institutions and criticizing those advocating judicial independence and Western-style legal reforms. Luo was worried that 'hostile forces' were trying to use legal institutions as an entry point for Westernizing and splitting China (see Liebman 2007).

Wang has placed much more emphasis on 'Chinese characteristics', 'mass line', and the 'Three Supremes'. Trevaskes has argued that Wang is engaged in a balancing act to facilitate 'not justice practice but also the power relationships that undergird it'. She describes the party's approach within China's changing political-legal system as 'legitimacy building':

> This legitimacy building does not entail separating party leadership and the policy-making process from the apparatuses of state power within the justice system; instead, quite the opposite. To improve the competence of judicial institutions so that they will gain citizens' confidence, the party requires the public security organs (police), procuratorates (public prosecution), and

> courts to develop their institutional authority as a group as well as individually, all under the party's overall leadership.
>
> (2011: 318)

In one way or another the party has always formally referenced the importance of meeting the needs of the people, but the recent adaptation to China's Confucian past has accentuated the relation between law, the politics of morality, and support for 'harmony' through 'judicial activism' that directly connects party and people. Under Wang the court has been more effusive than under Xiao in its wholesale subscription to the 'Three Supremes' (*sange zhi shang*). This secular trinity places the party cause and the needs of the people on the same level as the supremacy of law. Wang has reiterated the importance of responding to the leadership of the CCP, especially its Central Political-Legal Committee. His statements and SPC planning documents may make mention of judicial independence and professionalism, but the focus is on an institutional response that reflects 'Chinese characteristics' in court responses to people's needs.

Court President Wang has directed provincial judges not only to understand the political impact of domestic conflicts but also 'to balance the rights and interests of different groups in areas concerning labor disputes, surging housing prices and disputes about housing demolition'.[3] Wang has also drawn on mass-line bias against too many court meetings and too many documents. His court reflects party frustration over delays in providing the masses with justice, but the immediate association with 'feelings' poses a dilemma for rule-of-law-making which requires ample time to work through impersonal and often unfamiliar due process. Wang's 'judicial activism' prefers flexibility and using quick extra-legal solutions to release pent-up social frustration. He wants the court system to invigorate its Chinese roots and relearn elements of the mass line.

With regard to the now-famous 2010 case of the lawyer Li Zhuang in Chongqing, for example, there is concern that the courts, public security, and the procuratorate were working solely on the basis of mutual cooperation (*huxiang peihe*) and that formally checking each other's functions (*huxiang zhiyue*) is undermined by practices that stress a direct mass-line relation with the people at the expense of professionalism. The close association of *gongjianfa* (public security, procuratorate, and courts) in Zhongqing raised the specter of a recidivist lapse into *tiqian jieru*, where the court ignores proper procedure and participates in the initial stages of investigation.

With Wang as SPC president the people's courts are encouraged to support party leadership by supporting the needs of the people. Court personnel are to demonstrate correct work style by immediately interacting with the people and focusing politically on their interests. Some reformers would like to restrain the SPC, perhaps to minimize its politicization while highlighting the importance of professionalism and judicial independence to support rights and interests.

In the past China's jurists raised concerns about extended judicial interpretation (*kuoda jieshi*) and the potential legislation-izing of judicial interpretation (*guifanxing falu jieshide lifahua*). Those similarly concerned today prefer that the SPC confine its activity to interpreting judicial matters rather than making policy. In recent years there has been a deliberate attempt to obviate National People's Congress (NPC) controversy over issuance of SPC interpretations. Now there is preemptive deliberation of recommended interpretations by a special NPC panel. In this way the system anticipates contradictions within the political-legal system and, presumably, fosters harmony rather than acrimonious disagreement between leadership institutions.

According to the constitution the SPC supervises the court system. This raises yet another set of questions. The SPC has been under fire for interfering with the 'freedom of judges' decisions' even as it perhaps legitimately addresses often wildly inconsistent local applications of the standards of justice. One of China's most senior jurists, Li Buyun, for example, has warned against 'the proliferation of wrongly judged cases, the uneven, and indeed the irrational, application of the centre's standards' (Li 2004: 259).' This is what Zhang described as the 'judicial syndrome' that is morbidly manifest in rampant 'local protectionism', low professional and ethical standards, and a highly centralized administrative model that is unable to fund local courts on its own terms (2003: 87). Human rights standards based on the rule of law require consistently supportive SPC decisions and interpretations, but the SPC is also part of the CCP strategy to ensure political and social stability through protection of rights and interests.

Reformers like Professors Chen Xingliang and Liu Yanhong have complained that the SPC is too concerned about general interpretations; it should stick to the specifics of individual cases. According to Chen (2003: 138) the tendency to general interpretation smothers the potential for 'freedom of judge's decision' (*fayuan ziyou cailiang*). These critics have slotted SPC interpretations of the 1997 Criminal Law into three categories: supplementing the details of legislative intent; revising stipulated crime, moving beyond original legislative provisions; and making new stipulations to facilitate the fight against crime.

The SPC dilemma: procedure versus populism

The SPC has often risen to the defense of national standards, but in doing so it sometimes seems to take its cues from the party and public opinion. One of the most notorious examples was the Liu Yong case, which was determined during the tenure of Chief Justice Xiao Yang, who is widely considered one of the staunchest advocates of professionalism and independent trial.

At his first trial Liu, an infamous kingpin of organized crime, was sentenced to death. After this trial, disgruntled public security officers revealed that his confession had been illegally extracted under torture (Keith and Lin 2006: 145). Chinese jurist reformers have often argued that capital punishment cases require the highest standards of evidence. At Liu's second trial, the High Court noted the illegal acquisition of evidence and reduced his death sentence to the lesser punishment of death with a two-year reprieve (which in practice almost always results in life imprisonment). The sentence reduction inflamed the public, who believed that clever procedure had thwarted justice and clamored for immediate execution. The sustained uproar resulted in a rare move by the SPC: It stepped in to revisit the revised death sentence by exercising its prerogative or 'retrial' (*zaishen*) a little–known 'reconsideration' procedure. Rather than returning the case to the trial court, the SPC in December 2003 changed the decision to a sentence of immediate execution.

Among some in the legal circles, there was disquiet that the SPC had never used its power of retrial before, and that, rather than returning the case to the court of second instance for reconsideration of its original verdict it directly overturned the latter's verdict and made the decision itself without the usual outside request from the SPP. The SPC's action did little to promote the cause for supremacy of law based upon principles of judicial justice and independence.

The larger issue regarding the SPC's right to supervise lower courts was addressed only in 2010 in 'Several SPC Notes Regarding Standard Relations Between Higher and Lower Courts in the Conduct of Trial Work Responsibilities'.[4] Article 1 affirmed the right of the higher level to supervise and guide lower courts. Article 2 affirmed that each level is to carry out 'trial work on the basis of judicial independence according to law' (*yifa duli xingshi shenpan quan*). There is perhaps a hint of judicialization in Article 3, which strengthens higher court supervision and guidance by specifying categories of cases that basic and middle-level courts should forward to the SPC, including 'important and complex' cases, 'new types' of cases, and cases that have general legal relevance.

Protection of rights and interests

Reform has stressed the importance of adjusting and protecting 'rights and interests'. The party mandated that the people's court system led by the SPC should facilitate such protection to ensure political and social stability. The 1996–97 reform of criminal and criminal procedural law was inspired by the need to facilitate China's new economy and protect the rights of designated newly emerging interests. Criminal procedural law was explicitly stated to be equal to the criminal law itself. Reform challenged the state's past reliance on 'flexibility', substituted analogy for legislated law, and called for comprehensive stipulation of all manner of crimes.

The intention was easily forgotten in the extreme political pressure that accompanied the National People's Congress Standing Committee (NPCSC) decision to eliminate Falun Gong activities. Acting together, the SPP and the SPC on 1 November 1999 issued an interpretation that grounded the reference in Article 300 to 'evil cults' in an urgently needed definition of related specific criminal behavior and established a new line of severe criminal punishments that could be used against adherents of Li Hongzhi (Keith and Lin 2003: 638).

Even with the disappearance of the criminal law on counterrevolution, there was thus a continuing CCP focus on using the law to ensure political action to support what the party decided would promote political stability. There was also new party interest in the use of law to protect new interests in society so as to support an orderly transition to the market economy that would avoid formation of festering social contradictions. Politically, the appeal to order in China cuts two ways. It may justify suppression, but it may also require protection of rights; and, as discussed below, it is in the latter sphere that there are inklings of judicialization.

Protection of education rights

In other areas of judicial activity the party has also encouraged the SPC to protect the rights and interests of the masses in the interest of ensuring social and political stability. The case of Qi Yuling offers some insight on the court's role in protecting rights: In an elaborate ruse by a corrupt official to secure college entrance under false pretenses for the daughter of an influential friend, a poor village girl was the victim of identity theft. Qi Yiling's *hukou*, or registration, was used by this privileged student, who on this illicit basis went on to acquire a highly desirable job. Qi later discovered the theft of her identity and lodged a suit against the local official and the college educational authority for having infringed on her rights to a personal identity and to education.

As there was no specific law supporting the constitution's guarantee of education rights, the Shandong Higher Court lodged a request with the SPC for instruction. The July 2001 SPC instruction favored Qi. The Shandong Higher Court's subsequent ruling referred explicitly not only to Qi's identity rights but also to the constitution's guarantee of education rights.[5] For a while China's legal reformers euphorically compared this case in its significance to the U.S. case of *Marbury* v. *Madison* as it seemed to imply that the court was asserting its independence to review constitutional law and the rights it protected. However, the SPC later withdrew its interpretation in deference to a new national law on education.

Peerenboom offers a plausible explanation for the inherently conservative approach of the courts to using constitutional law: 'Constitutional law developments ... have the potential to alter the balance of power among state organs and challenge the basic principles of the political system' (2009: 53).

There is more than one way to influence the course of justice, however. In its recent circulation of leading cases in administrative law the SPC drew attention to a 1999 High Court decision regarding a student who sued his university because on being caught cheating in an exam he was issued not a degree but a certificate. The case raised two important questions: First, could a student sue the university, which is part of the state administration? Second, did the student's argument that the university had to give him a degree have merit? The High Court supported the lower court judgment that a student has a right to sue the university but also that in this case the university had acted properly in refusing the degree as punishment for cheating.[6]

The utility in describing this as a leading case is twofold. It protected the student's right to sue, and courts throughout China acquired important, though non-binding, advice that could reduce future laborious requests to the SPC for instruction as to the status of universities in administrative law. This was a rational and just streamlining of a system where there is no history of case law, and it supports SPC leadership in ensuring national standards of applied justice.

Rape and due process

Perhaps the most politically sensitive issues for the SPC arise from the criminal law. In 2003, for example, the SPC was caught up in a storm of public opinion about a sensational case in which several officials had raped an underage girl. Proceedings in the Liaoning High People's Court had bogged down over an apparent gap in the criminal law. Both antagonists and protagonists were fascinated by the procedure and privilege issues. Criminal Law Article 236 makes it very clear that rape occurs where a man has intercourse with a woman under the age of 14 and is aware of the victim's age. The defense argued that the alleged intercourse was with consent and that all six defendants were fooled by the girl's relatively mature appearance and were unaware of her real age.

Since Article 236 did not state what to do in that situation, the High Court's request for SPC instruction was reasonable. The SPC reaffirmed Article 236, Section 2, but went on to add that criminal rape had not occurred if the accused were unaware of the victim's true age and the attendant circumstances were not 'severe'. Though the reasoning focused on *mens rea* and the question of social harm, some reformers suspected that the SPC's judgment was skewed to protect the officials.

Rights and interests are often examined through a time-sensitive prism of social stability. The Wang Shengjun presidency has carried over the work of the Xiao Yang presidency that established SPC panels to review all death penalties. The emphasis has been on strict application of the highest technical standards in the professional administration of justice. However, the SPC is well aware of party concern about mistreatment of the floating population and the relevance to social stability of protecting their rights. In 2010, for example, the court confirmed the death penalty for very grievous crimes of family rape and murder in Anhui and Henan involving the women and children of husbands who had gone to the city for work.[7]

Because these cases were extraordinarily severe the death penalty would probably have been upheld in any event, but the SPC used the cases to instruct lower courts that they should apply the death penalty with particular vigilance in such cases because they reflect a growing social problem that has catalyzed the spread of violent crime in rural areas. In this sense, the court was acting out of concern for social policy to support the rights of the floating population as well as for the sake of justice for the individuals concerned. Jurists have been debating whether policy considerations sometimes supplant the judicial dimensions of the trial process and whether this is not only a misappropriation of NPC legislative authority but also an inappropriate example of 'administration-ization of court organization' (*fayuan tizhde xingzhenghua*).

Judicialization and judicial independence

In his reflection on a popular account of the politics of the U.S. Supreme Court, SPC Judge He Fan has suggested that China's SPC does not have the same luxury to focus on rights issues like abortion, racism, and states rights. China's SPC, he argues, is in the 'first stage of the rule of law' (Toobin 2010: x). The SPC is immediately concerned with creating a viable institutional framework that will support 'justice, efficiency and authority'.

In thinking about the progress of China's legal system and the interpretation of 'judicial independence' and 'judicialization' in China, Peerenboom (2010: 4, 7) detects some weakness in Western generalizations, adding that 'blanket denunciations of the lack of meaningful independence in China fail to recognize the more complex reality'. He sees 'substantive disagreement in China about how independent the courts should be and whether the courts are the appropriate forum for resolving certain types of disputes, notwithstanding the global trend toward judicialization' (2010: 4, 7, 9). Reflecting on He Xin's work on 'married-out women' who after marriage leave their home villages and are then denied home village benefits, he notes that the courts have diverged from the global trend to judicialize such disputes, preferring to push them back to state agencies whose decisions are then subjected to court review under the administrative litigation law. Peerenboom is impressed with the savvy, the 'strategic sophistication', of the courts:

> [By claiming the right to review the government's decisions in administrative litigation] the courts retain an advantageous position in the power relationship with the government. Moreover, as the cases inevitably leave some groups dissatisfied, the court can avoid public displeasure by forcing the government to make the decision. [He Xin] concludes that the Chinese courts are capable of deliberating about transforming their situation by strategically interpreting the law and negotiating with superior powers.
>
> (2010: 9)

Much of foregoing analysis suggests that under party leadership, the SPC and the court system it supervises are disinclined to challenge state organizations directly through a process of justiciability, but that the court system takes seriously the importance of political and social stability and has responded using indirect means, such as judicial interpretation and ex post facto review of administrative decisions.

The contemporary focus of party leadership on rebalancing makes it difficult to project a direct pattern of SPC judicialization; however, the system reflects self-correcting initiative even within the assumptions of the political-legal system. Wang Shengjun may have made less reference to professionalism than Xiao Yang, but he has nonetheless endorsed the current focus of reform on law enforcement and judicial transparency. A brief look at SPC-led reform in these two areas suggests, however, that there are serious barriers to the SPC effort to establish a 'socialist rule of law' in China.

Judicial transparency[8]

If justice must be seen to be done, then transparency is necessary to instill confidence in the public and thus reinforce the legitimacy of government. In 1999 the SPC issued new regulations (*guiding*) on enforcement of open trial proceedings. These regulations confirmed that citizens could gain access to court hearings by producing identification. In 1999 and 2004 the SPC acted in support of standardizing judgments so that they will stand up to public scrutiny, issuing two judicial interpretations, 'The Style Template of the Criminal Law Judgment of the Court' and the 'First-Instance Judgment of Administrative Law Courts'. Furthermore, regulations in the SPC's Second Five-Year Reform Outline addressed the standard of judgment requiring that judges improve their professional skills, especially with regard to legal writing and reasoning and careful sifting of the evidence.

In 2007 the SPC issued an 'opinion' (*yijian*) on the matter of open trials. This SPC interpretation set out for the first time the principles that trials must be conducted according to law, without delay, and be open in all respects. Wang Shengjun's court then reinforced the emphasis in 2009 with two more opinions and new regulations. The SPC committed to placing its judgments online and to broadcasting court trials live over the Internet.

Wang had no problem in picking up on Party Leader Hu Jintao's new emphasis on 'transparency' even as he reaffirmed the close relationship between politics and law, commenting in the *Guangming ribao*: 'Judicial power as an important ruling power is a significant way for the Party and the people under its leadership to administer state and social affairs'.[9] The emphasis on openness was designed to generate trust in China's legal system and thus enhance the legitimacy of the regime in meeting the people's needs for fair and timely justice. Openness could also further the cause of education among legal circles and the general public. Indeed, openness could generally enhance law-consciousness—though it might also draw attention to the issue of judicial competence in a legal system struggling with corruption and extraordinary societal transitions and contradictions.

The SPC has acted to assert its capacity to supervise courts with one eye on opening up the trial process, thus ensuring greater trust despite growing corruption, and the other eye on raising the standards for judgment. Judicial transparency is expected to facilitate improved legal reasoning, although reporting on the latter is still truncated.

Wang has made it clear that he wants to clear the backlog of cases to meet the need of the masses for prompt justice. Justice must therefore not only be openly seen to be done, but it must also have expeditious policy results. Addressing provincial judges, Court President Wang announced that the SPC would in 2011 reduce its meetings and documents by one-third and, drawing on mass-line preferences for the simplicity and clarity of law, he targeted 'pure formalism' throughout the court system.[10] Wang advised the courts to keep only records that might have a bearing on future cases.

Judicial enforcement

The legitimacy of the legal system is tied to publicly perceived outcomes. There is growing public concern that justice is only for the wealthy and powerful despite any constitutional notions of 'equality before the law' and 'independent exercise of judicial power'. What should the SPC do when the poor cannot defend themselves from the wealthy, and the wealthy indulge in wild, conspicuous consumption? When wealthy, privileged interests are brought to trial and are ordered to make restitution to those whose interests have been damaged, the integrity and dignity of the legal system are at stake. Failure to enforce compliance has exposed the justice system to popular disdain, particularly in cases where wealthy developers manipulated the 'public interest' by pushing long-time residents out of their homes to make way for what cartoonists have depicted as 'the great mall' of China.

The SPC's 17 May 2010 remedial regulations, however, did not enforce restitution of lost benefits as originally ordered by the courts. Instead, they appear to be a public relations exercise designed to indirectly make the recalcitrant rich uncomfortable and thus appease public feelings. Article 5 confirms that courts can issue instructions to deprive the wealthy of the enjoyment of their wealth. In what appears to be a strategy of public shaming they can seek the cooperation of employers and also inform the media of bad behavior. The wealthy are to be made to compensate for the lack of harmony. They are denied air flights, the privilege of soft seats in railway cars, the purchase of luxury real estate, the rental of high-rise offices, the sending of their children to expensive private schools, etc.[11]

But does this kind of displaced enforcement link a particular punishment to a particular crime? Rather than focusing on restitution to those who have been harmed, it looks like an opportunistic political attempt to mollify outraged public opinion. Moreover, if it were truly carried out, it could create staggering operational costs, extraordinarily intrusive violations of privacy, and aggravated interventions in the social order. There is also the question of whether such a system can really assuage public feelings.

The court system is already in serious budgetary difficulty. A real solution to the budgetary dynamic that supports continuing local protectionism is elusive. The new regulations on 'enforcement' seem to be a kind of moral ministration—politicization with 'Chinese characteristics'—rather than a rational, cost-efficient legal strategy.

Yu Lingyu, director general of the SPC Division for Law Enforcement, has defended the new regulations. He maintained that even though they would not result in restitution to those who had been harmed, they would serve as a wake-up call to the wealthy who think they are above the law and immune from court decisions.[12] The legal system continues to address *minfen*, public feeling or outrage. Mass-line populism continues to challenge Western-based procedural reform. However, Renda Law Professor Tang Weichen is of the opinion that if the regulations were applied zealously they might jeopardize rather than reinforce social stability. He has argued that in effect pervasive surveillance could raise issues of the 'Big Brother' state and might lead to violence.

Conclusion: heavy politicization, light judicialization

Eric Ip has suggested that the SPC has already achieved considerable latitude through its interpretation process:

> The SPC has self-consciously redefined its mandate to manage state-sponsored legal reforms by performing an expansive range of new functions, such as issuing abstract rules, tightening control over lower courts, and crafting a constitutional jurisprudence of its own at the expense of other powerful state actors. It is asserting more than ever its own vision of how law should develop in the contemporary People's Republic of China (PRC). SPC action can be broadly consistent with the Chinese Communist Party (CCP) interests, autonomous and expansive at the same time. However, the SPC's reform initiatives are inevitably constrained by the vested interests of major bureaucratic players as well as the Party's insistence on maintaining the Court as an integral administrative agency of its public security system.
> (2010: 1)

'Asserting more than ever its own vision of how law should develop' may conflict with SPC participation in the public security system, but does it suggest more than light judicialization? This chapter's analysis suggests that the 'political-legal system' has undergone substantive change and that the notion of 'judicial activism' has meant different things at different points in the cycles of SPC reform. Judicial interpretation is still important to the continued functioning of China's huge legal system; however, SPC ability to issue interpretations depends on negotiation with the NPC panel, and institutional limitations prevent court comment on the validity of law. Moreover, in future, as the SPC's system of leading cases evolves, there may be less institutional need for judicial interpretation.

For now, the comparative priority of judicial interpretation has to be seen in appropriate perspective. According to SPC regulations of 13 July 2009, if the legal system is taken as a whole, 'judicial interpretation' ranks behind law (*falu*), legislative interpretation (*falu jieshi*), provincial People's Congress regulations (*guiding*), and autonomous regional regulations (*guiding*). There is otherwise no formal tolerance for judges making decisions about conflicts in the law.

The 13 July 2009 meeting of the SPC Judicial Committee moved to reinforce the law on legislation.[13] Article 7 of the motion explicitly precluded People's Courts from making judgments on the comparative validity of conflicting law. Perhaps in its distinctive deferral to principles of democratic centralism the SPC wanted to avoid a situation where People's Court judges would attempt to determine the efficacy of law. If conflict between laws became evident in a court proceeding, the court was obliged to report it to higher 'authorities' without making its own determination. Essentially this avoided challenges to the decisions of People's Congresses and preserved the superiority of the NPC's exclusive legislative power. While sometimes interested in protecting rights and interests, the courts have not created a system of formal review of related law.

As Judge He Yan indicates in the preface to his translation of the recent analysis of the U.S. Supreme Court, because China's SPC is in a formative stage of development, it does not have the same luxury as the U.S. court to deal directly with hot-button rights issues. It is not capable of shaping 'pure politics'. It has not addressed 'deadlocked politics'. However, does this mean that there is no judicialization at all? The SPC is still a dynamic agency that is becoming influential through improvised judicial activism. Judicial interpretation, requests for instruction, and the selection of leading cases are necessary to the delivery of what justice there is in China, and there is a new awareness of the importance of openly protecting rights and interests in society so as to ward off unrest and instability that could undercut CCP legitimacy and China's continued economic success.

Emblazoned across the SPC's masthead are the 'Three Supremes', but to some degree the SPC persists in its own Chinese understandings of professionalism and judicial independence as it tries to compensate for weaknesses in the nation's court system in a time of profound transition in China's society and economy when there is great need for institutions to cope with extreme stress.

The SPC is a political court. It has a political mandate established through CCP guidance and leadership. By Western liberal democratic standards this represents a massive politicization of the judiciary. However, the Chinese terms of reference are what Zhu Suli describes as 'general and diffuse'. Unity is the message. Political instability is anathema but stability requires the protection of rights and interests within national economic development. These factors inform any concrete organizational tendency on the part of the SPC to carve out tentative areas of professional autonomy for itself as institutions around it modernize.

The SPC has declined to participate in open 'judicialization', though there is a modicum of opaque judicialization occurring insofar as the court creatively moves within the CCP mandate to create new formats of interpretation and supervision so as to provide more consistent and transparent justice in protecting rights and interests. The party has asked the SPC to meet the needs of the people, but how it does this is analytically interesting, reflecting as it does tendencies towards semi-independent institutional responsibility within a formally politicized system that must adapt to the requirements of party discourse and ideology.

Notes

1 'Zhongyong zhengfa wei tongzhi yaoqiu zhengfa xitong xuexi shiqi da jingshen' (The Central Legal and Political Affairs Committee Passes a Motion to Study the Political-Legal Affairs System in the Spirit of the 17th National Party Congress, http://cpc.people.com.cn/GB/64093/64094/6467746.html, 31 October 2007 (accessed 9 February 2012).

2 The 'mass line' generally requires political leaders to listen to the masses and to create conditions supportive of the masses' participation in political processes. In terms of the legal system over time this included the masses' actual participation in judicial processes alongside judges as 'people's assessors'. Related recent reference to the mass line calls upon judges to listen to the masses and to get close to the feelings and needs of the masses. Such emphases may challenge formal legal emphases that stress judicial independence and the supremacy of the law.

3 *China Daily*, 21 December 2010, 4.

4 *Guanyu guifan shangxia ji fayuan shenpan yewu guanxi de ruogan yijian* (Several SPC Notes Regarding Standard Relations Between Higher and Lower Courts in the Conduct of Trial Work Responsibilities), available online at http://wsl2010.fyfz.cn/art/905747.htm (accessed 9 February 2012).

5 Hou Meng, 'Suowei de "xianfa sifa hua diyian"—Qi Yuling an jieshao' (The First Case of So-called Constitutionalism—Qi Yuling), available online at http://flhshkx.fyfz.cn/art/609287.htm (accessed 3 March 2011).

6 Chu Ming Su Tianjin Shifan Daxue bu luxing shouyu xueweizheng fading zhize an (The Case of Chu Ming v. Tianjin Normal University for Refusing its Legal Duty to Award a Bachelor Degree), available online at http://court.dl.gov.cn/info/136_49005.vm.

7 Bai Long, *Zuigaofayuan hezhun sanqi qinhai nongmin liushou funu ertong sixing anjian* (The SPC Approved Three Death Penalty Cases Relating to the Violation of the Rights of Stay-at-home Women and Children), available online at http://legal.people.com.cn/GB/13201328.html (accessed 3 March 2011).

8 The following argument on judicial transparency follows closely on the analysis in Shumei Hou and Ronald C. Keith, 'A New Prospect for Judicial Transparency in China?', *China Information*, 26 (1), March 2012, 61–86.

9 'Wang Shengjun zai quanguo zhengfa gongzuo dianshi dianhua huiyi shang qiangdiao: shizhong jianchi "sange zhishang" gongzuo zhidao sixiang nuli shixian renmin fayuan gongzuo xin fazhan' (Wang Shengjun stressed in a national television and radio conference on political and legal affairs the consistency of the Three Supremes as our guiding work principle in achieving the new development of the people's courts), *Guangming ribao*, 19 December 2009, 2.

10 'Fewer Meetings and Fewer Documents', *China Daily*, 21 December 2010, 4. Mao Zedong used to complain of 'three too-manys': 'too many officials, too many meetings and too many documents'.

11 SPC document no. 8 (2010), 17 May 2010, *Zuigaofayuan guanyu xianzhi bei zhixingren gaoxiaofei de ruogan guiding* (SPC Regulations on Restricting High Consumer Lifestyle).

12 Chen Fei, 'Zuigaofayuan ni chutai xianzhi gaoxiaofeiling yingdui zhixingnan' (The SPC will issue a regulation to restrict the high consumer lifestyle), available online at www.gsly6.com/ShowArticle.shtml?ID=200991810492357739.htm (accessed 4 March 2011).

13 SPC document no. 14 (2009), *Zuigarenminfayuan guanyu caipan wenshu yinyong falu, fagui deng guifanwenjian de guiding* (SPC Regulations on Applying the Law, Regulations and Other Legal Documents in Judgments).

References

Administrative Office of the Supreme People's Court (2010) *Zuigao renmin fayuan lirenyuan zhang wenxian, (Selected Works of the Successive Presidents of the Supreme People's Court)*, Beijing: Renmin Fayuan Chubanshe.

Backer, L. C. (2009–2010) 'A Constitutional Court for China Within the Chinese Communist Party: Scientific Development and a Reconsideration of the Institutional Role of the CCP', *Suffolk University Law Review*, 43: 593–624.

Cabestan, J. P. (2005) 'The Political and Practical Obstacles to the Reform of the Judiciary and the Establishment of a Rule of Law in China,' *Journal of Chinese Political Science*, vol. 10, no. 1, April 2005.

Chen Xingliang (ed.) (2003) *Zhongguo xingshi sifa jieshi jiantao* (*Examining Chinese Judicial Interpretations of Criminal Legislation*). Beijing: Zhongguo Jiancha Chubanshe, p. 138.

Deng Xiaoping (1993) *The Selected Works of Deng Xiaoping*, Vol. III. Beijing: Foreign Languages Press.

Dong Likun (1980) 'No One Can Stand Above the Law: A Discussion of the Relationships Between the Law, Individuals, the Party, the Government and Policies', *Shehui kexue*, no. 1 (February) in Joint Publications Research Service, 77155, no. 155, p. 14.

Hou Meng, (2010) 'Suowei de "xianfa sifa hua diyian" Qi Yuling' (The First Case of So-called Constitutionalism—-Qi Yuling). Available online at http://flhshkx.fyfz.cn/art/609287.htm (accessed on 3 March 2011).

Hou Shumei and Keith, R. (2011) 'The Defense Lawyer in the Scales of Chinese Criminal Justice', *Journal of Contemporary China*, 20: 379–95.

Hou Shumei and Keith, R. (2012) 'A New Prospect for Judicial Transparency in China', *China Information*, 26 (1) March 2012, 61–86.

Hirschl, R. (2006) 'The New Constitutionalism and Judicialization of Pure Politics Worldwide', *Fordham Law Review*, 75:2 721ff.

Ip, E. C. (2010) 'The Supreme Court and the Making of Public Policy in Contemporary China', *Michigan Journal of Public Affairs*, vol. 7, Spring 2010: 1–15.

Keith, R. C. (1994) *China's Struggle for the Rule of Law*, London: Macmillan.

Keith, R. C. and Zhiqiu Lin, (2001) *Law and Justice in China's New Marketplace*, London: Palgrave.

Keith, R. C. and Zhiqiu Lin (2003) 'Falun Gong Problem: Politics and the Struggle for the Rule of Law in China', *China Quarterly*, no. 175: 623–42.

Keith, R. C. and Zhiqiu Lin (2006) *New Crime in China: Public Order and Human Rights*, London and New York: Routledge (Taylor and Francis).

Keith, R. C. and Zhiqiu Lin (2009) 'Judicial Interpretation of China's Supreme People's Court as "Secondary Law" with Special Reference to Criminal Law', *China Information*, 23: 223–55.

Li Buyun (2004) *New Constitutionalism in China*, Beijing: Falu Chubanshe.

Liebman, B. (2007) 'China's Courts: Restricted Reform', *The China Quarterly*, no. 191: 620–38.

National People's Congress of the People's Republic of China (2000) *The State Constitution of the People's Republic of China, 1982*, Beijing: Foreign Languages Press.

Peerenboom, R. (ed.) (2004) *Asian Discourse on the Rule of Law*, London: Routledge Curzon.

Peerenboom, R. (2010) 'Between Global Norms and Domestic Realities: Judicial Reforms in China', Social Science Research Network, Working Paper Series. SSRN paper. Available online at http://papers.ssrn.com/sol3/papers.cfm?abstract_id=1401232 (accessed 3 May 2011).

Peerenboom, R. and Xin He (2011) 'Dispute Resolution in China: Patterns, Causes and Prognosis', *East Asia Law Review*, 4: 53ff.

Schubert, G. (2005) 'Reforming Authoritarianism in Contemporary China. Reflections on Pan Wei's Consultative Rule of Law Regime', *ASIEN*, 94: S. 7–24.

Toobin, J. (2010) *Jiuren: Meiguo zuigao fayuan fengyun* (The nine: inside the secret world of the supreme court), trans. by He Fan. Shanghai: Shanghai Joint Publishing Co.

Trevaskes, S. (2011) 'Political Ideology, the Party, and Politicking: Justice System Reform in China', *Modern China*, 37: 315–44.

Zhang Qianfang (2003) 'The People's Court in Transition: The Prospects of Chinese Judicial Reform', *Journal of Contemporary China*, 12: 69–101.

Zhu Suli (2007) 'Political Parties in China's Judiciary', *Duke Journal of Comparative and International Law*, 17: 533–60.

10 Cambodia's judiciary

Heading for political judicialization?

Kheang Un and Sokbunthoeun So

Introduction

For some scholars, certain international justice mechanisms can contribute to judicialization at the national level. Hirschl (2008) has proposed that judicialization of mega-politics may account for the growing phenomenon of judicial activism, embracing 'everything political', from 'judicial scrutiny of executive branch prerogatives' to rulings on electoral processes, restorative justice, and regime legitimacy (p. 98). For Cambodia, establishment of the Khmer Rouge Tribunal, a hybrid court, would fit Hirschl's definition of judicialization of mega-politics in the case of transitional justice (Hirschl 2008: 93–8). However, it might not justify an assumption of further judicialization of the Cambodian court system. Because the tribunal is embedded in the political system, its impact on the Cambodian judiciary generally is minimal and is unlikely to bring any substantial change to the Cambodian courts (Un and Ledgerwood 2010).

Judicialization of politics requires not only a larger judiciary role and supportive laws but also an independent, efficient, and effective judiciary. The Cambodian judiciary suffers from institutional weakness as a result of limited capacity and low remuneration and also lacks independence. Legacies of war and authoritarian and radical communist revolution have left the Cambodian judiciary in a poor state; it lacks the ability even to appropriately perform its functions. Like most courts outside established democracies, the Cambodian judiciary has historically been highly politicized, and also highly subservient to the executive power and responsive to the interests of the ruling elite. An effective, efficient, independent judiciary would create an intra-system tension that could challenge elite domination and therefore compromise the concentration of power in elite hands that is free of institutional checks (see Solomon 2007: 123).

The lack of necessary judicial capacity and independence renders it unlikely that there will be any judicialization of politics in Cambodia. The situation is reminiscent of Guillermo O'Donnell's remarks (2004, p. 40) in reference to Brazilian President Getulio Vargas (in office 1930–45, 1950–54): 'For my friends, everything; for my enemies, the law'. In Cambodia the elites use legal instruments to marginalize political opposition and quell outspoken critics rather than allowing a shift toward judicialization of politics.

Various legal and judicial reforms since the early 2000s—such as projects to build institutional capacity, new laws and regulations, new buildings, and increased salaries for judges and prosecutors—have failed to established the rule of law that guarantees procedural fairness, judicial review of executive acts, equality before the law, and access to justice. For instance, though use of the courts has recently increased, the legal proceedings do not suggest that the judiciary functions independently. The lawsuits have mainly consisted of defamation and disinformation charges against opposition politicians and members of civil society, such as journalists and human rights workers. The suits were orchestrated to strengthen the position of the ruling elites, undermine opposition political parties, and constrict civil and political liberties. Rather than constituting a transition to the judicialization of politics, they represent a continuation of the politicization of the judiciary.

This chapter makes two propositions: (1) the increase in laws and regulations adopted in a series of reforms in the last decade may clarify or broaden the court's role, but the missing element is judicial independence, without which the judiciary cannot be transformed into an effective tool for checking executive power, and promoting rights and liberties, but will simply reinforce Cambodia's illiberal democracy and crony capitalism; (2) persistent judicial weakness and lack of independence is related to general political and economic conditions that inhibit emergence of an efficient and professionalized judiciary, preventing the possibility of judicialization beyond cosmetic assertions in formal documents.

We first briefly discuss the history of the modern legal system in Cambodia as background for a discussion of contemporary judicial issues. We then discuss judicial weaknesses and a range of cases brought against Cambodian political opposition leaders, members of nongovernmental organizations (NGOs), and journalists. Next we identify political drivers of the rise in these types of lawsuits, arguing that the trend is driven in part by a change in incentives, leading Cambodian political elites to adopt a more subtle and 'legitimate' strategy for politically and economically marginalizing their opponent. We also show that political elites are able to use the courts for this purpose because the judiciary, as a result of institutional, structural, and cultural factors, is very weak. We conclude by identifying where Cambodia's judiciary is positioned in the universe of judicial politics.

The modern Cambodian legal system

Considering its tumultuous history Cambodia has had a relatively short experience of a modern legal system. The French as colonial rulers introduced a modern legal system in the late nineteenth century. Before the French arrived, the legal system was based on customary law, with mediation the mechanism for settling disputes. Though the French introduced a civil code system nationally, the traditional system remained in use at the local level (Broadhurst, Bouhours and Keo 2010: 59). After Cambodia became independent in 1953, two post-independence governments (under Sihanouk, 1954–70, and Lon Nol, 1970–75) maintained the system. However, during these two regimes, the majority of Cambodians had no contact with the judicial system; those who were accused of crimes were confronted with imprisonment and possible execution without judicial review (Amnesty International 2002; Chandler 1991).

The judicial system entirely ceased to function in 1975, when Cambodia fell under the radical regime of Democratic Kampuchea (DK). Finding no value or necessity in law, the DK regime terminated the legal system. That regime, historian Michael Vickery writes, did not have even the 'pretense of legality' (1986: 120). Almost all Cambodians with legal backgrounds were killed; other legal resources, such as schools, texts, and court buildings, were either destroyed or converted to other uses. Arrests, sentencing, and executions were arbitrarily decided by DK cadres who acted in the name of *Angkar* ('the organization'), resulting in summary executions and grave systematic violations of human rights. The death toll was over two million people (Chandler 1991).

Thus when the People's Republic of Kampuchea (PRK) came to power in 1979, there was no legal system in place. The PRK, following Vietnamese and Soviet models, reestablished a judicial system so that Cambodia had at least the pretense of legality (Amnesty International 2002). Because of staff shortages, the PRK set up short-term training courses for would-be judges and prosecutors (Donovan 1993: 81–2). However, because the regime considered the legal system an integral part of the ruling party apparatus, the training emphasized Marxist-Leninist doctrine over legal subjects (Gottesman 2003: 243). Prosecutors and judges were usually former schoolteachers and other literate Cambodians with 'good biography'—no political connection to the previous regime (Gottesman 2003).

The PRK was slowly able to create a formal court system. However, as in other communist states, judges were subservient to the party and the government (Donovan 1993; Gottesman 2003). The official party line demonstrated a complete lack of trust in the courts, and the distrust opened space for both central and provincial government officials to interfere regularly in judicial processes.[1] The party or powerful individuals, not the law, determined the course of proceedings and the verdicts of trials. A former minister of justice complained during a meeting of the Council of Ministers in 1986: 'Sentencing depends on the influence of persons offering an opinion, not on the law' (Gottesman 2003).

In 1989, soon after Vietnamese troops departed, in anticipation of a possible pluralistic electoral contestation and to dissociate itself from a communist- and Vietnamese-dominated past, the PRK initiated a series of reforms, some of which were cosmetic and others more substantial. The government took a new name, the State of Cambodia (SOC), and promulgated a new constitution that emphasized fundamental freedoms and the rule of law. However, under the SOC government the overlap between the judicial and executive branches persisted (as in the colonial system), and the judicial branch was again subordinated to the party. A Supreme Court report to the National Assembly revealed this fundamental problem:

> The People's Supreme Court ... is not competent to resolve the suits itself, has only examined them ... so that they may be turned over to the competent organs to be dealt with. This is because we felt that the work of receiving and resolving suits is a matter of ideology.
>
> (Fernando 1988: 60)

Given Cambodia's unique history as the site of one of the twentieth century's greatest human tragedies, a concern to prevent 'a return to the policies and practices of the past' was central to the negotiations for the Paris Peace Agreement (Doyle 1995). The agreement ensured that protection of fundamental human rights consistent with the Universal Declaration of Human Rights and other relevant instruments, including the United Nations Basic Principles on the Independence of the Judiciary, was to be enshrined in the constitution of the government to be formed after UN-sponsored elections. These basic principles include 'due process and equality before the law, protection from arbitrary deprivation of property or deprivation of private property without just compensation, and freedom from racial, ethnic, religious or sexual discrimination' (United Nations 1996: 145).

After the 1993 democratic elections, Cambodia adopted a system of checks and balances in which judicial independence was enshrined in the constitution. Article 128 specifies that the judicial body 'shall be an independent power and shall guarantee and uphold impartiality and protect the rights and freedoms of the citizens'. Article 130 stipulates that 'Judicial power shall not be granted to either the legislative or the executive branch'.

To safeguard the constitution and protect citizens' fundamental rights, complex judicial institutions were established to review laws, impartially adjudicate laws, and enforce constitutional provisions on equal protection and the defense of civil and social rights. These judicial institutions, however, do not function appropriately because both state and non-state actors failed to systematically implement and follow laws and regulations. At the same time, government's politicized decisions are expeditiously and regularly implemented. As such, Cambodia has seen the judiciary politicized and the principle of judicial independence violated, abused, and neglected. To use Gillman's phrase, the judiciary serves as 'an extension of a regime's power and not a shield against it' (Gillman 1994: 60).

Institutional structure

The Cambodian court system encompasses a range of institutions: (1) the Constitutional Council (CC) has review and veto power to exercise its responsibility for ensuring the constitutionality of laws and regulations; (2) the constitutional role (articles 132 and 133) of the Supreme Council of Magistracy (SCM) is to help the king ensure the independence of the judiciary and recommend judges and prosecutors for royal appointment, dismissal, and discipline; and (3) there are three tiers of regular courts—courts of first instance, an appeals court, and the Supreme Court.

All Cambodian courts suffer from lack of independence and resources and from politicization. They are embedded in neopatrimonial structures in which an overarching system of patronage coexists with formal state institutions. As in other branches of the government, merit counts for little within the judiciary—appointments and promotions are based on patronage. Cambodians consider the courts to be unresponsive and servants of party interests, and a 2004 survey revealed that 66 percent of the Cambodian electorate then considered the judiciary to be corrupt (International Republican Institute 2004). Close to a decade later, little has changed. In the 2008 *Global Integrity Report*, on judicial accountability Cambodia received a score of just 17 out of a possible 100 (2008).

The CC was part of the 1993 Constitution influenced by the liberal ideas stipulated in the 1991 Paris Agreement which set the objective to ensure both vertical and inter-institutional accountability, and political and civil liberties.

The CC, whose constitutional role is 'to safeguard respect for the constitution, to interpret the constitution, and laws passed by the National Assembly', has thus far, to quote a Cambodian legal expert Lao Mong Hay, not yet 'made any decision that could affect the policy of the government or protect the constitutional rights of the people' (2008). According to the CC Secretariat, from 1998 to 2007 the CC considered or ruled on only 137 cases[2] of which, according to Lao, 'perhaps only one … of all the petitions [the council received] met with a positive decision' (Lao 2008). Further, the principle of judicial review has not been fully applied because many 'nonorganic' laws were not submitted to the CC for review before they were sent to the king for promulgation (Kato *et al.* 2000: 25–6). In 2009, a penal code was adopted without any known reaction from the CC even though code articles define broadly and criminalize defamation and disinformation, which have been alleged in lawsuits—a practice that threatens the constitutional guarantee of freedom of expression.

The CC is also generally silent toward the executive's expedient use of subdecrees 'without the approval of the National Assembly' and constitutional review with power of law (Transparency International 2006). The practice is to manipulate the generally vague legislature with patronage and rent-seeking. Land policy demonstrates how judicial muteness, or politicization, affects human rights and helps perpetuate corrupt and patronage-based allocation of natural resources, developments that help sustain Cambodia's illiberal democracy. By law 'state land' is divided into 'state private lands' and 'state public lands'. The former can be sold or transferred into private hands but the latter are reserved for the benefit of the public. However, by executive fiat, state public land can be reclassified as private and legally sold or transferred to private hands. There has been no judicial review of the executive's reclassification of land and its transfer (Un and So 2011).

The issue of CC legitimacy surfaced on the first day of its inception. First, the CC members are alleged to be pro-Cambodian People's Party (CPP), the dominant party that has controlled Cambodia since 1979. The CC's absence of independence from the CPP is a product of the imbalanced power configuration among the various political parties which enables the dominant party to prevent the creation of an independent institution which might curb its power in the future (Peou 2000). The CPP employed its control over other institutions to intervene in the selection of members of the CC to ensure a majority of CPP supporters. The CC was formed in 1998, five years after the promulgation of the Constitution and only after pressure from the international community following the 1997 violent conflict during which the CPP ousted the duly elected First Prime Minister Norodom Ranariddh (Brown and Timberman 1998). The international community wanted a functioning CC ready to adjudicate conflicts that might emerge from the 1998 elections. The CC has nine members, who hold staggered nine-year terms. Among them three are appointed by the king, three are appointed by the National Assembly and the remaining three are appointed by the SCM. Only three members are considered to be apolitical and highly qualified because they were appointed by the king, who has been seen as neutral. The other six members are considered to be affiliated with and thus biased towards the CPP (Lao 2001).

The political climate surrounding the period leading up to the establishment of the CC was marred by fear and uncertainty. Some leaders of the United National Front for an Independent, Neutral, Peaceful, and Cooperative Cambodia (FUNCINPEC) and the Buddhist Liberal Democratic Party (BLDP), which were CPP's coalition partners, were boycotting the National Assembly, following the violent coup d'état orchestrated by the CPP the preceding year. The members of FUNCINPEC and BLDP who remained in the National Assembly were alleged to have been co-opted by the CPP through monetary incentives. It was a National Assembly dominated by the CPP and some 'renegade' BLDP and FUNCINPEC members which selected the three members of the CC (Ashley 1998). Some CC members appointed by the National Assembly did not meet the constitutionally required qualifications.[3]

Many see the SCM, whose role is to help the king to ensure the independence of the judiciary, as politically dependent, subject to CPP influence, and functionally ineffective. It is often criticized for procedural irregularities. The SCM has eight members and is chaired by the king. Currently its members are: the Minister of Justice, the President of the Supreme Court, the Prosecutor General of the Supreme Court, the President of the Court of Appeals, the Prosecutor General of the Court of Appeals, and the three magistrates elected by their peers. The SCM has also been accused of violating its own procedures. According to SCM Law, three appointments to the council are reserved for members elected by the judges. The term for this appointment is five years and the person can be reelected. According to the Office of the United Nations High Commission for Human Rights (UNHCHR) 'no elections have ever been held for these three elected positions' (UNHCHR 2007).

The appointments and replacement of judges have also apparently not followed constitutional procedures. Although the Constitution stipulates that appointments and disciplinary actions against judges and prosecutors must be decided by the SCM, past appointments appeared to violate these principles. For instance, the 2007 replacement of the President of the Court of Appeals was made not on the recommendation of the SCM; rather it was decided on the recommendation of the executive branch, which in the UNHCHR's view, contravened 'the separation of executive and judicial powers specified in the Constitution' (UNHCHR 2007).

Most of its current members, except for the king and the prosecutor-general of the Supreme Court, are senior members of the CPP and some even sit on the party's powerful Central Committee (Lao 2001). The SCM's lack of independence and transparency can influence a judge's decisions and behavior. A judge whose decision deviates from what is expected could be transferred to remote provinces, a punishment judges have to keep in mind in sensitive cases. Despite the notoriously corrupt and erratic nature of the rest of the court system, SCM action against corrupt practices and judicial misconducts is rare.

This study focuses on the regular courts, where contentious and controversial legal battles occur. They are the first and most frequent contact point for Cambodians who seek justice when civil and social rights are violated. And the highest court has never, to the best of our knowledge, overturned a lower court verdict in a political case.

The politics of lawsuits

The last decade saw a surge in suits against members of political opposition parties, NGO leaders, and journalists (see Table 10.1). The cases have weakened opposition parties and suppressed civic space and political and civil liberties. In discouraging the activities of civil society actors, they have suppressed democratic aspirations.

The surge in lawsuits coincided with the decline in political violence and coercion which characterized the elections in the 1990s. The decline is a consequence of the CPP's increased strength in two areas. First, the party is confident in its popularity and the legitimacy of its rural development projects and gift-giving, not only during but also between elections. Second, the CPP can systematically employ the courts as a legitimate means to undermine opposition parties and suppress outspoken critiques. This latter strength is driven by the weaknesses, lack of professionalism, and politicized nature of Cambodian courts. Their shortcomings are multidimensional, with institutional, cultural, and structural factors all closely intertwined.

Members of the Sam Rainsy Party (SRP), the only major opposition party in Cambodia, have suffered severely from successive legal battles. In 2005 four SRP members—Cheam Channy, Chea Poch, Khom Piseth (former member), and Rainsy were charged with establishing a 'shadow army' that made 'the grenade attack in 1997' and with defamation. Rainsy was sentenced in absentia to 18 months in prison and required to pay 56 million riels in fines. All charges were dropped after Rainsy wrote a letter of apology to the prime minister, and King Norodom Sihamoni issued a royal pardon. In 2010 Rainsy, who is now in self-imposed exile, was again convicted, this time for destruction of public property after his removal of a few Cambodia–Vietnam border markers in an October

2009 protest of alleged Vietnamese encroachment on Cambodian soil and for disinformation and falsification of public documents after he published evidence of 'alleged Vietnamese encroachment on Cambodian territory in video press conferences and on the SRP website' (Sokchea and O'Toole 2010). He was sentenced to two years' imprisonment by the Svay Rieng Provincial Court on the first charge and to 10 years' imprisonment and over US$15,000 in fines and damages by the Phnom Penh Municipal Court (Sokchea 2011a).

Lawsuits filed by opposition party members against any of the ruling elites have little chance of being successful, and the party lodging the complaint risks a counter-suit. For example, SRP member Mu Sochua's legal battle began when she filed a defamation suit against the prime minister for 'derogatory comments about a female parliamentarian' in Kampot Province in April 2009, remarks that Mrs. Mu viewed as directed against her and as an insult to Cambodian women. The prime minister counter-sued and the court ordered her to pay 16.5 million riels in compensation and fine, to be deducted from her salary. The fine was paid off in November 2010 (Sokchea 2011b).

Since the domestic legal arena has been closed off, opposition parties are turning to foreign venues to redress their grievances. Realizing the weaknesses and partiality of the Cambodian courts, Rainsy allegedly filed or planned to file at least two complaints against ruling party members in foreign courts, including a criminal complaint against the prime minister in a U.S. court in New York for alleged involvement in a 1997 grenade attack that killed 19 people and wounded more than a hundred (Strangio and Sokchea 2010) and 'an international complaint accusing Hun Sen of crimes against humanity in connection with the K5 plan' in October 2010 (Sokha 2010). K-5 was the unpopular and abusive policy the People's Republic of Kampuchea (1979–89) designed to prevent the Khmer Rouge and other resistance forces from infiltrating Cambodia's interior by creating a defensive line along the Thai–Cambodian border. At the height of the project in 1985 about half a million people were conscripted to mine, demine, construct roads, transport military equipment, and clear jungle under harsh conditions in malaria-infected areas with insufficient food and medical care. Deaths totaled 25,000 to 30,000, and tens of thousands were infected with malaria or maimed (see Gottesman 2003; Slocomb 2001). His reactions may not yield a favorable outcome for Rainsy, but they do raise his profile in the media.

Institutional factors

A range of institutional weaknesses exacerbates the lack of professionalism within the Cambodian judiciary. First, the courts face a severe shortage of resources. Budgetary allocations for the judicial system are channeled through the Ministry of Justice (MOJ); only a small fraction of its annual budget of 0.1 percent of GDP went to the courts. In actual monetary terms, the 2007 budget for the MOJ was projected to be US$5 million (Ministry of Economy and Finance 2005). Although there have been some improvements in the physical infrastructure in recent years, Cambodian courts still face a variety of resource

Table 10.1 Opposition party members, NGO leaders, and journalists who have been sued

No.	*Sam Rainsy Party (SRP)*	*Charges and disposition*	*Year*	*Status*
1	Sam Rainsy, SRP president and Member of Parliament	1. Sentenced in absentia to 18 months in prison and fined 56 million riels for criminal charges (creating a 'shadow army, grenade attack in 1997') and for defamation relating to a radio interview alleging that Prince Ranariddh had received US$50 million and an aircraft from Prime Minister Hun Sen to form a coalition government with the CPP in 2004.	2005	Charges dropped following a royal pardon.
		2. Sentenced in absentia to two years' imprisonment and fined eight million riels (US$1,972) on 25 April 2011 for defamation in a lawsuit brought by Foreign Minister Hor Namhong for a 2008 public comment which allegedly suggested that the minister had served as supervisor of a work camp under the Khmer Rouge regime.	2008	continuing
		3. Sentenced in absentia to two years' imprisonment for racial incitement and destruction of public property for uprooting a border marker post (No. 185) 25 August 2009.	2010	continuing
		4. Sentenced in absentia to 10 years' imprisonment and fined US$16,000 for disinformation and forgery for publicly disputing the location of the Cambodia–Vietnam border.	2010	continuing
2	Cheam Channy, leading SRP parliamentarian	Sentenced by a military court to seven years' imprisonment for forming an illegal 'shadow army'.	August 2005	Criminal charges dropped; royal pardon after serving one year.
3	Chea Poch, SRP Member of Parliament	Charged with 1. creating a 'shadow army' 2. defamation: sued by Prince Norodom Ranariddh for allegedly stating that the prince had accepted bribes to form a coalition government with the CPP.	2005	Charges dropped following a royal pardon.
4	Khom Piseth, former SRP member	Sentenced in absentia to five years' imprisonment on a criminal charge for creating a 'shadow army'.	2005	Charge dropped for him and three others accused of the same crime.
5	Ho Vann, SRP Member of Parliament	Charged with defaming defense officials.	9 August 2009	Acquitted 9 September 2009 following pressure from civil society and international donors.
6	Mu Sochua, SRP Member of Parliament	Charged with defaming Prime Minister Hun Sen; ordered to pay roughly 16.5 million riels in compensation and fine.	2009	Fine and compensation deducted from her salary; no prison time.

Human Rights Party (HRP)	*Charges and disposition*	*Year*	*Status*
Kem Sokha, HRP president and former director of the Cambodian Center for Human Rights (CCHR)	Arrested for allegedly defaming the prime minister in handwritten comments on banners displayed during International Human Rights Day (10 December 2005) while CCHR director.	2005	Released 17 January 2006 after widespread protests from national and international NGOs and pressure from foreign diplomats.
	Complaint filed by a former CCHR employee resulted in a request from the prosecutor that Sokha's parliamentary immunity be removed.	2006	No further public information concerning the case.
	New complaint filed 30 August 2010 based on the one filed four years previously accusing Sokha of embezzling donor funds while CCHR president.	2010	Appeared in court 21 October 2010 to answer questions; denied wrongdoing.
Norodom Ranariddh Party (NRP)	*Charges and disposition*	*Year*	*Status*
Norodom Ranariddh, NRP president and former president of FUNCINPEC	Convicted in absentia by the Military Court for conspiring to overthrow the government and sentenced to 30 years' imprisonment plus US$54 million for damages caused in the coup that ousted him in July 1997.	1998	Pardoned three days after his trial and returned to Cambodia to participate in 1998 national election as FUNCINPEC leader.
	Charged by the Phnom Penh Municipal Court with breach of trust in relation to the alleged illegal sale of former FUNCINPEC headquarters; sentenced in absentia to 18 months in prison plus US$150,000 in fines (18 December 2006). Appeal in 2007 was rejected.	2006 and 2007	Self-imposed exile; sought royal pardon.
	Charged by Phnom Penh Municipal Court with adultery	2007	Self-imposed exile; sought royal pardon.
Journalists and Civil Society Leaders	*Charges and disposition*	*Year*	*Status*
Rong Chhun, president, Independent Teachers' Association	Arrested for defaming the prime minister in critiques of the government on the Cambodian–Vietnam border issue.	2005–06	Released on bail in January 2006 following pressure from civil society and the international community.
Pa NgounTieng, deputy director, CCHR Yeng Virak, director, Community Legal Education Center	Both arrested on defamation charges.	2005–06	Released in January 2006 after widespread protest from national and international NGOs and pressure from foreign diplomats.

Source: Author compilation from ADHOC (The Cambodian Human Rights & Development Association), LICADHO (Cambodian League for the Promotion and Defence of Human Rights), and newspaper reports 2005–11.

shortages. Consequently, superiors instruct court staff to ask litigants for a 'contribution'—an informal fee—to cover materials and supplement their meager incomes (the problem is more prevalent in the provincial courts).

The acute lack of resources is also obvious from the poor physical condition of court buildings. In a 2002 annual report, Dith Munty, head of the Supreme Court and co-chairman of the Council on Legal and Judicial Reform, described the general physical state of Cambodian court houses as follows: 'Working places are located in apartments or in people's residents [*sic*] built partly from bricks and partly from wood [and now] are in old, almost collapsed, narrow, and crowded conditions which [are] not suitable as a valuable place for finding justice for the people' (Council on Legal and Judicial Reform 2002).

Such physical conditions have made courts, in the words of one prosecutor, 'the cottage of justice', not 'the palace of justice'.[4] Because of the need for resources for such vital physical infrastructure as roads and bridges, court buildings have never been a priority on the Cambodian government agenda. However, capitalizing on the recent rise in real estate values in metropolitan areas, the government has more recently undertaken (nontransparent) arrangements to swap old court buildings for new buildings in areas where real estate is less valuable.

The Cambodian legal system also faces a severe shortage of human resources. In 2006 Cambodia had 225 judges—17 per one million people—and fewer than 300 practicing lawyers (Transparency International 2007: 186). One reason for the shortages was the Khmer Rouge-era execution of lawyers, judges, and legal scholars. Since 2002, as part of the judicial reform process, however, the government has been training additional lawyers and prosecutors. By 2010 the number of judges had risen to 309 and of lawyers to 594.[5] This is helping to slightly ease human resource constraints in the Cambodian legal system.

However, as the *Cambodia Daily* noted, 'From highly educated to unschooled, Cambodian judges are a mixed pot' (McEvens and Ana 2000). One judge commented that 'The court began from point zero in 1979. There were very few lawyers left. Judges have little education. Talking about the judicial system, [foreigners, especially Westerners] laughed at us. Our society is poor; in other countries, they wouldn't let me hold this position [director of a provincial court]'.[6] As a result, judges often find themselves incapable of resolving legal issues. Cambodian lawyers also possess widely varying educational backgrounds. Some were certified as lawyers after they gained experience serving in the legal system, usually as clerks.

Limited legal experience and knowledge of the law and legal procedures, like corruption, negatively affect the quality of legal representation. Based upon his own observations of court hearings in Cambodia, a Western embassy staff member, trained as a lawyer, noted that Cambodian lawyers are not competent and did not present solid evidence. He added, 'No evidence presented by the lawyers would stand up in any other court'.[7] One co-author observed, after attending many court sessions over several months in 2003 and others more recently, that there was little cross-examination during trials. Lawyers are either fearful or too inexperienced to challenge prosecutors or judges. The fear derives from concerns—real or perceived—that judges will rule arbitrarily against their clients in the current or future trials.

The recent increase in the number of trained judges, prosecutors, and lawyers has increased human resources within the legal system, but the continued subordination of the judiciary to the executive is less the result of a lack of human resources than of the government's lack of political will to grant real independence to the judiciary.

There is also little intra-institutional cooperation. The justice police are an auxiliary of the court assisting on judicial issues like investigations and execution of court warrants and rulings. By law, the prosecutors are responsible for supervising the justice police as they work with the court.[8] However, the court and the justice police are in constant confrontation with each other, and have been since the 1980s. At that time top PRK leaders debated the relative role of the two institutions, and the outcome was a general tendency to protect law enforcement from rival branches of government, including the judiciary (Gottesman 2003: 252–3). This legacy has continued into the present: the police threaten, ignore, or at best offer lukewarm support to the court. The prosecutor general in his 2002 annual report stated, 'Prosecutors have difficulty because of a lack of cooperation from local authorities', which includes the judicial police. Commenting on the report, a prosecutor from Sihanoukville stated, 'What the Prosecutor General has raised hits the main point, and that is that prosecutors throughout the country and the judicial police seem not to be on good terms. This is the truth' (Council on Legal and Judicial Reform 2002).

The poor relationship between the judiciary and the police may have roots in both administrative and political factors. The administrative problem derives from the justice police chain of command. Although by law the justice police are under the control of prosecutors, their salaries, promotions, and demotions are under the control of the Ministry of the Interior. Thus, a prosecutor explains, 'If the activities of prosecutors or judges affect the interests of their superiors, [the justice police] would not participate in these activities'.[9] Police interference appears to have declined slightly, however, since the 2008 death of Hok Longdy, the allegedly brutal and corrupt national police chief.

Politically, the state is unwilling to grant the judiciary its independence, which means that other institutions, especially the police, feel free to interfere in court affairs. There have been numerous instances as well as allegations in which the justice police refused to execute court warrants or rulings. This is a major problem, said a prosecutor, adding that 'In some cases the higher authorities defended the police when the police did not execute court orders'.[10] The courts have now been firmly incorporated into the CPP patronage networks, which channel resources to rural voters. This could place the courts on a better footing with other government institutions, such as the justice police, who might begin to see the courts' actions and behavior as serving party interests.

Structural factors

There can be little or no judicial independence when the judiciary forms part of a large power configuration. As in many other developing countries, the Cambodian state is built on patrimonialism, a political pattern in which a leader's power comes from his ability to capture and maintain the loyalty of key sections of the political elite by distributing perquisites that fulfill their material aspirations (Pak 2011; see also King 2000: 609). In a patrimonial arrangement, merit counts for little, within the judiciary or in any other state institution. On the contrary, appointments and promotions are based on patronage and bribery.[11] This situation perpetuates corruption within the judiciary and further undermines the credibility of the courts.

Judges, prosecutors, and other court officials often state that, as in other state institutions, low salaries contribute to the prevalence of corruption in the judiciary. Until 2002 the average monthly salary for judges, prosecutors, and other court officials was about US$24. That was never anywhere nearly sufficient to support an individual court official, let alone a family. As part of judicial reform, salaries of judges and prosecutors have been substantially increased; they now start at US$250 a month and exceed US$600 depending on seniority (World Bank 2003: 25).

However, the salary increases did not solve the problem of judicial corruption, and the public perception of the judiciary is still negative.

The prevalence of corruption within the judiciary may be based on a combination of uncertain job security for judges and prosecutors, the absence of institutional restraints, and general structural issues. Job security for judges and prosecutors obviously cannot be guaranteed when patronage and bribes are preconditions for appointment and promotion. This uncertainty, together with an absence of institutional restraints, has led many judges to maximize their personal gains whenever opportunities permit. As in other countries, when judges, prosecutors, and clerks have to buy their positions, they need to recoup their investment (Pepys 2007). Furthermore, judges and prosecutors are required to contribute to ruling-party patronage-based development projects, such as constructing schools and rural roads, and pre-election gift-giving.

Patrimonial power structures also allow the executive branch to readily intervene. The executive branch sometimes pressures the court to arrest and imprison people. On 21 September 2002, the chief of the Cambodian National Police ordered the arrest of the editor of *Chak Kroval Newspaper* and one of his staff. The police asked the prosecutor to file the charge and a judge to issue an arrest warrant because the newspaper had published an article 'defaming' the police chief.[12] Because of the power of General Hok Lundy in the government and as a member of the Central Committee of the CPP, a prosecutor said, 'The court had to do it even though according to the law, the judge should not issue a detention order. In normal cases, the accused can be released on bail until the trial. But because Hok Lundy ordered the arrest the judge must follow'.[13] Regarding the same issue, another judge commented, 'The detention was not done according to the will of the judge. He did it in order to please a senior police officer. This is a violation of human rights'.[14] Shortly after the detention order was issued, when the suspects were about to be sent to the detention center, news of the arrest reached Prime Minister Hun Sen, who ordered the police to release the two 'within 20 minutes'. Immediately, an advisor to the prime minister worked diligently with the court to secure release of the two suspects.

The politicized nature of Cambodian governance makes a neutral judicial system impossible. One prosecutor stated: 'The characteristics of politics determine the peculiarity of the court system'.[15] Because judges and prosecutors owe their careers to their parties or their patrons, when they make any decision, they must, as one court official put it, think of 'who offered them the seat'.[16] Consequently, 'it is unavoidable that court officials serve the interests of political parties and that the judicial system serves politics'.[17] Generally in political cases government leaders can order up the verdict of their choice. Citing a former president of the Cambodian Bar Association, a joint study by three human rights organizations shows that in political cases evidence is not needed; 'advice' from the top alone is sufficient for making judgments (ADHOC *et al.* 1999: 20).[18]

Norms and ideas

The patronage factors that characterize the functioning of the patrimonial system also shape the way judges perceive and deal with corruption and respond to executive branch interventions. Experiences from other countries indicate that when corrupt practices are thought to be the norm, as is the case with patrimonialism, even if judges are clean they still must bear up under the pressure caused by the political, cultural, and societal conditions of which they are a part. Pressure comes not only from politicians and political institutions but also from groups with which they are associated (Kurkchiyan 2007:103).

The absence of institutional constraints coupled with a sociopolitical environment dominated by patronage and corruption blurs even judges' perceptions of what is legal and illegal, or moral and immoral. Judges interviewed did not reject the allegation that the courts are corrupt, but they defended their actions by arguing forcefully that sometimes receiving money from litigants does not constitute corruption. These monetary transactions, they argued, should rightfully be called 'fees'. Accepting a fee is not wrong—if not legally, at least morally. Despite their claims of moral conduct, however, interviews and conversations with clerks, lawyers, and litigants revealed that judges often manipulated those who came into contact with them to ensure maximum payoffs. The office of the former governor of Phnom Penh, for instance, alleged that seven Phnom Penh Municipal Court judges accepted US$310,000 in bribes in exchange for releasing 20 criminals (Pen Khon 2000: 44). Corruption within the judicial system is still a major concern.

When high-ranking government officials intervene, judges and prosecutors generally acquiesce, either from 'affection' or fear. Affection is the product of reciprocal relationships in which people return favors for favors done for them; such relationships are a standard practice that is difficult to avoid in a patronage-based society like Cambodia. This desire to maintain a personal relationship and the need to retain backing from higher authorities in the long run contrasts with how 'corruption' is often conceived in the West, as a purely financial transaction.

Conclusion

Through its efforts to end conflict in Cambodia, the international community successfully instituted a political system characterized, at least in theory, by constitutionally ordained separation of powers, independent judicial review, and oversight authority. In reality, however, the executive branch has manipulated and thus violated the notion of judicial independence.

Reasons for the lack of judicial independence are numerous. The first is historical; Cambodia has never experienced rule of law as sustained by an independent judiciary. Consequently, while de jure the rules guarantee the independence of the courts, de facto they fail to do so because the elites manipulate a vicious cycle of patronage, corruption, abuse of power, and impunity that perpetuates their power.

The absence of judicial independence is also a product of the social, political, and economic environment of post-conflict Cambodia. Although the public has little trust in the judiciary, many give transparency, accountability, and rule of law a low priority because their immediate concern is political stability and economic growth. This attitude relieves any pressure on the government to grant the judiciary meaningful independence. Therefore, instead of instituting real judicial reform, the executive intervenes in court affairs by, for example, rearresting people the courts have released. Such actions may demonstrate the government's effectiveness, but they are counter-productive for judicial independence.

Furthermore, because under CPP control the government emphasizes economic development and political order rather than civil and political liberties, the party has employed its control over the judiciary to restrict these liberties, leading to the regression of democratic development. Within the global universe of judicial politics, the Cambodian judiciary is still in the process of evolving, making it difficult to categorize. However, it clearly falls somewhere between judicial muteness and politicization. There is little judicial independence and there is also little judicial involvement in such mega-political activities as reviewing the constitutionality of legislation, or the results of elections.

Recent hints of judicial activism are not an indication that Cambodia might eventually be a candidate for judicialization of politics; they are simply the continuation of an instrumentalization of the judiciary. On the other hand, trends towards politicization of the judiciary can be seen in the involvement of judges in patronage-based electoral politics, with court officials contributing resources to the CPP's rural infrastructure development program using resources extracted from those who come into contact with the court. As court interests and power can best be served by siding with the ruling party, in the foreseeable future Cambodia will see far more politicization of the courts than judicialization of politics.

The politicization of the judiciary will limit any effort to promote democratic governance, rule of law, and civil society for it hinders vertical and inter-institutional accountability mechanisms. The case of politicization of the judiciary highlights that an analysis of the role of the judiciary in politics requires contextual analysis that embeds court behavior in a country's existing cultural, economic, and political configurations. Configurations that are dominated by patronage politics, absence of a culture of judicial independence, and poverty permit the cooptation of the judiciary preventing the judicialization of politics.

Notes

1 Author's interviews with court officials during his fieldwork revealed that such interference was indeed extensive. Officials consistently used the phrase 'they act like during the communist era', when they were frustrated with interference from powerful individuals and other institutions, particularly the police (Fieldnotes September–December, 2002). See also Gottesman 2003: 250–4.

2 Ten cases were classified as 'consultation or request'; 46 as 'electoral litigation'; 21 as 'interpretation of the constitution and laws'; 52 as 'constitutional review'. For details see www.ccc.gov.kh/english/index.php.

3 For instance, Eric Pape and Sareth Sopha, 'That Separation of Powers Thing', *The Phnom Penh Post*, May 22–4 June 1998, reported that Yang Sem, a CC member appointed by the National Assembly in 1998, did not have academic credentials. While his file notes that he received a bachelor's degree in economics from California State University in 1997, his biography stated that he was enrolled at the university from 1963 through 1968.

4 Interview, Phnom Penh, 27 September 2002.

5 This information is extracted from the Bar Association of Cambodia website, available online at www.bakc.org.kh/km/lawyer-statistic.html and www.bakc.org.kh/km/2011-09-12-08-55-34.html (accessed 11 February 2012). It should be noted that there is a high number of judges partly because Cambodia has adopted the French-style system, which has two categories of judges—investigative and presiding.

6 Interview, 10 March 2003. This judge is highly regarded by many people, foreigners and Cambodians within and outside the legal system, as one of the few highly qualified judges.

7 Foreign diplomat, interview, Phnom Penh, 6 June 2003.

8 Interview, 27 September 2002.

9 Interview, 29 September 2002.

10 Interview, 14 May 2002.

11 This view is based on one author's observations and conversations with various sources in Cambodia since 2002.

12 For details of the story see Koh Santpheap (2002), 'Samdech Hun Sen orders the police to immediately release the journalists! Mr. Oam Yin Teang escorts Keo Sophoan from the site of abusive arrest', 25 September.

13 Interview, 25 September 2002.

14 Interview, 9 October 2002.

15 Interview, 25 September 2002. According to later research, although such remarks were made some years ago, they still apply.

16 Interview, 20 November 2001.

17 Interview, 2 October 2002.

18 The recent increase in law suits against opposition party leaders is evidence of political interference.

References

ADHOC, LICADO, and Human Rights Watch (1999) *Impunity in Cambodia: How Human Rights Offenders Escape Justice*. Phnom Penh.

Amnesty International (2002) 'Kingdom of Cambodia: Urgent need for judicial reform'.

Ashley, D. (1998) 'The Failure of Conflict Resolution in Cambodia: Causes and Lessons', in Brown, F. Z. and Timberman, D. G. (eds) *Cambodia and the International Community: The Quest for Peace Development and Democracy*, Singapore: Institute of Southeast Asian Studies, pp. 49–78.

Broadhurst, R., Bouhours, T., and Keo, C. (2010) 'Cambodia' in Newman, G. (ed.) *Crime and Punishment Around the World: Asia Pacific*, Santa Barbara, CA: ABC Clio/Greenwood.

Brown, F. Z. and Timberman, D. (eds) (1998) *Cambodia and the International Community: The Quest for Peace Development and Democracy*, Singapore: Institute of Southeast Asian Studies.

Chandler, D. (1991) *The Tragedy of Cambodian History: Politics, War, and Revolution Since 1945*, New Haven, CT: Yale University Press.

Council on Legal and Judicial Reform (2002) *Report on the Situation of Courts*, Phnom Penh.

Donovan, D. A. (1993) 'The Cambodian legal system: An overview', in Brown, F. (ed.), *Rebuilding Cambodia: Human Resources, Human Rights, and Law*, Washington, DC: Foreign Policy Institute, Paul H. Nitze School of Advanced International Studies, Johns Hopkins University.

Doyle, M. (1995) *UN Peacekeeping in Cambodia: UNTAC Civil Mandate*, Boulder, CO: Lynne Rienner.

Fernando, B. (1988) *Problems Facing the Cambodian Legal System*, Hong Kong: An Asian Human Rights Commission Publication.

Gillman, H. (1994) 'On constructing a science of comparative judicial politics: Tate & Haynenie's "Authoritarianism and the Functions of Courts" ', *Law & Society Review*, 28: 901–922.

Global Integrity Report, Cambodia: Integrity Indicator Scorecards 2008, available online at http://report.globalintegrity.org/Cambodia/2008/scorecard (accessed 27 May 2011).

Gottesman, E. (2003) *Cambodia After the Khmer Rouge: Inside the Politics of Nation Building*, New Haven, CT: Yale University Press.

Hirschl, R. (2008) 'The judicialization of mega-politics and the rise of political courts', *Annual Review of Political Science*, 11: 93–118. International Republic Institute (2004), 'Poll results', Phnom Penh.

International Republican Institute (IRI) (2004) *Poll Results*, Phnom Penh: IRI.

Kato, Toshiyasu and Kaplan, J. A., Chan Sophal and Real Sopheap (2000) *Cambodia Enhancing Governance for Sustainable Development*, Phnom Penh: Asian Development Bank.

King, D. (2000) 'Corruption in Indonesia: A curable cancer?', *Journal of International Affairs*, 53: 603–624.

Kurkchiyan, M. (2007) 'Judicial corruption in the context of legal culture', in Transparency International, *Global Corruption Report 2007: Corruption in Judicial Systems*, Cambridge: Cambridge University Press, 99–107.

Lao Mong Hay (2001) 'Institutions for the rule of law and human rights in Cambodia', available online at: www.article2.org/mainfile.php/0501/223 (accessed 29 January 2008).

McEvens, K. and Ana, P. (2000) 'Disorder in the courts: From highly educated to unschooled, Cambodian judges are a mixed pot', *Cambodian Daily*, 4–5 May.

Ministry of Economy and Finance (2005) *The Medium-Term Expenditure Framework for Cambodia 2005–2007*, Phnom Penh: MEF.

O'Donnell, G. (2004) 'Why the rule of law matters', *Journal of Democracy*, 15: 32–46.

Pak, K. (2011) 'A dominant party in a weak state: How the ruling party in Cambodia has managed to stay dominant', doctoral dissertation, Australian National University.

Pen Khon (2000) *Phnom Penh Before and After 1997*, n.p.

Pepys, M. N. (2007) 'Corruption within the judiciary: Causes and remedies', in Transparency International, *Global Corruption Report 2007: Corruption in Judicial Systems*, pp. 4–5, Cambridge: Cambridge University Press.

Peou, S. (2000) *Intervention and Change in Cambodia: Towards Democracy?* Singapore: Institute of Southeast Asian Studies.

Slocomb, M. (2001) 'The K5 gamble: National defence and nation building under the People's Republic of Kampuchea', *Journal of Southeast Asian Studies*, 32: 195–210. See also: http://journals.cambridge.org/action/displayAbstract?fromPage=online&aid=86521

Sokchea, M. (2011a) 'High Court Hears Rainsy Case', *The Phnom Penh Post*, 23 February.

Sokchea, M. (2011b) 'Lawmakers fights for immunity', *The Phnom Penh Post*, 11 January.

Sokchea, M. and O' Toole, J. (2010) 'Sam Rainsy gets ten years', *The Phnom Penh Post*, 23 September.

Sokha, C. (2010) 'PM warns political rival', *The Phnom Penh Post*, 9 December.

Solomon, P. H. (2007) 'Court and judges in authoritarian regimes', *World Politics* 60: 122–145.

Strangio, S. and Sokchea, M. (2010) 'Rainsy to file complaint against PM', *The Phnom Penh Post*, 22 September.

Transparency International (2006) *Country Study Report, Cambodia 2006*, available online at www.transparency.org/policy_research/nis/nis_reports_by_country.

Transparency International (2007) *Global Corruption Report 2007: Corruption in Judicial Systems*, Cambridge: Cambridge University Press.

Un, K. and Ledgerwood, J. (2010) 'Is the trial of Duch a catalyst for change in Cambodia's courts?', *Asia Pacific Issues*, 95: 1–12.

Un, K. and So, S. (2011) 'Land rights in Cambodia: How neopatrimonialism restricts land policy reforms', *Pacific Affairs*, 84: 289–308.

United Nations Department of Information (1996) *The United Nations and Cambodia, 1991–1995*, New York, NY: United Nations.

The United Nations High Commission for Human Rights (2007) 'Joint Public Statement: The United Nations Special Representatives of the Secretary General for Human Rights in Cambodia and the Special Rapporteur on the Independence of Judges and Lawyers Express Concern Over Judicial Independence in Cambodia in the Light of Recent Judicial Appointment', Geneva: UNHCHR.

Vickery, M. (1986) *Kampuchea: Politics, Economics, and Society*, Boulder, CO: Lynne Reinner.

World Bank (2003) *Cambodia: Legal and Judicial Sector Assessment.* Phnom Penh: Legal Vice Presidency, World Bank.

11 Malaysia

Limited and intermittent judicialization of politics

Chandra Kanagasabai

Introduction

This chapter argues that the 'judicialization of politics', described by Hirschl (2006: 721) as 'the ever accelerating reliance on courts and judicial means for addressing core moral predicaments, public policy questions and political controversies' has seen only limited and intermittent appearance in Malaysia as compared to other Asian countries like the Philippines, Thailand, and India.

Logically, for the judicialization of politics to occur a gradual transfer of power from representative institutions to the judiciary is required. This trend, described by Hirschl as a transition to 'juristocracy' (see Hirschl 2004: 71), in turn, is often driven by the adoption of new constitutional arrangements that include a strengthened bill of rights, increased powers of judicial review and/or the setting up of a constitutional court.

In Malaysia, while the Federal Constitution adopted at independence in 1957 contains a number of constitutionally entrenched fundamental rights, in Part Two from Article 5 to Article 13, these rights can be restricted in certain conditions as laid out in the Constitution. However the conditions for restrictions on these rights are so broad as to render the rights themselves meaningless (Thomas 1987: 97);[1] (Freedom of assembly under Article 10 (1) (b) restricted by Article 10 (2) and the Police Act 1967 which requires a permit if three or more persons wish to gather in public; Freedom of association entrenched under Article 10(1) (c) is constrained by the limitation in Article 10 (2) and by the amendments in 1982 to The Societies Act 1966; Over and above, Article 149 and 150 of the Federal Constitution provide for passing of laws which will be deemed valid despite inconsistencies with the rights in Part Two of the Constitution).

Unlike some of its Asian counterparts, Malaysia's relative stability and single party dominance since independence has left the parameters for judicial activism constrained. More important, a clash with the executive in 1988 has left the powers of the judiciary further constrained and its independence weakened (Abas and Das 1989; Lawyers Committee for Human Rights 1989). Following the assault, amendments to the Constitution and other legislation relating to fundamental rights were passed ousting judicial review, which further whittled judicial power thereby limiting juristocracy and truncating tentative attempts towards the judicialization of politics. The result in the period after the 1988 assault and up to the end of Dr. Mahathir's premiership as I attempt to show was growing politicization and declining professionalism among Malaysia's judiciary.

The latest imbroglio occurred in September 2007 when opposition leader Anwar Ibrahim released a video clip of a senior lawyer purportedly brokering justice with a senior member of the judiciary. The matter, only the latest in a string of scandals rocking the judiciary over the last decade, became the subject of a Royal Commission of Inquiry in January 2008, with the Commission recommending investigations against key parties in the allegations including members of the judiciary and politicians.[2]

These developments marked not only a new low point in public perception but also a sharp deviation from the past. Known for its independence and professionalism in the first decades following independence in 1957, the Malaysian judiciary has arguably undergone a major transformation in reaction to the assault by the executive in 1988, which has left powerful path dependencies behind. Decisions of the Malaysian judiciary in the post-Mahathir period (2003–present) illustrate a broader reluctance to engage with areas of 'mega-politics'. While this is not to say that there are no occasional instances of judicial assertiveness, such interventions have primarily occurred after Dr. Mahathir (1982–2003) retired as Prime Minister, and even then, such decisions have in most cases not been upheld by the Federal Court (the present apex court after the Supreme Court was renamed in 1994) leaving the public guessing about the direction of the judicial branch.

To illustrate these developments and advance the above arguments, this chapter is structured as follows. I start by tracing the various permutations of the Malaysian judiciary since independence by first examining the period from 1957 to the 1980s, highlighting in particular how during the Mahathir period (1982–2003) intra-elite struggles propelled the judiciary into the political fore eventually prompting the 1988 executive assault of the judiciary. I then evaluate the post-Mahathir period showing through case law deconstruction that the judiciary has lost its ability to play the role of an effective veto player in the political system. Based on the historical account, I then highlight some critical drivers behind the judicialization trend (or lack thereof) in the Malaysian case, concluding with a brief discussion on the effects of these developments for judicial and democratic governance in Malaysia and its wider implication for the literature on this subject.

I Judicial pattern in Malaysia: a brief history

The early years (1957–82): strict legalism

The early independence period was marked by growing indigenization of the judiciary. By the 1970s all foreign High Court judges appointed by the colonial administration had retired.[3] Meanwhile, the new senior judges, having been trained abroad, struggled to find a balance between protection of individual rights and the newly independent state's attempts to enforce its authority—which were challenged perhaps most notably in 1969 by widespread multiethnic riots.

With the judiciary sharing the national ambitions of the newly independent state, and the judiciary walking a careful line of strict legalism, the relationship between the judiciary and the executive during this period was inordinately smooth. In cases involving fundamental rights or constitutional issues, the judiciary followed strictly the parameters of the constitution. In the case of fundamental rights, the constitution allowed for restriction by legislation even where the legislation in question rendered the constitutional right illusory.

Thus in 1975 in *Arumugam Pillai v. Government of Malaysia* ([1975] 2 MLJ: 29) Chief Justice Gill commenting on Article 13 (the constitutional right not to be deprived of property in accordance with law) held:

> The result is that whenever a competent legislature enacts a law to the extent on any of its legislative powers destroying or otherwise depriving a man of his property, the latter is precluded from questioning its reasonableness by invoking article 13 (1) of the Constitution, however arbitrary the law might possibly be.

Exercising strict judicial legalism and deference to parliamentary sovereignty, judicial intervention in political matters remained limited despite occasional opportunities. An illustration is the formation of Malaysia (incorporating the states of Sabah and Sarawak), which prompted for the first time a challenge to the Federation by a State. When the ruler of Kelantan challenged the formation on the ground that he had not given his consent,[4] his case was rejected, with Chief Justice Thomson stating that:

> The Constitution is primarily to be interpreted within its own four walls and not in the light of analogies drawn from other countries such as Great Britain, the United States of America or Australia.[5]

The Kelantan ruler's contention that the Malaysia Act would in effect abolish the Federation of Malaya Agreement and thus would require the consent of the rulers was not without legal merit (see Hickling 1978: 10; Suffian *et al.* 1986). In fact, an eminent constitutional law expert has described this period as an uneasy decade because it breached the concept of equality on which the original compact of federation was founded (Hickling 1978: 10).

The path of strict legalism was also apparent in cases pitting the individual against the state. These included rulings that the Internal Security Act (which provides for detention without trial) was not in violation of Article 5 of the Constitution on the deprivation of personal liberty (*PP* v. *Yee Kim Sen* [1983] 1 MLJ: 252); affirming that detention under the Banishment Act 1959 remains valid until revoked, where the two applicants had remained in detention for five and eight years because no other country was willing to accept them (*Minister of Home Affairs* v. *Chu Choon Yong* [1977] 2 MLJ: 20); upholding the power of the Attorney General to choose the statute under which to charge the accused, one statute which carried the death penalty and the other a term in prison (*Johnson Tan Han Seng* v. *PP* [1977] 2 MLJ: 66); and upholding that the rights given by Article 10 of the Constitution on freedom of speech were subject to laws passed by parliament (*Lau Dak Kee* v. *Public Prosecutor* [1976] 2 MLJ: 229).

However, this is not to say that the judiciary during this period did not rule in favor of the individual. Cases where it ruled against the state included the decision that a detention order under the Sarawak Preservation of Public Order was unlawful as the detainee was outside Sarawak at the time the order was made (*Ministry of Home Affairs* v. *Datuk James Wong Kim Min* [1976] 2 MLJ: 245); allowing the application of a developer that the government had no power to make the developer give up a freehold title in exchange for a 99-year lease (*Pengarah Tanah & Galian* v. *Sri Lempah Enterprise [*1979] 1 MLJ: 135); and granting leave to a Company to challenge Section 100 of Chapter 1 of the National Land Code (*East Union Malaya Sdn Bhd* v. *Government of State of Johor & Government of Malaysia* [1980] 2 MLJ: 145).

Apart from case law, two major amendments to the Constitution during this period further consolidated the powers of the ruling coalition. The first is the Thirteenth Schedule added to the constitution in 1962, which set out the principles for the delimitation of single-member constituencies for parliament. In effect it transferred the power of delimitation from the Election Commission (EC) to the legislature, thereby not only undermining the independence of the EC but also allowing the ruling coalition to further cement its power through gerrymandering and electoral malapportionment—a trend that continued long after.[6] The second change, in 1971, was amending Article 153 in direct response to the racial riots of 1969.[7] Passed after the emergency was lifted, the amendment makes it a crime for members of parliament to question the rights of protected people. Combined, these two institutional changes laid the foundation for single-party dominance in Malaysia.

The Mahathir era (1982–2003): capping judicial power

By the 1980s fundamental changes were engulfing Malaysia, most notably in the form of an Islamic resurgence and growing demands from civil society. The former is best illustrated by the emergence of fundamentalist Islamist parties like *Parti Islam Malaysia* (PAS), which rapidly gained support among rural Malays that made it a credible opposition party[8] and thereby forced the ruling coalition to adopt an Islamic strategy of its own (Ahmad 2005).[9] At the same time, new social movements such as *Aliran, Hakam* and *Suaram* also exerted growing pressure on the government to strengthen civil rights regimes and further liberalize. In reaction, the government proposed several sweeping amendments to the 1966 Societies Act, which although partially successfully resisted by opposition political parties and the Malaysian Bar, had the effect of further restricting freedom of association.

These broader changes did not leave Malaysia's judiciary unaffected. The judiciary attempted to follow the earlier path of strict legalism and interpret the laws fairly in the face of growing state repression in areas of civil and political liberties. However the attempts of holding the government authorities in strict compliance with procedural rules brought the judiciary increasingly in conflict with the executive—a conflict that would grow once the judiciary attempted to chart a more distinctly independent course.

Early decisions reflecting this trend include the Sessions Court admonishing and discharging 42 lawyers who had been charged for illegal assembly under the Police Act 1967 for marching to parliament to present a memorandum protesting the proposed amendments to the Societies Act in 1981 (*PP* v. *Cheah Beng Poh & Ors* [1984] 1 CLJ: 117); the High Court dismissing the charges under the Societies Act against the Baitiangong group that was not registered as a society under The Societies Act 1966 and were practicing a religion professing to contain elements of Christianity and Islam (*PP* v. *Chew Choon Ming & Ors* [1987] 2 MLJ: 522] the Supreme Court affirming the High Court decision allowing the habeas corpus application of a detainee on the ground that he was detained at a place other than that stated in the detention order (*PP* v. *Koh Yoke Koon* [1987] 2 MLJ: 522); the High Court allowing the challenge of a person accused of being a leader of a secret society and detained under the Emergency (Public Order and Prevention of Crime) Ordinance 1969 *(Yit Hon Kit* v. *Minister of Home Affairs* [1988] 2 MLJ: 638).

The *Yit Hon Kit* case ([1988] 2 MLJ: 638) illustrates the dominant judicial reasoning at the time; in it trial judge Edgar Joseph stated (following the Federal Court in *Dato James Wong Kim Min* ([1976] 2 MLJ: 245), 'A matter of deprivation of liberty ... requires meticulous compliance with the law'.[10] The judge allowed the applicant's challenge on the ground that Constitution Article 5 (3) had not been complied with because he had not been informed of the grounds of his arrest, and because the criminal activities alleged were too remote to justify the detention order. In support, his lordship quoted Lord Atkin in *Liversidge* v. *Anderson* ([1942] A.C.: 206 p. 244): 'It has long been one of the pillars of freedom ... that the judges are no respecters of persons *and stand between the subject and any attempted encroachment on his liberty by the executive alert to see that any coercive action is justified by law'* (emphasis added).

Then-Prime Minister Mahathir did not receive these decisions happily; he publicly denounced them as going against executive prerogative and will. In an interview with *Time Magazine* in 1986, he commented:

> ...the judiciary says although you passed a law with certain things in mind, we think your mind is wrong and want to give our interpretation. If we disagree the courts say, we will interpret your disagreement. If we go along we are going to lose our power of legislation. We know exactly what we want to do. But once we do it, it is interpreted in a different way and we have no means to interpret it our way. If we find that a court always throws us out on its own interpretation, if it interprets contrary to why we made the law *then*

> *we will have to find a way of producing a law that will have to be interpreted according to our wish* (emphasis added).[11]

The overt threat however did not result in an end to possible clashes with an increasingly brash executive. In fact, while strictly enforcing the observance to procedural rules in civil rights cases, the courts provided further upsets to the executive. Particularly when the Supreme Court upheld the quashing of the revocation of the employment pass of a foreign journalist on the ground that he had not been given the right to be heard when his permit was revoked (*J.P. Berthelsen* v. *Director General of Immigration* [1987] 1 MLJ: 134); the High Court rejecting the Home Minister's reasons for not granting a licence to a social movement (*Aliran*) to publish a magazine in Malay (*Persatuan Aliran* v. *Minister of Home Affairs* [1988] 1 MLJ: 440); the Supreme Court reaffirming the High Court decision that the detention under the Internal Security Act of an employee for mismanagement of a Bank was unlawful (*Inspector General of Police* v. *Tan Sri Raja Khalid* [1988] 1 MLJ: 182); the Supreme Court upholding the High Court decision that Section 418 (A) of the Criminal Procedure Code empowering the Attorney General to transfer cases from the subordinate Courts to the High Court was unconstitutional as Article 121 of the Constitution had vested judicial power in the High Court (*PP* v. *Dato Yap Peng* [1987] 2 MLJ: 311).

While these early decisions still fell short of broader judicial activism in areas of mega-politics, a number of subsequent cases illustrate an increasing involvement of courts in more pronounced political conflict, including the testing of existing boundaries. For instance, the case brought by opposition parliamentarian (*Lim Kit Siang* v. *United Engineers* [1988] 1 MLJ: 35) seeking an interim injunction to restrain the defendant company and the government from signing the RM 3.4 billion North South Highway project, marked a first attempt at public interest litigation in Malaysia. On the issue whether Lim had locus standi (legal standing) to file the suit, the High Court's affirmation was later reversed on appeal by the Supreme Court. The High Court's refusal to impose on Lim an undertaking in damages as requested by the government might have been construed as an attempt to liberalize public interest litigation (Khoo 1999: 216).

Growing political infighting within the component partners of the ruling coalition also meant increasing political involvement of the courts throughout the 1980s, as illustrated in the cases of Parti Gerakan (*Lee Liong Chan* v. *Tan Sri Tek Ewe Lim* [1985] 2 MLJ: 138) or the Malaysian Chinese Association (*Kok Wee Kiat* v. *Chong Hon Nyan* [1985] 2 MLJ: 130). However, none of these cases was matched in significance by the one involving the leadership contest at the helm of the United Malays National Organization (UMNO)—Malaysia's most important political party—which ultimately paved the way for a concerted assault on Malaysia's apex judiciary.

At stake here was nothing less then the political survival of Prime Minister Dr. Mahathir himself who won reelection as UMNO president only by a slim majority (amidst allegations of irregularities) in 1987. The defeated faction took the matter to the High Court which ruled UMNO illegal for non-compliance with the Societies Act (*Mohamed Noor bin Omar* v. *Mohamed Yusof* [1988] 2 MLJ: 129). In reaction, Mahathir chose not to appeal the decision but instead formed a new political party—UMNO Baru—while at the same time excluding his main political rival Tengku Razaleigh and his faction.

The defeated faction decided to appeal the High Court decision. Before the full panel of nine Supreme Court judges could hear the appeal, Lord President Salleh Abas was suspended and a tribunal set up against him (Abas and Das 1989). When five Supreme Court judges granted an application to stay proceedings of the First Tribunal they themselves were subject to a Second Tribunal for not attending a scheduled sitting in another state (Abas and Das 1989). Eventually the Lord President and two Supreme Court judges, Justice Wan Suleiman and Justice George Seah, were dismissed. The other three judges were subject to disciplinary action.

It was clear to observers that the timing of the Tribunal against the Lord President was not accidental. Earlier decisions by the Supreme Court had evidenced a split judiciary with a slim majority of 3:2 against the government (*PP* v. *Dato Yap Peng* [1988] 1 MLJ: 31 1); *Government of Malaysia* v. *Lim Kit Siang* [1988] 1 MLJ: 35). Indeed with Mahathir's own political survival an issue too risky to be left to a split judiciary to decide, control over the top judiciary was critical. On 9 August 1988, a day after Tun Salleh Abas was dismissed, the UMNO appeal brought by Dr. Mahathir's political rival was heard and dismissed by the newly constituted court.[12]

This critical blow to the judiciary was bolstered by further attempts to subjugate the judiciary through constitutional amendments to constrain the powers and scope of the courts. In June 1988, Article 121 of the Federal constitution was amended, replacing the words 'judicial powers of the Federation vests in two High Courts and such inferior courts as might be provided by Federal law' with 'There shall be two High Courts of co-ordinate jurisdiction and ... the High Courts ... shall have such jurisdiction and powers as might be conferred by Federal laws', thereby effectively restricting the powers of the High Court. The amendment had also a direct bearing on the Supreme Court ruling in Dato Yap Peng's case, which had held that judicial power to transfer cases could not be conferred on any other organ of government other than the judiciary—by this amendment the executive had effectively removed the judiciary's ability to act as a bulwark against executive transgression of legislation.

While some critics may argue that the judiciary is not restricted by this amendment, it must be remembered that these amendments occurred in the immediate aftermath of the assault on the judiciary, which had left it vulnerable and threatened and thus unlikely to interpret the Article 121 amendment as not limiting its powers. In fact, the Federal Court has in two cases after this amendment reiterated that its jurisdiction could be removed or restricted under Article 121 (1) by Parliament enacting a Federal law.[13] In *PP* v. *Kok Wah Kuan*, the Federal Court in 2007 examined Article 121 before the 1988 amendment, and stated:

> After the amendment there is no longer a specific provision declaring that the judicial power of the Federation shall be vested in the two High Courts. What it means is that there is no longer a declaration that judicial power of the Federation as the term was understood prior to the amendment vests in the two High Courts. If we want to know the jurisdiction and powers of the two High Courts we will have to look at the federal law.[14]

The second amendment passed in 1988 was the addition of Article 121 (1A). The new clause stated that civil courts have no jurisdiction in respect of matters within the jurisdiction of the Syariah courts, thereby effectively ensuring that Muslims bring their matrimonial-related disputes, like custody of children issues, before the Syariah court. Although largely perceived as a 'house-keeping' amendment (Ahmad 2005: 24) given that these issues had been previously brought before the civil courts by Muslims (see *Myriam* v. *Mohd. Arif* [1971)] 1 MLJ 165) the amendment had far-reaching effects for the functioning of the judiciary as it would stir future controversy in a series of cases in the first decade of the millennium as discussed later.

The executive also further curtailed the powers of courts to uphold the rights of citizens by amending the 1984 Printing Presses and Publications Act (PPPA), as well as the Internal Security Act of 1960. This was done by ousting judicial review (making the matter non-challengeable in court) through Section 13A (1) in the case of the PPPA 1984 so that the Minister's decision to revoke or suspend the license or permit to publish could not be challenged in court. In the case of detentions without trial under the Internal Security Act, a new amendment by way of section 8 (B) precluded judicial review of any act done by the Agong (King) or Minister in the exercise of their discretionary power unless it related to procedural rules. In effect, this meant that several of the cases in the past where the court had decided against the government (i.e. the *Aliran* matter in the case of the PPPA and some of the habeas corpus applications under the Internal Security Act) would be prohibited by these amendments.

Combined, the changes not only curtailed the scope of judicial activity but ultimately undermined judicial independence, as illustrated in *Insas Bhd.* v. *Ayer Molek* [1995] 3 AMR). This case was criticized for 'judge-choosing': the case was filed and heard in the court of the judge who was in charge of the administration of justice and whose court was designated for appellate and special powers. In reaction the London-based *International Commercial Litigation Journal* published 'Malaysian Justice on Trial' (Samuels 1995: 10), which brought into focus allegations of irregular procedural speed and judge-choosing in other Malaysian cases. This in turn prompted a series of defamation cases against those who had been interviewed for the article (e.g. *MBF Capital Bhd.* v. *Tommy Thomas & Another* [1999] 1 MLJ 139]; *MBF Capital* v. *Param Cumaraswamy* ([1997] 3 MLJ 824); and *Raphael Pura* v. *Insas Berhad* [2000] 4 AMR 4475), which spotlighted the declining standard for judicial accountability. The decline continued, with judges threatening contempt charges against lawyers in a case when recusal of a judge was sought[15] and an actual charge of contempt against a counsel in another case.[16]

Also publicized were other alleged judicial improprieties, such as an application requesting recusal of the Chief Justice because of his close connection with counsel for a plaintiff company (*MBF Bhd* v. *Param Cumaraswamy;* see Das and Chandra 2003: 190) and an application in *Insas Bhd* v. *Raphael Pura*[17] where the defendant alleged that in a previous case the decision had been written by opposing counsel (an application that was eventually dismissed).[18]

Growing concerns about the deteriorating independence and professionalism of the Malaysian judiciary was also expressed by an International Bar Association fact-minding mission; its report *Justice in Jeopardy: Malaysia* (2000),[19] identified as one of the root causes of the problems an executive who had shown disregard for the other branches of government identified with the separation of powers.

Concern about the Malaysian judiciary in international legal circles continued in *MBF Bhd* v. *Param Cumaraswamy*, where the International Court of Justice (ICJ) ruled on the issue of whether the defendant, the United Nations Special Rapporteur on the independence of judges and lawyers, was immune from being sued.[20] These developments seem to have encouraged the judiciary to reassert some of its lost authority.

Following a regional judicial accountability workshop in 2002 in Kuala Lumpur under the auspices of the Commonwealth Lawyers Association[21] and attended by several Malaysian judges, a decision in the area of aboriginal peoples' land rights emerged, which could be seen as testing again judicial boundaries. One of the participant judges gave a decision in (*Sagong Bin Tasi* [2002] 2 MLJ: 591) finding in favor of native title, (based on the trend in Commonwealth countries and the earlier Malaysian decision of *Adung Bin Kuwau* [1997] 1 MLJ: 418] which had recognized the right of indigenous people to native title—a decision upheld by both the Court of Appeal and the Federal Court.

The Court of Appeal decision in the *Adung and Sagong Bin Tasi* case are particularly important as they sought to reconcile the pre-independence law, namely The Aboriginal Peoples Act 1954, with the constitutional right of citizens under Article 13 not to be deprived of their property without adequate compensation. However, as will be elaborated further, such trends towards greater judicial involvement in politically sensitive matters have remained sporadic and largely dependent on individual judges hearing the case. It must also be noted that these cases occurred late in Dr. Mahathir's premiership when pressure was mounting on him to retire. Finally, it must be remembered that aboriginal land rights cases have limited ripple effects in other areas; they seem to merely follow the trend in other Commonwealth countries towards upholding the rights of weak and defenseless people considered wards of the state.

The judiciary in the post-Mahathir period (2003–present): testing the ground?

Dr. Mahathir retired on 23 October 2003, and while it could be argued that there have been signs of judicialization at the tail end of his premiership, it was only after his retirement that the judiciary was propelled once more to address highly contentious public policy questions. During the more accommodating premiership of Prime Minister Abdullah Badawi (2003–09), adjudication on the earlier amended Article 121 (1A) of the constitution which provides that civil courts have no jurisdiction in matters relating to Syariah law came up.

A legacy of the Mahathir period, it caused unanticipated problems in cases where a non-Muslim married under civil law converts to Islam. Non-Muslims in Malaysia are governed by the 1976 Law Reform (Marriage and Divorce) Act (which provides for marriage, divorce, and maintenance issues). When a non-Muslim, who had contracted a civil marriage converted to Islam, the non-converting spouse[22] was left without access to justice as the civil courts have refused to hear their applications on the ground that Article 121 (1A) precludes them from hearing cases where Syariah law is concerned (the converted spouse would now be governed by Syariah law).

The issue that caused most negative ramifications was the conversion and custody of minor children. In the highly publicized case of *Shamala Satiyaseelan* v. *Dr. Jayaganesh* ([2004] 2 CLJ) the High Court refused to hear the mother's application and held that the father had the right to convert the minor children. The decision left the mother with no redress, as the High Court recognized, that as a non-Muslim she could not fall under the jurisdiction of the Syariah court; the judgement stated that 'it is not for the court to legislate and confer jurisdiction to the civil court but for parliament to provide the remedy'.[23]

While the decision explicitly followed precedent (see *Majlis Agama Islam* v. *Shaik Zolkaffily & Ors* [2003] 3 CLJ 289) it left unresolved the constitutional right of a non-Muslim parent to decide on the religion of a minor child under Articles 12 and 4 of the Federal Constitution, as well as Section 5 of the Guardianship Act 1961 (the High Court interpreted the parental right to decide on the religion of a minor child in the singular and not as a joint decision by both parents). The decision also conflicts with the Convention on the Elimination of all Forms of Discrimination Against Women (CEDAW) and the Convention on the Rights of the Child, to both of which Malaysia is a signatory.[24]

When the *Shamala* case was brought before it in 2010, the Federal Court refused to decide it because Shamala had left the country with her two infant children—a decision that the Malaysian Bar Council criticized, stating that in 'sidestepping these significant issues, the Federal Court failed to be decisive and abdicated its role as the ultimate arbiter in disputes involving constitutional questions and jurisdictional conflict'.[25]

Leaving aside the unwillingness of the judiciary to tackle some of the most pertinent constitutional questions, there is also little doubt that the addition of Article 121 (1A) has reduced the efficacy of existing Malaysian laws such as the

Law Reform Act 1976. Prior to the constitutional amendments, non-Muslims to whom this law applied had the equal protection of the law in the case, for instance, of a divorce resulting from one spouse's conversion and equitable division of family property in addition to guardianship and custody rights of children. The decisions raise apprehensions that a de facto act of conversion to Islam by one spouse denies all the protection of the civil laws to the non-Muslim spouse. The interpretation by the court of Article 121(1A) allows the converting spouse to escape all the antecedent liabilities under civil laws which governed him when he was a non-Muslim.

It could be argued that the judiciary's refusal to reconcile existing civil laws relating to non-Muslims with Article 121 (1A) of the Constitution amounts to a form of 'shadow boxing' with the executive. Article 121 (1A) was passed in 1988 at the same time Article 121 was amended restricting the powers of the judiciary. In taking a literal interpretation of Article 121 (1A) and not attempting to resolve the rights of non-Muslims whose spouses have converted to Islam, the question is whether the judiciary is attempting to show that because its powers had been constrained under Article 121, it could only take the literal interpretation when it came to Article 121 (1A).[26] Alternatively, it can be interpreted as a continuation of the practice of judicial restraint in deeply controversial cases.

No matter what view one follows, further criticism leveled against the decision in conversion cases included the fact that they are invariably heard by Muslim judges. This is a result of the higher proportion of Muslim judges as compared to non-Muslim judges.[27] Critics have also noted that it is difficult for Muslim judges to adjudicate on these matters as it means judging on Islamic law or having to expound on Islamic law principles to which they do not have Federal law to be guided by or may be conversant with (Ahmad 2005). The issues require the judges to maintain a 'critical distance' which within the sociopolitical structure of Malaysia is difficult. Indeed it should be recalled that one of the charges against Lord President Tun Salleh at the First Tribunal was that he adjourned sine die the habeas corpus application by a father in the case of a minor who had converted to Islam (Teoh Eng Huat; Abas and Das 1989: 174). The minor was a few days short of attaining 18 (the age of majority) and since she could not be found and produced before the court, the court had to adjourn the case sine die (to a date to be fixed). Once the majority age was reached, the court decision would have been academic as constitutionally the parental right to decide on the religion of the minor under Article 12 ends at the age of majority.

Aside from this, several actions taken under the premiership of Abdullah Ahmad Badawi also indicate efforts by the executive branch to reconcile the injustices perpetrated on the judiciary and the consequent rift with the public. On 2 September 2004, the Federal Court by a majority of 2:1 overturned the sodomy conviction of opposition leader Anwar Ibrahim, and in June 2006 the Court of Appeal set aside the conviction of Sukma Dermawan, the foster brother of Anwar on the charge of allowing himself to be sodomized by Anwar (although he had already served the sentence). These two decisions can be categorized as constrained judicialization of politics as they were brought up by way of judicial review after the time frame for the appeal process in both cases was over.

The government also responded to the release of the video clip alleging judicial improprieties with the creation of a Royal Commission of Inquiry. Beginning proceedings in 2008 it has implicated several judges and politicians, though its findings are still pending judicial review. In April 2008 the government also proposed a Marriage Reform Act that seeks to tackle jurisdictional problems between Civil and Syariah courts. It was followed by the creation of a Judicial Appointment Commission, better terms of service and remuneration for judges and ex-gratia payments for the judges in the 1988 crisis. In April 2009 the Cabinet issued a directive that children should not be converted from their original religion without the joint consent of both parents. However the relevant legislation has not been amended to date. The fact that the ruling party no longer has the two-thirds majority required to amend the Constitution may account for this but does not explain why amendments were not instituted during the years 2004–2008 when the Barisan Nasional had a clear majority.

Benefiting from the new political space under Prime Minister Badawi, the courts also continued to show occasional signs of new assertiveness at the beginning of the premiership of Najib Razak (2009–present) though hardly in a linear fashion. In December 2009, in an unprecedented decision, in an application by the Catholic Church the High Court ruled that the word 'Allah' predates Islam (*Titular Roman Catholic Archbishop of Kuala Lumpur* v. *Menteri Dalam Negeri & Anor* [2010] 2 MLJ: 78). The Catholic Church, in its monthly magazine *The Herald* (published in the Malay language), used the word Allah to denote God. Its permit to publish the magazine was subject to a condition that it refrains from using the word Allah. The court held that Section 13 (A) of the Printing Presses and Publications Act (PPP) 1984, which ousts the jurisdiction of the court, cannot apply to judicial review which corrects errors of law by an administrative body or tribunal illustrating the High Court's willingness to scrutinize the impugned act and not to merely accept without question that the amendment to the PPP Act 1984 ousting judicial review applied. The case is pending appeal as this chapter is written.

Finally, in the political struggle that engulfed Perak state after the 2008 elections (which saw the Barisan Nasional losing its two-thirds majority), the High Court ruled in favor of the incumbent Chief Minister Nizar who was from the opposition party. The grounds for this was that (after three of its council members had left the party, and thrown their support behind the ruling coalition who were three members short of forming the state government) the Chief Minister had requested for dissolution of the Legislative Assembly under Article XXXVI (2) of the Perak state constitution. However the Court of Appeal reversed the finding of fact which was upheld by the Federal Court (*Dato Seri Mohd. Nizar* v. *Dato Seri Zambry* [2010] 2 CLJ: 925) on the ground that the request for dissolution could only be made in accordance with Article XVI (6) of the Perak state constitution which gives the discretion solely to the Sultan. The result was that the opposition lost control of the state to the ruling coalition. The decision alters the concept of a constitutional monarchy and swings the balance against the democratic will of the people in favor of the Monarch.

In summary, despite occasional signs of judicial assertiveness in highly contested political and religious matters, recent events suggest that Malaysia's judiciary is searching for its proper role post-Mahathir. Against the background of a remarkable trajectory of judicial politics in Malaysia that saw the judiciary gradually shed its cloak of judicial restraint to take on a more activist stance before being muted by the executive, recent developments suggest a new stage that is perhaps best described simply as a period of uncertainty.

II Evaluating drivers and effects of judicialization

Given this convoluted history, Malaysia offers interesting insights into the drivers and effects of the judicialization phenomenon—or the lack thereof. Three drivers seem to stand out, helping to explain changes in the patterns of judicial politics over time in Malaysia.

Leadership: It seems clear from the case that the actions of the executive branch as well as its judiciary played a critical role in determining the parameters for the latter. That should not be surprising because Malaysia's Westminster type political system not only allows for executive dominance but also encompasses a strong legacy of parliamentary sovereignty. Moreover personality traits of the various prime ministers have played an important role in shaping executive–judicial relations. While the early generation of prime ministers in Malaysia (Tengku Abdul Rahman, Tun Razak, Tun Hussein Onn) were all trained lawyers, who respected the rule of law and independence of the judiciary, this cannot be said for the next generation (Mahathir). As shown in the case of Mahathir, a medical doctor, one might even detect a certain degree of contempt for the judicial branch and its workings (if not the rule of law), particularly in relation to executive actions. Leadership dimensions are a critical variable for understanding the strategic behavior of the executive branch in relation to judicial politics.

Institutional Changes: There is little doubt that some of the institutional changes in respect of the scope and powers of the judiciary have provided important limitations on the ability of the judiciary to engage in areas of mega-politics. Malaysia lacks a proper constitutional court with powers comparable to those of Thailand or Indonesia. Unlike the Philippines, where constitutional amendments gave greater powers to the judiciary, thus enhancing juristocracy,[28] institutional changes in Malaysia during the 1980s have meant new limitations on juristocracy. These occurred in the form of new constitutional constraints relating to the judiciary (Article 121); amendments to legislation relating to fundamental rights like the PPP Act 1984, the Societies Act 1988 ousting judicial review or the recent practice of appointing judges to positions as judicial commissioners for two years before confirmation as judges (thus leaving them more vulnerable), if not the wider interference with the judicial appointment process (during Dr. Mahathir's premiership) that led to a widely perceived weaker judiciary. Combined, there is no doubt that these changes have further muted the judiciary vis-à-vis the executive, and undermined its professionalism and independence.

Ideas: Finally, there are ideational aspects to consider. For instance, adhering to principles of strict legalism in the early independence period was critical in shaping judicial behavior in politically contested cases. Likewise, before the assault on the judiciary in 1988, it relied on jurisprudential doctrines like the separation of powers that can be viewed as generally supportive of decisions encompassing judicialization.[29] However, since 1988 the judiciary has arguably sought to distance itself from such doctrines, as shown in *PP* v. *Koh Wan Kuan*, where the Federal Court stated: 'So in determining the constitutionality or otherwise of a statute under our Constitution,… *it is the provision of our Constitution that matters, not a political theory by some thinker'* (Abdul Hamid FCJ) (emphasis added). Referring to Article 121 (1) and the doctrine of the separation of powers,[30] the decision reflects the Federal Court's decision not to exceed the parameters provided by the executive in amending Article 121 (1) to limit the powers of the judiciary to what the legislature prescribes. Decisions like these seem to suggest an ideational acceptance of new limitations and rejection of a larger role for the judiciary in line with the separation of powers. This in turn has a direct bearing on judicial willingness to engage with issues of mega-politics.

Overall, in Malaysia there seems to be a complex interplay between factors such as leadership, institutional changes, and ideational foundations that has affected how the judiciary has behaved since independence. Combined with a political environment where a single party dominates, this has produced only sporadic judicial engagement in areas of mega-politics.

It is not easy to evaluate how such developments affect aspects of democratic governance, rule of law, or legitimacy. There is little doubt that the increasing muteness of the judiciary has meant a decline in its independence and respect from the public, as indicated by recent scandals. More important, though, such perceptions of the judiciary, particularly in cases relating to political power struggles, has meant that Malaysia lacks an effective arbiter in politically charged cases and thus also has little ability to transform political conflict into constitutional dialogue. There is little indication in this period of uncertainty how things will play out in the long run.

III Conclusion

Judicialization of politics in Malaysia has surfaced sparingly. The result is that Malaysia is one of the few Asian countries where no discernable trend is evident. However the substantial changes in judicial behavior over time, judicial restraint, nascent activism, muteness, and indications of growing politicization provide a particularly rich resource for the general academic debate on the drivers and effects of the judicialization phenomenon as it unfolds in Asia. Indeed with judicial politics increasingly in flux in contemporary Malaysia, one is well advised to keep a close eye on the case in the near future. While the current trajectory is difficult to predict, there is little doubt that what happens in Malaysia will have an impact within the region that may inform the scholarly debate for years to come.

Notes

1 See Thomas (1987: 54): 'The courts have ... consistently upheld the validity of Acts of Parliament ... [even] where parliamentary action has rendered meaningless, for practical purposes, fundamental liberties enshrined in the Constitution'.
2 See *The Star*, 14 May 2008, p. 3, for the findings of the Royal Commission.
3 In 1958 out of 11 judges 8 were expatriates; by 1970 all the judges were Malaysian-born. *Malayan Law Journal* 1958 and 1970, cover pages.
4 *Government of the State of Kelantan* v. *Government of the Federation of Malaya and Tunku Abdul Rahman* ([1963] MLJ 355).
5 Ibid., p. 358.
6 The constitution was amended in 1963 when Malaysia was formed; again in 1969 after the communal riots and for similar reasons in 1984; in 1994 when a delimitation exercise was carried out; and in 2003 when the ruling coalition asked the EC for a proposal for new electoral boundaries to reflect changing demographics.
7 The riots of 13 May 1969 occurred after the general elections where the opposition deprived the incumbent Alliance Party of its two-thirds majority for the first time since independence. In 1971 Art. 63 of the Constitution which protects free speech in parliament was amended by the insertion of clause 4 which states that protection will not be accorded to a person charged under law passed under Art. 10 (4) or the Sedition Act 1948. See also (*Mark Koding* v. *PP* [1982] 2 MLJ: 160).
8 In 1969 at national elections PAS won 12 Federal seats and a majority in the state of Kelantan, enabling it to form the state government.
9 These include co-opting the Dakwah movement and subsidizing pilgrimages to Mecca, the setting up of the International Islamic University and an Islamic think tank.
10 [1988] 2 MLJ: 638 p. 640.
11 *Time Magazine*—November 1986, p. 21.
12 See [1988] 2 MLJ: 129 for the High Court decision.
13 See *Danaharta Urus Sdn Bhd* v. *Kekatong Sdn Bhd.* [2004] 2 MLJ 259; *PP* v. *Kok Wah Kuan* [2008] 1 MLJ 1.
14 Ibid., *PP* v. *Kok Wah Kuan, Per Abdul Hamid Mohd*, PCA p. 17.
15 1999 1 MLJ: 139, where one defendant, Skrine & Co., had filed an application to disqualify the High Court judge because he had made a pre-judgment of the most pivotal point affecting that defendant. The Court of Appeal took the view that the application was misconceived and intemperate and if not immediately withdrawn a notice for contempt would have to issue.
16 *PP* v. *Zainur Zakaria* (2001) 3 MLJ: 305.
17 2000 4 CLJ p. 830.
18 The defendant applied to amend his defence, alleging that in a previous case of libel, *Tan Sri Vincent Tan & Anor* v. *Haji Hamzah & Others* ([1995] 1 MLJ 39) the judgment was typed in the lawyer's office, corrected by him, and the final draft forwarded to the judge on a floppy disc.
19 The mission comprised four international organizations: The International Bar Association, the International Court of Justice Centre for the Independence of Lawyers and Judges, the Commonwealth Lawyers Association and the Union International Des Avocats.
20 On 29 April 1999 the ICJ by a 14:1 majority held the Special Rapporteur was immune from prosecution.
21 N 18, Das and Chandra (2003) Kuala Lumpur for a compilation of the papers.

22 *Shamala Satyaseelan* v. *Dr. Jayaganesh* 2004 2 CLJ:416.

23 Ibid, pp. 426, 427.

24 Article 14 of CEDAW enjoins state parties to eliminate discrimination against women in relation to marriage on a basis of equality of men and women, and 14(f) asserts the same rights and responsibilities with regard to guardianship of children has been infringed. Similarly in the Convention on the Rights of the Child, Article 30, which deals with minorities, and Article 2, which deals with religious rights of the child, were infringed.

25 Press release 17 November 2010. See also *Subashini Rajasingam* v. *Saravanan Thangathoray* ([2008] 2 MLJ: 147), where the Federal Court held that the High Courts have jurisdiction to decide in conversion cases but reiterated that the converted spouse could file for custody in the Syariah court and convert minor children unilaterally.

26 Conversely in *Chan Ah Mee* v. *Jabatan Hal Ehwal Agama Islam* [2003] 5 MLJ: 106 the Sabah High Court held that as a state court it had jurisdiction over all state matters including Islam and determined the conversion of a two-year-old infant by his father was void.

27 For statistics, sec www.kehakiman.gov.my.

28 The Philippines constitution was amended in 1987 by adding Section 1 Article VIII vesting judicial power in the court. It states explicitly that it shall be the duty of the courts to settle controversies involving rights which are legally demandable and enforceable and to determine if there has been abuse of discretion amounting to lack or excess of jurisdiction by any branch of government.

29 See *PP* v. *Dato Yap Peng* ([1988] 1 MLJ 311) where the Supreme Court upheld the decision that Section 418A of the Criminal Procedure Code empowering the Attorney General to transfer cases from subordinate courts to the High Court was unconstitutional, explicitly referring in doing so to Article 121 of the Constitution and the term 'judicial powers' as well as to the doctrine of separation of powers.

30 Background: The Federal Court here overruled the Court of Appeal, which had released a child convicted of murder. The Court of Appeal had held that the 1988 amendment of Article 121 (1) did not divest the courts of the judicial power of the federation. In overturning the attempt by the Court of Appeal to reclaim judicial power, the Federal Court held that the jurisdiction and powers of the two High Courts are not dependent on the interpretation of the term 'judicial power' (which had been removed by the amendment).

References

Abas, T. M. S. and Das, C. (1989) *Mayday for Justice*, Kuala Lumpur: Magnus Books.

Ahmad, S. (2005) 'Islam in Malaysia: Constitutional and human rights perspectives', *Muslim World Journal of Human Rights*, vol. 2, issue 1: 7–27.

Das, C. and Chandra, K. (eds) (2003) *Judges & Judicial Accountability*, Kuala Lumpur: Printworks.

Hickling, H. R. (1978) 'An overview of constitutional changes in Malaysia 1957–1977' in Suffian, T., Lee, H. P., and Trindade, F. A. (eds), (1986) *The Constitution of Malaysia Its Development: 1957–1977*, Kuala Lumpur: Oxford University Press.

Hirschl, R. (2004) *Toward Juristocracy: The Origins and Consequences of the New Constitutionalism*, Cambridge, MA: Harvard University Press.

Hirschl, R. (2006) The New Constitutionalism and the Judicialization of Pure Politics Worldwide, *Fordham Law Review*, 75: 721–54.

International Bar Association (2000) *Justice in Jeopardy: Malaysia 2000*, www.ibanet.org/humanrights.Malaysia.cfm.

Khoo, B. T. (1999) 'Between law and politics' in Jayasuria, K. (ed.), *Law, Capitalism and Power*, Brisbane: Griffith University Press.

Ross, J. D. (1989) 'Malaysia, Assault on the Judiciary', Lawyers Committee for Human Rights, New York, N.Y.

Samuels, D. (1995) 'Malaysian justice on trial', *International Commercial Litigation Journal*, 10–15.

Suffian, T., Lee, H. P., and Trindade, F. A. (eds) (1986) *The Constitution of Malaysia. Its Development: 1957–1977*, Kuala Lumpur: Oxford University Press.

Thomas, T. (1987) 'The Role of the Judiciary', *Aliran*, vol. 1: 54–108.

12 Leadership, law, and legitimacy

Reflections on the changing nature of judicial politics in Asia

Haig Patapan

Constitutional courts and supreme courts of final appellate jurisdiction are unique institutions. As the principal courts in the legal hierarchy of the state, they represent the apex of the law, the fundamental institution that addresses and resolves the most important legal disputes, and thus the body entrusted with responsibility for supervising the legal contours of the regime. But to the extent that they exercise judicial review, overturning executive and legislative initiatives for inconsistency with the constitution, they are also inevitably political institutions whose decisions affect the character of the regime.

This twofold aspect of the highest courts, and the extent to which their judgments favour one over the other, has been a concern of political and legal scholars.[1] The phrase 'judicialisation of politics' seeks to capture their increasingly political role and therefore the potentially undemocratic exercise of their authority, while 'politicisation of the judiciary' suggests political usurpation of the legal authority of the court in ways that undermine its expertise, independence, and judgment. As these phrases suggest, students of judicial politics are fundamentally concerned with questions about democratic and liberal constitutionalism and the extent to which the judiciary may be said to strengthen or limit democratic accountability. Consequently, the study of judicial politics is inevitably an examination of its legitimacy, specifically within the context of the unique constitutionalism of each state and more generally within the theoretical conceptions that comprehend and frame the judicial role.

Because of the historical origins of liberal and democratic constitutionalism and the theoretical reflections that have shaped constitutional changes, it is perhaps inevitable that scholarship has focused predominantly on Western jurisprudence and constitutionalism. The far-reaching influence of the American constitution as the first modern experiment in self-government has obviously shaped much of the research on judicial politics.[2] Through their colonial influences, Westminster 'responsible' government and European conceptions of the rule of law have also had an important role in directing this scholarship. Consequently, when the focus has shifted to Asia, these conceptions of constitutionalism (and implicitly judicial politics) have informed models for constitutional reform and thus have become the basis for comparative evaluations by students seeking to understand judicial politics in the region (see, for example, Ginsberg 2003;

Ginsberg and Moustafa 2008; and Peerenboom 2004; Ginsburg and Chen 2009; Harding and Nicholson 2010). The question of whether courts are usurping powers that properly belong to the political domain ('judicial activism'), which is the prevailing concern of Western students of judicial politics, is therefore inevitably asked as well about the judiciary in Asia.

The usefulness of this question is evident from the complex and subtle assessments of judicial politics revealed in the essays in this book. In this survey of judicial politics in 10 Asian countries, students of Western judicial politics will see many familiar aspects of constitutionalism, which confirm the importance, perhaps even the primacy, of the legal and constitutional over the cultural, historical, ethnic, and religious. Yet these chapters are instructive not only because they confirm what we already know; they also reveal crucial differences that warrant closer scrutiny. The examination of judicial politics in Asia in this book therefore yields significant insights not only into the nature of judicial politics—indeed politics generally—in each country analysed; these insights allow us to revisit questions and concerns that have always been present in the study of judicial politics and constitutionalism but have perhaps been overshadowed by the focus on judicial activism.

In the concluding chapter to this book I draw upon the preceding essays to explore three aspects of judicial politics that warrant closer attention from students of judicial politics and comparative constitutionalism. The first aspect concerns the importance of judges taking leadership in shaping judicial politics. I do not intend to revisit the perennial—and not always helpful—'structure vs. agency' problem that concerns certain subdisciplines of the social sciences. My point is more modest: the cases in this book reveal that in some instances who judges are and the unique decisions they take influence the shaping of both judicial institutions and constitutionalism.

The second theme I take up concerns the law itself. Students of judicial politics and constitutionalism have to some extent forgotten that the judiciary is a *legal* institution. It must therefore act, to a greater or lesser degree and depending on its constitutional and political mandate, like a legal institution. Our notion of an 'activist' court comes predominantly from our preconceptions about what is properly 'legal' and therefore what constitutes 'improper' activism when a judge or a court steps beyond the strictures we perceive to be legal.

My third theme, which in one sense comprehends the first two, is the question of legitimacy. The legitimacy of the judiciary is, I contend, fundamentally different from the legitimacy of other institutions, precisely because it has both legal and political dimensions. This creates a complex and acutely difficult environment for judges and the courts, who have to negotiate between contending demands of legitimacy: to the people, to the law or constitution, to elected representatives, whether legislative or executive. How well they negotiate this fine balance is the core theme of my analysis.

My focus on these three questions is not meant to suggest that they are the only three. No doubt other factors can be seen to be equally important—for example, the role in each country of religion, or traditions and history, in shaping judicial politics (on the importance of historical and ideational factors see Hilbink 2008 and McCann 2009). It is simply that, in examining the fine-grained studies in this book, these three aspects of judicial politics stand out as worthy of further investigation, not only in Asia but also in the West.

Leadership

It would seem obvious that who a judge is—the judge's character—would be important for understanding the nature of judicial politics and therefore of evolving constitutionalism. Our general reluctance to ask this question is in part informed by our understanding of the law and justice as 'blind', that is, impartial and disinterested. Though it should not matter who the judge is, extensive research on attitudinal data and the biographies of judges reveals the continuing importance to the bench of individual character, discretion, and judgment (on attitudinal research see Pritchett 1948; Schubert 1965; and Segal and Speath 2002). Certainly, politicians are acutely conscience of the importance of who is appointed, often not for publicly salutary reasons; hence the use of institutional bodies such as judicial commissions to limit the influence of politicians in the judicial appointment process.

The importance of individual judges can be seen in appointments to the court in recently democratising states. Because they are likely to be drawn from those who advocated democracy and human rights, they are inevitably opposed to the previous authoritarian regime. For example, the Philippines Supreme Court as reconstituted in 1987 had an anti-Marcos predisposition; at least five of its original members were reputed to be Marcos critics.[3] When they have the power to appoint judges, politicians will naturally be tempted to choose those who favour their cause and are pliable, or at least neutral. Jarun Pukditanakul and other judges appointed to the Thai Constitutional Court in 2008 were known Thaksin critics. Musharraf's appointment of the Dogar Court in 2007 to reconstitute the Pakistan Supreme Court was clearly aimed at political control over the judiciary. Similarly, in 2009 commentators began to speak of the Arroyo Court, because in her nine years in office Arroyo appointed 23 justices to The Philippines Supreme Court and before she left office appointed a subordinate and ally, Renato Corona, as Chief Justice.

It is in crucial junctures of political or legal evolution, such as constitutional foundings when courts have just been created, or in periods of major constitutional change, that judicial leadership assumes particular significance.[4] There are notable examples in Asia of individual judges influencing judicial politics. The first Indonesian Chief Justice, Jimly Asshiddique, a respected professor of constitutional law at the University of Indonesia, proved crucial to the future legitimacy of the court. Not only did he bring the court significant political support, he also secured a sizeable budget and impressive new buildings; perhaps more importantly, he was instrumental in ensuring that the court's decisions were better reasoned and more accessible. He was especially influential in establishing the court's jurisprudential reasoning, in crafting Indonesia's version of the rule of law (the *negara hukum*, or law state) as an underlying constitutional principle, and in upholding human rights and democratic principles.

Perhaps the most striking example of how the actions of individual judges can have major implications is Pakistan's Ifthikar Muhammad Chaudhry, who was apparently considered reliable and unexceptional when Musharraf appointed him Chief Justice in 2005. Soon after his appointment, however, Chaudhry set up a Human Rights Office in the Supreme Court and instructed court employees to track media reports of crimes against women and children, abuses of justice, corruption, and abuses of power by civil servants and elected public officials. He then claimed jurisdiction to investigate such situations and issue judicial orders if warranted. Suspended from office in 2007, Chaudhry refused to resign and contested the decision, triggering demonstrations by lawyers and members of opposition political parties. His stance resulted in the Supreme Court declaring Musharraf's actions to be illegal and lifting Chaudhry's suspension.

Though Chaudhry demonstrates how the character of judges can make a major difference in judicial politics, usually its influence is mitigated by a range of institutional structures that attempt to limit the unpredictability of judicial discretion. One of the most significant, as noted, is the appointment process. The Japanese process of appointment and promotion, involving education in a Supreme Court Institute, appointments throughout the country, and 10 years of service before elevation to full judge shows the powerful potential of organisational selection in judicial appointments. The philosophical presuppositions of what a judge should do, derived from tradition, history, or in the case of Japan from Prussian scholars like Otto von Gierke and Georg Jellinek during the Meiji era, can be a powerful means of limiting judicial discretion. Similarly, the fact that Malaysian judges tend to be lawyers influenced by Westminster traditions explains their 'legalistic' jurisprudence. In the extreme case of Cambodia, the Khmer Rouge execution of lawyers, judges, and legal scholars meant that thereafter the quality of Cambodian judges ranged from the highly educated to the totally unschooled. By 2006 Cambodia had just 225 judges—17 per one million people—and fewer than 300 practising lawyers.[5]

Judges may arrogate to themselves the power of appointment, as did the Chief Justice of India and four senior judges in 1993 (who also mandated that criminal investigation of judges required judicial consent). But generally such procedures are subject to legislative or constitutional provisions. A wider appointment process may encourage more individual discretion. The Korean Constitutional Court (KCC) consists of nine justices appointed by the president, but the mixed appointment system means that of the nine, three are selected by the National Assembly and three are nominated by the Chief Justice of the Supreme Court, resulting in a more diverse bench. Combined with an increasingly large, active, and powerful Korean bar, it would seem that Korean judges might exercise greater discretion. But their short six-year terms may make them more sensitive to the opinions of those who appoint them. The Thai attempt to combine career and non-career judges on the bench may have provided room for greater independence. But the fact that Constitutional Court judges are appointed for a single non-renewable term and are further term-limited by age may have had the unintended consequence of undermining institutional continuity and therefore of augmenting executive influence on the court.

Indeed, the conditions of appointment, including pay, term limits, and general independence seem to heavily influence the nature and extent of the discretion individual judges exercise. This can be seen in the Philippines, where the leadership of individual judges has not been as significant, arguably because judges there do not have life tenure, have relatively low pay, and are appointed by the president. Similarly, poor pay, corruption, lack of job security, and patronage make Cambodian judges vulnerable to outside influence and thus corruption.

The most extreme lack of judicial authority is evident in China, where the judiciary is seen as an arm of the Communist Party of China (CPC). What is interesting there, however, is that this politicisation of the judiciary gives the office of chief justice greater importance. Until 2008 decisions of the Supreme People's Court (SPC) were influenced by the Court Presidency of Xiao Yang (1999–2008), who was largely faithful to Deng Xiaoping's reforms that stressed the 'rule of law', 'trial independence' and professionalism as against inappropriate CPC intervention and misapplication of checks and balances within the justice system. But since Wang Shengjun became Court President in 2008, politicization of the SPC and the court system based on party leadership has been enhanced.

Law

To understand the nature of judicial politics, it is essential to appreciate the juridical or legal foundations of the judiciary. All aspects of law and justice, such as the ideas of jurisdiction, proceedings, actions and submissions, deliberation, judgments and orders, will more or less influence how judges exercise their authority. Perhaps most important, three aspects of the judiciary at the highest level make it a unique institution: it must act according to procedures and laws; it must exercise its authority openly, subjecting itself to public scrutiny and examination; and generally speaking it must give reasons for its judgments, that is, it must persuade using arguments rather than decide by the pure exercise of will, untrammelled by the requirements of reasoning.

Since the law is usually respected, the judiciary, clothing itself in the vestments of such august authority, is a powerful institution that can make far-reaching and influential decisions because its verdicts have the imprimatur of the law. At the same time, however, the law, with its unique requirements, places powerful limitations on the exercise of authority by the judiciary. These limitations can be summarised under the general rubric of 'the rule of law', which implicitly assumes '*not* the rule of men'. Consequently, judges are assumed to protect the constitution by *interpreting*, not *making*, the law.

This overriding presumption has a number of aspects. For example, the assumption that the court will treat like cases alike underscores the requirement that courts will act consistently and follow their previous decisions. The idea of *stare decisis* thus becomes both a powerful resource and a limitation on what judges and courts can do in a specific case. Similarly, the presumptions that unconstitutionality cannot be 'prospective' and that impugned laws are invalid as of their enactment (and not from the judgment date), that judges cannot simply 'redraft' legislation to make it valid, and finally that decisions have to be made public and persuade through legal reasoning—all these are significant limits the law imposes on the judiciary.[6]

The exercise of judicial review—the authority to declare executive or legislative regulations or enactments unconstitutional—is perhaps the judiciary's most powerful source of authority. Judicial review, the power exercised by courts founded on liberal constitutionalism, is constitutionally conferred on the judiciary in Thailand, the Philippines, Korea, Japan, Indonesia, and India, though the power can be limited. For example, the Indonesian MK can only review the constitutionality of statutes enacted by the national parliament and therefore it cannot review most Indonesian law, which is found in executive and departmental regulations.[7] In contrast, in the Philippines the 'pro-people, pro-poor, and pro-Filipino' nature of the Constitution has meant that its Supreme Court has an extensive constitutional mandate that not only entrenches judicial review of cases related to human rights, including such new rights as those of indigenous peoples, it also allows the court to define economic policy and social justice. As a result the court was able to invalidate major reform initiatives of the Ramos government.[8]

Ramos assumed the presidency in 1992 with the intention of transforming the Philippines into a newly industrialized country by 2000. To achieve that end, he advocated economic reforms based on, among other things, liberalization, deregulation, and privatization policies. The court's decisions undermined these reforms. For example, in *Manila Prince Hotel* v. *Government Service Insurance System* (1997), the court allowed a Filipino corporation to match the winning bid of a Malaysian company for 51 per cent of Manila Hotel shares, justifying its decision as upholding the 'Filipino First Policy' espoused by the 1987 Constitution. In *Tatad* v. *Secretary of Energy* (1997), the court also invalidated the 1st Oil Deregulation Law on the ground that it violated the economic rights of the Filipino people. Importantly, in *Santiago* v. *Comelec* (1997) the court ruled that the Initiative Referendum Act was not a sufficient support for amending the Constitution, thwarting efforts to remove from the text of the Constitution alleged economic protectionist or nationalist provisions as well as term limits for elected officials.[9]

This form of judicial review, where the court can hold enactments unconstitutional, should be distinguished from ideas of the administration of the law that are specific to legal-political institutions in China, Cambodia, and Malaysia. In those countries the judiciary is seen as an arm of the ruling party which is expected to ensure that party demands are recognized and enforced. We can see the contrast clearly in Malaysia, where the Supreme Court at first emphasised the importance of separation of powers in its jurisprudence, only to abandon that 'political theory' after the 1988 assault on it by Dr. Mahathir and the United

Malays National Organization (UMNO).[10] But even where there is judicial administration rather than review, the court's power can vary significantly. In China, where there is no judicial review and the court is under direct political control, jurisprudence still matters. Thus the Wang Shengjun Court has endorsed the 'Three Supremes' (*sange zhi shang)*, placing the party's cause and the needs of the people on the same level as the supremacy of law. While reiterating the importance of the CPC, especially the leadership of its Central Political-Legal Committee, Wang refers to judicial independence and professionalism (though in the form of an institutional response that reflects 'Chinese characteristics').

The importance of the legal nature of the judiciary becomes especially apparent when scholars seek to examine judicial activism—whether the judiciary has assumed too much power and thereby intruded improperly into the political arena. To some extent the very use of the word activism presumes that there is a 'proper' scope of judicial review that has clearly limned boundaries to demarcate between judicial quiescence and judicial overreach. I would argue that it is an implicit conception of the rule of law (with its jurisprudential and procedural assumptions) that allows scholars to argue in terms of activism. The more judges and courts seem to overstep, go beyond, or subvert principles of the rule of law, the more they will appear to be acting politically rather than legally and will therefore seem 'activist'. For example, because the Japanese Supreme Court has rarely exceeded strict legal principles, it is widely regarded as not an activist court.

In contrast, it is perhaps because the KCC in Korea has relied on traditional jurisprudential techniques, such as proportionality, to balance interests that scholars questioned the basis of its decision in the Relocation of the Capital City Case. One of the central issues in the 2002 presidential election was the pledge by Roh Moo-Hyun of the ruling New Millennium Democratic Party to move the capital away from Seoul to promote balanced development across the country. In the 2004 Capital City Case, the KCC held that the legislative act to move the capital was unconstitutional, basing its decision on the grounds that an operative though unwritten 'customary constitution' held Seoul to be the capital. This customary constitution could only be revised by following constitutional procedures (Article 130) that require a national referendum. The KCC decision striking down the act evoked both wide-ranging political and legal debates and the charge of judicial activism, precisely because, I contend, the concept of a customary constitution seemed to overstep the rule of law as previously understood.

Similarly, Thai constitutional court decisions were not challenged until a series of them seemed to go beyond the rule of law, suggesting improper activism. The court's decision to uphold Prime Minister's Thaksin's innocence was interpreted as political, even though the 1,200-page judgment seemed to suggest that unusual voting rules may have transformed minority opinions into a majority ruling. Subsequent cases raised more substantial concerns. The decision in May 2006 to annul the April general elections was questioned because of unusually broad legal reasoning. The 2007 dissolution of the Thai Rak Thai party, soon after adoption of the post-coup constitution, seemed political because the justices abruptly ended testimony by defence witnesses—and then returned just hours later with a verdict less than three pages long that ignored vital questions, such as how vote-buying might be considered anti-democratic behaviour as defined by relevant law or how court dissolution of a party could be reconciled with the constitutionally guaranteed freedom to form a party. Finally, in the Samak case, the court forced the resignation of the first prime minister elected under the 2007 constitution by relying on a dictionary definition of 'employee' rather than the actual definitions set out in Thailand's civil code and labour laws.

These examples from Korea and Thailand are not unique. Many examples of such verdicts can be found in other countries in the region. What they reveal, however, is that it is the very basis of its authority—the law—that lays the foundation for evaluating what the judiciary does and thereby sets the standard for assessing judicial activism or 'creativity'.

Legitimacy

The discussion above has revealed the importance of individual judges in shaping judicial politics. It has also shown the important role of the idea of the rule of law in determining both the opportunities for and the constraints on judicial discretion. In addition to these factors, it is clear that the judiciary as an institution is significant for our understanding of judicial politics. The institutional aspect especially, its origins, history, and continuing influence on how the law and politics evolve, has far-reaching implications for both the discretion of individual judges and the jurisprudence of the court. Though each element—individual, jurisprudential, and institutional—may decide or influence important aspects of judicial politics, to understand the comprehensive nature of judicial politics in any country requires an appreciation of the dynamic interplay between these three elements. This more dynamic understanding of the determinative role of the judiciary in politics is suitably comprehended, I would argue, in the idea of legitimacy.

Legitimacy is a complex notion that takes into account diverse conceptions of power and authority (see generally Kane and Patapan 2009; Kane *et al.* 2011). Where judicial institutions are vitally concerned with the administration of justice, legitimacy is refracted through the lens of the 'law' and therefore assumes a complexity not evident in other institutions. This is perhaps most evident in criminal law, where the decisions of judges on both culpability and sentencing are most obviously evaluated in terms of just outcomes. But where questions involve more subtle notions of constitutionalism, such as ideas of rights, freedoms, and the rule of law generally, whether any single decision is just becomes more complex to discern and evaluate. As a result, the judiciary here finds itself in an especially difficult situation in trying to ascertain how far it can exercise its power while preserving its legitimacy. Because the role of the judiciary is both legal *and* political, judges need to be especially mindful of the unique demands the exercise of judicial review makes on them.

These demands are complicated not only by the uniquely political and legal role of the courts but also by contending sources of legitimacy. Foremost, of course, are the constitution and the rule of law that gives the court its most powerful mandate. Legitimacy is therefore most readily secured in complying with and defending the rule of law, as we saw above in discussing the jurisprudence of the courts and the claims made for and against judicial activism. But the judiciary is aware that its decisions defending the rule of law also have political consequences. The reason for this, though apparently paradoxical, is simple: In a sense, the less authority the court exercises, the greater its legitimacy and influence. Consequently, the more a court intervenes in both law and politics, the more it looks like any other arm of government or political institution and the more vulnerable it becomes to strident and sometimes immoderate political critique.

Judicial legitimacy is thus both very powerful and quite fragile, easily undermined by suspicions of impropriety and corruption. Therefore, in considering the consequences of its decisions, the judiciary will defend its own legitimacy not just for apparently self-seeking purposes but in order to defend the rule of law more generally. Because the judiciary is the interpreter of the rule of law, its legitimacy reflects fundamentally on the law itself. But in seeking to ensure that its legitimacy is not undermined by its judgments, the judiciary will look not only to the rule of law, including the larger community of lawyers and judges, but to other sources of legitimacy. Here we consider the two major sources: the 'people' and the executive or government.[11]

One of the crucial sources of judicial legitimacy is the people. This democratic mandate is especially clear in Asia, where constitutional reform and the entrenchment of judicial review were seen as a part of a democratic process to overthrow previously authoritarian regimes. Post-colonial independence and constitutional innovation were fundamentally democratic in intent in Thailand in 1987, India in 2003, the Philippines in 1987, South Korea in 1988, Indonesia in 2003, and Malaysia in 1957. It is therefore not surprising that people in those countries would see the judiciary as a bulwark against authoritarian rule and expect judges to exercise their judgment against encroachments on rights and freedoms.

Such a mandate is a powerful source of authority and legitimacy that can sustain the courts for a long time. Indeed, popular legitimacy is so powerful that it is even evident in countries that do not have much sense of judicial review. Even in China the importance of public sentiment is such that in the Liu Gong case the SPC changed its decision to accommodate it. Thus the SPC, though it has often risen to the defence of national standards, sometimes appears to take its cue directly from public opinion as well as the party.[12]

But this democratic source of legitimacy can impose highly complex demands on individual judges and courts seeking to defend their moral authority and protect their institutional power while dispensing justice. The Philippines court in a sense owed its origins to people power. Yet in its 2001 decision to remove Joseph Estrada from the presidency, the court seemed to go against the people's wishes in order to protect the integrity of the constitution. Subsequent attempts by mostly poor pro-Estrada supporters to launch their version of 'People Power' in May 2001 ended in violence, destruction of property, and declaration of a state of rebellion. It also led in mid-2003 to attempts to impeach members of the court. The legislature's impeachment of Chief Justice Hilario Davide in November 2003 resulted in the court using its constitutional powers to pre-empt the impeachment process. These decisions seemed to challenge the democratic credentials of the court, apparently aligning it with the administration of Estrada's successor and rival, Gloria Macapagal-Arroyo. Similarly, the Thai court's decisions on electoral laws appeared to go against the view of the majority of the public, making the court seem to be part of the entrenched powers.

Beyond such instances, it is clear that the changing nature of politics will elicit different public expectations. As Korean society has become more pluralistic, with a larger civil society and a more sophisticated community of lawyers, democratic expectations of the judiciary have become more subtle and nuanced. Thus the goodwill of the people as a source of legitimacy and authority based on seemingly neutral decisions of the courts may be limited by the type of cases decided, such as Korea's capital city and impeachment cases. The risk is that as its decisions become increasingly contentious, the court will look no different from the executive and the bureaucracy.

In addition to its democratic legitimacy, the judiciary is aware of the importance of securing legitimacy within the overall framework of the new constitutional settlement. This means that in questioning or even overriding executive decisions, the judiciary is aware of the need to preserve its legitimacy before the legislature and the executive. Especially in its early period when a court's authority may be uncertain, the judiciary is often wary of imposing difficult, if not impossible, demands on the executive. The success of Indonesian democracy is arguably attributable in large measure to the judgment and discretion of the Indonesian Constitutional Court, whose 'strategic pragmatism' has gained it the title of guardian of Indonesia's democracy. Although the court has employed legal means to limit the government, it has also appreciated the difficulties the executive faces in enforcing such limits. The use of prospective invalidation, decrees of invalidity that recognised further attempts at compliance, and invalidity subject to deadline, show a court that is cognisant of the limits of democratic principles in an emerging democracy.

Similarly, the Indian Supreme Court has handed down judgments that have expanded free access to anti-retro-virals for AIDS patients, created a right to food, allowed Delhi to enact anti-pollution policies, provided justification for an education guarantee scheme, and created new mechanisms for regulating blood banks and processing medical negligence claims. It has issued interim orders mandating provision of cooked midday meals in all primary schools and of 35 kilos of grain each month at highly subsidized prices to 15 million destitute households, but these decisions have also recognised government financial constraints and the fact that the executive may be unable to implement more ambitious judgments.

The need for considered exercise of judicial review to protect judicial legitimacy arises from the complex and often fraught relationship between the judiciary, the legislature, and especially the executive. A court may have the authority to deem provisions unconstitutional, but this alone is not sufficient. It is not simply the possibility that the executive will disregard the court's judgment and thus undermine its authority; there is also the fear that the executive will take direct action to limit the court's power. What happened in Malaysia is instructive. The first three prime ministers after independence in 1957 (Tengku Abdul Rahman, Tun Razak, and Tun Hussein Onn), who were all lawyers, showed respect for the judiciary by not commenting on its decisions or attempting to limit its constitutional powers. In contrast, the premiership of the medical doctor Mahathir, Malaysia's fourth and longest-serving prime minister (1982–2003), saw major constitutional and legislative limitations imposed on the judiciary. Soon after assuming office, Mahathir in 1985 abolished civil appeals to the Privy Council and began criticising the judiciary for making decisions contrary to the intentions of the executive, threatening to create a law the judiciary would have to follow. Mahathir felt so constrained by judicial decisions that in 1988 he dismissed the Lord President and two other Supreme Court judges. This incident, in addition to the absence of a major opposition party in Malaysia, has resulted in a judiciary that has largely deferred to the executive, at significant cost to its own legitimacy.

These dangers suggest that the judiciary may be tempted to avoid executive attack by simply endorsing or upholding executive decrees. But this has the potential of crucially undermining the legitimacy of the courts. In India on 25 June 1975 Prime Minister Indira Gandhi suspended Article 21 of the Constitution and imprisoned hundreds of people (mainly political opponents and civil society activists) under an executive order proclaiming a state of emergency. Nine high courts found the order unconstitutional. They were overruled by the Supreme Court. That decision has had far-reaching implications for the Supreme Court's legitimacy as a guardian of civil liberties. Subsequent attempts by the prime minister to pack the court with pliable judges, superseding judges who were seen as anti-regime and transferring those perceived to be hostile to her policies, further undermined the legitimacy of the court. The court has been trying ever since to regain its legitimacy but, mindful of its experience, has been using a more nuanced approach. As the cases of Malaysia and India show, it takes considerable time for a court to recover lost legitimacy.

Perhaps the question of judicial legitimacy is resolved or made easier where there is no clear-cut separation between the political and the legal, so that the question of judicial legitimacy does not arise. China's system has been described as political-legal—the antithesis of the American separation of powers doctrine.[13] Indeed, according to Article 3 of the 1980 State Constitution, all state organizations, including the SPP and SPC, are subject to 'democratic centralism'. Yet the SPC still has the ability to 'supervise' and 'guide' the people's court system. It also has an informal capacity to improvise review through judicial interpretation of the law, even if it has no formal power to review national legislation. It is true that the role of the SPC has changed over time. Recent attempts to emphasise 'Chinese characteristics', 'mass line', and the 'Three Supremes' demonstrate the importance of the judiciary as a form of 'legitimacy building': by improving the competence of judicial institutions the CCP hopes to enhance citizen confidence in leadership by the party.

A similar account can be given for Cambodia, where the courts are used to implement political decisions. After democratic elections in 1993 Cambodia adopted a system of checks and balances that enshrined judicial independence in the Constitution. But the judiciary has been too weak to resist the Cambodian People's Party (CPP), which employs the courts to weaken opposition parties and suppress outspoken critics. Consequently, Cambodians see the courts as corrupt and serving party interests. Legal reforms since the early 2000s, such as institutional capacity-building projects, new laws and regulations, new buildings, and increased salary for judges and prosecutors, have all been initiated to enhance judicial power and legitimacy. Yet because they have not secured basic aspects of the rule of law, such as procedural fairness, equality before the law, and equal access to justice, their success has been limited.

Leaving aside cases of rule *by* law, courts that have extensive powers of judicial review and are secure in established constitutional regimes in effect have two paths to securing legitimacy: the Japanese and the Korean. The Japanese Supreme Court, aware of the continuing dominance until recently of the Liberal Democrats, has been unwilling to challenge policies of the Diet. It has decided to ensure its legitimacy by limiting its exercise of judicial review. Korea's KCC has taken the alternative and potentially more difficult path of more extensive use of judicial review without obvious direct challenge of the executive. For example, in the landmark impeachment of President Roh Moo-Hyun the court attempted to satisfy the opposition parties and their supporters by finding that President Roh had committed illegal and unconstitutional acts that would justify the motion of impeachment, but it also tried to please the president's side by allowing him to keep his office despite the recognized violations. In doing so it decided that the court was the final authoritative arbiter of whether or not impeached public officials should be dismissed, even if they had been found guilty of illegal activities.

Judicial legitimacy in Asia

It is perhaps inevitable that the extraordinary diversity in history, culture, and political traditions in Asia raises considerable obstacles to any attempts to generalize about the nature of judicial legitimacy in Asia. Nevertheless, as we have suggested, there are certain major themes and ideas that are consistent in all these countries, allowing us to discern important commonalities in judicial politics in the region. Useful starting points for understanding judicial politics in Asia can be found in the character and discretion of individual judges; the autochthonous jurisprudential and rule of law principles that define, empower, and constrain their discretion; and the institutional aspects of the judiciary, such as the degree of judicial independence, how judges are appointed (and dismissed), and more generally the character of constitutionalism in each nation.

But perhaps the most important aspect, as I have suggested, is the question of legitimacy. The essential foundation of the judiciary is legitimacy, since its very authority is derived not from its access to financial or political power but from the respect accorded to the rule of law. The judiciary in every country is therefore acutely aware of its own legitimacy and engaged in securing and enhancing it. Yet any such attempt is inevitably complicated by the dual nature of the judiciary. In exercising judicial review courts at the highest level are in effect both a political and a legal institution. They are therefore inevitably in a difficult situation, attempting to secure legitimacy by negotiating this duality, defending the rule of law and constitutionalism while considering the larger implications of their jurisprudence for the other branches of government, and the people generally.

Legitimacy is the fundamental concern of every court in the region. How they negotiate this problem reveals much about the state's constitutionalism. In states with entrenched principles of liberal constitutionalism, it is possible to discern a sophisticated judiciary that has successfully negotiated the contending demands of facilitating executive policy ambitions while defending the principles of rule of law and constitutionalism. Japan, Korea, and more recently Indonesia have shown the deft touch necessary for pursuing prudent accommodation and compromise. In other cases we see how such attempts can fall short, either in favouring the executive, as in Thailand and the Philippines, or by succumbing to direct executive initiatives, as in Malaysia. The unusual case of Pakistan shows how in rare cases the judiciary may successfully counter attempts at manipulation. But in general the courts are relatively weak and therefore vulnerable to concerted and powerful political attacks. For this reason there are at the other extreme courts that de facto, if not de jure, exercise little or no judicial review. In China and Cambodia the principle of 'rule *by* law' means that the judiciary is effectively an arm of government. There notions of legitimacy are inevitably tied to the hopes and ambitions of the reigning regime or party.

Thus judicial politics in Asia demonstrates an extraordinary diversity that traverses the spectrum from liberal constitutionalism to the one-party state. This diversity warns against a too-ready application to Asian courts of principles and insights, such as judicial activism, that are familiar to Western students of constitutionalism. Yet this very diversity allows us to raise for future research fruitful questions about leadership, law, and legitimacy that may yield greater insights into the unique nature of judicial politics.

Notes

1 On the general trend see Tate and Vallinder (1995). On challenges to the trends from both progressive and conservative perspectives, see Ely (1980); Hirschl (2004); Mandel (1989); Morton and Knopff (2000); Bork (1990); Tushnet (1999).

2 On the theoretical origins of the founding of America, see Stoner (1992). On the international influence of the American constitution, see Henkin and Rosenthal (1990).

3 As Ciencia notes above, Claudio Teehankee Sr. and Vicente Abad Santos were dissenters in the Marcos-era Supreme Court. Pedro Yap, as a delegate to the 1971 Constitution Convention, voted against the transitory provisions of the 1973 Constitution that gave Marcos total control of the government. Marcelo Fernan was an opposition member in the Batasan Pambansa (National Legislature), and Andres Narvasa was part of the Agrava fact-finding body which found the military culpable for the assassination of Benigno Aquino Jr. in 1983. The rest of the court consisted of reputed independent-minded legal scholars and human rights or libertarian advocates.

4 It is notable that the judgment that established the principle of judicial review in America, Chief Justice Marshall's opinion in *Marbury* v. *Madison*, 5 U.S. (1 Cranch) 137 (1803), was one of the earliest Supreme Court decisions.

5 As Un So notes above, since 2002 as part of the judicial reform process the government has trained more lawyers and prosecutors so that by 2010, there were 309 judges and 594 lawyers.

6 On the jurisprudential problems raised by void *ab initio* vs progressive overruling, as well as 'advisory' opinions, see Patapan (2000: 102–104).

7 Examples of these, as Butt notes above, include government regulations, presidential regulations, and ministerial decrees. The court also lacks jurisdiction to review the many thousands of by-laws that local governments have enacted since decentralisation.

8 As Ciencia notes, the court did uphold the constitutionality of the Ramos-endorsed value-added tax in *Tolentino* v. *Secretary of Finance* (1995) and sustained the Philippine Senate's ratification of the World Trade Organization in *Tañada* v. *Angara* (1997).

9 It also has law-making powers. For example, in 2008, the Supreme Court promulgated the writ of *amparo* to contain the rise in extrajudicial executions in the Philippines, and in April 2010 promulgated the writ of *kalikasan* to address urgent environmental concerns.

10 Mahathir sacked the Lord President and two Supreme Court justices, subjected judges to disciplinary action, and finally amended the Constitution to limit the powers of the judiciary.

11 It is tempting to consider the influence on the courts in terms of concentric or overlapping circles, with the centre dominated by peers; then legal communities, such as bar associations; human rights advocates and NGOs, as well as the international legal community; and finally the encompassing political communities (see, for example, Epp 1998 and Baum 2006). Though useful as a heuristic device, such an approach would not give sufficient attention to the influence of ideas (legal, indigenous, religious, cultural) on decisions and to the unpredictability of political contestations and struggles, which could constantly disrupt such a neat typology.

12 See, for example, Hou and Keith's discussion above of the 2007 SPC 'opinion' (*yijian*) on the three principles of open trial (according to law, open trial without delay, and open trial in all respects), as well as the Wang Shengjun court's 2009 regulations (*guiding*) on broadcasting live court trials over the Internet.

13 The SPC, as Hou and Keith note, has to cope with the institutional realities of 'judiciary and administration are inseparable' (*sifa yu xingzheng bufen*).

References

Baum, L. (2006) *Judges and Their Audiences: A Perspective on Judicial Behavior*, Princeton: Princeton University Press.

Bork, R. H. (1990) *The Tempting of America: The Political Seduction of the Law*, New York: Free Press.

Ely, J. H. (1980) *Democracy and Distrust: A Theory of Judicial Review*, Cambridge: Harvard University Press.

Epp, C. R. (1998) *The Rights Revolution: Lawyers, Activists, and Supreme Courts in Comparative Perspective*, Chicago: University of Chicago Press.

Ginsberg, T. (2003) *Judicial Review in New Democracies: Constitutional Courts in Asian Cases*, Cambridge: Cambridge University Press.

Ginsburg, T. and Chen, A. H. Y. (eds) (2009) *Administrative Law and Governance in Asia*, London and New York: Routledge.

Ginsburg, T. and Moustafa, T. (2008) *Rule by Law: The Politics of Courts in Authoritarian Regimes*, Cambridge and New York: Cambridge University Press.

Harding, A. and Nicholson, P. (2010) *New Courts in Asia*, Oxford and New York: Routledge.

Henkin, L. and Rosenthal, A. J. (eds) (1990) *Constitutionalism and Rights: The Influence of the United States Constitution Abroad*, New York: Columbia University Press.

Hilbink, L. (2008) 'Assessing the new constitutionalism', *Comparative Politics* 40: 227–45.

Hirschl, R. (2004) *Towards Juristocracy: The Origins and Consequences of the New Constitutionalism*, Cambridge, MA: Harvard University Press.

Kanc, J. and Patapan, H. (2010) 'Recovering justice: Political legitimacy reconsidered', *Politics and Policy*, 38: 3, 589–610.

Kane, J., Loy, H. C., and Patapan, H. (eds) (2011) *Political Legitimacy in Asia: New Leadership Challenges*, New York: Palgrave Macmillan.

Mandel, M. (1989) *The Charter of Rights and the Legalisation of Politics in Canada*, Toronto: Thompson.

McCann, M. (2009) 'Interests, ideas, and institutions in comparative analysis of judicial power', *Political Research Quarterly*, 62: 834–9.

Morton, F. L. and Knopff, R. (2000) *The Charter Revolution and the Court Party*, Peterborough, ON: Broadview Press.

Patapan, H. (2000) *Judging Democracy: The New Politics of the High Court of Australia*, Cambridge: Cambridge University Press.

Peerenboom, R. (ed.) (2004) *Asian Discourses of Rule of Law*, London: Routledge.

Pritchett, H. C. (1948) *The Roosevelt Court*, New York: Macmillan Co.

Schubert, G. (1965) *The Judicial Mind: The Attitudes and Ideologies of Supreme Court Justices, 1946–1963*, Evanston IL: Northwestern University Press.

Segal, J. A. and Spaeth, H. (2002). *The Attitudinal Model Revisited*, Cambridge: Cambridge University Press.

Stoner, J. R. (1992) *Common Law and Liberal Theory: Coke, Hobbes, & the Origins of American Constitutionalism*, Lawrence: University Press of Kansas.

Tate, N. and Vallinder, T. (eds) (1995) *The Global Expansion of Judicial Power*, New York: New York University Press.

Tushnet, M. (1999) *Taking the Constitution Away from the Courts*, Princeton: Princeton University Press.

Index

Abad Santos, Vicente 119
Abdur Razzaq Aamir v. *Federal Government of Pakistan* 144
activism, judicial *see* judicial activism
activist courts 7
Adung Bin Kuwau case 210
Agabin, P. 123–4, 126
Agan Jr. v. *Philippine International Air Terminals Co., Inc.* 121
Al-Jehad Trust v. *Federation of Pakistan PLD* 160n47
analysis framework of judicialization: drivers and effects of judicial patterns 7–11; effects evaluation 11–12; typology of judicial politics 3–7
Anwar Ibrahim 203, 212
apoliticism, Hilbink's findings 17–18
Aquino & Robredo v. *Comelec* 130
Aquino, Benigno III 119, 129–30
Aquino, Corazon 117–20, 133
Arroyo, Dato 130
Arroyo, Gloria 121, 127–8, 131–2, 134, 221, 228
Arroyo, Mikey 130
Arumugam Pillai v. *Government of Malaysia* 204
Asma Jilani v. *Government of Punjab PLD* 158n5
assassinations: Benazir Bhutto 150; Benigno Aquino Jr 119; Indira Gandhi 65; Zia ul-Haq 142
Asshiddique, Jimly 101–2, 221
Association of Small Landowners v. *Secretary of Agrarian Reform* 120
Austin, G. 66
autonomy 2, 6, 9–10, 20, 69, 153

Badawi, Abdullah 211, 213
Bajrakitiyabha, Princess 92
Bakker, J. W. 127
Bali Bombing case 108
Bank of Punjab v. *Haris Steel Industries* 155
Bautista, Elena 130
Bautista v. *Salonga* 119
Baxi, U. 63, 67
BAYAN v. *Ermita* 121
Begum Nusrat Bhutto v. *Chief of Army Staff and Federation of Pakistan PLD* 158n3
Bhutto, Benazir 145, 148, 150–1
Biraogo v. *Truth Commission* 129–30
Bowsher v. *Synar* 35n28
Brillantes v. *Yorac* 119

Cabestan, J. P. 164
Cambodia: decline in political violence 190; independence 185; institutional structure 187–90; institutional weaknesses 191, 194–5; judicial legitimacy 230–1; modern legal system 185–7; opposition party members, NGO leaders, and journalists who have been sued *192*; patrimonialism 196–7; political climate 189; the politics of lawsuits 190–8; prevalence of corruption in the judiciary 196–7; vulnerability to corruption 223; *see also* Khmer Rouge
Centre for Public Interest Litigation and others v. *Union of India* 73n26, 73n29, 74n50
Chatterjee, Somnath 70
Chaudhry, Ifthikar Muhammad 139, 147, 154, 222
Chavez v. *Public Estates Authority - Amari* 121
Chen Xingliang 172

Cheong Wa Dae 41
Chilean judicial quiescence, Hilbink's account 17–18
China, judicial legitimacy 229–30
China's Supreme People's Court: approach to law and politics 165, 168; and the Cultural Revolution 166; judicial enforcement 178–9; and judicial independence 166; judicial transparency 177; judicialization and judicial independence 176; Liu Yong case 172–3; opinion on open trials 177; procedure versus populism dilemma 172–3; protection of education rights 174–5; rape and due process 175; recent leadership 169, 172; reforms management 179; rights and interests protection 173–5
Choudhary, S. 57
Chu Ming v. *Tianjin Normal University* 181n6
Chulalongkorn, King of Siam (Thailand) 81
Chun Doo-hwan 38, 43
Citizens United v. *FEC* 23
Civil Liberties Union v. *Executive Secretary* 119
civil rights protection, as measure of constitutionalism 48
Coelho judgment (*I.R. Coelho* v. *Union of India*) 66, 70, 73
Common Cause Reg, Soc v. *UOI* 71n7
conciliation, Japanese system 20–1
constitutional adjudication, Korea's adoption 38
constitutional rights jurisprudence 3
Corona, Renato 128, 132, 221
courts, visibility in the Asian political landscape 1

Das Genossenschaftsrecht (Von Gierke) 29
Dastoor v. *Federation of Pakistan PLD* 159n11
Dato Seri Mohd. Nizar v. *Dato Seri Zambry* 213
David v. *Arroyo* 122
de Castro v. *JBC* 130
De Leon, H. S. 124
death penalty, Chinese perspective 172, 175
Deng Xiaoping 166–7, 169, 223
detention without trial, Malaysian perspective 204, 209
Divine Retreat Centre v. *State of Kerala* 72n23
Dogar Court 149–53, 221
Dong Likun 166
Dr. M. Oslam Khaki v. *Syed Muhammad Hashim PLD* 158n7
Dr. Subramanian Swamy v. *Union of India* 73n29
drivers and effects of judicial patterns: behaviour clusters 7; interplay between institutional, ideational, and structural factors 8; liberalization and democratization 8
drivers of judicialization, literature review 2

East Union Malaya Sdn Bhd v. *Government of State of Johor & Government of Malaysia* 205
The Economic and Political Weekly 56
Ejaz Akbar Kasi v. *Ministry of Broadcasting and PTV* 155
electoral alternation, as key factor for judicialization in Japan 27
electoral malapportionment, and judicialization in Japan 22
environmental rights jurisprudence, Indian perspective 57
Estrada, Joseph 121, 131, 133, 227
Estrada v. *Arroyo* 121, 122, 131

Falun Gong 168, 173
federalism 3, 64
Federation of Pakistan v. *Mian Nawaz Sharif PLD* 159n34
Federation of Pakistan v. *Muhammad Shahbaz Sharif PLD* 159n34
Federation of Pakistan v. *Muhammad Siafullah Khan PLD* 158n6
Ferejohn, J. 66
Fernan, Marcelo 119
Francisco Jr. v. *House of Representatives* 121
Francisco v. *House of Representatives* 131
freedom of religion, Indonesian perspective 104–5
freedom of speech, Indonesian perspective 99, 102
Funa v. *Ermita* 130

Gadbois, G. 57
Gandhi, Indira 65–6, 229
Garcia v. *Board of Investments* 119
Gierke, O. von 29, 222

Gillman, H. 187
Ginsburg, T. 27
Golak Nath case 65
Government of Malaysia v. *Lim Kit Siang* 208
Govt of Punjab v. *Abid Hussain et al.* 154
Gutierrez, Merceditas 130, 134
Gutierrez v. *House of Representatives* 130

Haji Naseer Mehmood v. *Mian Imran Masood et al.* 160n42
Haley, J. 18–19
Hansen's disease (leprosy), Japanese perspective 25
He Xin 176
hegemonic preservation model 5, 27
Hilbink, L. 17
Hirschl, R. 1, 5, 27, 39, 45, 57, 79, 93, 118, 134–5, 163, 184, 202
Hok Longdy 195–6
Hu Jintao 163, 170, 177
human rights: Cambodian perspective 187–8; Chinese perspective 169; Indonesian perspective 102–3, 109; Pakistani perspective 154–6
Human Rights Commission of Pakistan v. *Government of Pakistan* 155
Hun Sen 197
Hunter, C. A. 57

impeachment 42, 47, 64, 69, 83, 89, 121, 124, 131, 230
India: Constitution 59; drivers of judicialization 63–8; judicial legitimacy 229; right to education legislation 57
Indian judiciary: basic structure doctrine 66, 68; civil society perspective 67; conservatism on health and education issues 69; constitutional perspective 63–4; expansion of powers 64–7; and governance 59–63; involvement in politics 58; judges' behaviour 7, 67–8; negative implications of judicialization 69–70; and the parliament 63–4; positive impact of judicialization 68
Indonesia: corruption scandals 100; judicial legitimacy 231; political landscape 110; Bill of Rights 98
Indonesia's constitutional court (MK): allegations of impropriety 102; background 99–102; Bali Bombing case 108; democracy-related cases 105–7; functions 98; as the 'guardian' of democracy 111; judicial review 102–5, 224; strategic pragmatism 108–9; tempering techniques 108–10; timidity and conservatism 107–8
Information Technology Foundation of the Philippines v. *Comelec* 121
INS v. *Chadha* 35n28
Insas Bhd. v. *Ayer Molek* 209
Insas Bhd v. *Raphael Pura* 210
Inspector General of Police v. *Tan Sri Raja Khalid* 207
institutional autonomy, Japanese example 20
institutional conservatism, in Japan 19
Ip, E. C. 179
I.R. Coelho v. *Union of India* 73
Ishihara, Shintaro 25
Islam, Indonesian perspective 104–5
Islamic Academy of Education and Anr v. *State of Karnataka and Anr* 71n4

Jamaat-i-Islami v. *Federation of Pakistan PLD* 159n24
Japan: declared goal of legal reforms 17; judicial legitimacy 230; trends in judicial decision-making 17
Japanese judiciary: origins 20; and rural landlord-tenant disputes 20; *see also* judicialization in Japan
Jarun Pukditanakul 92, 221
Jellinek, G. 29, 222
Jiang Zemin 163, 168, 170
Johnson Tan Han Seng v. *PP* 205
J.P. Berthelsen v. *Director General of Immigration* 207
judicial activism: Chinese perspective 169; Choudhary and Hunter's definition 57; Filipino perspective 125–6; as growing phenomenon 184; Islamization and 142–4; Korean perspective 225; Malaysian perspective 202, 207; Shankar's definition 57–8; Thai perspective 91–2, 225–6
judicial apoliticism, Hilbink's focus 17
judicial behaviour, and regime type 8
judicial empowerment: ambiguity of the effects of 2; Hirschl's theory 5, 27
judicial independence, greatest danger to 66
judicial muteness 6
judicial performance, questions about dramatic variations in 2
judicial politics, typology 3–7
judicial restraint 6, 11, 83, 89, 91, 212, 214
judicial review: constitutional perspective

224; Indonesian perspective 102–5, 224; Philippines perspective 224; place in the democratic process 227, 229; Thai perspective 81–5
judicialization, relationship between regime type and 8
judicialization in Japan: adjudicating history 24–5; cases 21–2; constitutional perspectives 21–2, 24–7; and corporate donations 22; and courts in the Meiji and Taisho eras 20–1; equality cases 25; explanations for limited 27; and Hansen's disease (leprosy) 25; Heisei era 23–7; and increasing public involvement 26; outward signs 26–7; postwar era 21–3; postwar retention of organ theory 30–2; Prussian origins of organ theory 28–30; recent SDF Cases 24; and reform 23; and the separation of powers 28, 30; Shrine Visit cases 24; status of 18, 20
judicialization of politics: analysis framework *see* analysis framework of judicialization; definition 1; vs politicization of the judiciary 219; significance 37
judicialization patterns 2, 8, 79; institutional variables' influence 8; interplay between institutional, ideational, and structural factors 8–11
judiciary: juridical/legal foundations 223–6; most powerful source of authority 224
juristocracy 5, 39, 63, 202, 214
Justice Ifthikar Chaudhry v. *President of Pakistan PLD* 159n20
Justice Khurshid Bhinder and others v. *Federation of Pakistan PLD* 159n37

Kanao v. *Hiroshima Election Management Commission* 22
KCC (Korean Constitutional Court): appointment system 222; areas of jurisdiction 47; composition 46; Comprehensive Real Estate Tax Act 49; Comprehensive Real Estate Tax Case 40; and Core National Policy 40–2; and electoral politics 42–3; equal rights protection role 40; establishment 38; Impeachment of President Roh Moo-hyun case 42; policy-making interventions 39; proportionality principle 40, 47; and the protection of civil liberties 40; public worries 48; and questions of nationhood 43–4; Relocation of the Capital City Case 40–1, 225; Residential Property Ownership Ceiling Case 52; and restorative justice 43; scope of review 39; and the war in Iraq 42; *see also* Republic of Korea
Keshavananda Bharati v. *State of Kerala* 73n42
Khawaja Muhammad Sharif v. *Federation of Pakistan PLD* 158n6
Khmer Rouge 184, 191–2, 194, 222
Kim Yong-sam 43
Kitokuro, Ichiki 29
Koizumi, Junichiro 24–5
Kok Wee Kiat v. *Chong Hon Nyan* 207
Korea, Republic of *see* Republic of Korea
Korean War 21, 45
Koshiyama v. *Tokyo Election Management Commission* 22
Kurokawa v. *Chiba Prefecture Election Commission* 22

La Bugal-B'laan Tribal Association, Inc. v. *Ramos* 121, 124
Lambino v. *Comelec* 122
Lao Mong Hay 188
Lau Dak Kee v. *Public Prosecutor* 205
Laurel v. *Garcia* 119
Law, D. 18–19
Lawyers' League for a Better Philippines v. *Corazon C. Aquino* 118
leadership, importance of judicial 221–3
Lee Liong Chan v. *Tan Sri Tek Ewe Lim* 207
Lee Myung-bak 40
legitimacy, judicial 226–31
leprosy *see* Hansen's disease
liberalization, and concerns about the rule of law 1
Lim Kit Siang v. *United Engineers* 207
Liu Yanhong 172
Liversidge v. *Anderson* 206

Macapagal-Arroyo, Gloria *see* Arroyo, Gloria
Madras v. *Dorairajan* 65
Mahathir Mohamad 203, 206–8, 211, 214, 224, 229
Mahmood-ur-Rehman Faisal v. *Secretary Ministry of Justice and Parliamentary Affairs PLD* 158n7
Majlis Agama Islam v. *Shaik Zolkaffily & Ors* 211

Malaysia: aboriginal land rights cases 210; constitutional amendments 205, 208–9; conversion and custody of minor children cases 211–12; defamation cases 209; evaluating drivers and effects of judicialization 214–15; formation 204; habeas corpus cases 206, 209, 212; independence 203; Islamic resurgence 205; judicial behaviour 7–8, 209–10; judicial legitimacy 229; judicial patterns in the early independence period 203–5; judicial patterns in the Mahathir era 205–10; multiethnic riots 204; post-Mahathir judicial patterns 211–14; social movements 205; Supreme Court judges dismissed 208
mandamus, Manmohan Singh's observations 56
Manila Prince Hotel v. *GSIS* 120, 224
Marbury v. *Madison* 174
Marcos, Ferdinand 119, 126, 135
Marcos v. *Manglapus* 120
Matsui, S. 19
MBF Bhd v. *Param Cumaraswamy* 210
MBF Capital Bhd. v. *Tommy Thomas & Another* 209
MBF Capital v. *Param Cumaraswamy* 209
M.C. Mehta v. *Union of India (UOI)* 72n22
mega-politics 3, 6–7, 11–12, 39, 43, 51, 57, 184, 207, 214; Hirschl's definition of judicialization of 184; typology of judicial politics in areas of **6**
Megawati Sukarnoputri 100, 107
Mietzner, M. 99
Minister of Home Affairs v. *Chu Choon Yong* 204
Ministry of Home Affairs v. *Datuk James Wong Kim Min* 205
Minobe, Tatsukichi 29–30
Mohamed Noor bin Omar v. *Mohamed Yusof* 208
Mongkut, King of Siam (Thailand) 81
Moro Islamic Liberation Front 122
Mubashir Hassan v. *Federation of Pakistan PLD* 159n26, 159n39
Muhammad Naseer Mahmood v. *Federation of Pakistan PLD* 159n33
Muhammad Rizwan Gill v. *Nadia Aziz et al. PLD* 159n40
Musharraf, Pervez 139, 145–51, 153, 222
Muted Courts 7
Myriam v. *Mohd. Arif* 209

Nadeem Ahmed v. *Federation of Pakistan PLD* 160n48
Naganuma Nike Missile Site case 21
Najib Razak 213
Najibullah v. *Aamir Yar PLD* 160n44
Nandini Sundar v. *Union of India 250/2009* 74n51
Narvasa, Andres 119–20
National Human Rights Commission v. *State of Gujarat* 72n23
Nawadzada Iftikhar Ahmed Khan v. *Chief Election Commissioner PLD* 160n43
Nawaz Sharif 144–6, 148, 151–2, 155
Nehru, Jawaharlal 65
neoliberalism, Hirschl's argument 135
Neri, Romulo 122, 131–2
Neri v. *Senate* 122, 131–2

O'Donnell, G. 184
Orosa, T. J. P. 125
Others v. *Secretary of Health, Government of Pakistan* 155
Ozawa Ichiro 26, 32

Pakistan: constitutional adjustments 156–7; constitutional background 139–42; constitutional reconstruction 145–7; coup 149; Dogar Court 149–53, 221; 'enlightened' military authoritarianism 144–5; general elections 150; human rights perspective 154–6; impeachment proceedings 151; Islamization and judicial activism 142–4; restoration of judiciary 152–3; suspension of the Chief Justice 147–9; Zardari's election 151
Pakistan Lawyers' Forum v. *Federation of Pakistan PLD* 159n18
Pakistan Muslim League (N) v. *Federation of Pakistan PLD* 148
Pakistan Muslim League (Q) v. *Chief Executive of Islamic Republic of Pakistan PLD* 159n33
Paris Peace Agreement 187
Park Chung Hee 38
Peerenboom, R. 167, 174, 176
Pengarah Tanah & Galian v. *Sri Lempah Enterprise* 205
People's Union for Civil Liberties v. *Union of India (UOI) and Anr.* 62
People's Union for Civil Liberties v. *Union of India (UOI) and Ors.* 74n49
Persatuan Aliran v. *Minister of Home Affairs* 207

Philippines: consequences of judicialization 126–8; drivers of judicialization 122–6; 'Hello Garci' scandal 121, 131; impeachment proceedings 121, 131; importance of judicial empowerment 8; judicial appointments process 133; judicial review 224; pertinent decisions and events 131–2; politicization of the Supreme Court 128–35; post-Marcos judicialization 118–22; provisions that safeguard the Court's independence 124–5; ratification of WTO membership 120; talk of an 'Arroyo Court' 129
political insurance 27
politicization of the judiciary, vs judicialization of politics 219
Politicized Courts 7
polygamy, Indonesian perspective 104
PP v. *Cheah Beng Poh & Ors* 206
PP v. *Chew Choon Ming & Ors* 206
PP v. *Dato Yap Peng* 207–8
PP v. *Koh Yoke Koon* 206
PP v. *Kok Wah Kuan* 208
PP v. *Yee Kim Sen* 204
Prajadhipok, King of Siam (Thailand) 82
Pridi Banomyong 82
PRK (People's Republic of Kampuchea) 186
property rights, Japanese perspective 23, 30
Province of North Cotabato v. *Government of the Republic of the Philippines* 122
Prussian legal thought, Meiji adaptation 17

Qazi Hussain Ahmed, Amir Jamaat-i-Islami v. *General Pervez Musharraf PLD* 159n17
Qi Yuling 174

Rainsy, Sam 190–1
Ram Jethmalani v. *Union of India* 72n23, 74n51
Ramos, Fidel V. 120, 127, 224
Ramseyer, M. J. 18–19, 27
Raphael Pura v. *Insas Berhad* 209
Relocation of the Capital City Case 225
Republic of Korea: causes of the judicialization of politics 44; early adoption of constitutional adjudication 38 (*see also* KCC); evaluation of political judicialization 48–50; macro factors in political judicialization 44–6; micro factors in political judicialization 46–8; number of licensed lawyers 46
restorative justice 37, 39, 43, 45, 184
Restrained Courts 7
Roh Moo-hyun 40, 41–2
Rubrico v. *Arroyo* 130
rule of law: and activism 225; Cambodian perspective 185–6, 198; Chinese perspective 167–9; Filipino perspective 127; Indonesian perspective 102
Russian crown prince, Japanese policeman's attempt on the life of the 20

S. P. Gupta v. *Union of India* 73n44
Sagong Bin Tasi case 210
Santiago v. *Comelec* 120, 224
Sanusi, Arsyad 102
Sarmiento v. *Mison* 119
Sathe, S. P. 63, 66
Senate v. *Ermita* 121–2, 132
separation of powers: Chinese perspective 163; Filipino perspective 118; in the French tradition 28; German tradition 28–9; Indian perspective 64; and judicial legitimacy 229
Shamala Satiyaseelan v. *Dr. Jayaganesh* 211
Shen Junru 165
Sindh High Court Bar Association v. *Federation of Pakistan PLD* 158n1, 159n36
Singh, Manmohan 56
S.P. Gupta and Ors. etc. etc. v. *Union of India and Ors. etc. etc.* 73n36
Spaeth, H. J. 132
Sri Radhy Shyam (Dead) through L.Rs. and Ors. v. *State of U.P. and Ors.* 74n50
State v. *Dosso PLD* 158n2
State v. *Zulfiqar Ali Bhutto and others PLD* 158n4
Suharto 98, 100–1, 110
Sukma Dermawan 212
Sunakawa case 21
supremacy of law, Chinese perspective 167
Supreme Court Advocates on Record Association v. *Union of India* 73n37
Swamy v. *Singh* 61

Tañada v. *Angara* 120
Tatad v. *Secretary of Energy* 120, 224
Tatad v. *Secretary of the Department of Energy* 136n4

Tate, N. C. 118, 131
Teehankee, Claudio 118
Thailand: coups 80, 82; dissolution of Thai Rak Thai 87–8; dissolution of the People's Power Party 88–90; election annulment 85–7; electoral impact of the rural poor 80; explaining judicial behaviour 91–2; frustrations about the functioning of democracy 79; judicial behaviour 7; looming royal succession crisis 92; monarchy 81; Political Party Act 90; roots of judicial review in 81–5
Thaksin Shinawatra 80, 84–6, 88, 90, 92, 221, 225
Thirayuth Boonmee 80
Tika Iqbal Muhammad Khan v. *Pervez Musharraf PLD* 159n31
Tinga, Dante 124
Titular Roman Catholic Archbishop of Kuala Lumpur v. *Menteri Dalam Negeri & Anr* 213
TMA Pai Foundation v. *State of Karnataka* 71n4
Tolentino v. *Secretary of Finance* 120
transitional justice 184
Trevaskes, S. 170

Uesugi, Shinkichi 29
Umil v. *Ramos* 119
Union of India v. *Association for Democratic Reforms* 62
Union of India v. *Sankalchand Himmatlal Seth* 73n38
Union of India v. *Sushil Kumar Modi and Ors.* 72n24
United Bank Limited v. *Farooq Brothers PLD* 158n7
United States v. *Carolene Products Company* 53n26
University of Kerala v. *Council, Principals* 71n9
Unnikrishnan v. *State of AP* 71n4

Valmonte v. *De Villa* 119
Vargas, Getulio 184
Venecia, Jose de 120
Vickery, M. 186
Vineet Narain v. *Union of India* 58, 73n25
Vishaka v. *State of Rajasthan* 57
Von Gierke, O. 29

Wahid, Abdurrahman 100
Wajihuddin Ahmed v. *Chief Election Commissioner PLD* 159n27, 159n29
Wang Shengjun 165, 170, 176, 223
Wen Xiaoli 168
Western jurisprudence, scholarly focus 219–20
Wikileaks 56

Xi Jinping 32
Xiao Yang 165, 169–70, 172, 176, 223

Yahata Steel Company case 22
Yahya Khan 141–2
Yamaguchi et al. v. *Tokyo Election Administration* 34n9
Yap, Pedro 119
Yasukuni Shrine, Tokyo 24
Yit Hon Kit v. *Minister of Home Affairs* 206
Yu Lingyu 178
Yudhoyono, Susilo Bambang 107

Zafar Iqbal Shagra v. *Federation of Pakistan* 155
Zardari, Asif 139, 140, 148
Zheng Tianxiang 167
Zhu Suli 164, 180
Zia ul-Haq 141–3, 145
Zulfiqar Ali Bhutto v. *State PLD* 158n4